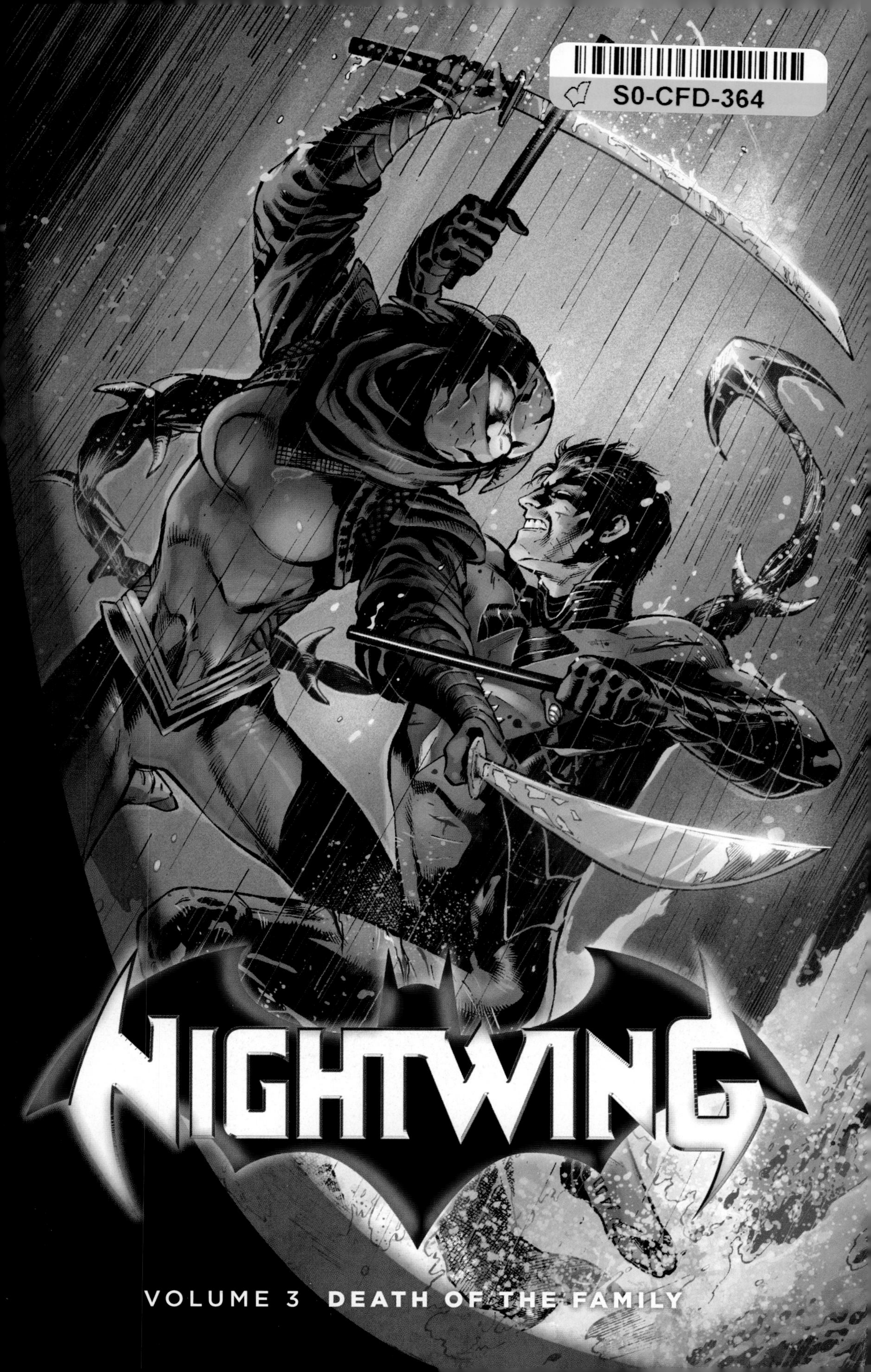

NIGHTWING

VOLUME 3 DEATH OF THE FAMILY

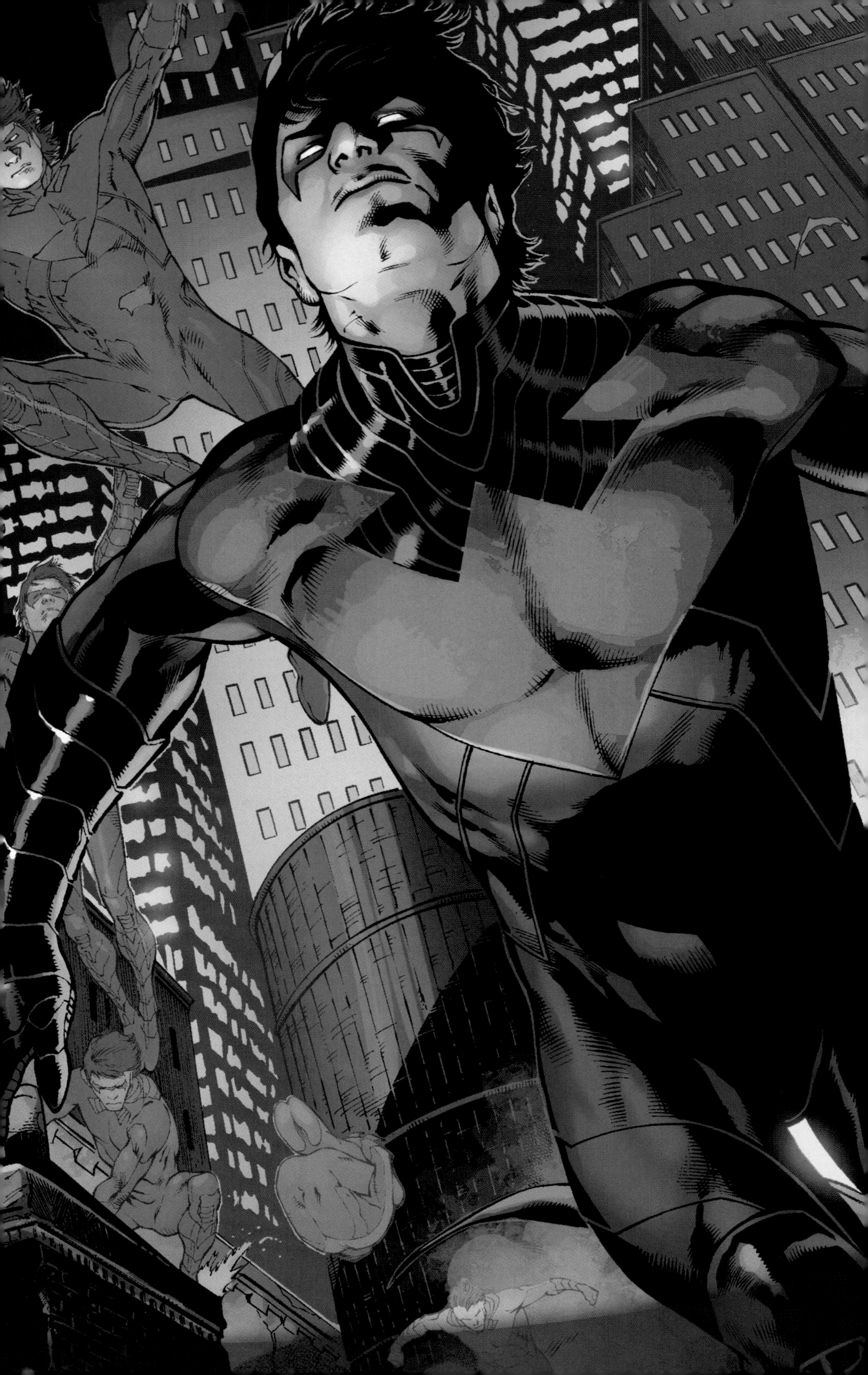

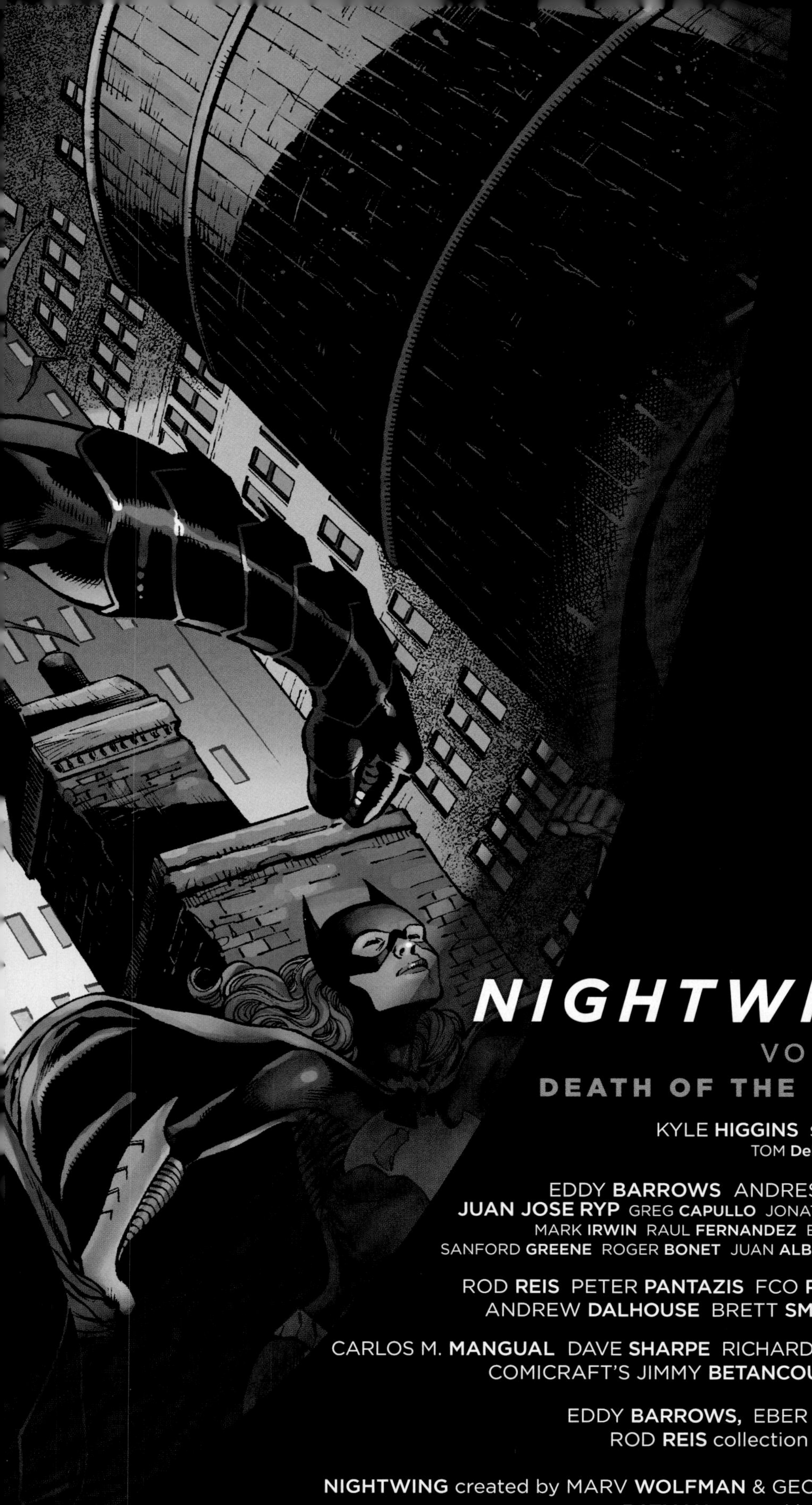

NIGHTWING

VOLUME 3
DEATH OF THE FAMILY

KYLE **HIGGINS** SCOTT **SNYDER**
TOM **DeFALCO** writers

EDDY **BARROWS** ANDRES **GUINALDO**
JUAN JOSE RYP GREG **CAPULLO** JONATHAN **GLAPION**
MARK **IRWIN** RAUL **FERNANDEZ** EBER **FERREIRA**
SANFORD **GREENE** ROGER **BONET** JUAN **ALBARRAN** artists

ROD **REIS** PETER **PANTAZIS** FCO **PLASCENCIA**
ANDREW **DALHOUSE** BRETT **SMITH** colorists

CARLOS M. **MANGUAL** DAVE **SHARPE** RICHARD **STARKINGS**
COMICRAFT'S JIMMY **BETANCOURT** letterers

EDDY **BARROWS,** EBER **FERREIRA** &
ROD **REIS** collection cover artists

NIGHTWING created by MARV **WOLFMAN** & GEORGE **PÉREZ**
BATMAN created by BOB **KANE**

MIKE MARTS BRIAN CUNNINGHAM SHELLY BOND Editors – Original Series
KATIE KUBERT Associate Editor – Original Series GREG LOCKARD Assistant Editor – Original Series
ROWENA YOW Editor ROBBIN BROSTERMAN Design Director – Books ROBBIE BIEDERMAN Publication Design

BOB HARRAS Senior VP – Editor-in-Chief, DC Comics

DIANE NELSON President DAN DIDIO and JIM LEE Co-Publishers
GEOFF JOHNS Chief Creative Officer
JOHN ROOD Executive VP – Sales, Marketing and Business Development
AMY GENKINS Senior VP – Business and Legal Affairs NAIRI GARDINER Senior VP – Finance
JEFF BOISON VP – Publishing Planning MARK CHIARELLO VP – Art Direction and Design
JOHN CUNNINGHAM VP – Marketing TERRI CUNNINGHAM VP – Editorial Administration
ALISON GILL Senior VP – Manufacturing and Operations HANK KANALZ Senior VP – Vertigo and Integrated Publishing
JAY KOGAN VP – Business and Legal Affairs, Publishing JACK MAHAN VP – Business Affairs, Talent
NICK NAPOLITANO VP – Manufacturing Administration SUE POHJA VP – Book Sales
COURTNEY SIMMONS Senior VP – Publicity BOB WAYNE Senior VP – Sales

NIGHTWING VOLUME 3: DEATH OF THE FAMILY
Published by DC Comics. Copyright © 2013 DC Comics. All Rights Reserved.

Originally published in single magazine form in NIGHTWING 13-18; BATMAN 17; YOUNG ROMANCE 1 © 2012, 2013 DC Comics.
All Rights Reserved. All characters, their distinctive likenesses and related elements featured in this publication are
trademarks of DC Comics. The stories, characters and incidents featured in this publication are entirely fictional.
DC Comics does not read or accept unsolicited ideas, stories or artwork.

DC Comics, 1700 Broadway, New York, NY 10019
A Warner Bros. Entertainment Company.
Printed by RR Donnelley, Salem, VA, USA. 3/12/14. Second Printing.

ISBN: 978-1-4012-4413-2

Library of Congress Cataloging-in-Publication Data

Higgins, Kyle, 1985- author.
Nightwing. Volume 3, Death of the Family / Kyle Higgins, Eddy Barrows.
pages cm. — (The New 52!)
Summary: "After having his face sliced off one year ago, the Joker makes his horrifying return to Gotham City! But even
for a man who's committed a lifetime of murder, he's more dangerous than ever before. The Joker sets his twisted sights on the
members of the Bat-Family and attacks them all where it hurts--and for Dick Grayson, that means going after the family he's
built up for the past year at Haly's Circus!"— Provided by publisher.
ISBN 978-1-4012-4413-2 (pbk.)
1. Graphic novels. I. Barrows, Eddy, illustrator. II. Title. III. Title: Death of the Family.
PN6728.N55H56 2013
741.5'973—dc23

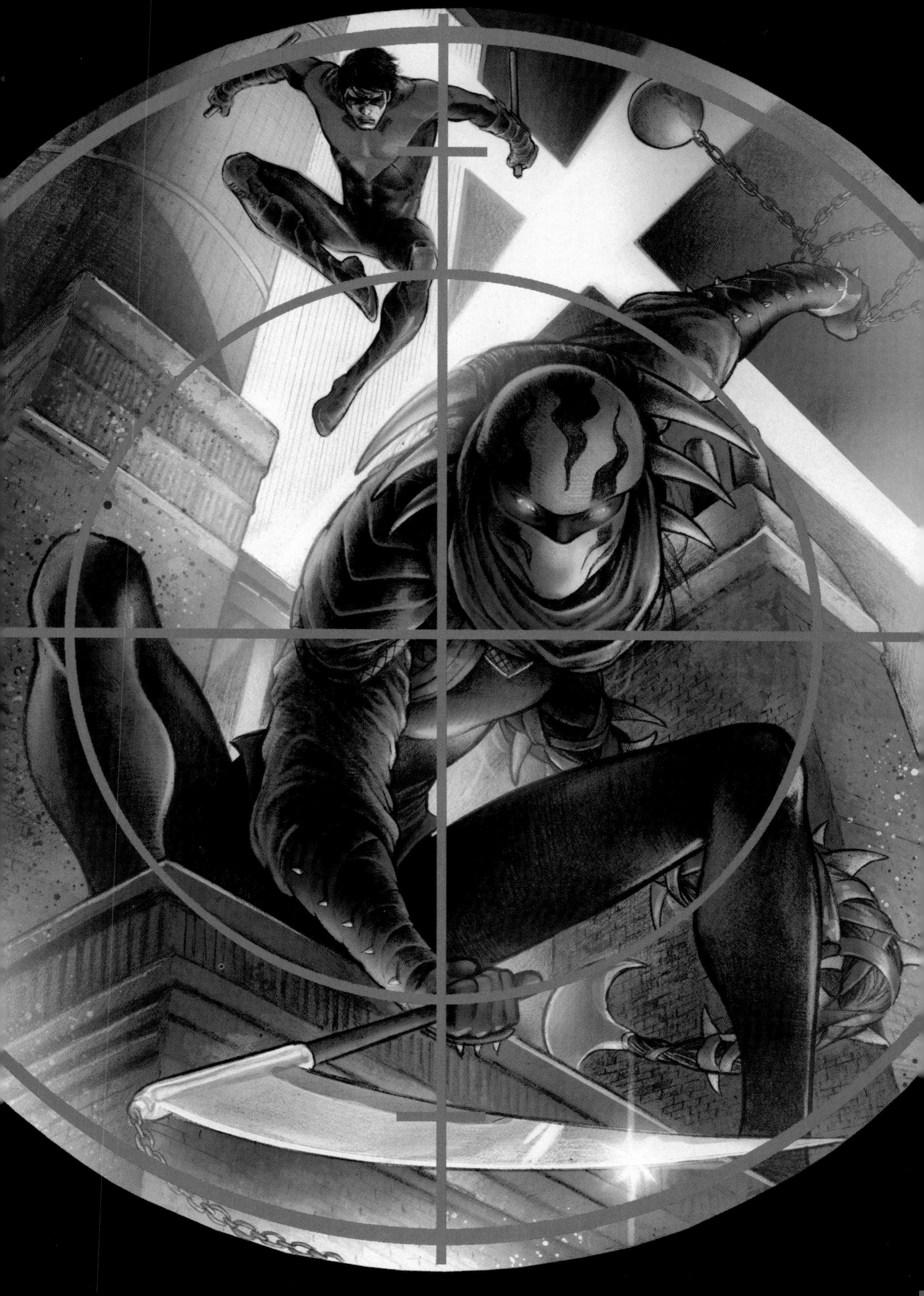

THE HUNTER

TOM DEFALCO writer **ANDRES GUINALDO** penciller **MARK IRWIN & RAUL FERNANDEZ** inkers cover art by **EDDY BARROWS & ROD REIS**

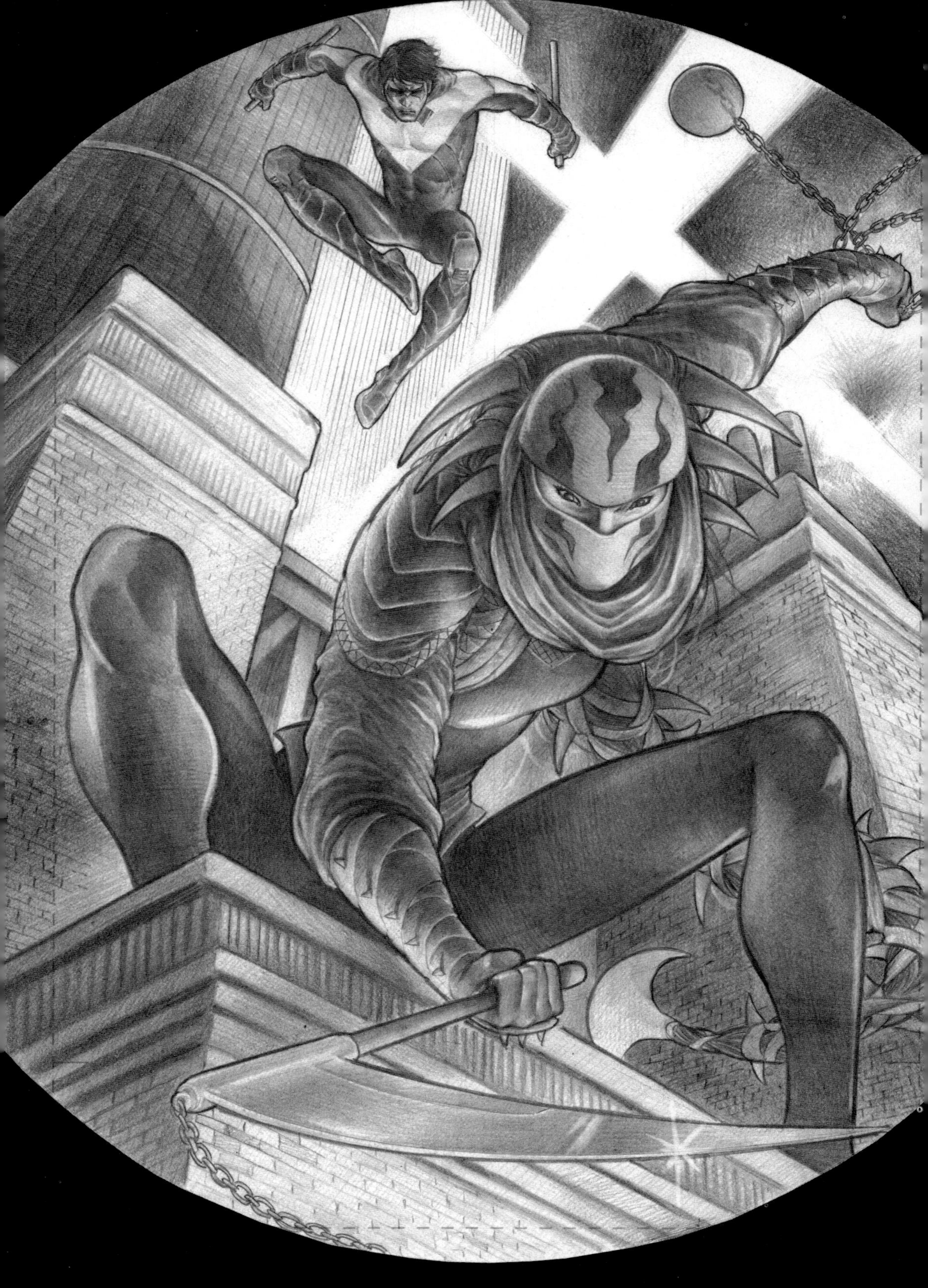

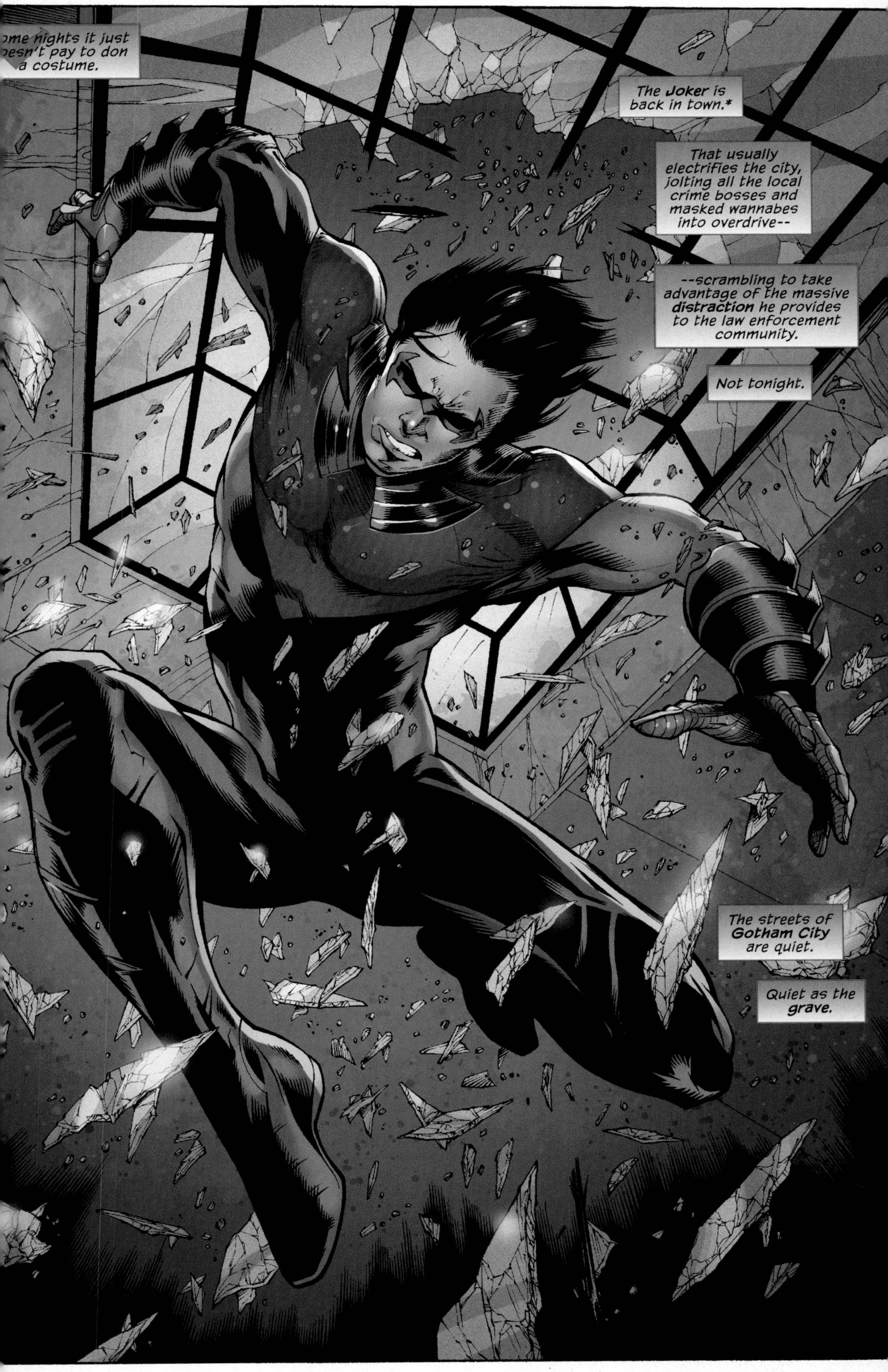
ome nights it just
oesn't pay to don
a costume.
The Joker is back in town.*
That usually electrifies the city, jolting all the local crime bosses and masked wannabes into overdrive--
--scrambling to take advantage of the massive distraction he provides to the law enforcement community.
Not tonight.
The streets of Gotham City are quiet.
Quiet as the grave.

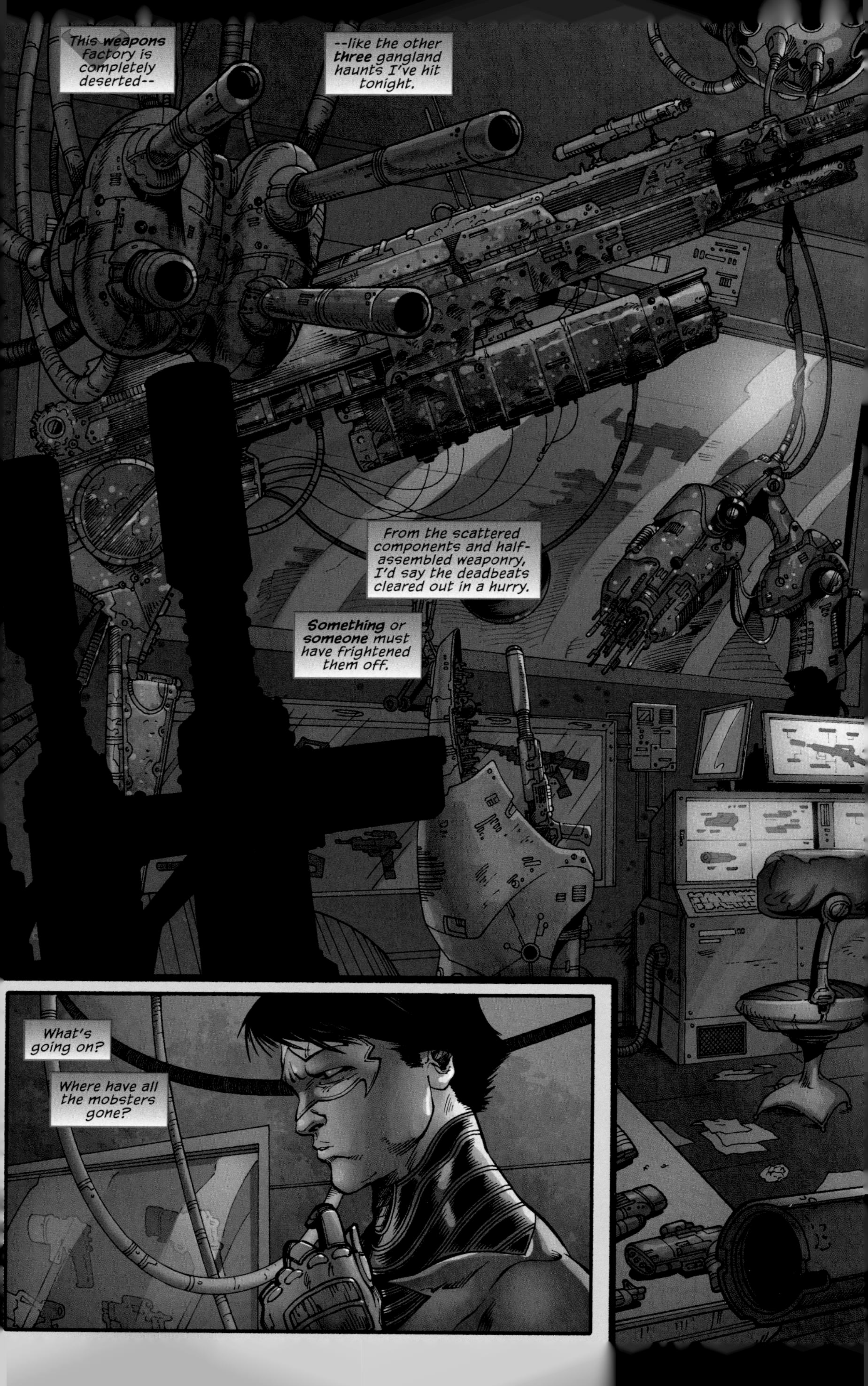
This weapons factory is completely deserted--
--like the other three gangland haunts I've hit tonight.
From the scattered components and half-assembled weaponry, I'd say the deadbeats cleared out in a hurry.
Something or someone must have frightened them off.
What's going on?
Where have all the mobsters gone?

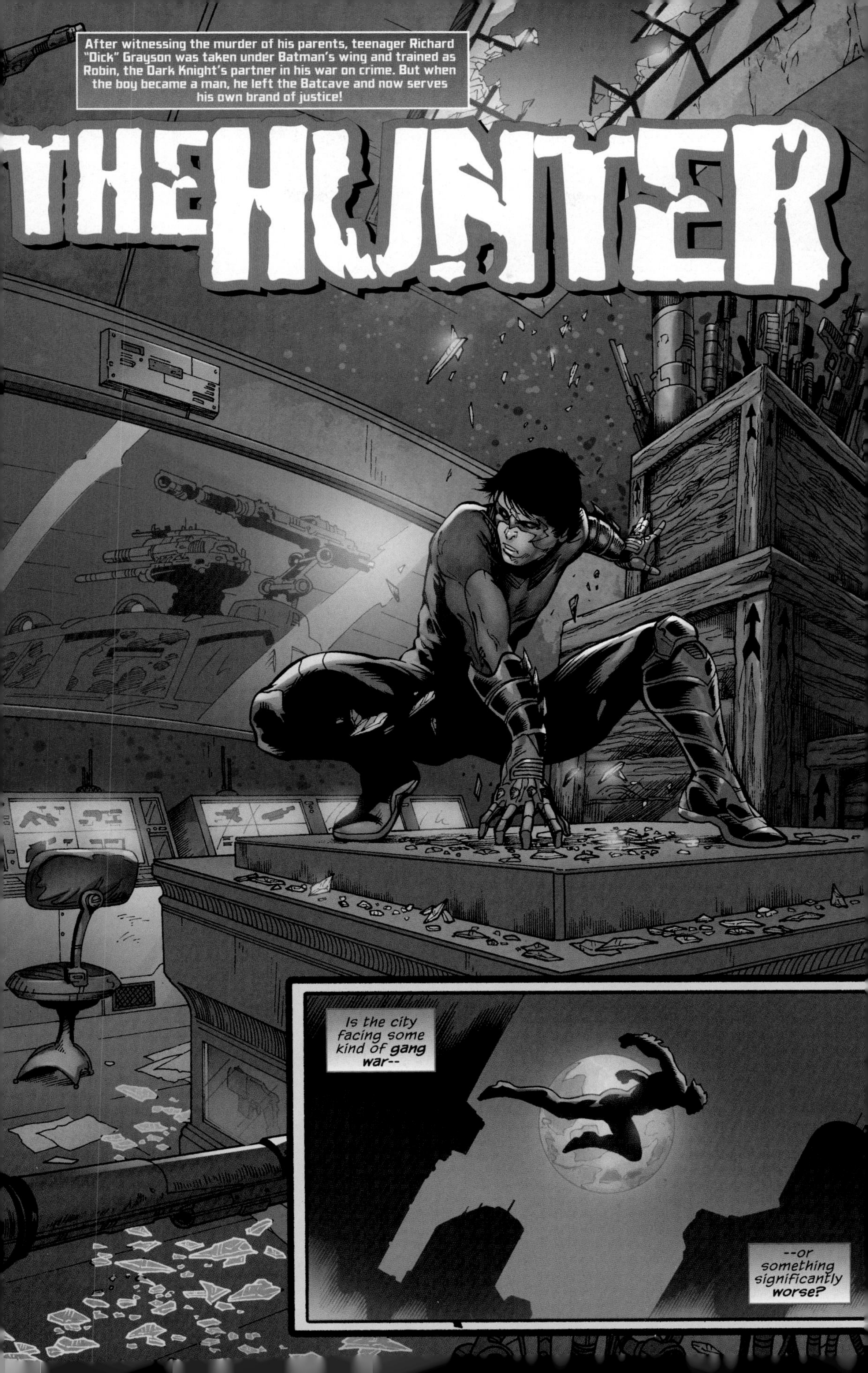

After witnessing the murder of his parents, teenager Richard "Dick" Grayson was taken under Batman's wing and trained as Robin, the Dark Knight's partner in his war on crime. But when the boy became a man, he left the Batcave and now serves his own brand of justice!
THE HUNTER
Is the city facing some kind of gang war--
--or something significantly worse?

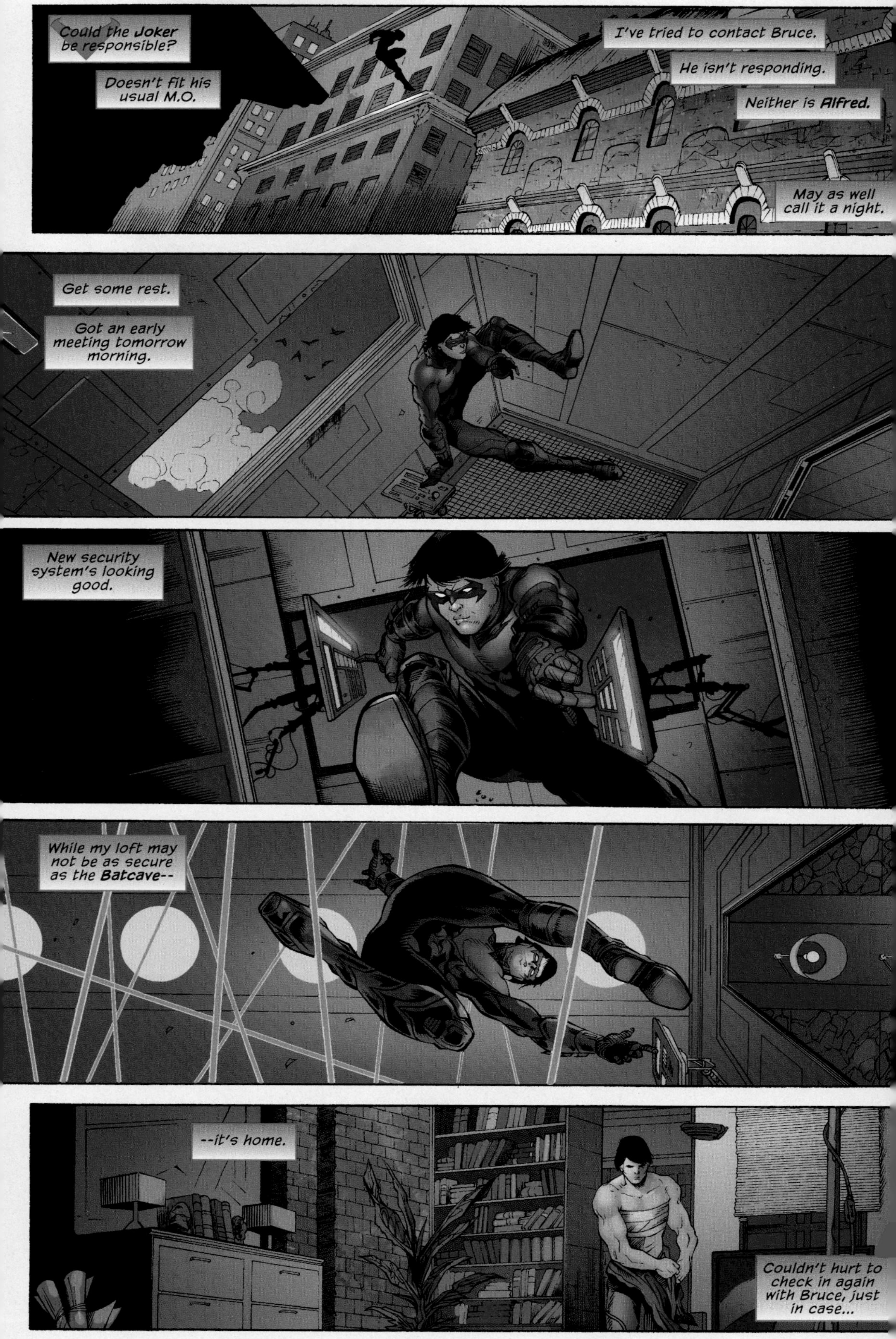
Could the Joker be responsible?
Doesn't fit his usual M.O.
I've tried to contact Bruce.
He isn't responding.
Neither is Alfred.
May as well call it a night.
Get some rest.
Got an early meeting tomorrow morning.
New security system's looking good.
While my loft may not be as secure as the Batcave--
--it's home.
Couldn't hurt to check in again with Bruce, just in case...

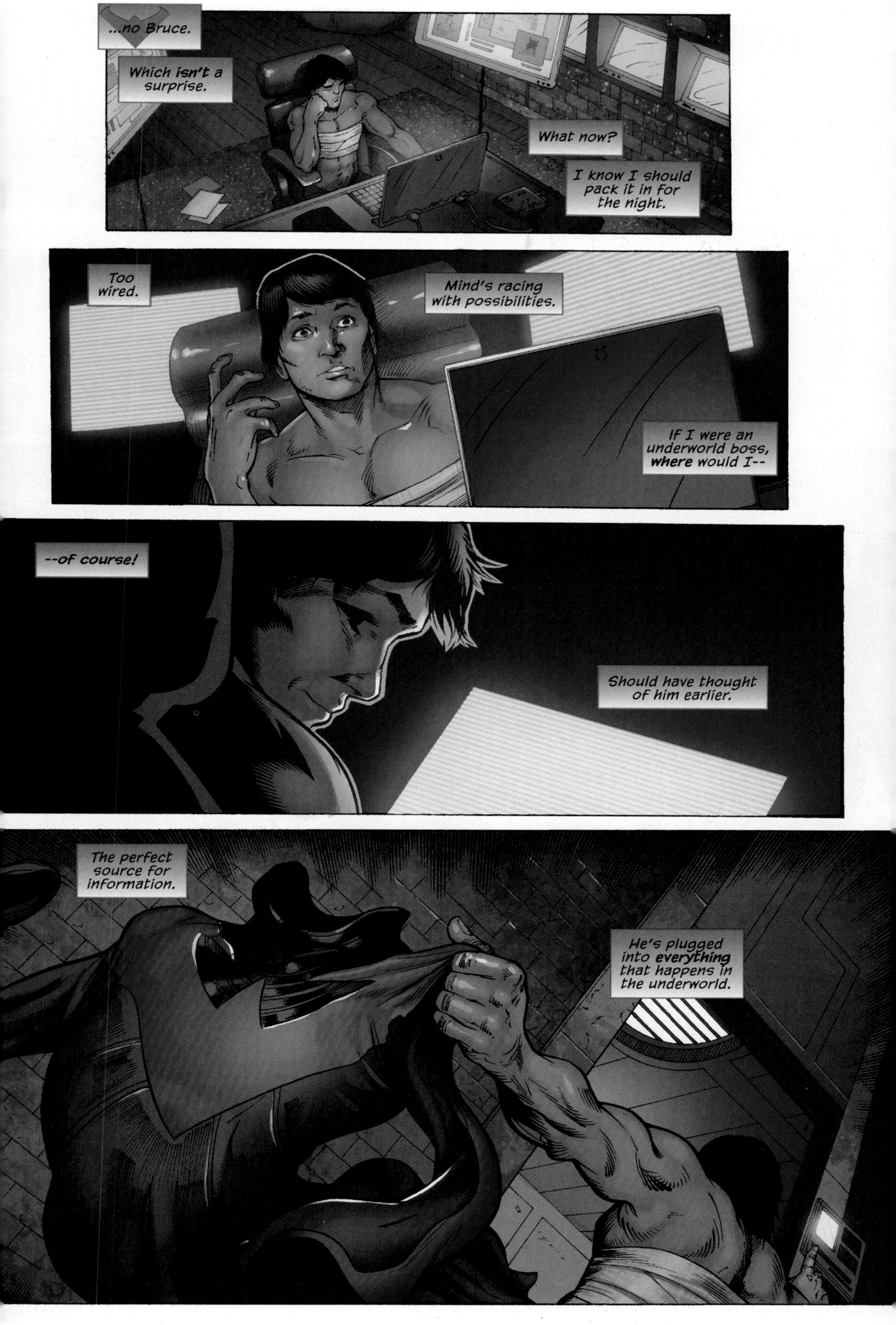
...no Bruce.
Which isn't a surprise.
What now?
I know I should pack it in for the night.
Too wired.
Mind's racing with possibilities.
If I were an underworld boss, where would I--
--of course!
Should have thought of him earlier.
The perfect source for information.
He's plugged into everything that happens in the underworld.

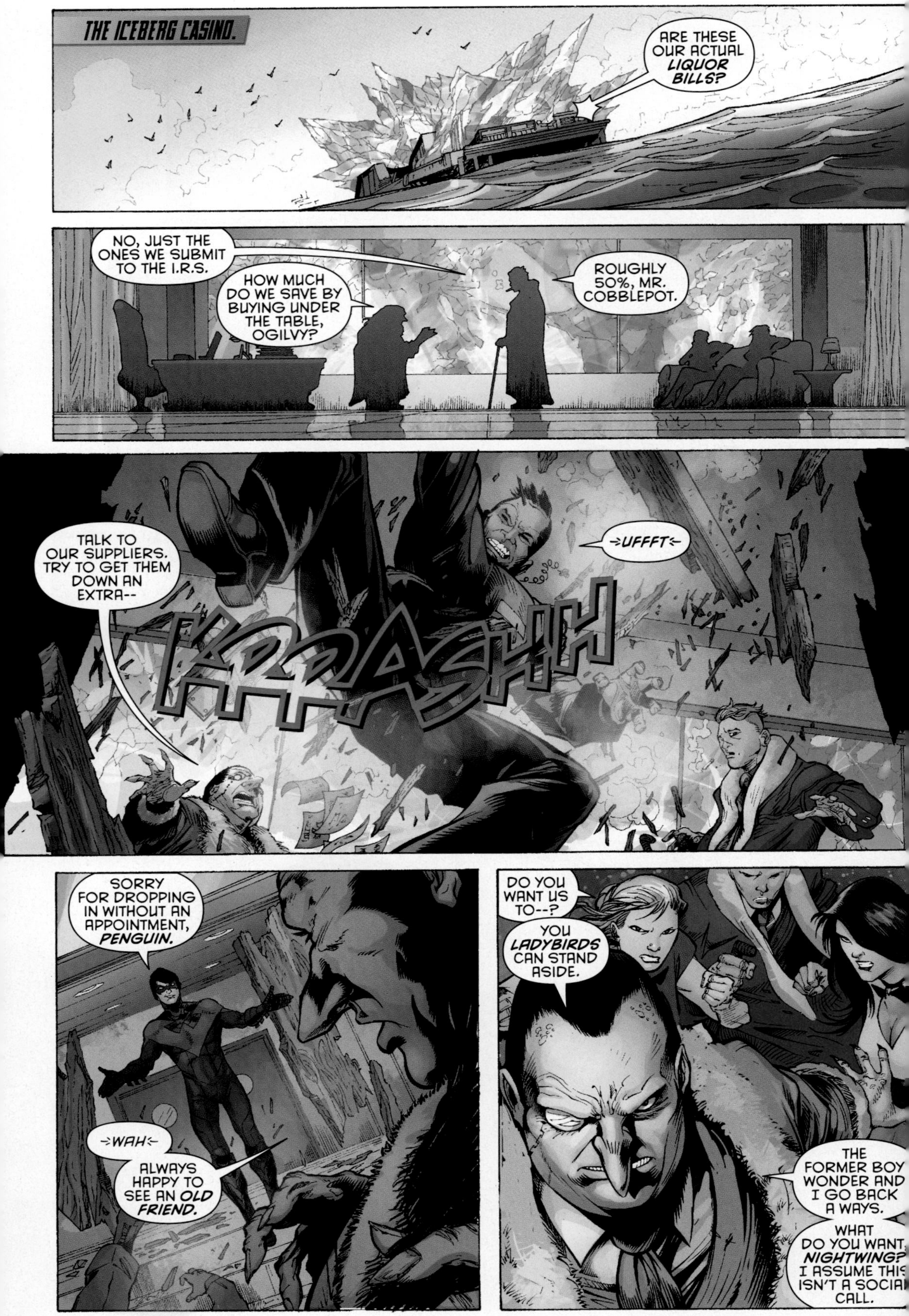
THE ICEBERG CASINO.
ARE THESE OUR ACTUAL LIQUOR BILLS?
NO, JUST THE ONES WE SUBMIT TO THE I.R.S.
HOW MUCH DO WE SAVE BY BUYING UNDER THE TABLE, OGILVY?
ROUGHLY 50%, MR. COBBLEPOT.
TALK TO OUR SUPPLIERS. TRY TO GET THEM DOWN AN EXTRA--
UFFFT
KRRASHH
SORRY FOR DROPPING IN WITHOUT AN APPOINTMENT, PENGUIN.
WAH
ALWAYS HAPPY TO SEE AN OLD FRIEND.
DO YOU WANT US TO--?
YOU LADYBIRDS CAN STAND ASIDE.
THE FORMER BOY WONDER AND I GO BACK A WAYS.
WHAT DO YOU WANT, NIGHTWING? I ASSUME THIS ISN'T A SOCIAL CALL.

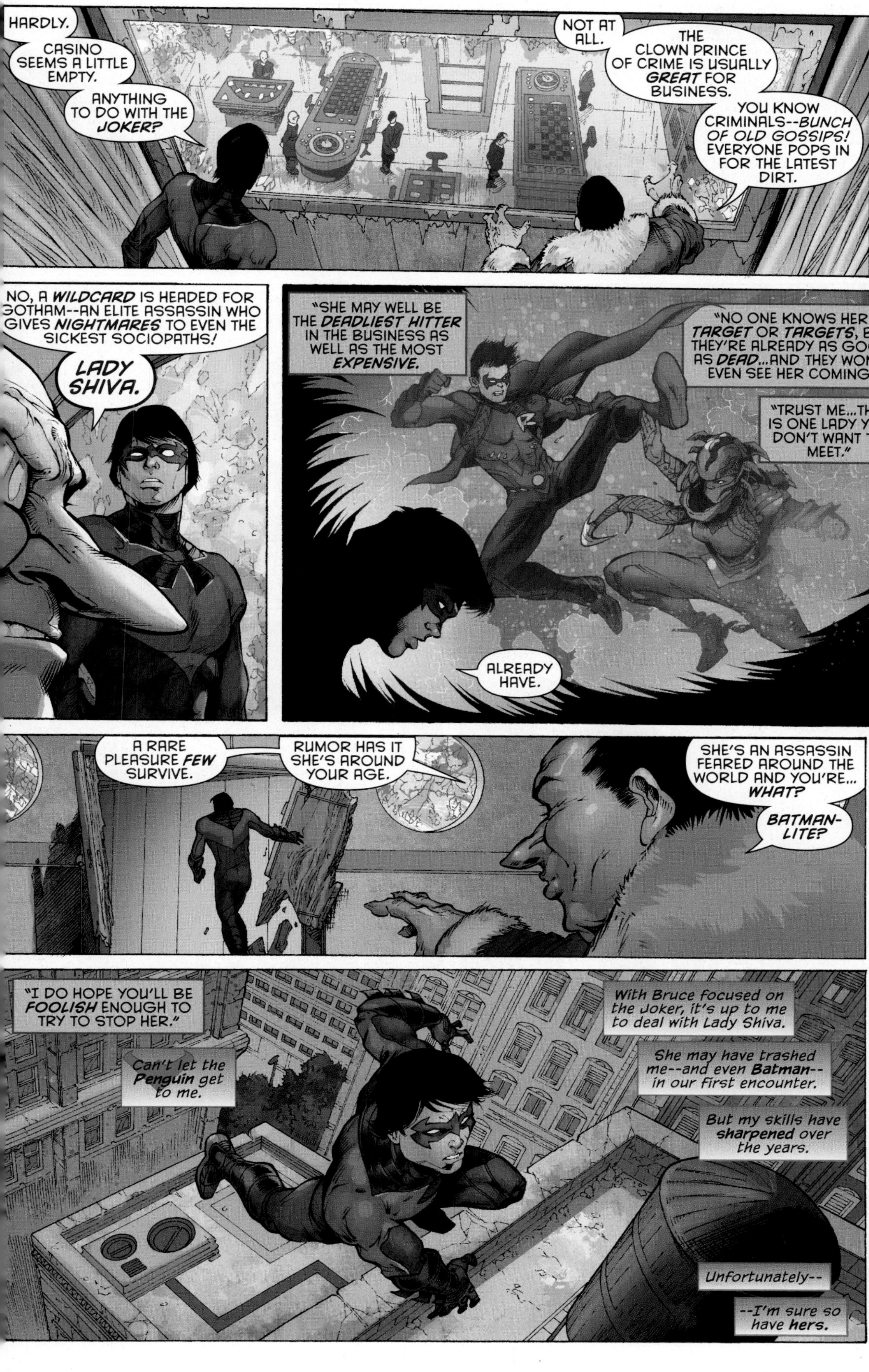
HARDLY.
CASINO SEEMS A LITTLE EMPTY.
ANYTHING TO DO WITH THE *JOKER?*
NOT AT ALL.
THE CLOWN PRINCE OF CRIME IS USUALLY *GREAT* FOR BUSINESS.
YOU KNOW CRIMINALS--*BUNCH OF OLD GOSSIPS!* EVERYONE POPS IN FOR THE LATEST DIRT.
NO, A *WILDCARD* IS HEADED FOR GOTHAM--AN ELITE ASSASSIN WHO GIVES *NIGHTMARES* TO EVEN THE SICKEST SOCIOPATHS!
LADY SHIVA.
"SHE MAY WELL BE THE *DEADLIEST HITTER* IN THE BUSINESS AS WELL AS THE MOST *EXPENSIVE.*
"NO ONE KNOWS HER *TARGET* OR *TARGETS*, BUT THEY'RE ALREADY AS GOOD AS *DEAD*...AND THEY WON'T EVEN SEE HER COMING.
"TRUST ME...THIS IS ONE LADY YOU DON'T WANT TO MEET."
ALREADY HAVE.
A RARE PLEASURE *FEW* SURVIVE.
RUMOR HAS IT SHE'S AROUND YOUR AGE.
SHE'S AN ASSASSIN FEARED AROUND THE WORLD AND YOU'RE... *WHAT?*
BATMAN-LITE?
"I DO HOPE YOU'LL BE *FOOLISH* ENOUGH TO TRY TO STOP HER."
Can't let the ***Penguin*** *get to me.*
With Bruce focused on the Joker, it's up to me to deal with Lady Shiva.
She may have trashed me--and even ***Batman****--in our first encounter.*
But my skills have ***sharpened*** *over the years.*
Unfortunately--
--I'm sure so have ***hers.***

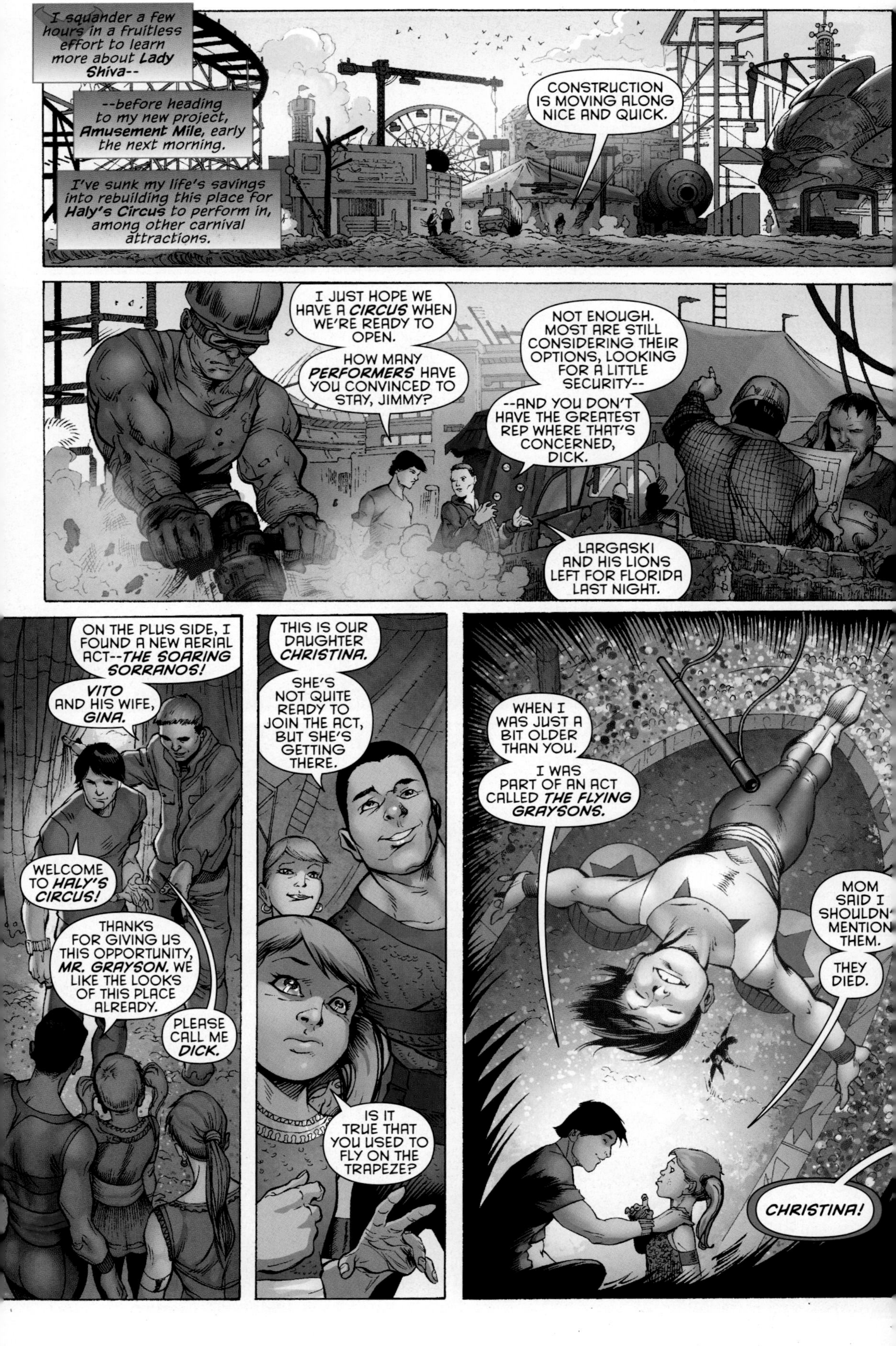

I squander a few hours in a fruitless effort to learn more about Lady Shiva--
--before heading to my new project, Amusement Mile, early the next morning.
I've sunk my life's savings into rebuilding this place for Haly's Circus to perform in, among other carnival attractions.
CONSTRUCTION IS MOVING ALONG NICE AND QUICK.
I JUST HOPE WE HAVE A CIRCUS WHEN WE'RE READY TO OPEN.
HOW MANY PERFORMERS HAVE YOU CONVINCED TO STAY, JIMMY?
NOT ENOUGH. MOST ARE STILL CONSIDERING THEIR OPTIONS, LOOKING FOR A LITTLE SECURITY--
--AND YOU DON'T HAVE THE GREATEST REP WHERE THAT'S CONCERNED, DICK.
LARGASKI AND HIS LIONS LEFT FOR FLORIDA LAST NIGHT.
ON THE PLUS SIDE, I FOUND A NEW AERIAL ACT--THE SOARING SORRANOS!
VITO AND HIS WIFE, GINA.
WELCOME TO HALY'S CIRCUS!
THANKS FOR GIVING US THIS OPPORTUNITY, MR. GRAYSON. WE LIKE THE LOOKS OF THIS PLACE ALREADY.
PLEASE CALL ME DICK.
THIS IS OUR DAUGHTER CHRISTINA.
SHE'S NOT QUITE READY TO JOIN THE ACT, BUT SHE'S GETTING THERE.
IS IT TRUE THAT YOU USED TO FLY ON THE TRAPEZE?
WHEN I WAS JUST A BIT OLDER THAN YOU.
I WAS PART OF AN ACT CALLED THE FLYING GRAYSONS.
MOM SAID I SHOULDN' MENTION THEM.
THEY DIED.
CHRISTINA!

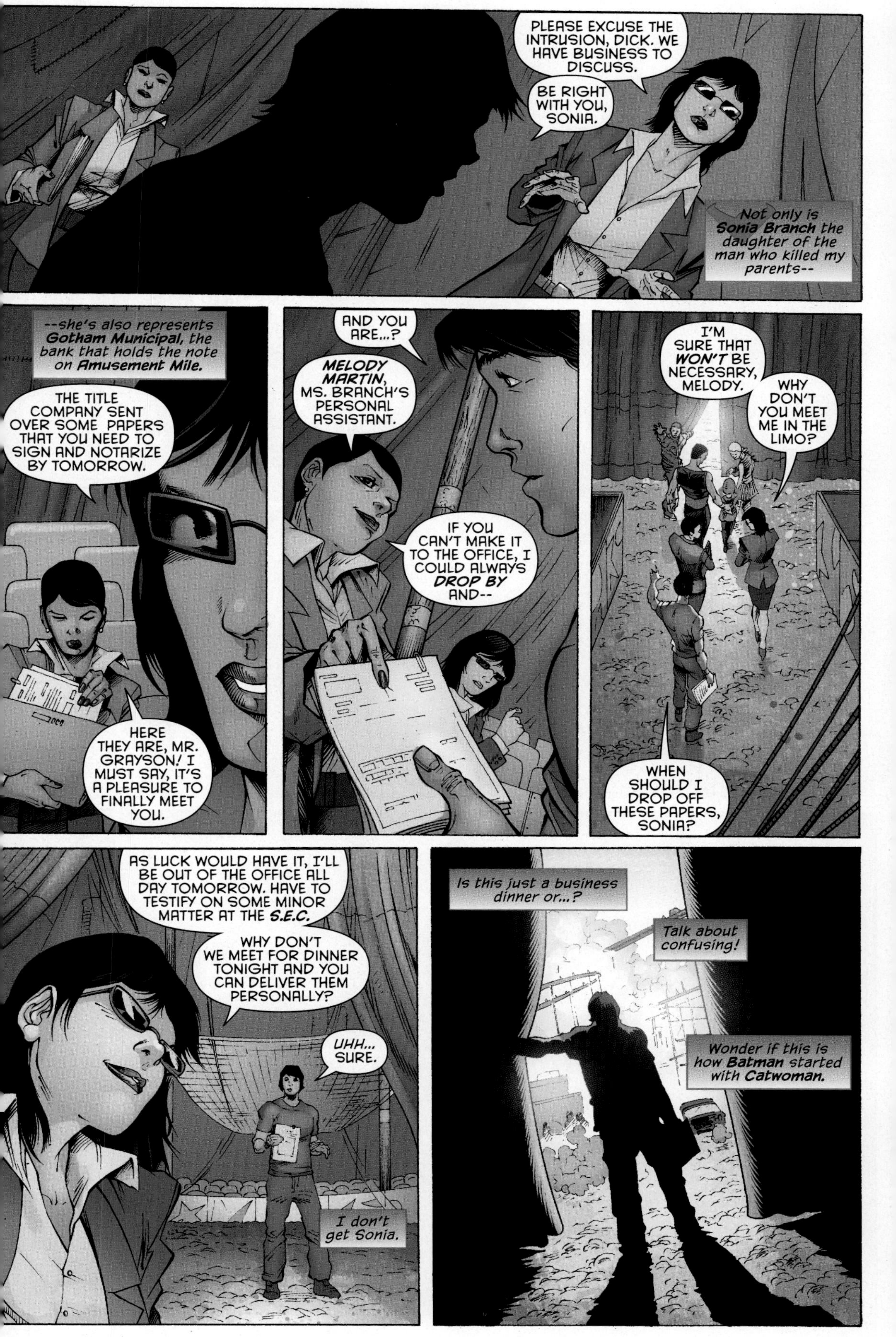
PLEASE EXCUSE THE INTRUSION, DICK. WE HAVE BUSINESS TO DISCUSS.
BE RIGHT WITH YOU, SONIA.
Not only is Sonia Branch the daughter of the man who killed my parents--
--she's also represents Gotham Municipal, the bank that holds the note on Amusement Mile.
THE TITLE COMPANY SENT OVER SOME PAPERS THAT YOU NEED TO SIGN AND NOTARIZE BY TOMORROW.
HERE THEY ARE, MR. GRAYSON! I MUST SAY, IT'S A PLEASURE TO FINALLY MEET YOU.
AND YOU ARE...?
MELODY MARTIN, MS. BRANCH'S PERSONAL ASSISTANT.
IF YOU CAN'T MAKE IT TO THE OFFICE, I COULD ALWAYS DROP BY AND--
I'M SURE THAT WON'T BE NECESSARY, MELODY.
WHY DON'T YOU MEET ME IN THE LIMO?
WHEN SHOULD I DROP OFF THESE PAPERS, SONIA?
AS LUCK WOULD HAVE IT, I'LL BE OUT OF THE OFFICE ALL DAY TOMORROW. HAVE TO TESTIFY ON SOME MINOR MATTER AT THE S.E.C.
WHY DON'T WE MEET FOR DINNER TONIGHT AND YOU CAN DELIVER THEM PERSONALLY?
UHH... SURE.
I don't get Sonia.
Is this just a business dinner or...?
Talk about confusing!
Wonder if this is how Batman started with Catwoman.

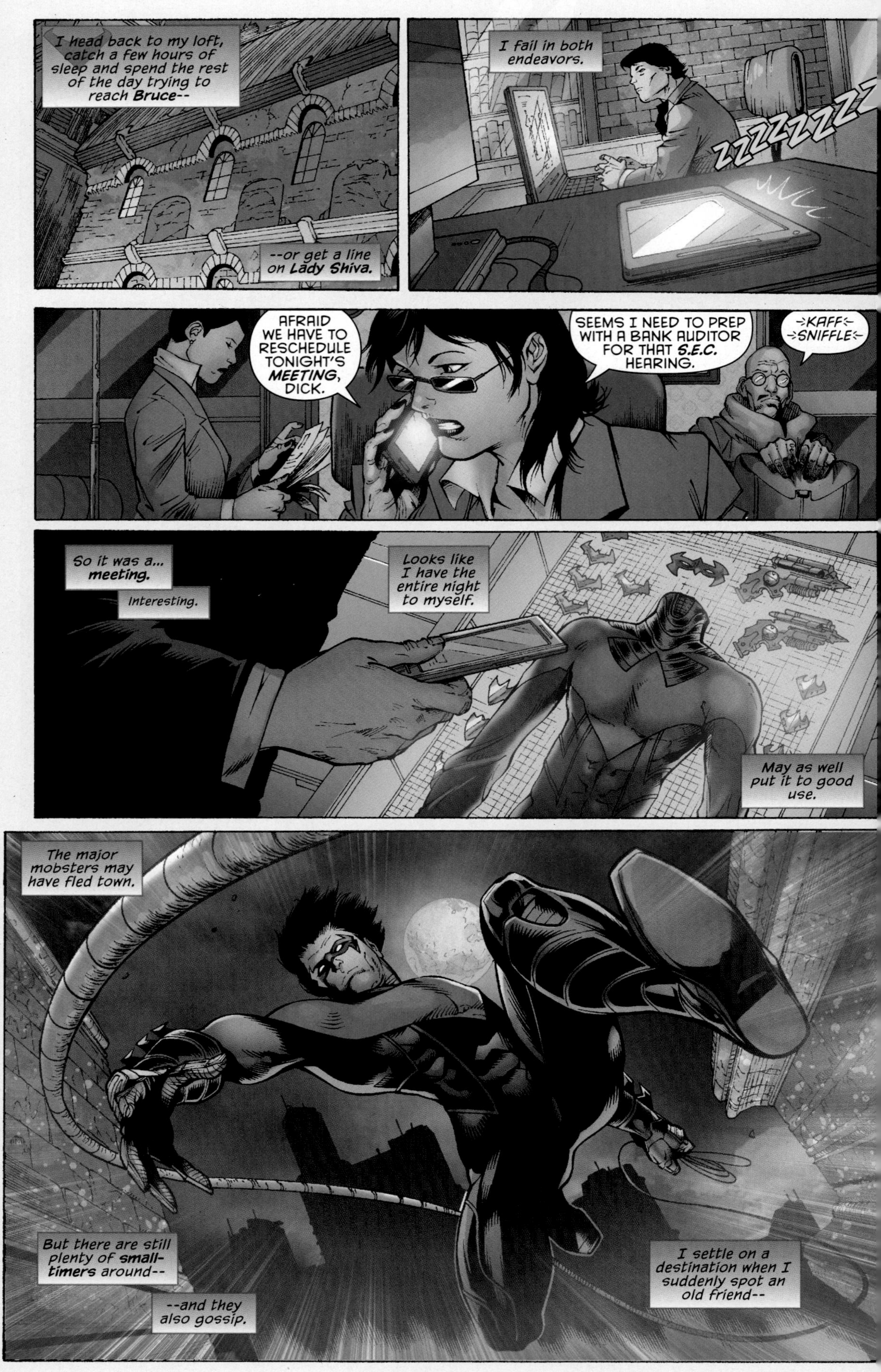
I head back to my loft, catch a few hours of sleep and spend the rest of the day trying to reach Bruce--
--or get a line on Lady Shiva.
I fail in both endeavors.
ZZZZZZZZZ
AFRAID WE HAVE TO RESCHEDULE TONIGHT'S MEETING, DICK.
SEEMS I NEED TO PREP WITH A BANK AUDITOR FOR THAT S.E.C. HEARING.
KAFF
SNIFFLE
So it was a... meeting.
Interesting.
Looks like I have the entire night to myself.
May as well put it to good use.
The major mobsters may have fled town.
But there are still plenty of small-timers around--
--and they also gossip.
I settle on a destination when I suddenly spot an old friend--

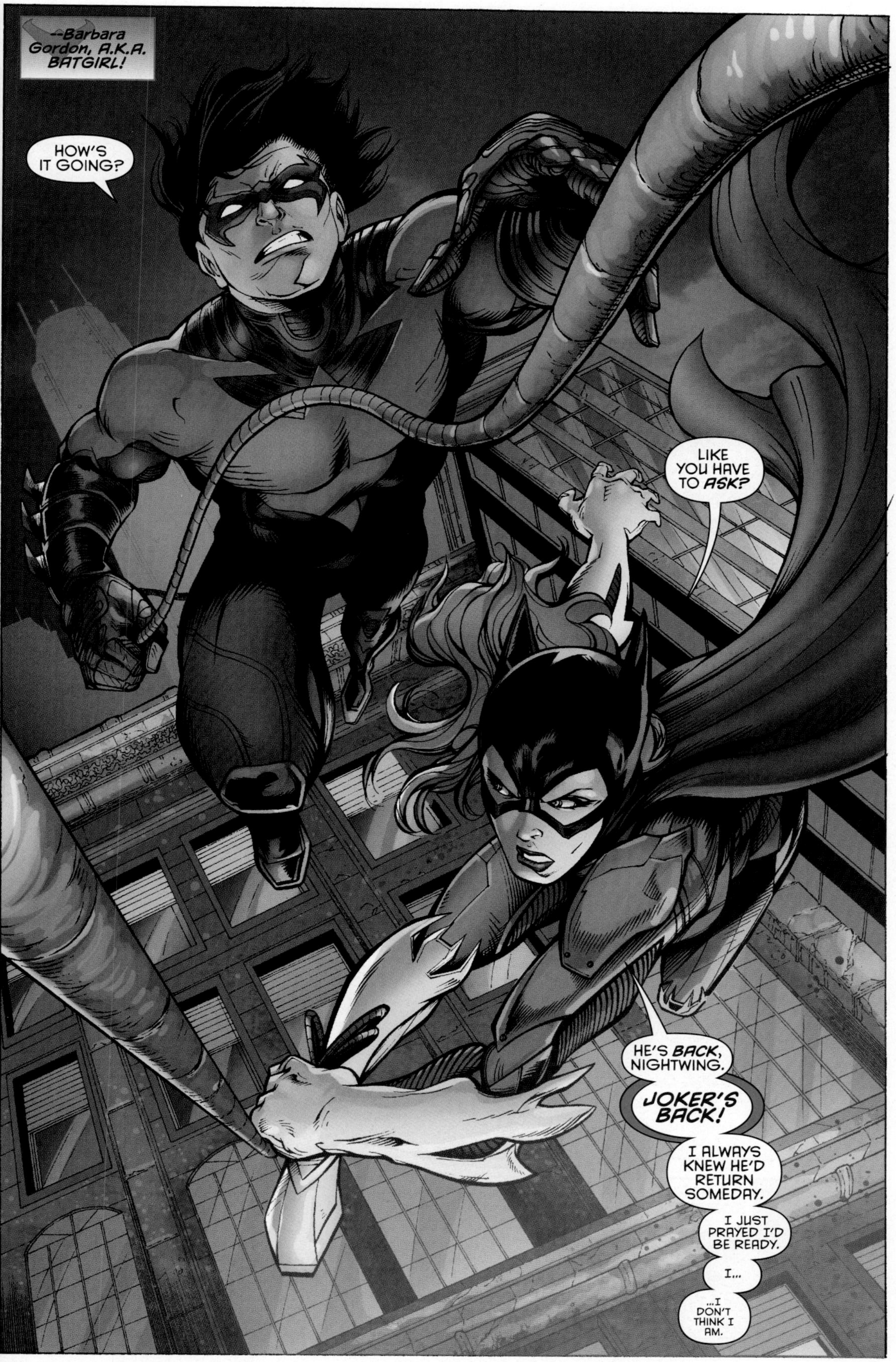

--Barbara Gordon, A.K.A. BATGIRL!
HOW'S IT GOING?
LIKE YOU HAVE TO *ASK?*
HE'S *BACK,* NIGHTWING.
JOKER'S BACK!
I ALWAYS KNEW HE'D RETURN SOMEDAY.
I JUST PRAYED I'D BE READY.
I...
...I DON'T THINK I AM.

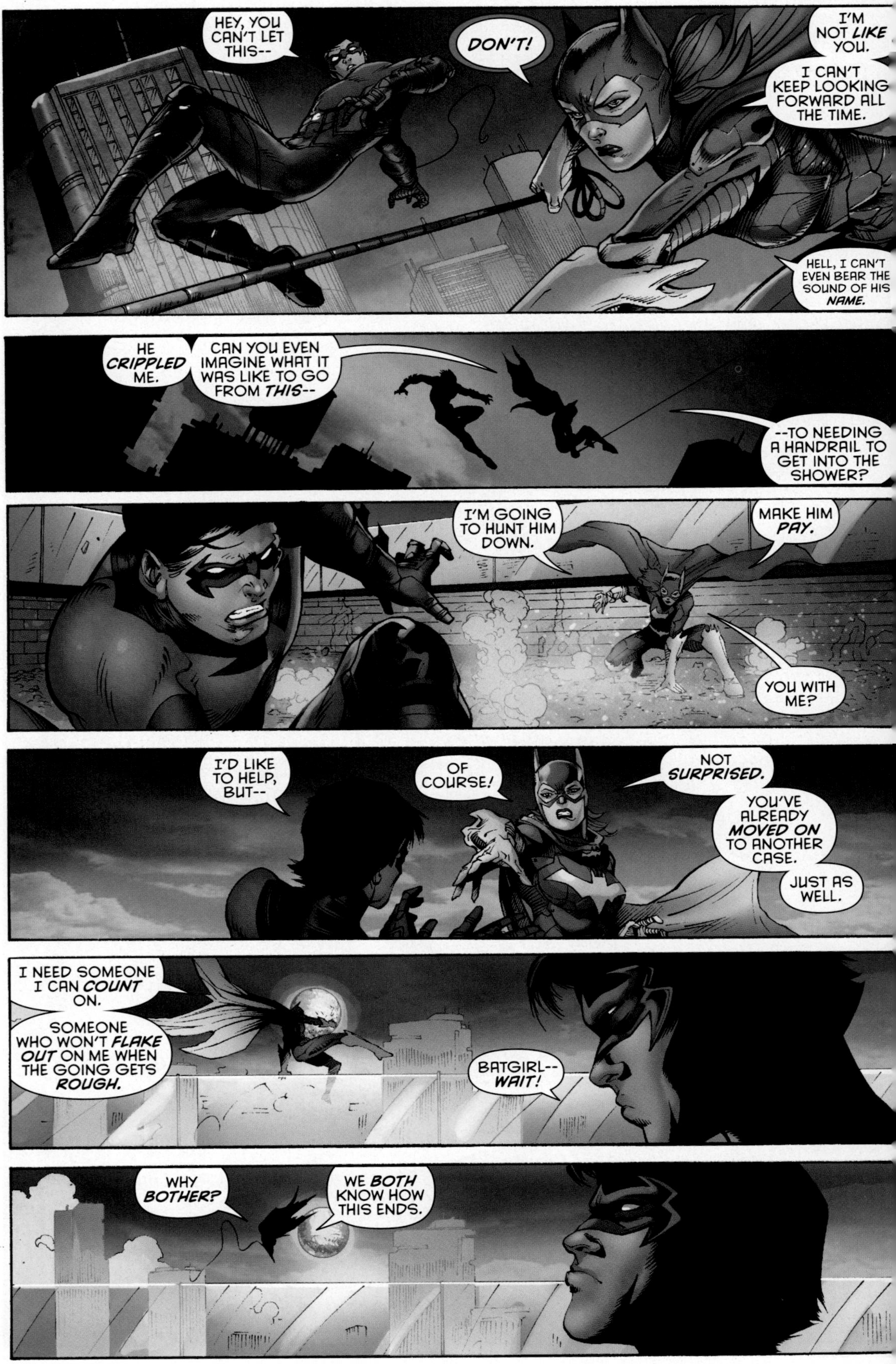
HEY, YOU CAN'T LET THIS--
DON'T!
I'M NOT *LIKE* YOU.
I CAN'T KEEP LOOKING FORWARD ALL THE TIME.
HELL, I CAN'T EVEN BEAR THE SOUND OF HIS *NAME.*
HE *CRIPPLED* ME.
CAN YOU EVEN IMAGINE WHAT IT WAS LIKE TO GO FROM *THIS*--
--TO NEEDING A HANDRAIL TO GET INTO THE SHOWER?
I'M GOING TO HUNT HIM DOWN.
MAKE HIM *PAY.*
YOU WITH ME?
I'D LIKE TO HELP, BUT--
OF COURSE!
NOT *SURPRISED.*
YOU'VE ALREADY *MOVED ON* TO ANOTHER CASE.
JUST AS WELL.
I NEED SOMEONE I CAN *COUNT* ON.
SOMEONE WHO WON'T *FLAKE OUT* ON ME WHEN THE GOING GETS *ROUGH.*
BATGIRL-- *WAIT!*
WHY *BOTHER?*
WE *BOTH* KNOW HOW THIS ENDS.

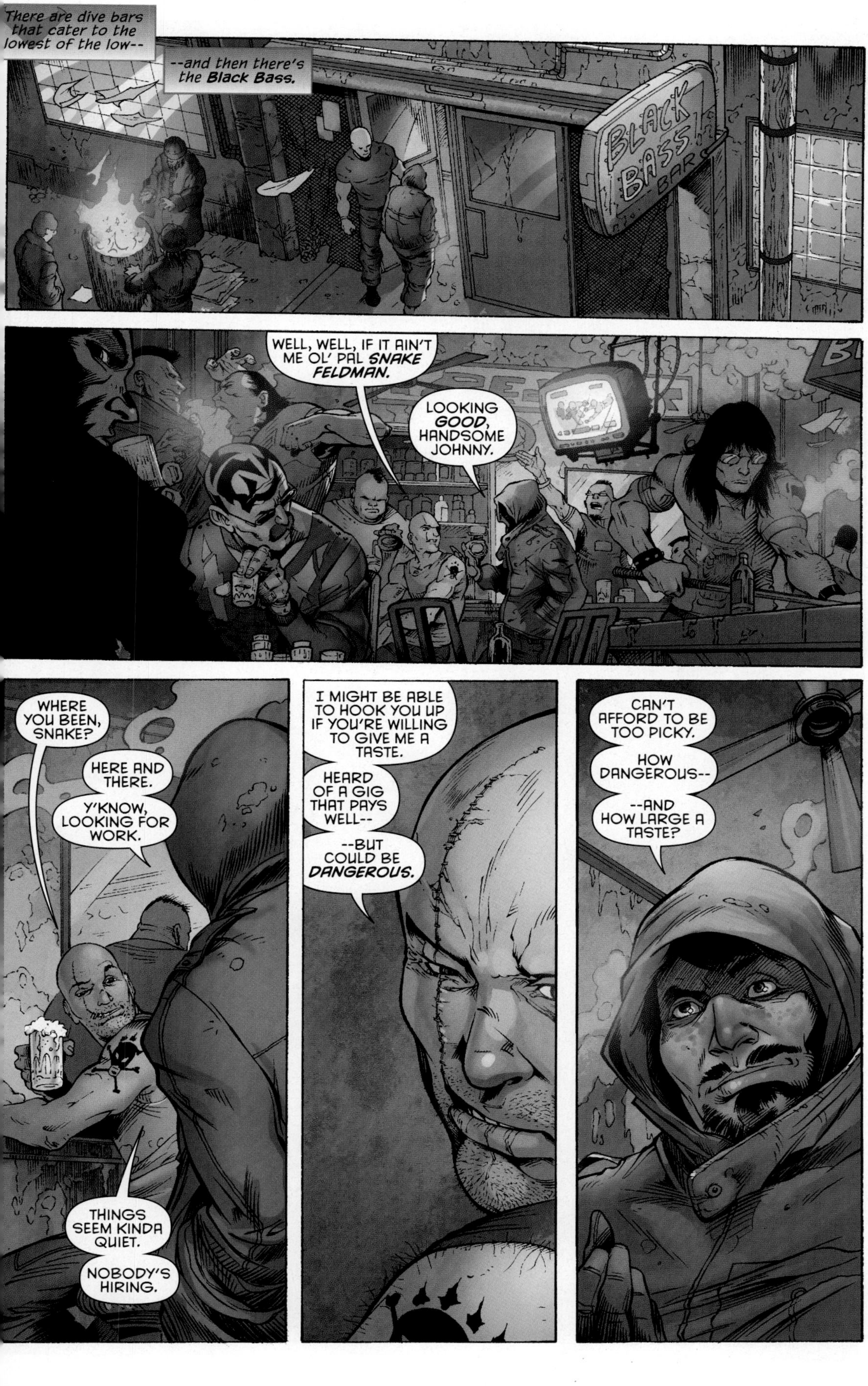

There are dive bars that cater to the lowest of the low--
--and then there's the Black Bass.
BLACK BASS! BAR
WELL, WELL, IF IT AIN'T ME OL' PAL SNAKE FELDMAN.
LOOKING GOOD, HANDSOME JOHNNY.
WHERE YOU BEEN, SNAKE?
HERE AND THERE.
Y'KNOW, LOOKING FOR WORK.
THINGS SEEM KINDA QUIET.
NOBODY'S HIRING.
I MIGHT BE ABLE TO HOOK YOU UP IF YOU'RE WILLING TO GIVE ME A TASTE.
HEARD OF A GIG THAT PAYS WELL--
--BUT COULD BE DANGEROUS.
CAN'T AFFORD TO BE TOO PICKY.
HOW DANGEROUS--
--AND HOW LARGE A TASTE?

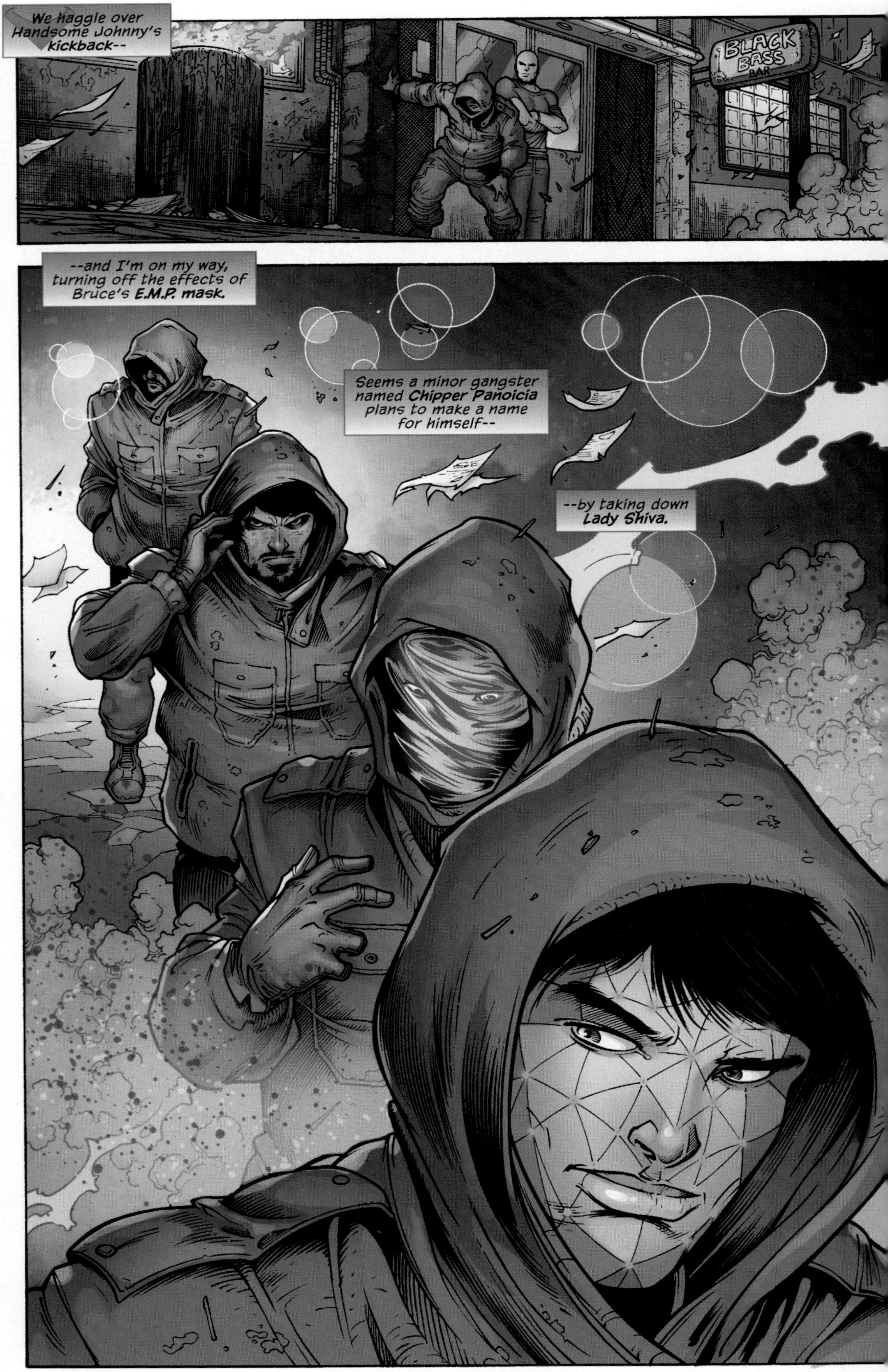
We haggle over Handsome Johnny's kickback--
BLACK BASS BAR
--and I'm on my way, turning off the effects of Bruce's E.M.P. mask.
Seems a minor gangster named Chipper Panoicia plans to make a name for himself--
--by taking down Lady Shiva.

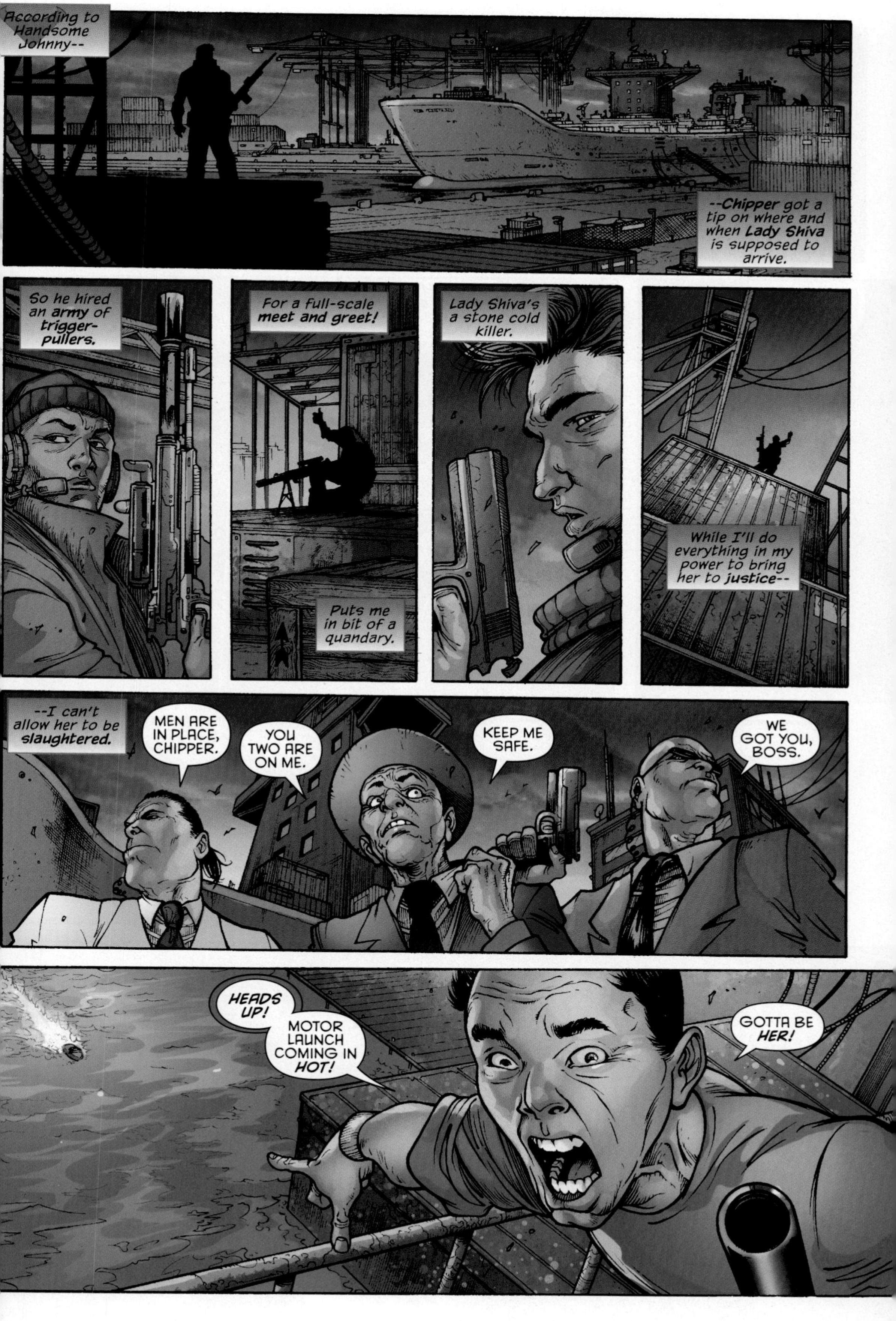
According to Handsome Johnny--
--Chipper got a tip on where and when Lady Shiva is supposed to arrive.
So he hired an army of trigger-pullers.
For a full-scale meet and greet!
Puts me in bit of a quandary.
Lady Shiva's a stone cold killer.
While I'll do everything in my power to bring her to justice--
--I can't allow her to be slaughtered.
MEN ARE IN PLACE, CHIPPER.
YOU TWO ARE ON ME.
KEEP ME SAFE.
WE GOT YOU, BOSS.
HEADS UP!
MOTOR LAUNCH COMING IN HOT!
GOTTA BE HER!

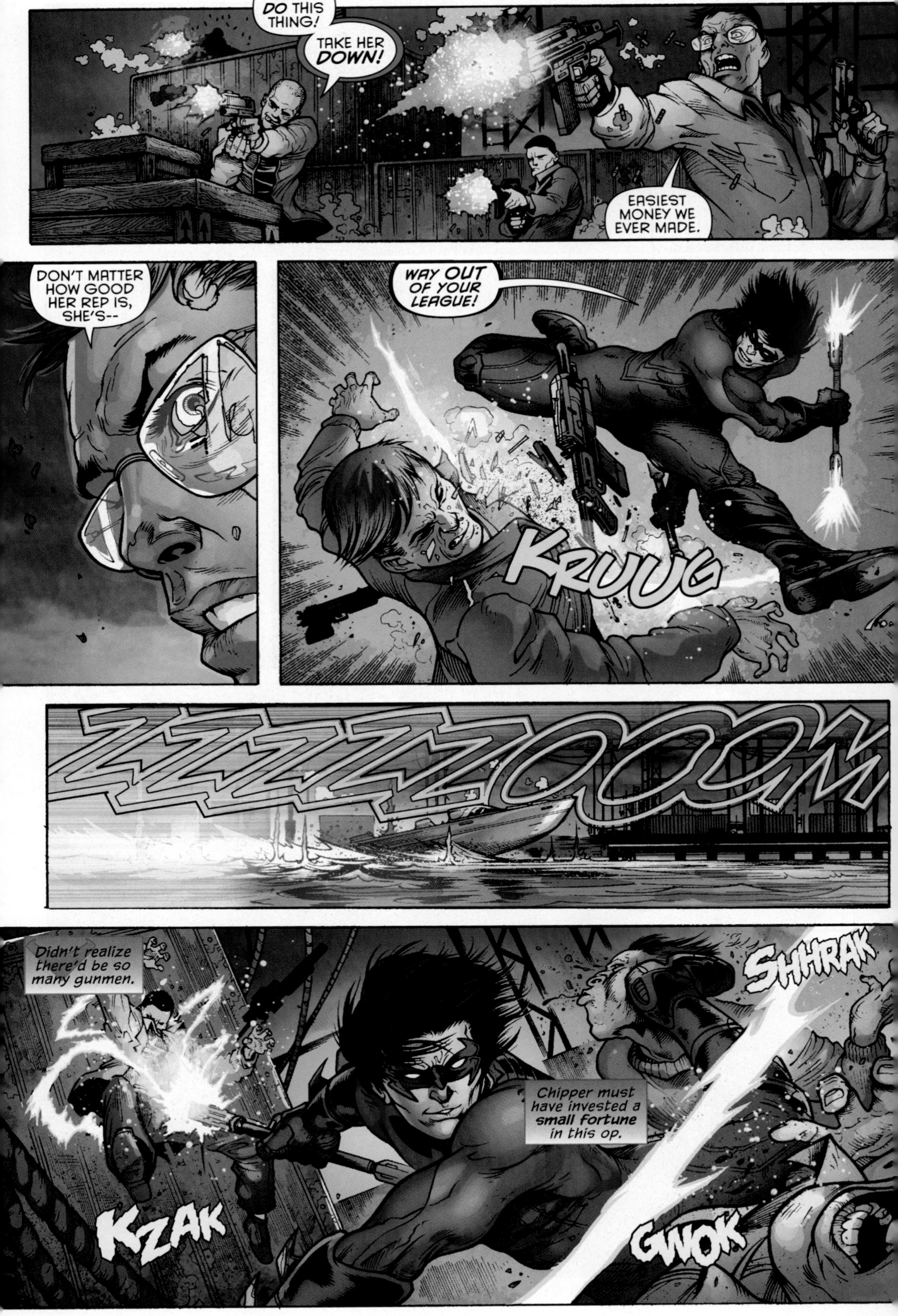
LET'S DO THIS THING!
TAKE HER DOWN!
EASIEST MONEY WE EVER MADE.
DON'T MATTER HOW GOOD HER REP IS, SHE'S--
WAY OUT OF YOUR LEAGUE!
KRUUG
ZZZZOOOM
Didn't realize there'd be so many gunmen.
SHHRAK
Chipper must have invested a small fortune in this op.
KZAK
GWOK

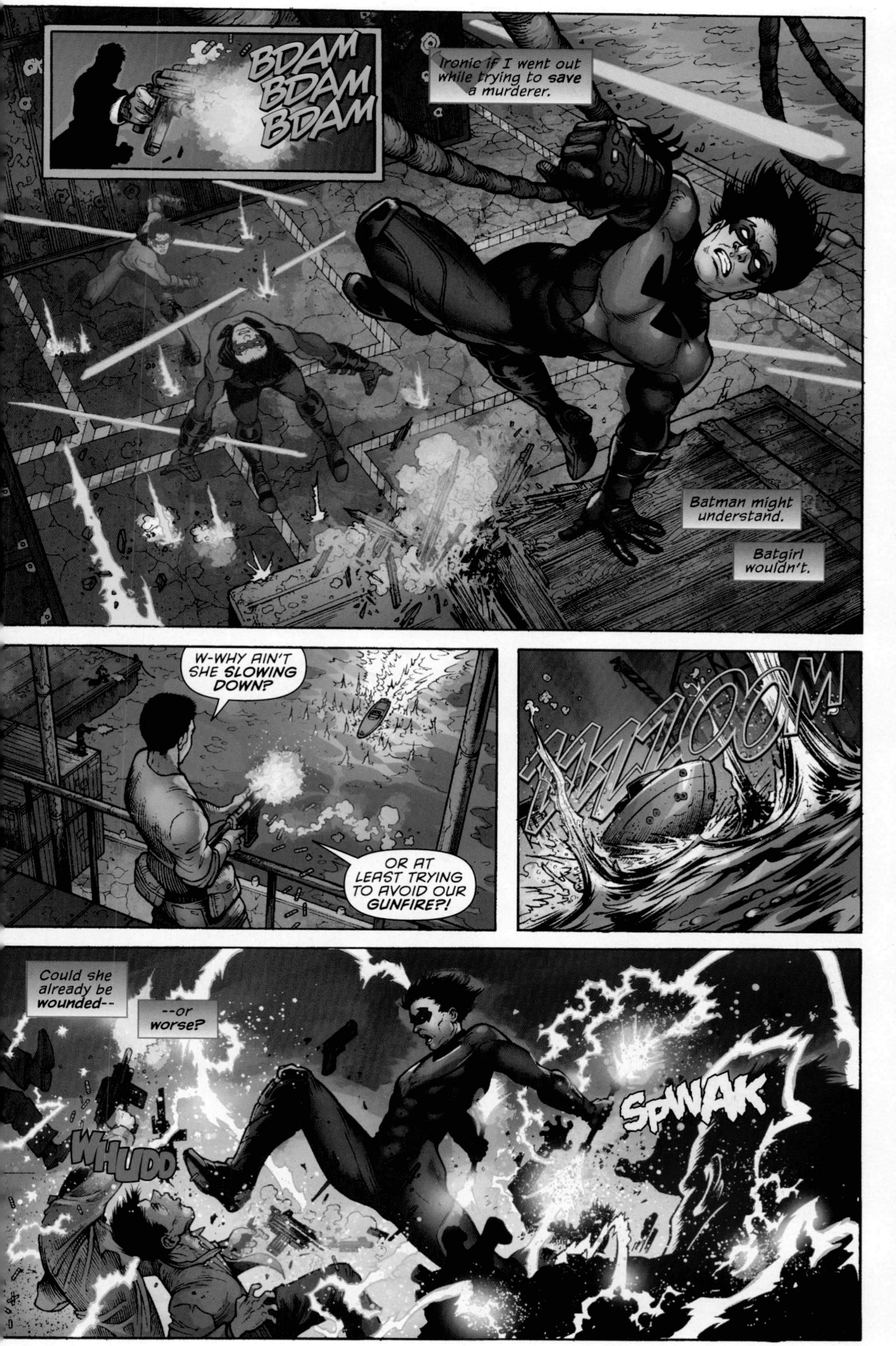
BDAM
BDAM
BDAM
Ironic if I went out while trying to save a murderer.
Batman might understand.
Batgirl wouldn't.
W-WHY AIN'T SHE SLOWING DOWN?
OR AT LEAST TRYING TO AVOID OUR GUNFIRE?!
KAWHOOM!
Could she already be wounded--
--or worse?
WHUDD
SPWAK

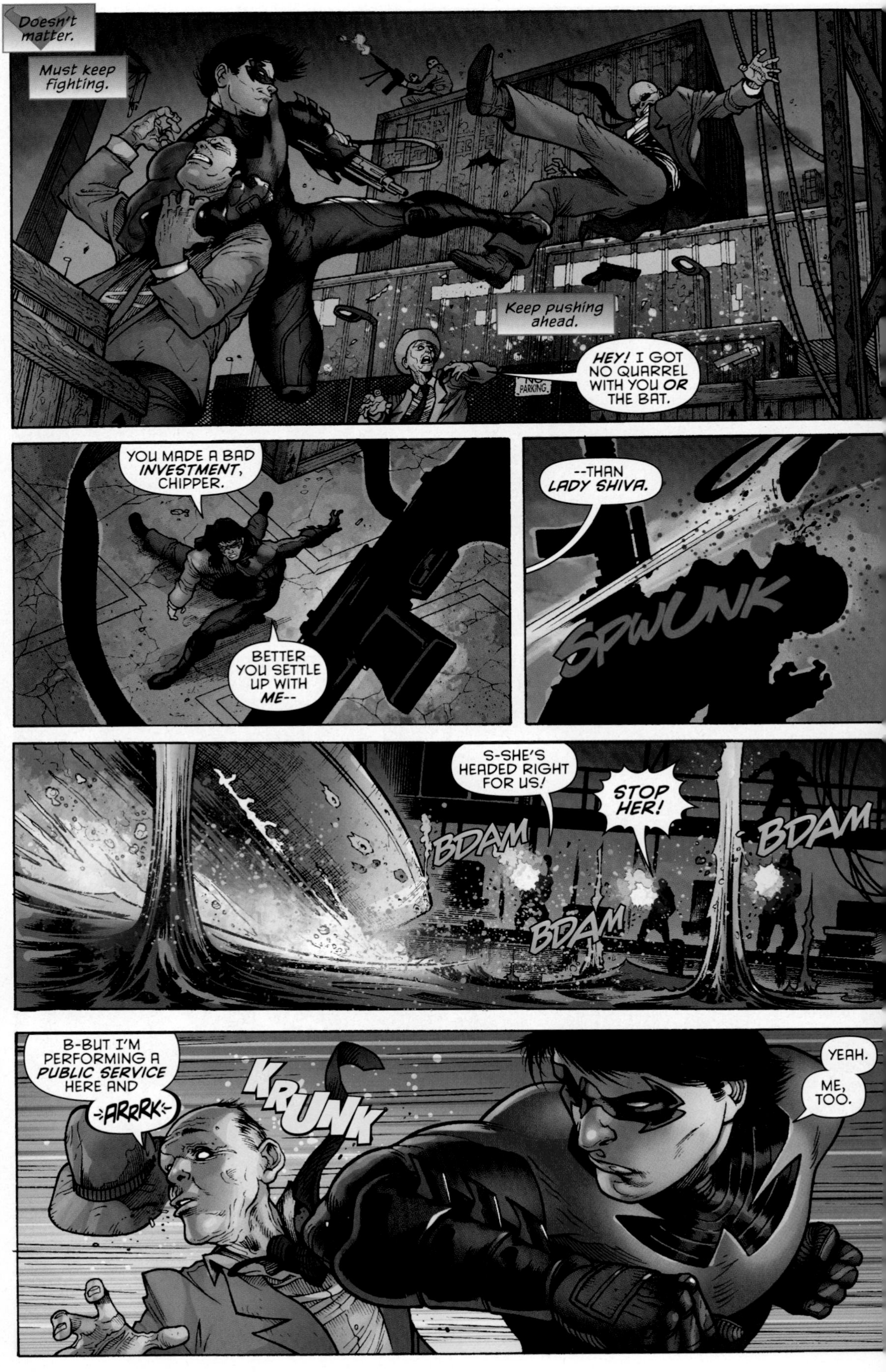

Doesn't matter.
Must keep fighting.
Keep pushing ahead.
HEY! I GOT NO QUARREL WITH YOU OR THE BAT.
NO PARKING.
YOU MADE A BAD INVESTMENT, CHIPPER.
BETTER YOU SETTLE UP WITH ME--
--THAN LADY SHIVA.
SPWUNK
S-SHE'S HEADED RIGHT FOR US!
STOP HER!
BDAM
BDAM
BDAM
B-BUT I'M PERFORMING A PUBLIC SERVICE HERE AND
ARRRK
KRUNK
YEAH.
ME, TOO.

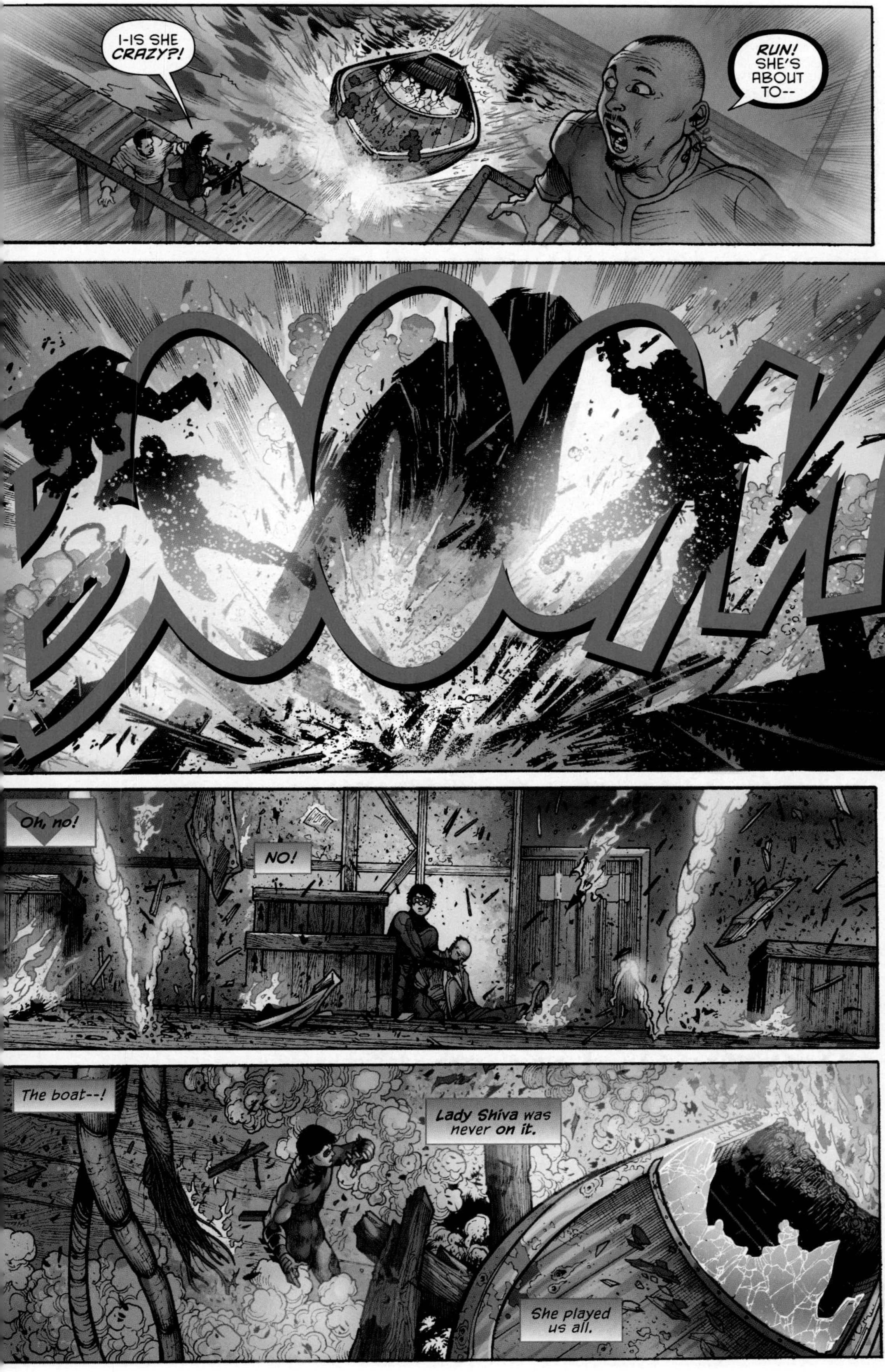

I-IS SHE CRAZY?!
RUN! SHE'S ABOUT TO--
BOOOM
Oh, no!
NO!
The boat--!
Lady Shiva was never on it.
She played us all.

Why?

‹KAFF›
‹KAFF›
‹SNIFFLE›

Where is she?

What's her real game?

SSSSWIK

‹URRK›

She's been ahead of me from the start.

How many targets does she have in Gotham?

Is it even possible to stop her--

--before she kills again?

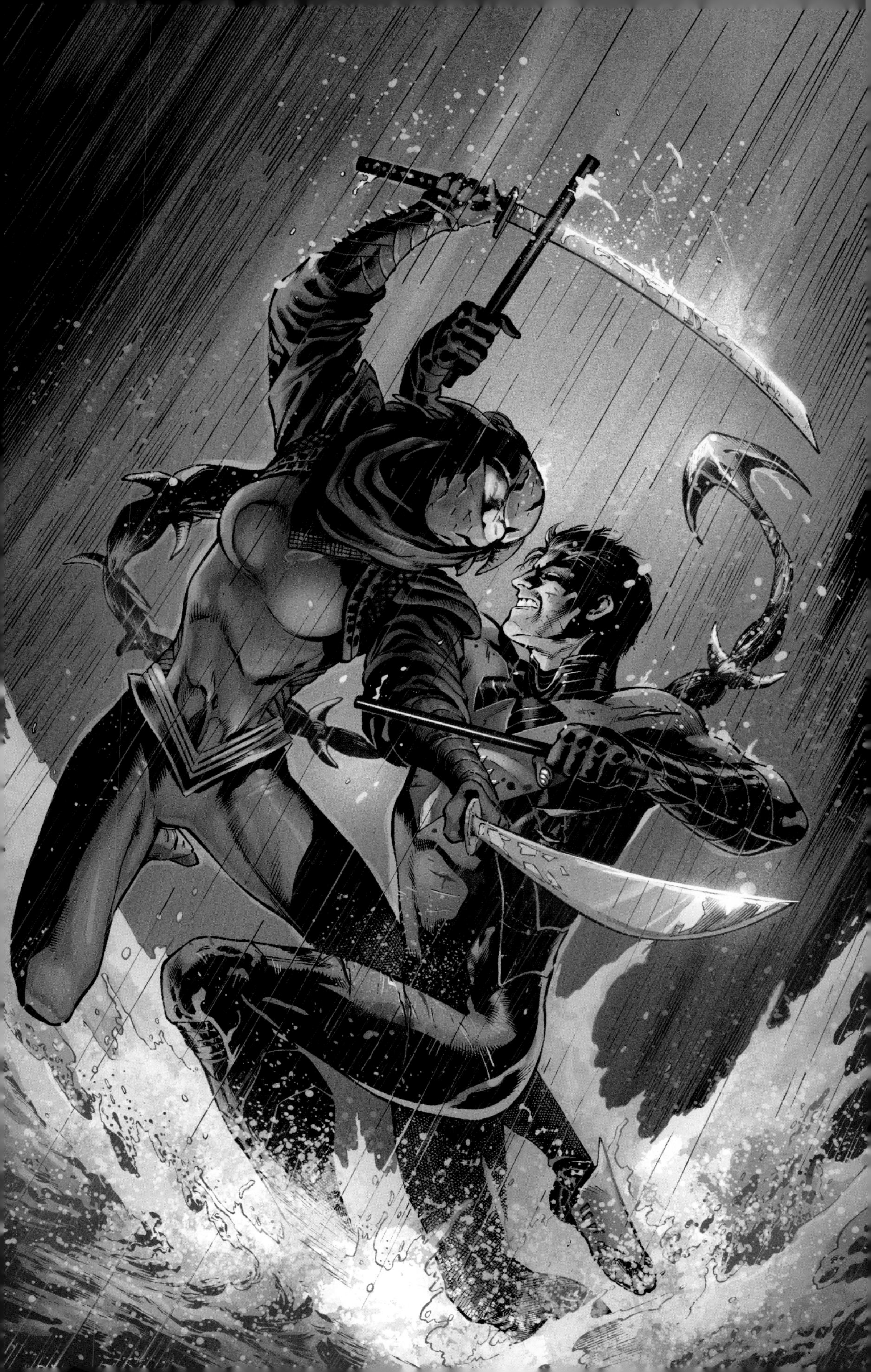

DIE FOR ME

TOM DEFALCO writer **ANDRES GUINALDO** penciller **MARK IRWIN** inker cover art by **EDDY BARROWS, EBER FERREIRA & ROD REIS**

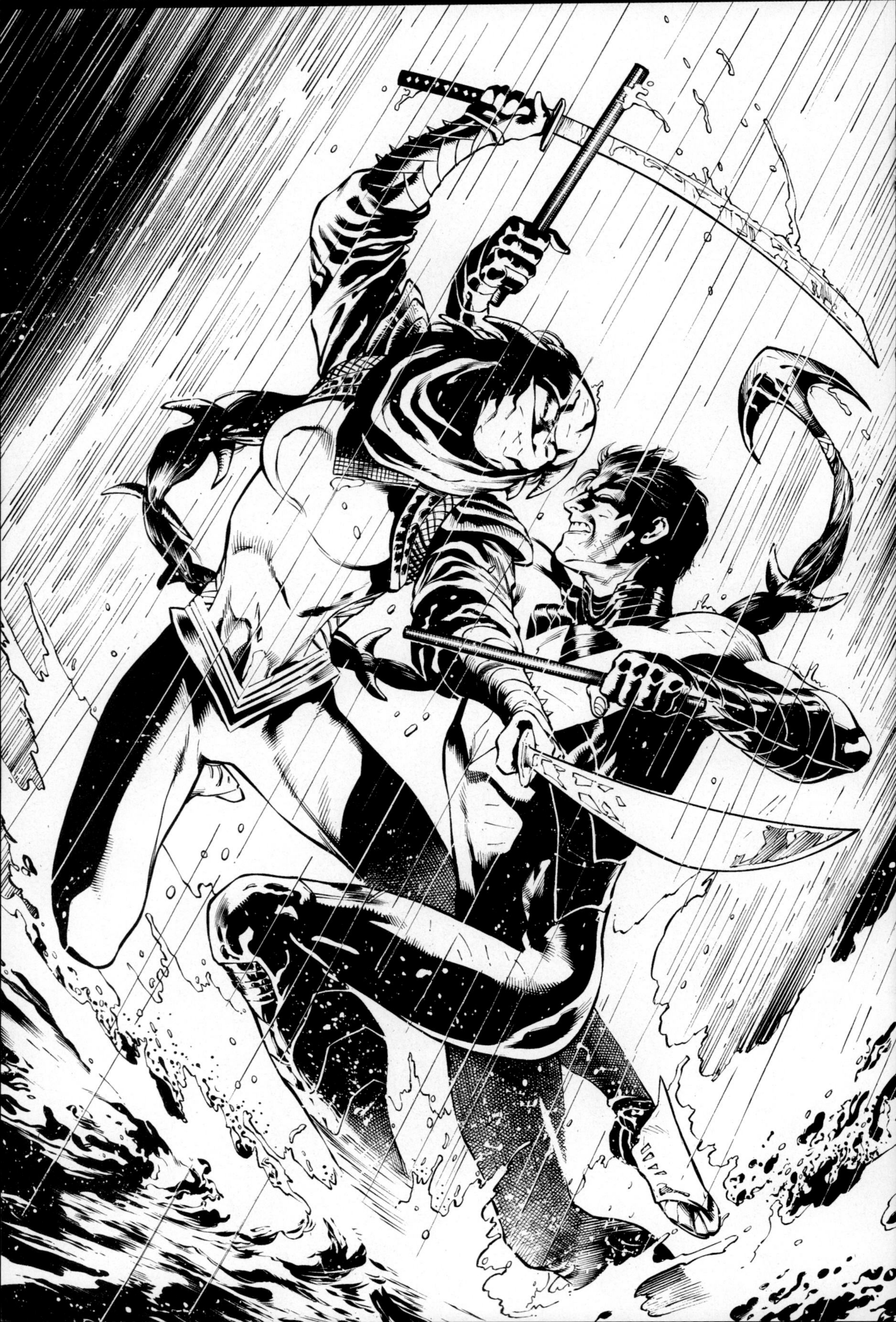

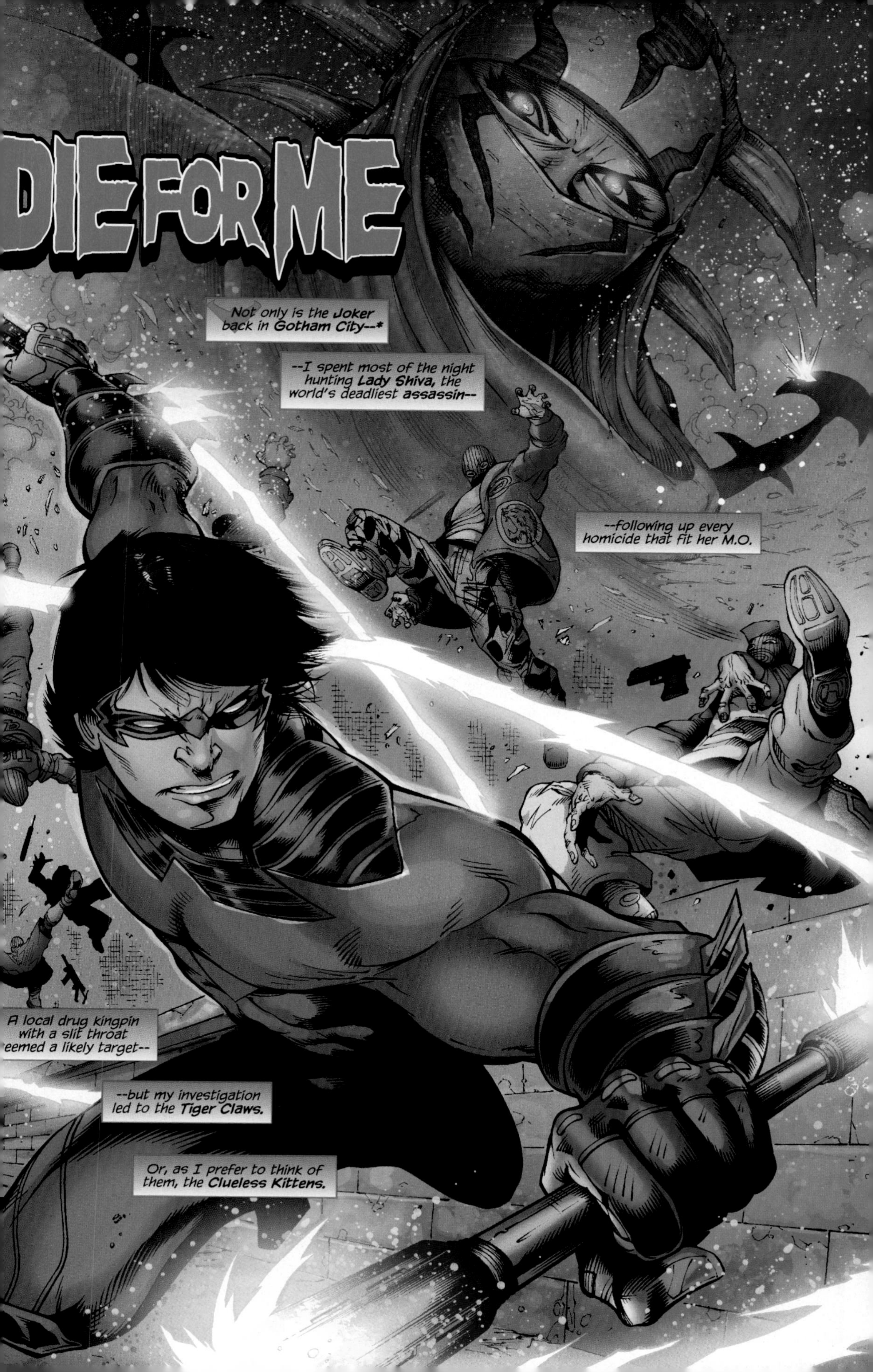
DIE FOR ME
Not only is the Joker back in Gotham City--*
--I spent most of the night hunting Lady Shiva, the world's deadliest assassin--
--following up every homicide that fit her M.O.
A local drug kingpin with a slit throat eemed a likely target--
--but my investigation led to the Tiger Claws.
Or, as I prefer to think of them, the Clueless Kittens.

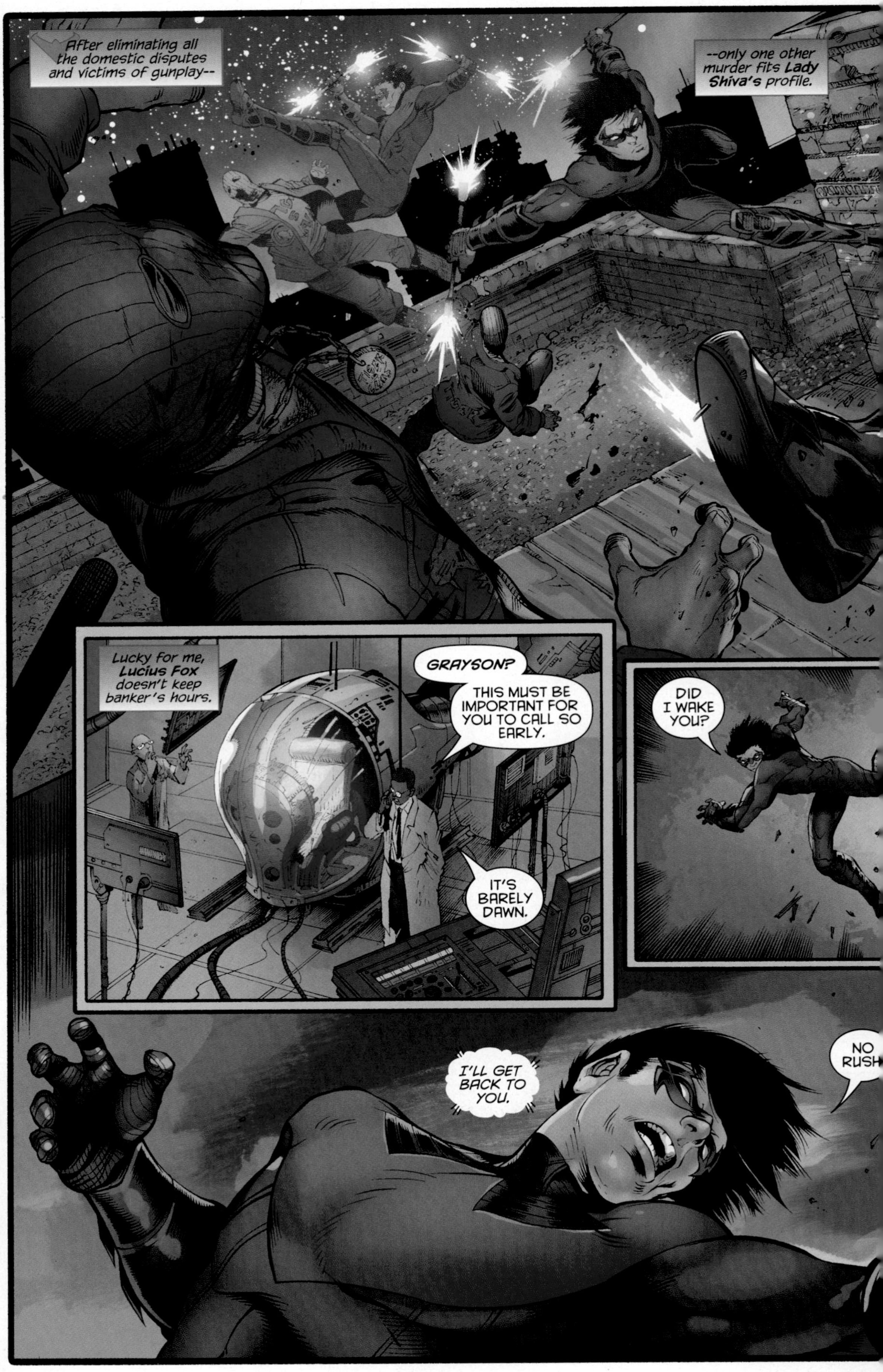
After eliminating all the domestic disputes and victims of gunplay--
--only one other murder fits Lady Shiva's profile.
Lucky for me, Lucius Fox doesn't keep banker's hours.
GRAYSON?
THIS MUST BE IMPORTANT FOR YOU TO CALL SO EARLY.
IT'S BARELY DAWN.
DID I WAKE YOU?
I'LL GET BACK TO YOU.
NO RUSH

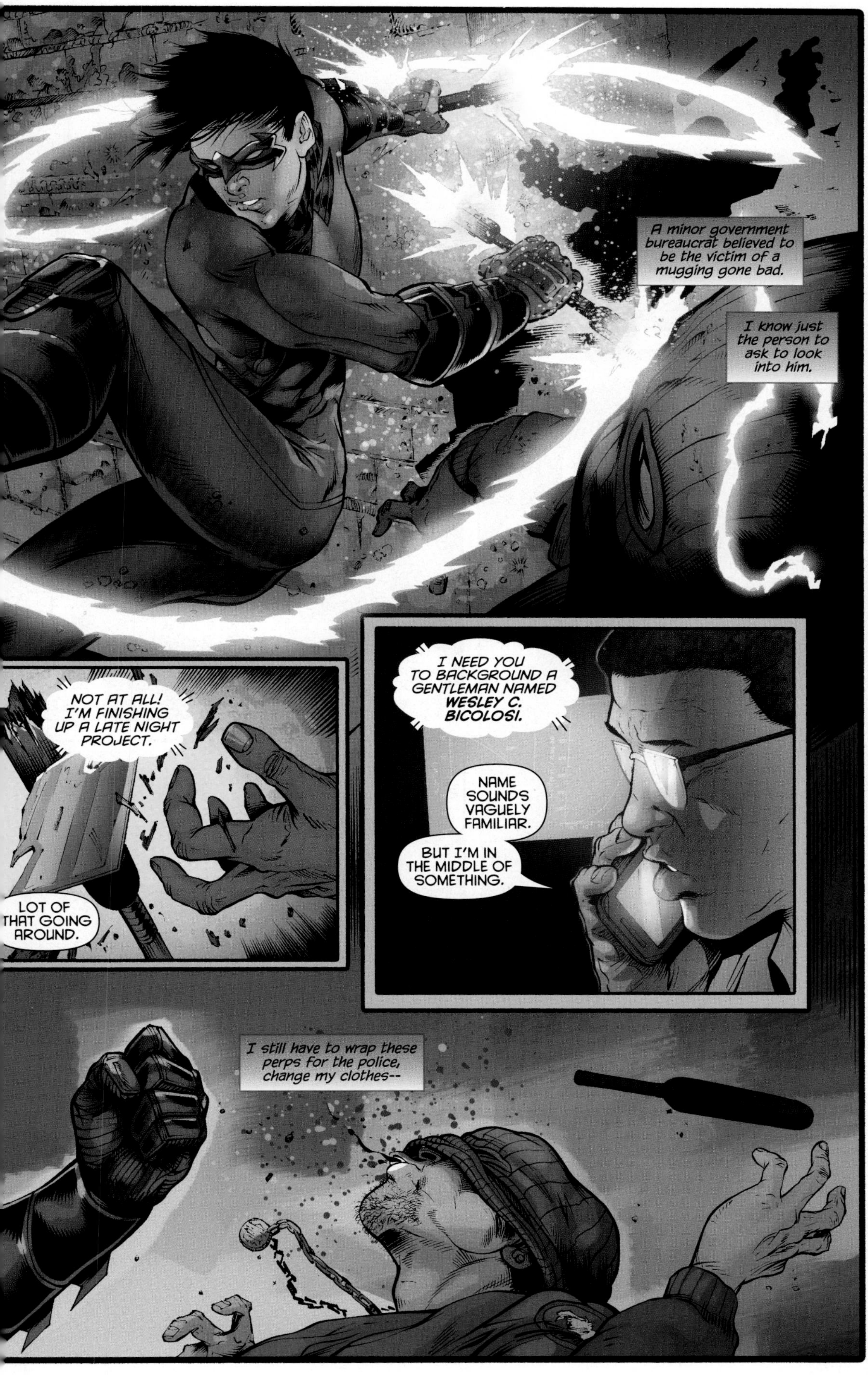
A minor government bureaucrat believed to be the victim of a mugging gone bad.
I know just the person to ask to look into him.
I NEED YOU TO BACKGROUND A GENTLEMAN NAMED WESLEY C. BICOLOSI.
NOT AT ALL! I'M FINISHING UP A LATE NIGHT PROJECT.
NAME SOUNDS VAGUELY FAMILIAR.
BUT I'M IN THE MIDDLE OF SOMETHING.
LOT OF THAT GOING AROUND.
I still have to wrap these perps for the police, change my clothes--

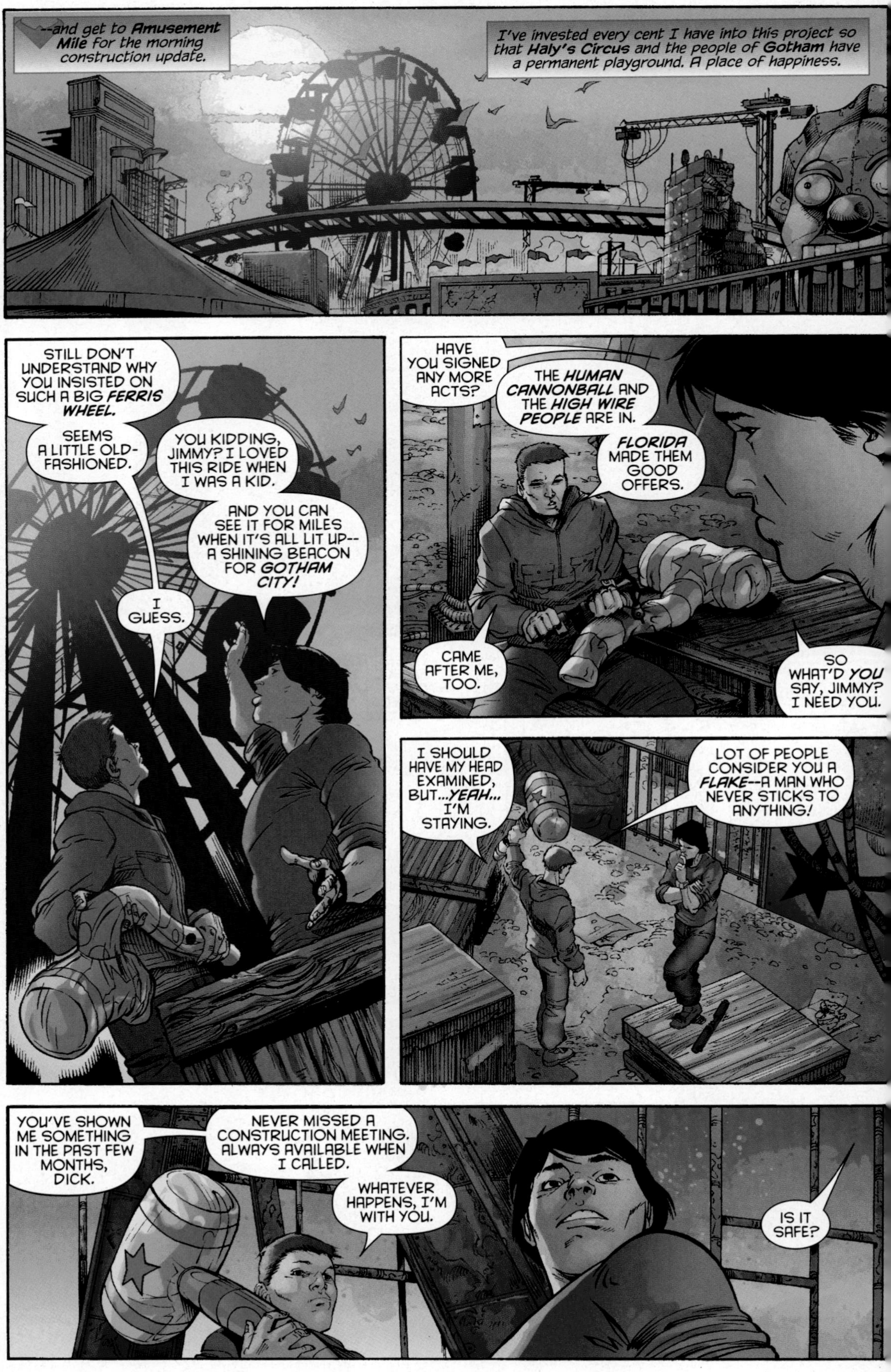

--and get to Amusement Mile for the morning construction update.
I've invested every cent I have into this project so that Haly's Circus and the people of Gotham have a permanent playground. A place of happiness.
STILL DON'T UNDERSTAND WHY YOU INSISTED ON SUCH A BIG FERRIS WHEEL.
SEEMS A LITTLE OLD-FASHIONED.
YOU KIDDING, JIMMY? I LOVED THIS RIDE WHEN I WAS A KID.
AND YOU CAN SEE IT FOR MILES WHEN IT'S ALL LIT UP--A SHINING BEACON FOR GOTHAM CITY!
I GUESS.
HAVE YOU SIGNED ANY MORE ACTS?
THE HUMAN CANNONBALL AND THE HIGH WIRE PEOPLE ARE IN.
FLORIDA MADE THEM GOOD OFFERS.
CAME AFTER ME, TOO.
SO WHAT'D YOU SAY, JIMMY? I NEED YOU.
I SHOULD HAVE MY HEAD EXAMINED, BUT...YEAH... I'M STAYING.
LOT OF PEOPLE CONSIDER YOU A FLAKE--A MAN WHO NEVER STICKS TO ANYTHING!
YOU'VE SHOWN ME SOMETHING IN THE PAST FEW MONTHS, DICK.
NEVER MISSED A CONSTRUCTION MEETING. ALWAYS AVAILABLE WHEN I CALLED.
WHATEVER HAPPENS, I'M WITH YOU.
IS IT SAFE?

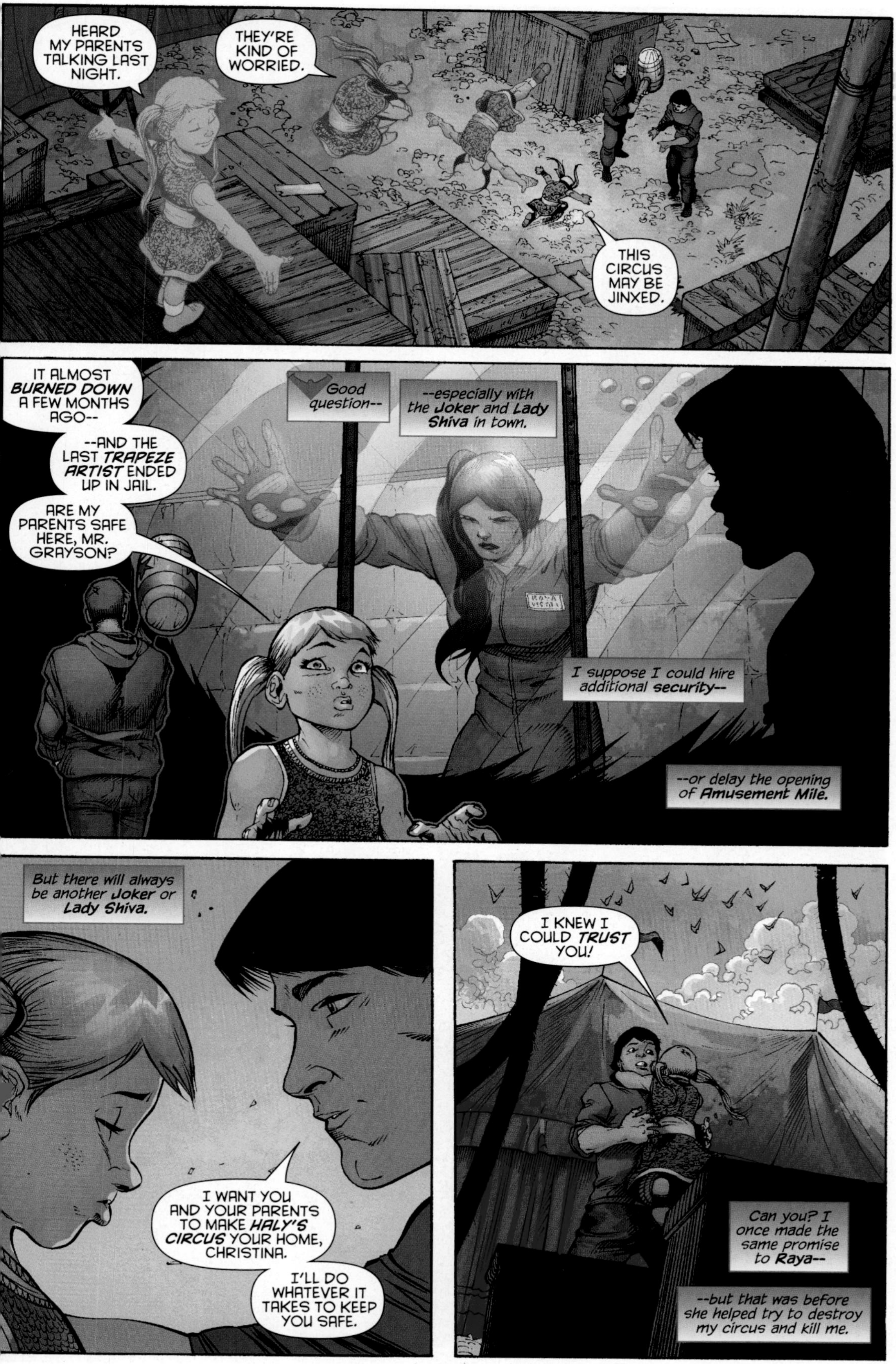

HEARD MY PARENTS TALKING LAST NIGHT.
THEY'RE KIND OF WORRIED.
THIS CIRCUS MAY BE JINXED.
IT ALMOST BURNED DOWN A FEW MONTHS AGO--
--AND THE LAST TRAPEZE ARTIST ENDED UP IN JAIL.
ARE MY PARENTS SAFE HERE, MR. GRAYSON?
Good question--
--especially with the Joker and Lady Shiva in town.
I suppose I could hire additional security--
--or delay the opening of Amusement Mile.
But there will always be another Joker or Lady Shiva.
I WANT YOU AND YOUR PARENTS TO MAKE HALY'S CIRCUS YOUR HOME, CHRISTINA.
I'LL DO WHATEVER IT TAKES TO KEEP YOU SAFE.
I KNEW I COULD TRUST YOU!
Can you? I once made the same promise to Raya--
--but that was before she helped try to destroy my circus and kill me.

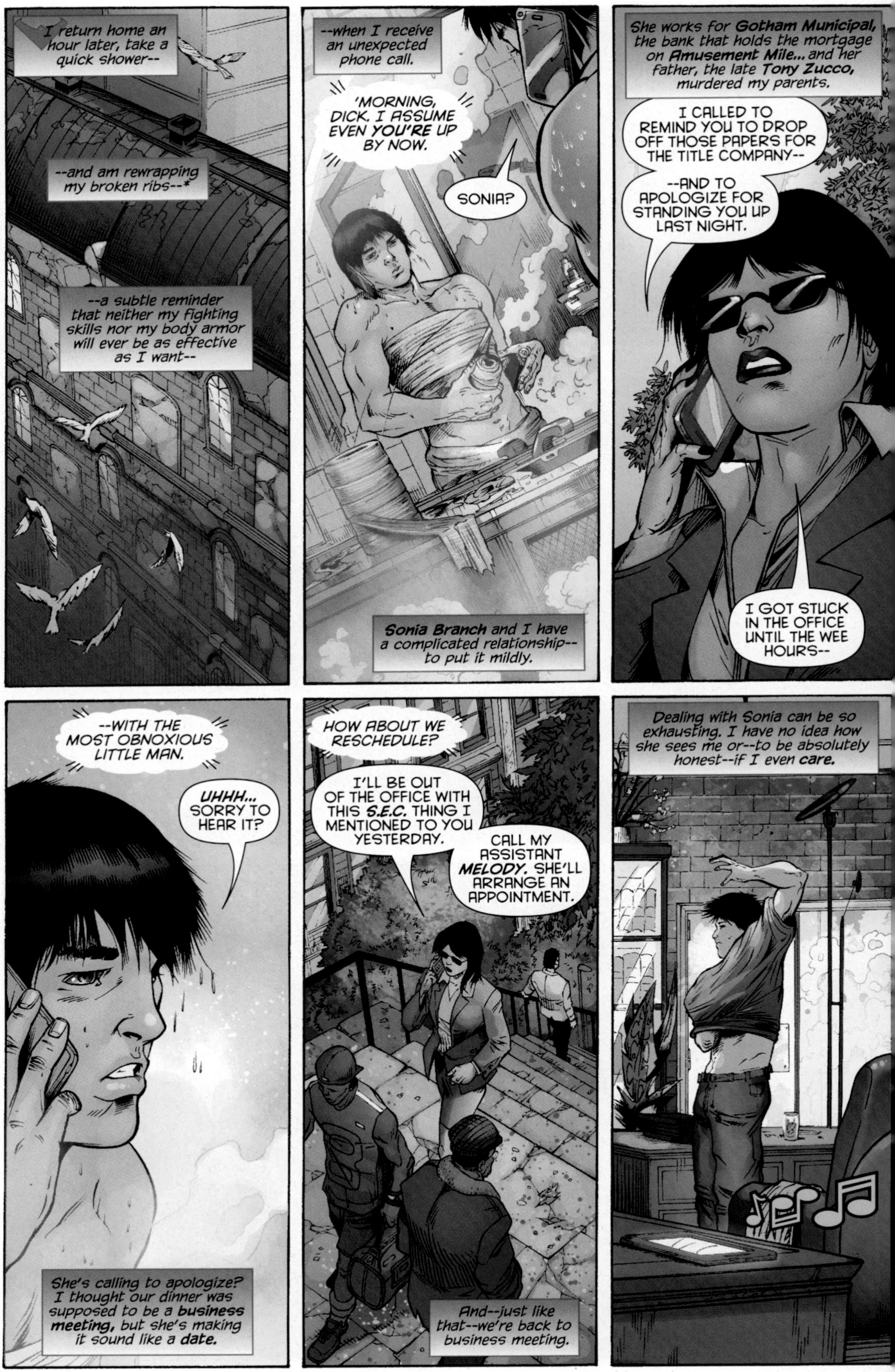
I return home an hour later, take a quick shower--
--and am rewrapping my broken ribs--*
--a subtle reminder that neither my fighting skills nor my body armor will ever be as effective as I want--
--when I receive an unexpected phone call.
'MORNING, DICK. I ASSUME EVEN YOU'RE UP BY NOW.
SONIA?
Sonia Branch and I have a complicated relationship--to put it mildly.
She works for Gotham Municipal, the bank that holds the mortgage on Amusement Mile... and her father, the late Tony Zucco, murdered my parents.
I CALLED TO REMIND YOU TO DROP OFF THOSE PAPERS FOR THE TITLE COMPANY--
--AND TO APOLOGIZE FOR STANDING YOU UP LAST NIGHT.
I GOT STUCK IN THE OFFICE UNTIL THE WEE HOURS--
--WITH THE MOST OBNOXIOUS LITTLE MAN.
UHHH... SORRY TO HEAR IT?
She's calling to apologize? I thought our dinner was supposed to be a business meeting, but she's making it sound like a date.
HOW ABOUT WE RESCHEDULE?
I'LL BE OUT OF THE OFFICE WITH THIS S.E.C. THING I MENTIONED TO YOU YESTERDAY.
CALL MY ASSISTANT MELODY. SHE'LL ARRANGE AN APPOINTMENT.
And--just like that--we're back to business meeting.
Dealing with Sonia can be so exhausting. I have no idea how she sees me or--to be absolutely honest--if I even care.

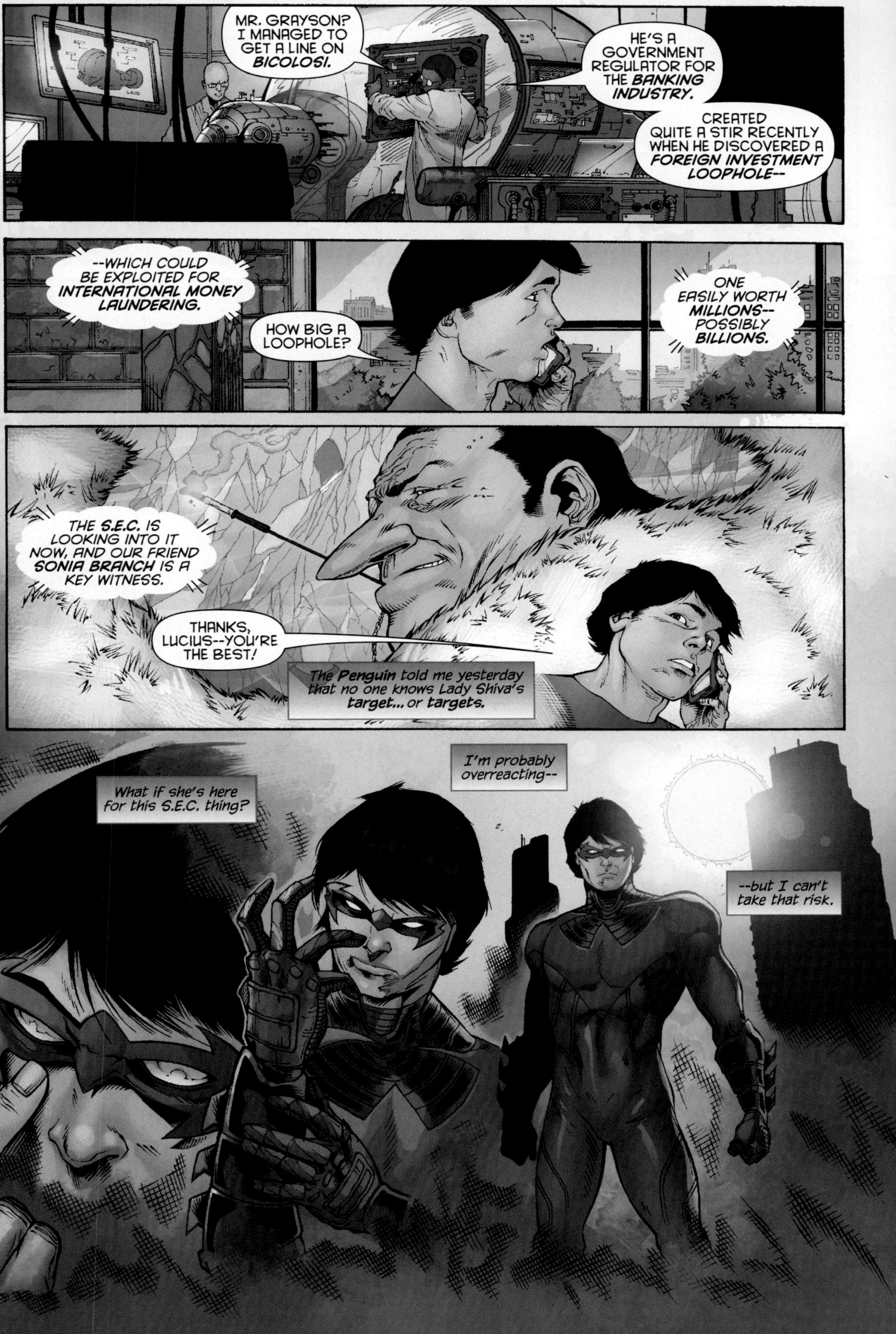
MR. GRAYSON? I MANAGED TO GET A LINE ON BICOLOSI.
HE'S A GOVERNMENT REGULATOR FOR THE BANKING INDUSTRY.
CREATED QUITE A STIR RECENTLY WHEN HE DISCOVERED A FOREIGN INVESTMENT LOOPHOLE--
--WHICH COULD BE EXPLOITED FOR INTERNATIONAL MONEY LAUNDERING.
HOW BIG A LOOPHOLE?
ONE EASILY WORTH MILLIONS-- POSSIBLY BILLIONS.
THE S.E.C. IS LOOKING INTO IT NOW, AND OUR FRIEND SONIA BRANCH IS A KEY WITNESS.
THANKS, LUCIUS--YOU'RE THE BEST!
The Penguin told me yesterday that no one knows Lady Shiva's target... or targets.
What if she's here for this S.E.C. thing?
I'm probably overreacting--
--but I can't take that risk.

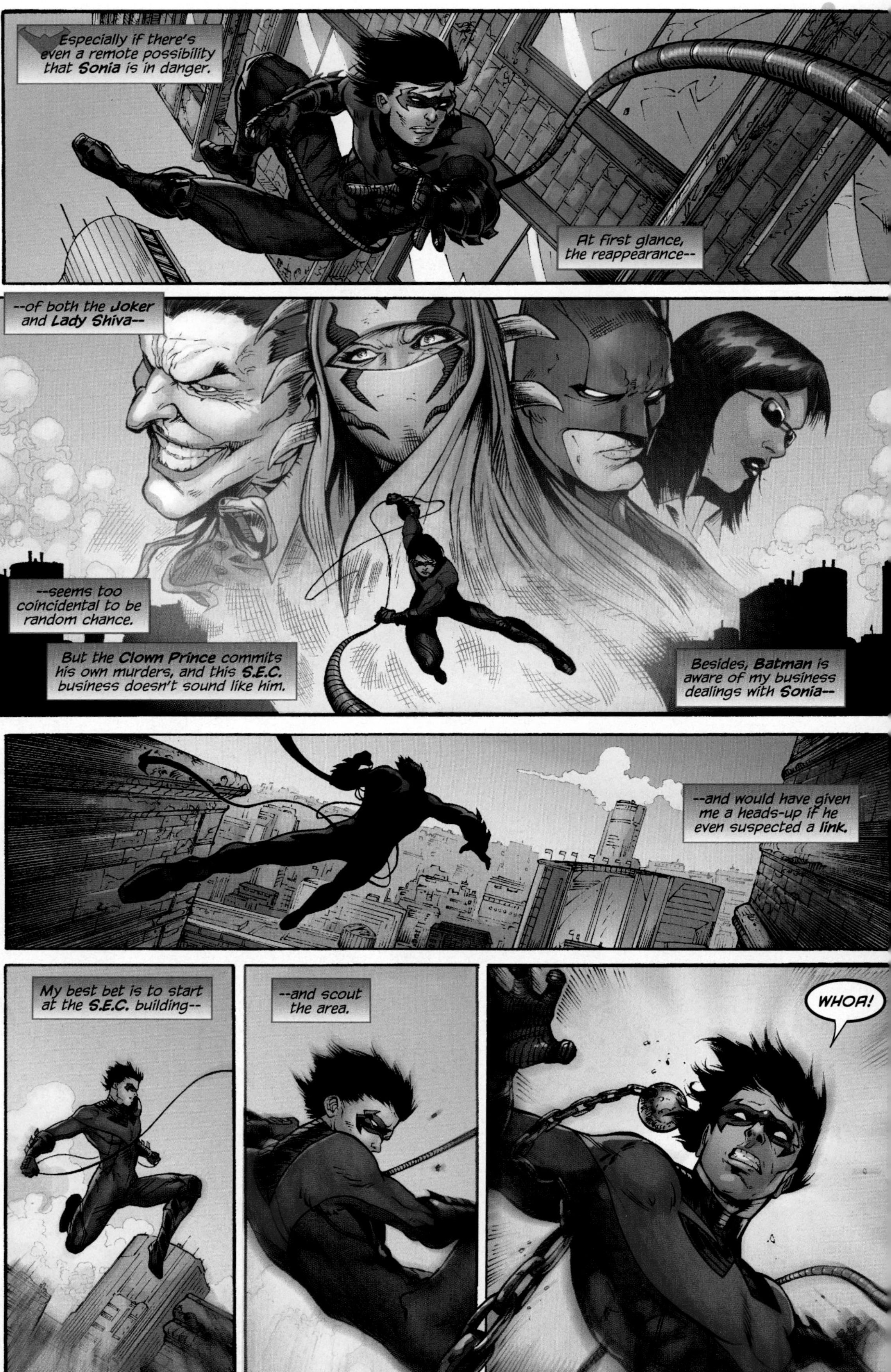
Especially if there's even a remote possibility that Sonia is in danger.
At first glance, the reappearance--
--of both the Joker and Lady Shiva--
--seems too coincidental to be random chance.
But the Clown Prince commits his own murders, and this S.E.C. business doesn't sound like him.
Besides, Batman is aware of my business dealings with Sonia--
--and would have given me a heads-up if he even suspected a link.
My best bet is to start at the S.E.C. building--
--and scout the area.
WHOA!

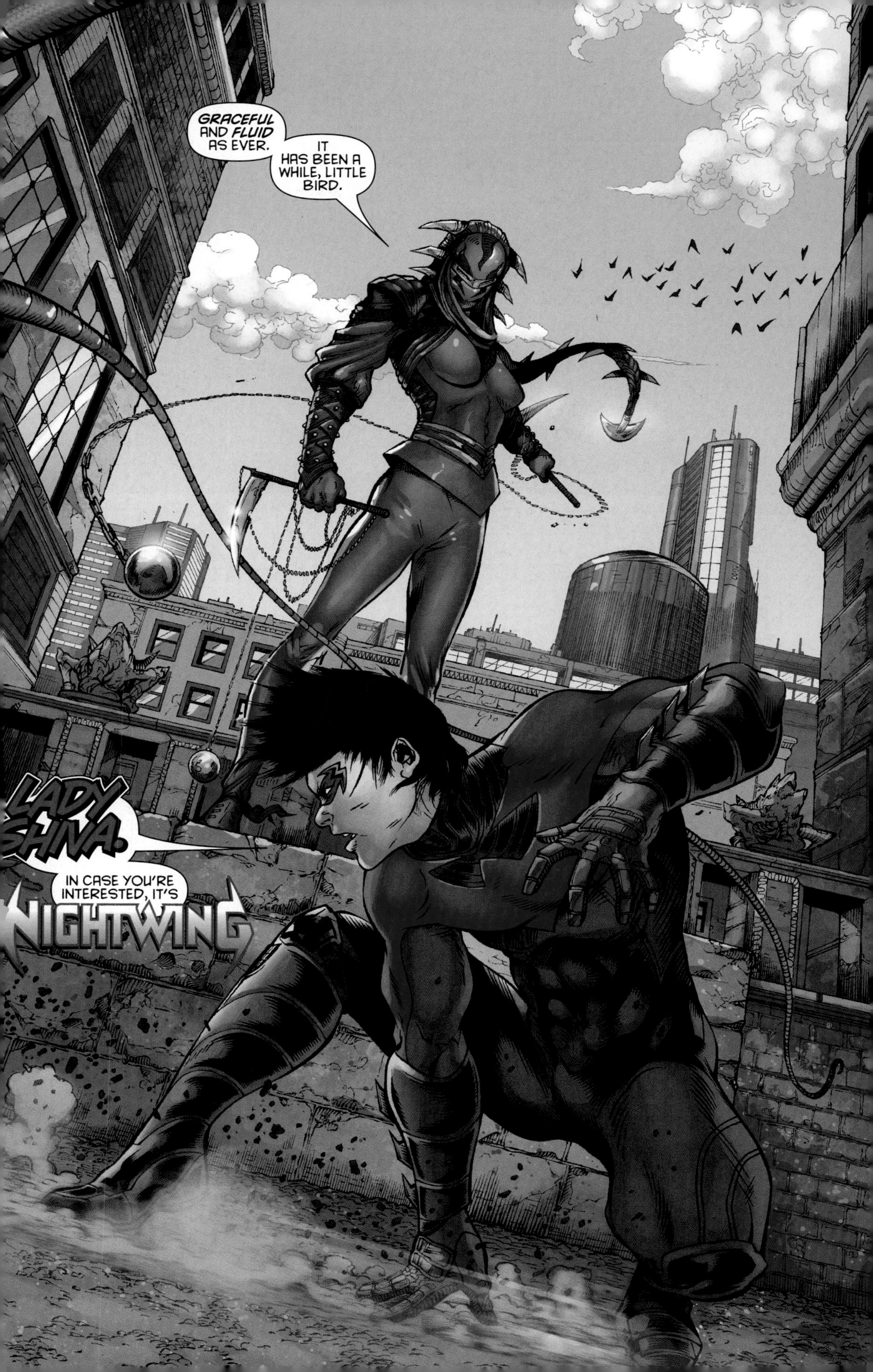
GRACEFUL AND FLUID AS EVER.
IT HAS BEEN A WHILE, LITTLE BIRD.
LADY SHIVA.
IN CASE YOU'RE INTERESTED, IT'S
NIGHTWING

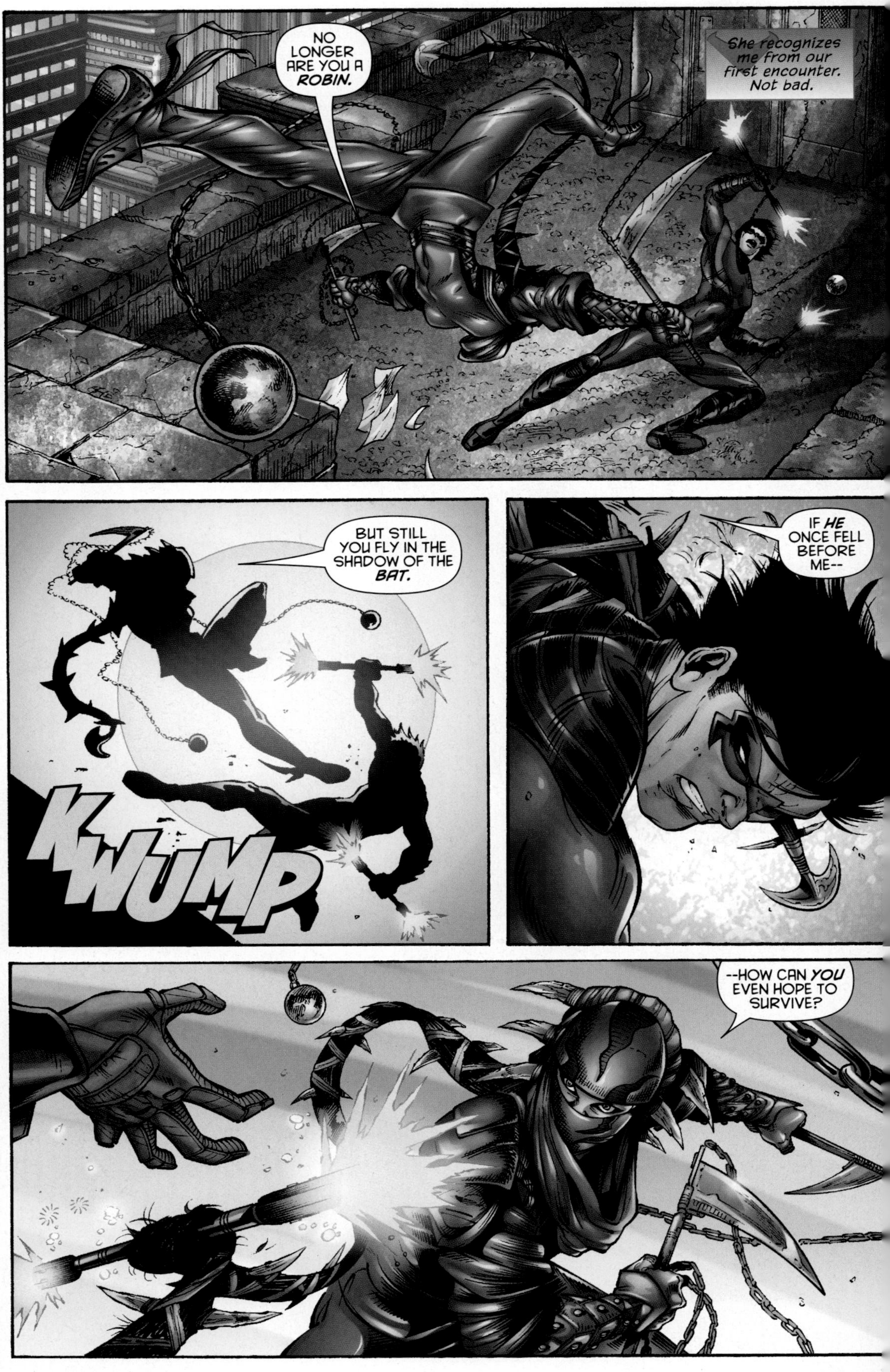
NO LONGER ARE YOU A *ROBIN.*
She recognizes me from our first encounter. Not bad.
BUT STILL YOU FLY IN THE SHADOW OF THE *BAT.*
KWUMP
IF *HE* ONCE FELL BEFORE ME--
--HOW CAN *YOU* EVEN HOPE TO SURVIVE?

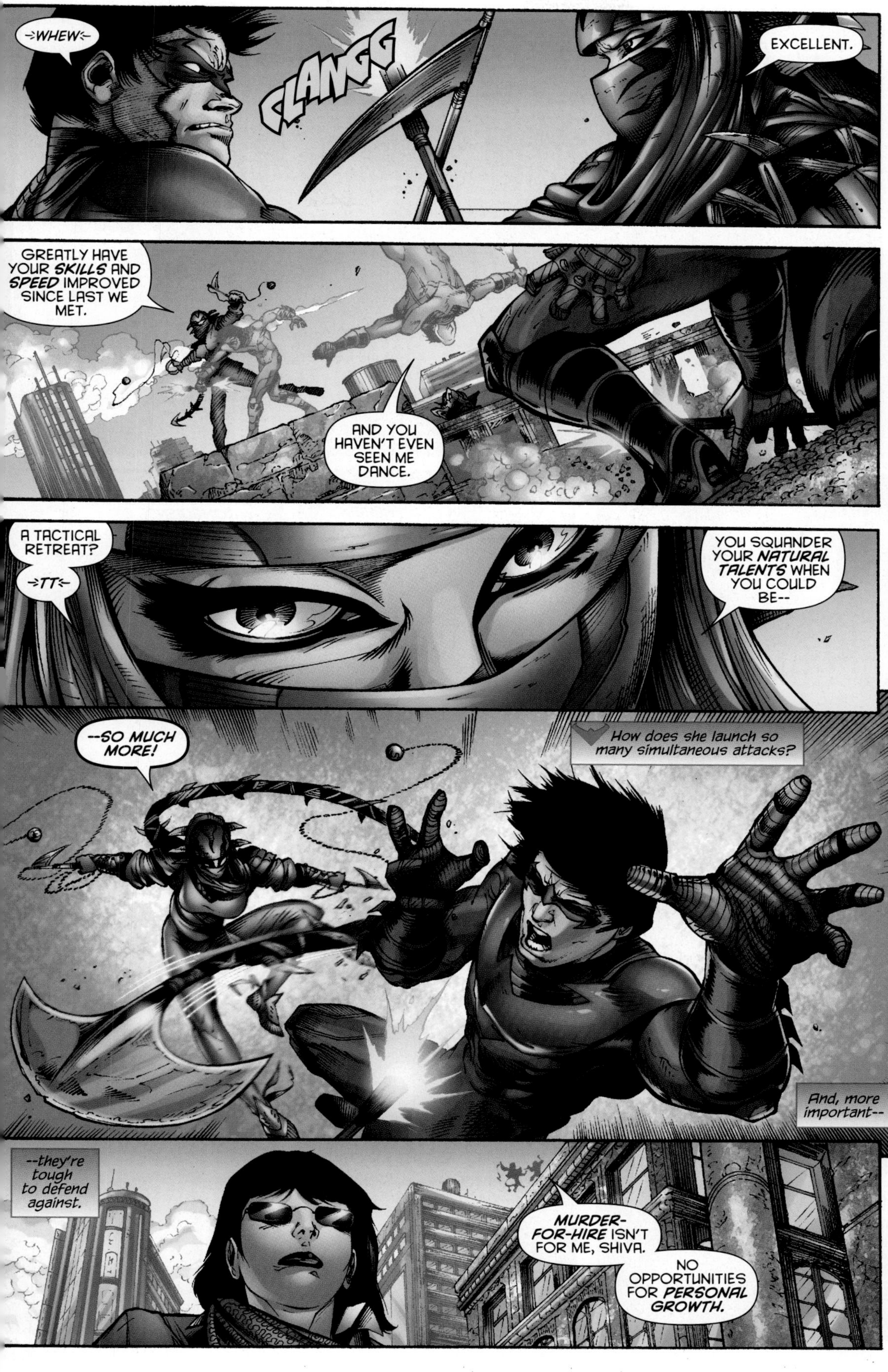

⇒WHEW⇐
CLANGG
EXCELLENT.
GREATLY HAVE YOUR **SKILLS** AND **SPEED** IMPROVED SINCE LAST WE MET.
AND YOU HAVEN'T EVEN SEEN ME DANCE.
A TACTICAL RETREAT?
⇒TT⇐
YOU SQUANDER YOUR ***NATURAL TALENTS*** WHEN YOU COULD BE--
--SO MUCH MORE!
How does she launch so many simultaneous attacks?
And, more important--
--they're tough to defend against.
MURDER-FOR-HIRE ISN'T FOR ME, SHIVA.
NO OPPORTUNITIES FOR ***PERSONAL GROWTH.***

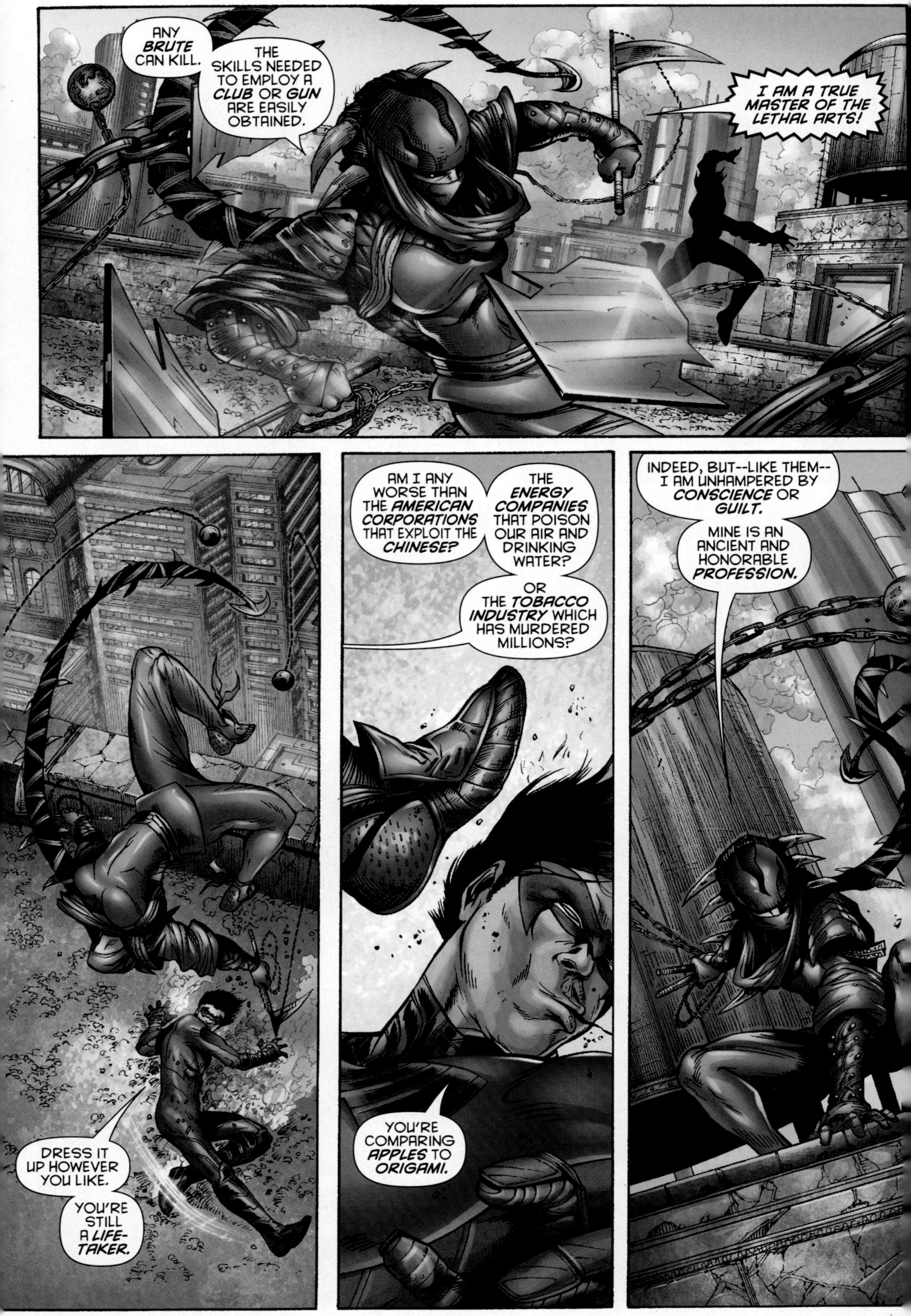
ANY *BRUTE* CAN KILL.
THE SKILLS NEEDED TO EMPLOY A *CLUB* OR *GUN* ARE EASILY OBTAINED.
I AM A TRUE MASTER OF THE LETHAL ARTS!
DRESS IT UP HOWEVER YOU LIKE.
YOU'RE STILL A *LIFE-TAKER.*
AM I ANY WORSE THAN THE *AMERICAN CORPORATIONS* THAT EXPLOIT THE *CHINESE?*
THE *ENERGY COMPANIES* THAT POISON OUR AIR AND DRINKING WATER?
OR THE *TOBACCO INDUSTRY* WHICH HAS MURDERED MILLIONS?
YOU'RE COMPARING *APPLES* TO *ORIGAMI.*
INDEED, BUT--LIKE THEM--I AM UNHAMPERED BY *CONSCIENCE* OR *GUILT.*
MINE IS AN ANCIENT AND HONORABLE *PROFESSION.*

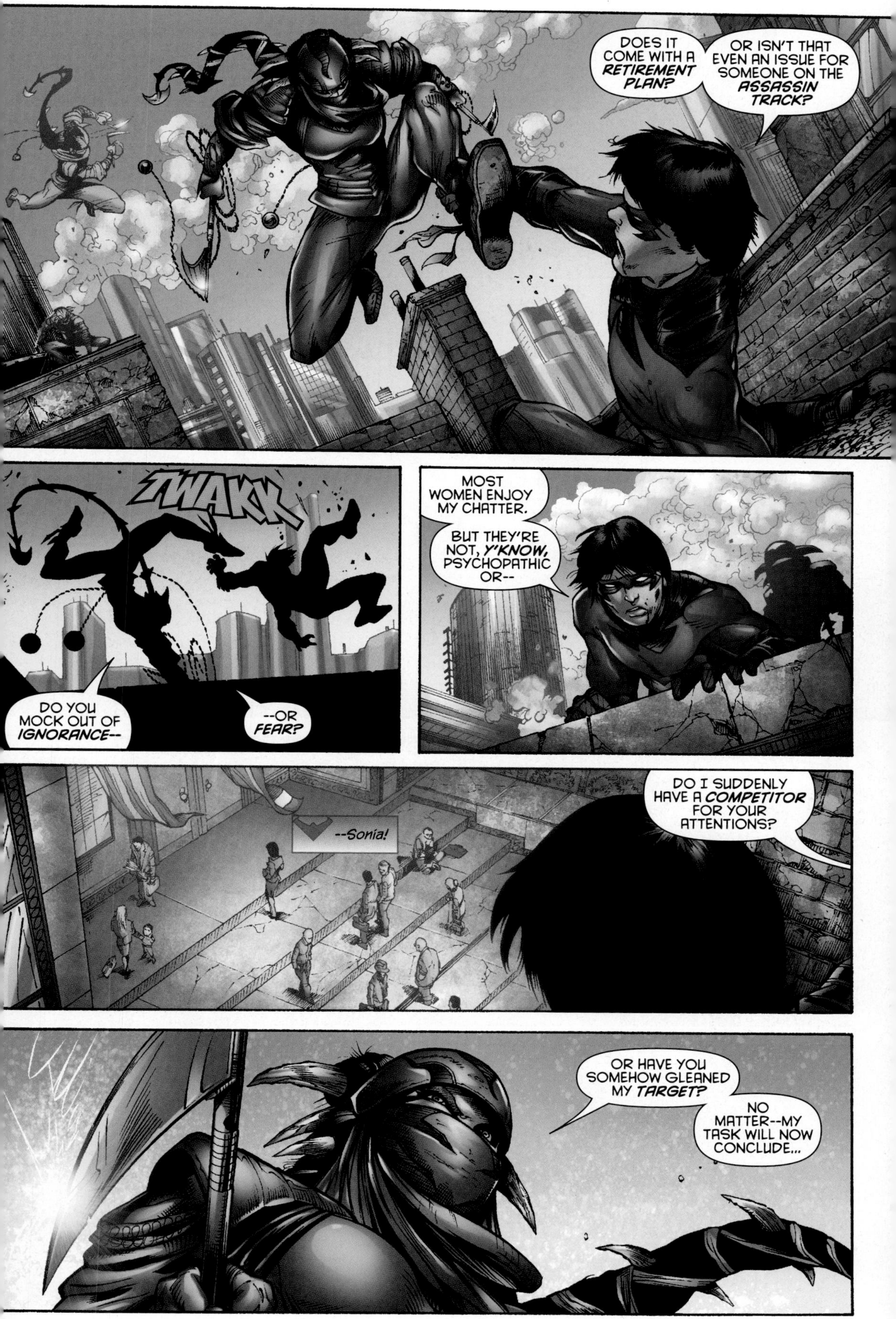
DOES IT COME WITH A RETIREMENT PLAN?
OR ISN'T THAT EVEN AN ISSUE FOR SOMEONE ON THE ASSASSIN TRACK?
TWAKK
DO YOU MOCK OUT OF IGNORANCE--
--OR FEAR?
MOST WOMEN ENJOY MY CHATTER.
BUT THEY'RE NOT, Y'KNOW, PSYCHOPATHIC OR--
DO I SUDDENLY HAVE A COMPETITOR FOR YOUR ATTENTIONS?
--Sonia!
OR HAVE YOU SOMEHOW GLEANED MY TARGET?
NO MATTER--MY TASK WILL NOW CONCLUDE...

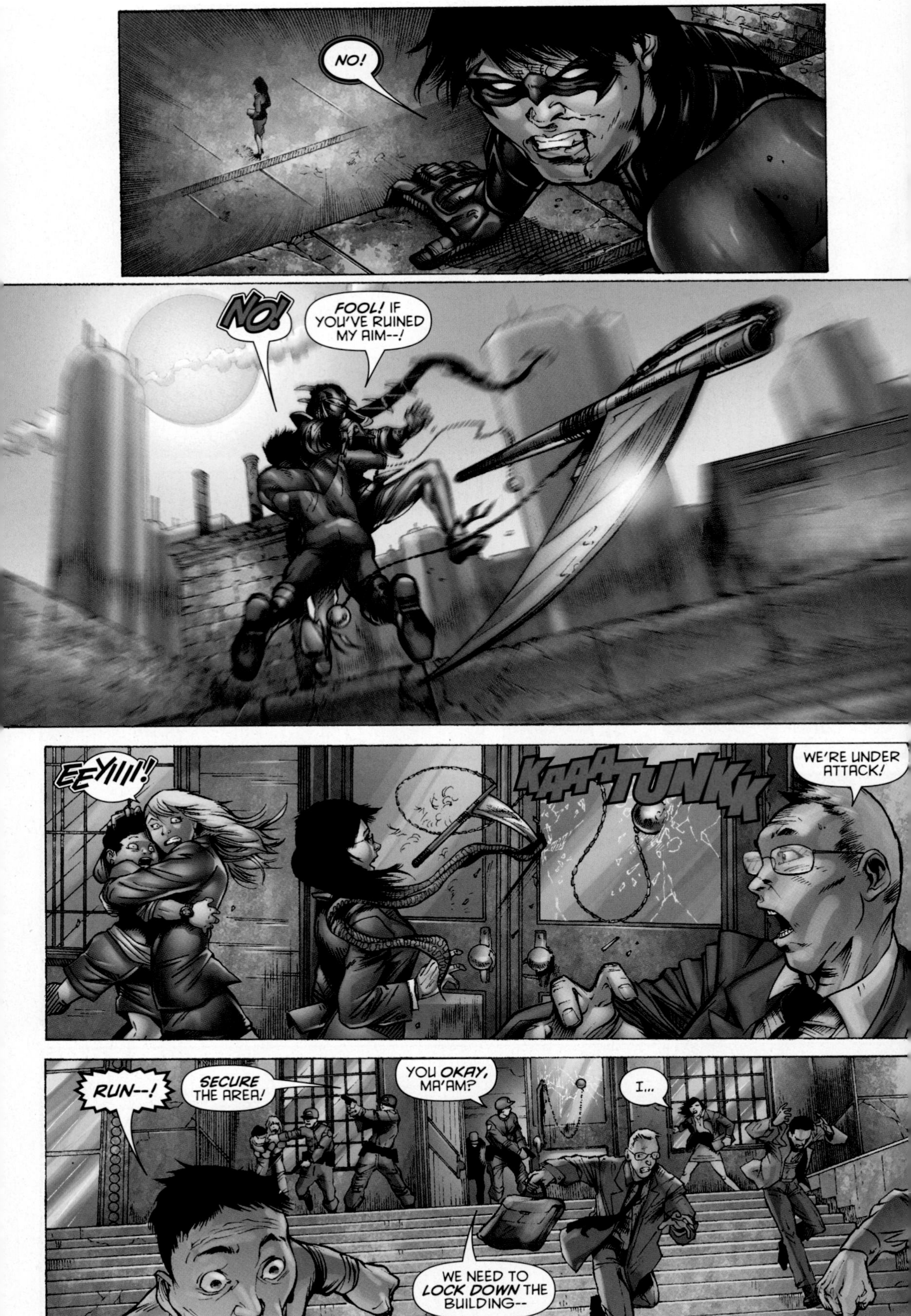
NO!
NO!
FOOL! IF YOU'VE RUINED MY AIM--!
EEYIIII!
KAAATUNKK
WE'RE UNDER ATTACK!
RUN--!
SECURE THE AREA!
YOU OKAY, MA'AM?
I...
WE NEED TO LOCK DOWN THE BUILDING--

--YOU *IN* OR *OUT?!*

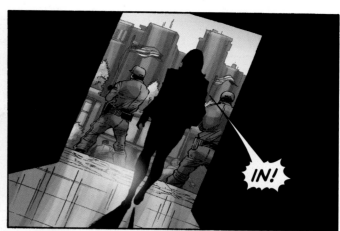

IN!

Sonia...

...she didn't let Shiva intimidate her.

She found a way to *finish* what she started.

So can I!

KWADDD

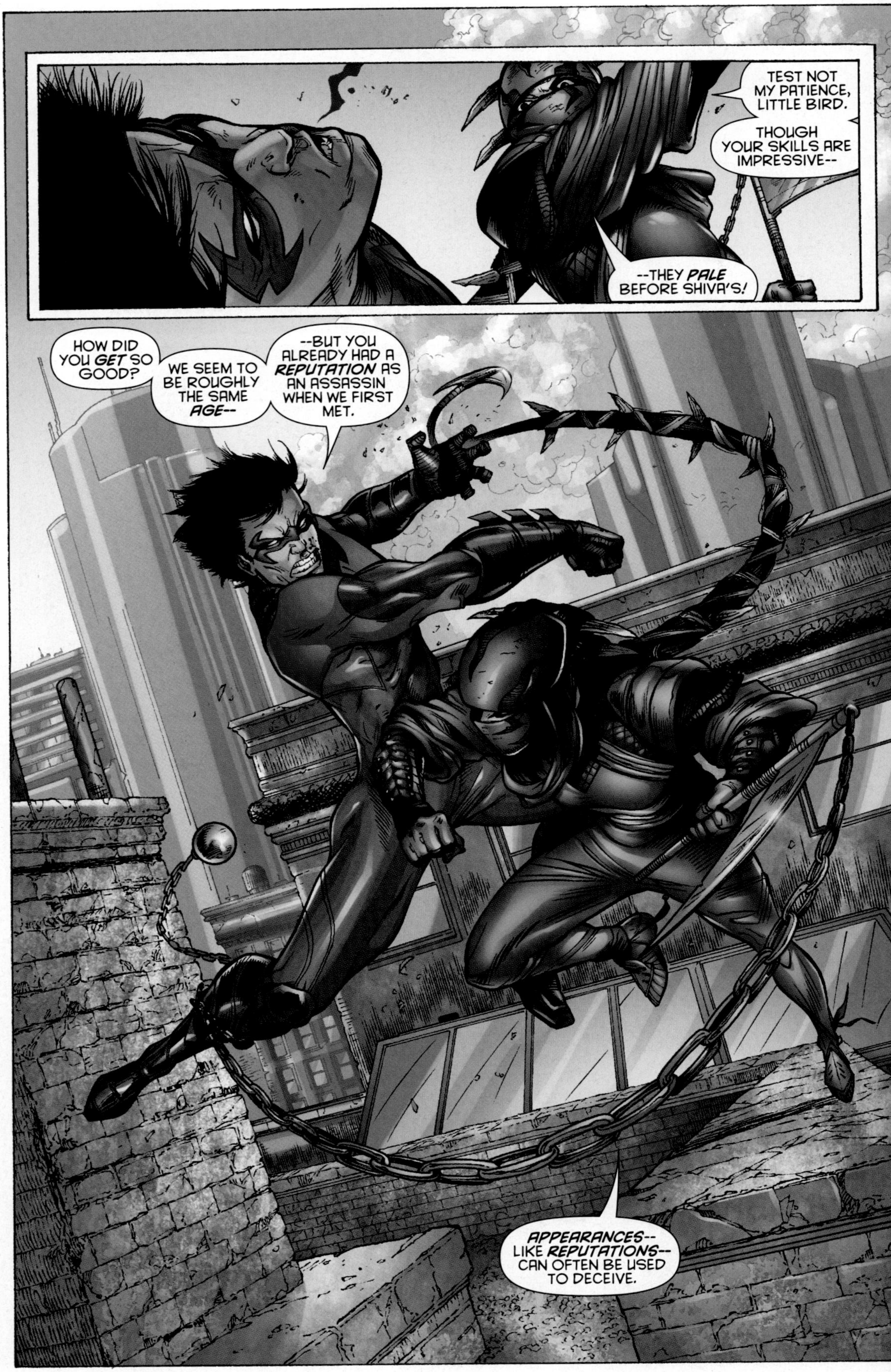
TEST NOT MY PATIENCE, LITTLE BIRD.
THOUGH YOUR SKILLS ARE IMPRESSIVE--
--THEY PALE BEFORE SHIVA'S!
HOW DID YOU GET SO GOOD?
WE SEEM TO BE ROUGHLY THE SAME AGE--
--BUT YOU ALREADY HAD A REPUTATION AS AN ASSASSIN WHEN WE FIRST MET.
APPEARANCES-- LIKE REPUTATIONS-- CAN OFTEN BE USED TO DECEIVE.

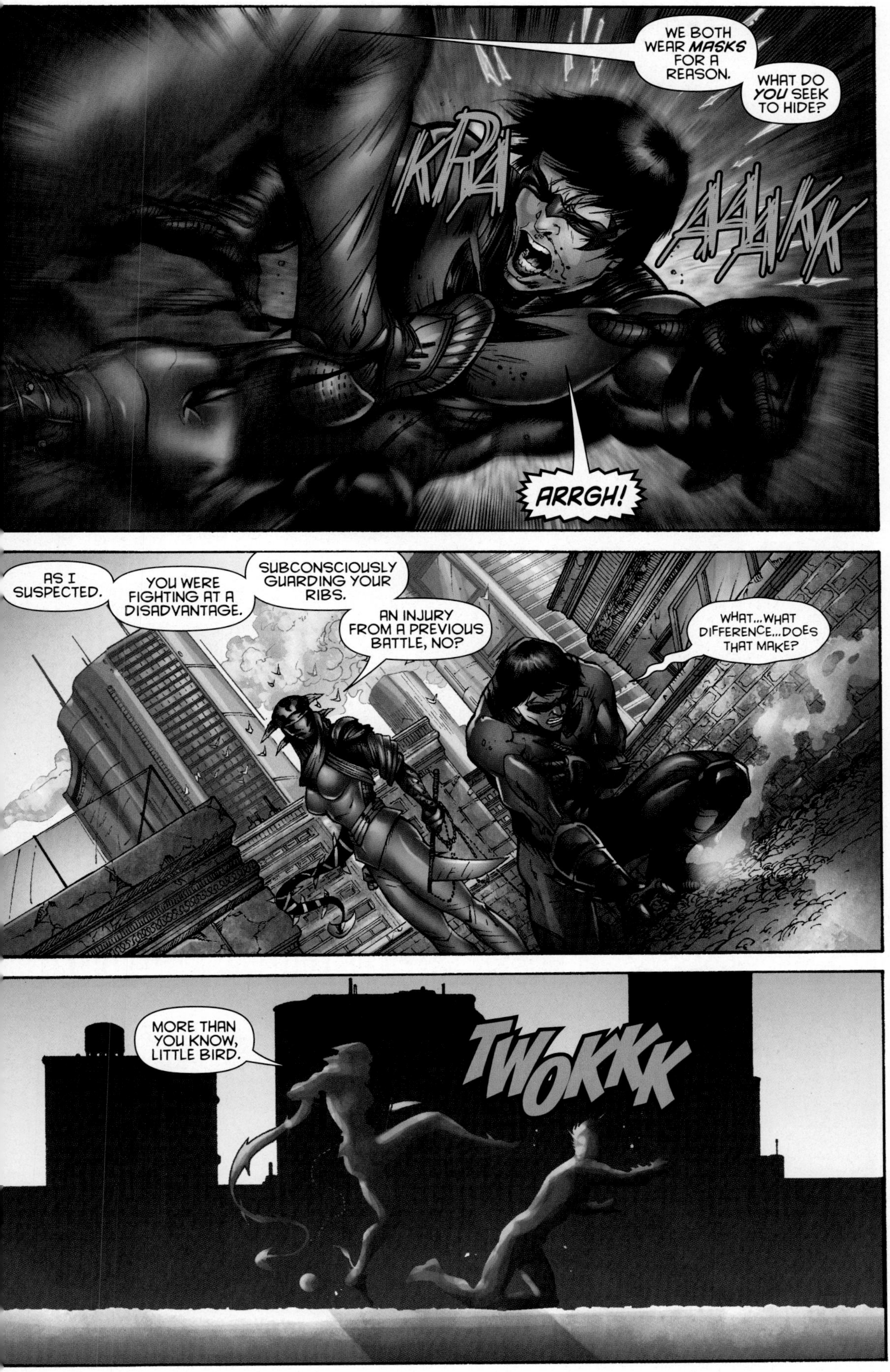
WE BOTH WEAR MASKS FOR A REASON.
WHAT DO YOU SEEK TO HIDE?
KRAAAAAKK
ARRGH!
AS I SUSPECTED.
YOU WERE FIGHTING AT A DISADVANTAGE.
SUBCONSCIOUSLY GUARDING YOUR RIBS.
AN INJURY FROM A PREVIOUS BATTLE, NO?
WHAT...WHAT DIFFERENCE...DOES THAT MAKE?
MORE THAN YOU KNOW, LITTLE BIRD.
TWOKKK

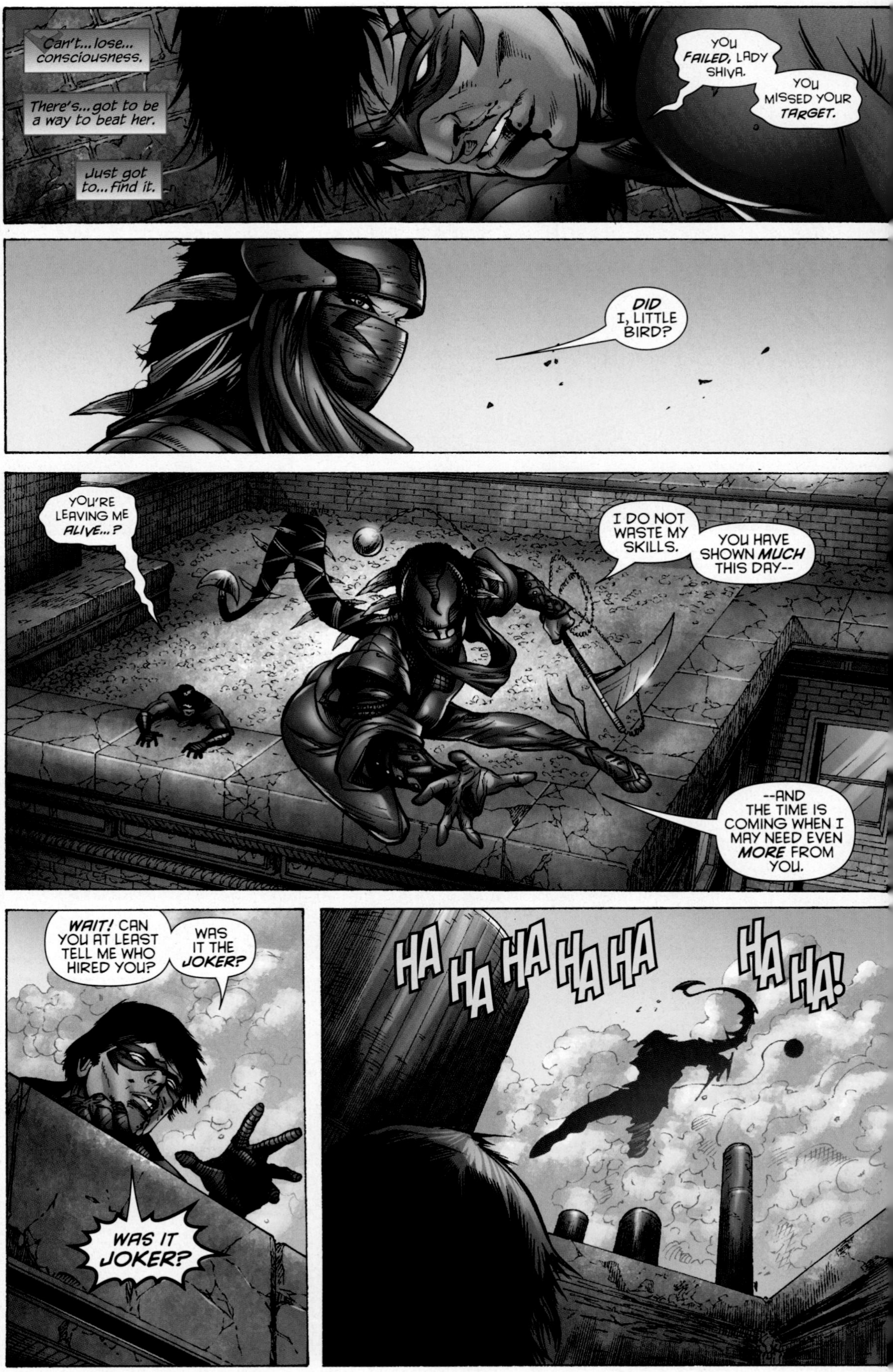
Can't...lose... consciousness.
There's...got to be a way to beat her.
Just got to...find it.
YOU FAILED, LADY SHIVA.
YOU MISSED YOUR TARGET.
DID I, LITTLE BIRD?
YOU'RE LEAVING ME ALIVE...?
I DO NOT WASTE MY SKILLS.
YOU HAVE SHOWN MUCH THIS DAY--
--AND THE TIME IS COMING WHEN I MAY NEED EVEN MORE FROM YOU.
WAIT! CAN YOU AT LEAST TELL ME WHO HIRED YOU?
WAS IT THE JOKER?
WAS IT JOKER?
HA HA HA HA HA HA HA HA!

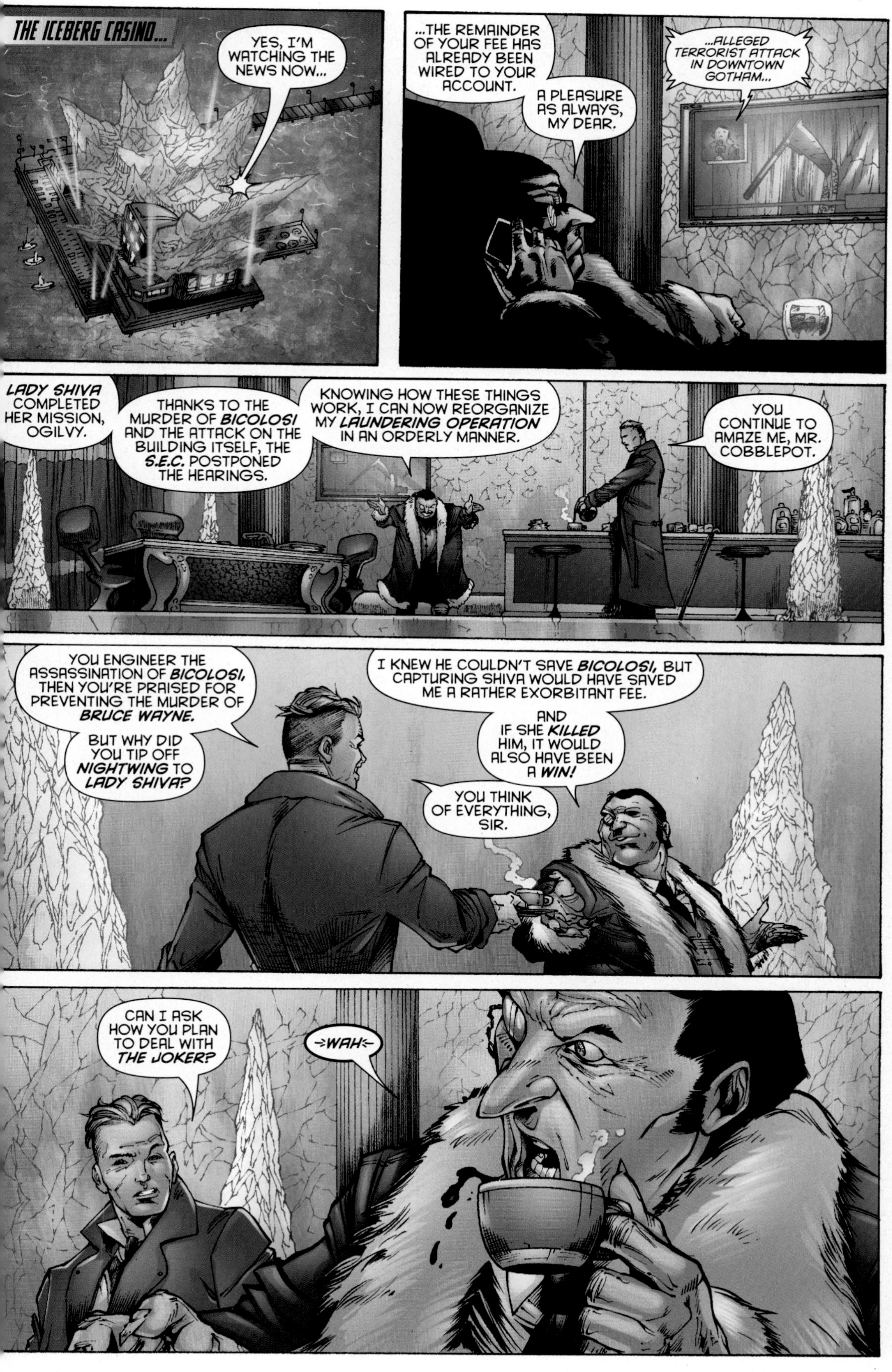
THE ICEBERG CASINO...
YES, I'M WATCHING THE NEWS NOW...
...THE REMAINDER OF YOUR FEE HAS ALREADY BEEN WIRED TO YOUR ACCOUNT.
A PLEASURE AS ALWAYS, MY DEAR.
...ALLEGED TERRORIST ATTACK IN DOWNTOWN GOTHAM...
LADY SHIVA COMPLETED HER MISSION, OGILVY.
THANKS TO THE MURDER OF BICOLOSI AND THE ATTACK ON THE BUILDING ITSELF, THE S.E.C. POSTPONED THE HEARINGS.
KNOWING HOW THESE THINGS WORK, I CAN NOW REORGANIZE MY LAUNDERING OPERATION IN AN ORDERLY MANNER.
YOU CONTINUE TO AMAZE ME, MR. COBBLEPOT.
YOU ENGINEER THE ASSASSINATION OF BICOLOSI, THEN YOU'RE PRAISED FOR PREVENTING THE MURDER OF BRUCE WAYNE.
BUT WHY DID YOU TIP OFF NIGHTWING TO LADY SHIVA?
I KNEW HE COULDN'T SAVE BICOLOSI, BUT CAPTURING SHIVA WOULD HAVE SAVED ME A RATHER EXORBITANT FEE.
AND IF SHE KILLED HIM, IT WOULD ALSO HAVE BEEN A WIN!
YOU THINK OF EVERYTHING, SIR.
CAN I ASK HOW YOU PLAN TO DEAL WITH THE JOKER?
WAH

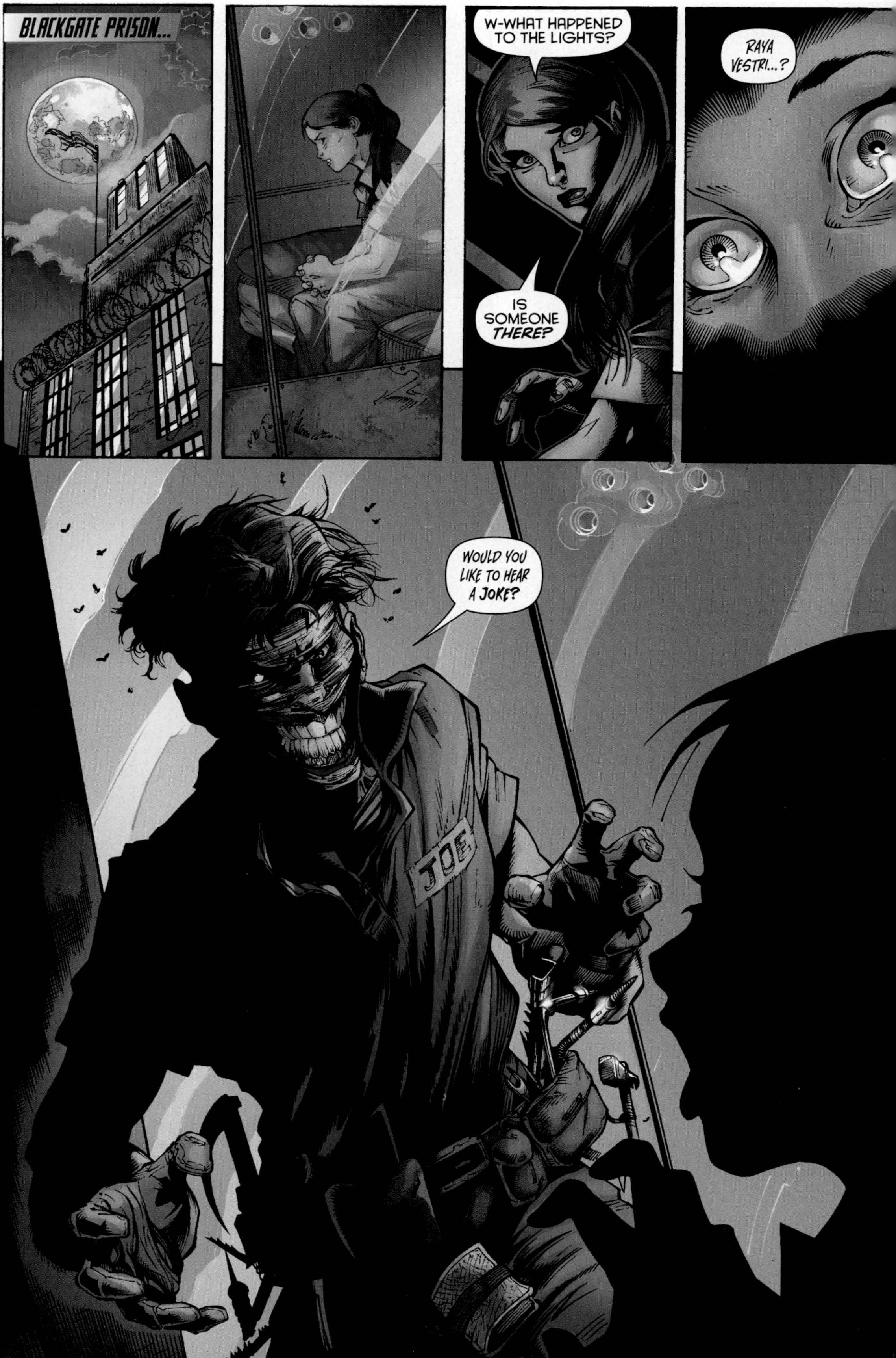
BLACKGATE PRISON...
W-WHAT HAPPENED TO THE LIGHTS?
IS SOMEONE THERE?
RAYA VESTRI...?
WOULD YOU LIKE TO HEAR A JOKE?
JOE

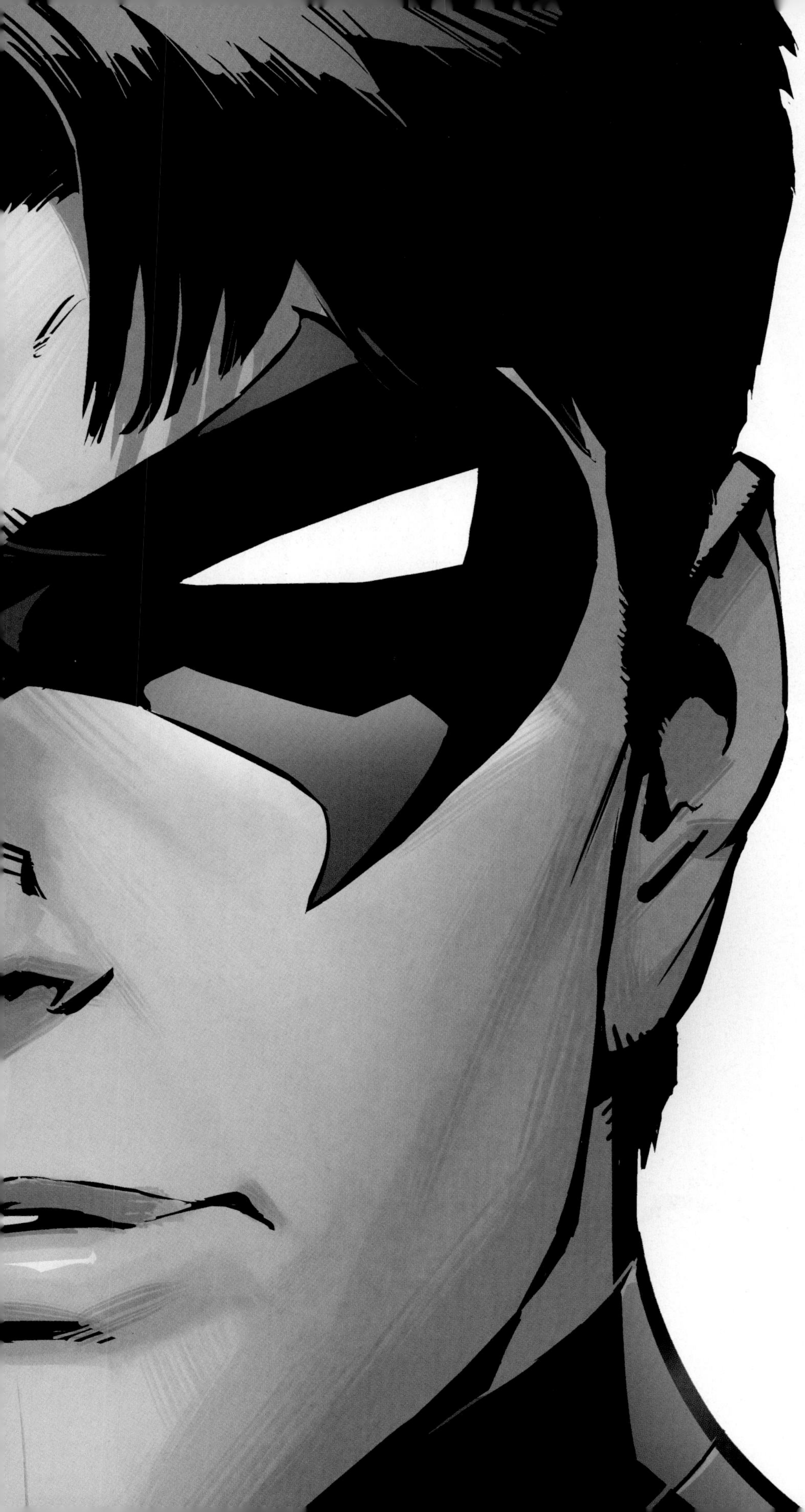

CLEANING HOUSE

KYLE HIGGINS writer **EDDY BARROWS** penciller **EBER FERREIRA** inker cover art by **GREG CAPULLO & FCO PLASCENCIA**

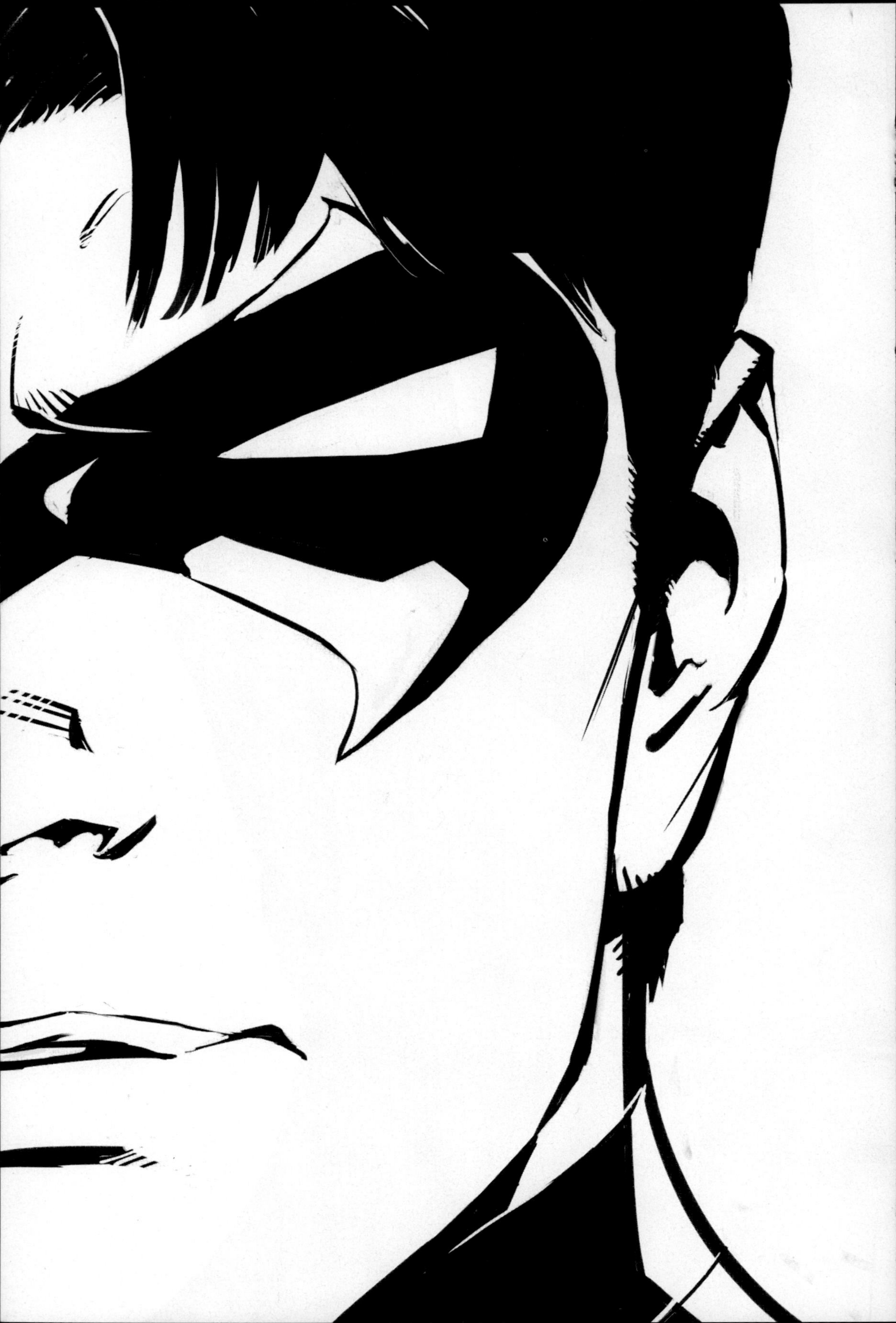

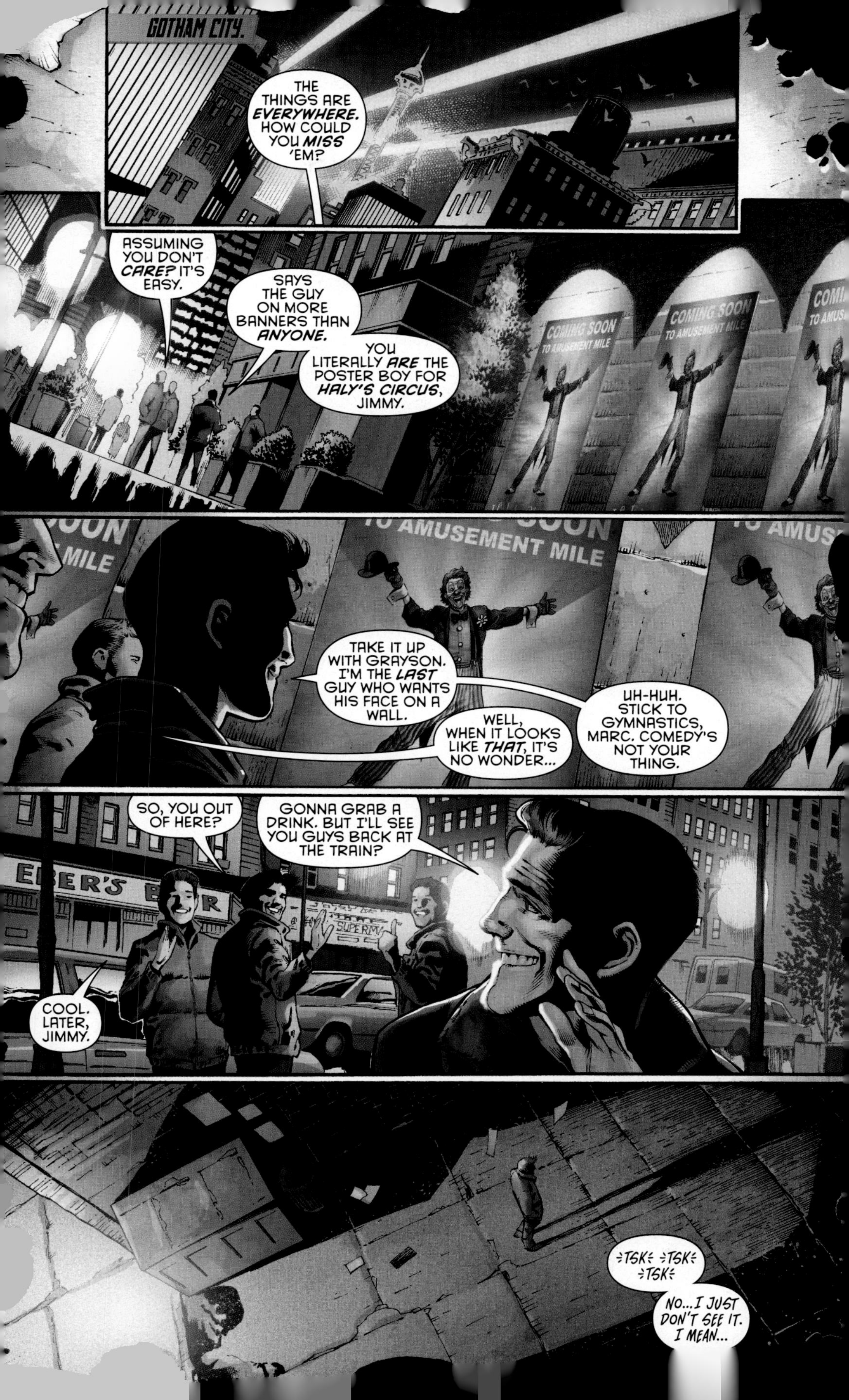
GOTHAM CITY.
THE THINGS ARE EVERYWHERE. HOW COULD YOU MISS 'EM?
ASSUMING YOU DON'T CARE? IT'S EASY.
SAYS THE GUY ON MORE BANNERS THAN ANYONE.
YOU LITERALLY ARE THE POSTER BOY FOR HALY'S CIRCUS, JIMMY.
COMING SOON TO AMUSEMENT MILE
TAKE IT UP WITH GRAYSON. I'M THE LAST GUY WHO WANTS HIS FACE ON A WALL.
WELL, WHEN IT LOOKS LIKE THAT, IT'S NO WONDER...
UH-HUH. STICK TO GYMNASTICS, MARC. COMEDY'S NOT YOUR THING.
SO, YOU OUT OF HERE?
GONNA GRAB A DRINK. BUT I'LL SEE YOU GUYS BACK AT THE TRAIN?
COOL. LATER, JIMMY.
TSK TSK TSK
NO...I JUST DON'T SEE IT. I MEAN...

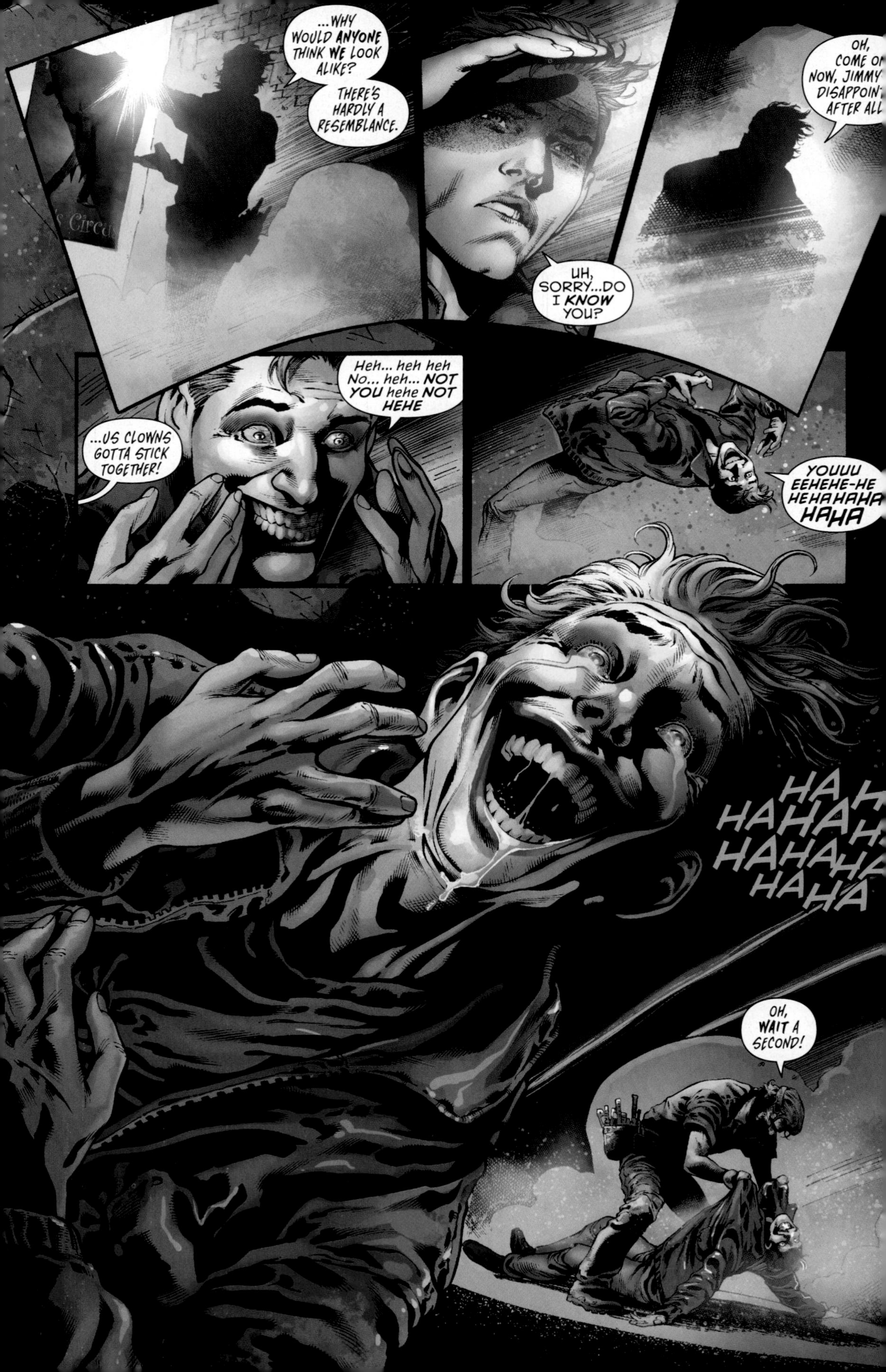

...WHY WOULD ANYONE THINK WE LOOK ALIKE?
THERE'S HARDLY A RESEMBLANCE.
UH, SORRY...DO I KNOW YOU?
OH, COME ON NOW, JIMMY DISAPPOIN AFTER ALL
Heh... heh heh No... heh... NOT YOU hehe NOT HEHE
...US CLOWNS GOTTA STICK TOGETHER!
YOUUU EEHEHE-HE HEHAHAHA HAHA
HA HA HAHAH HAHAHA HAHA
OH, WAIT A SECOND!

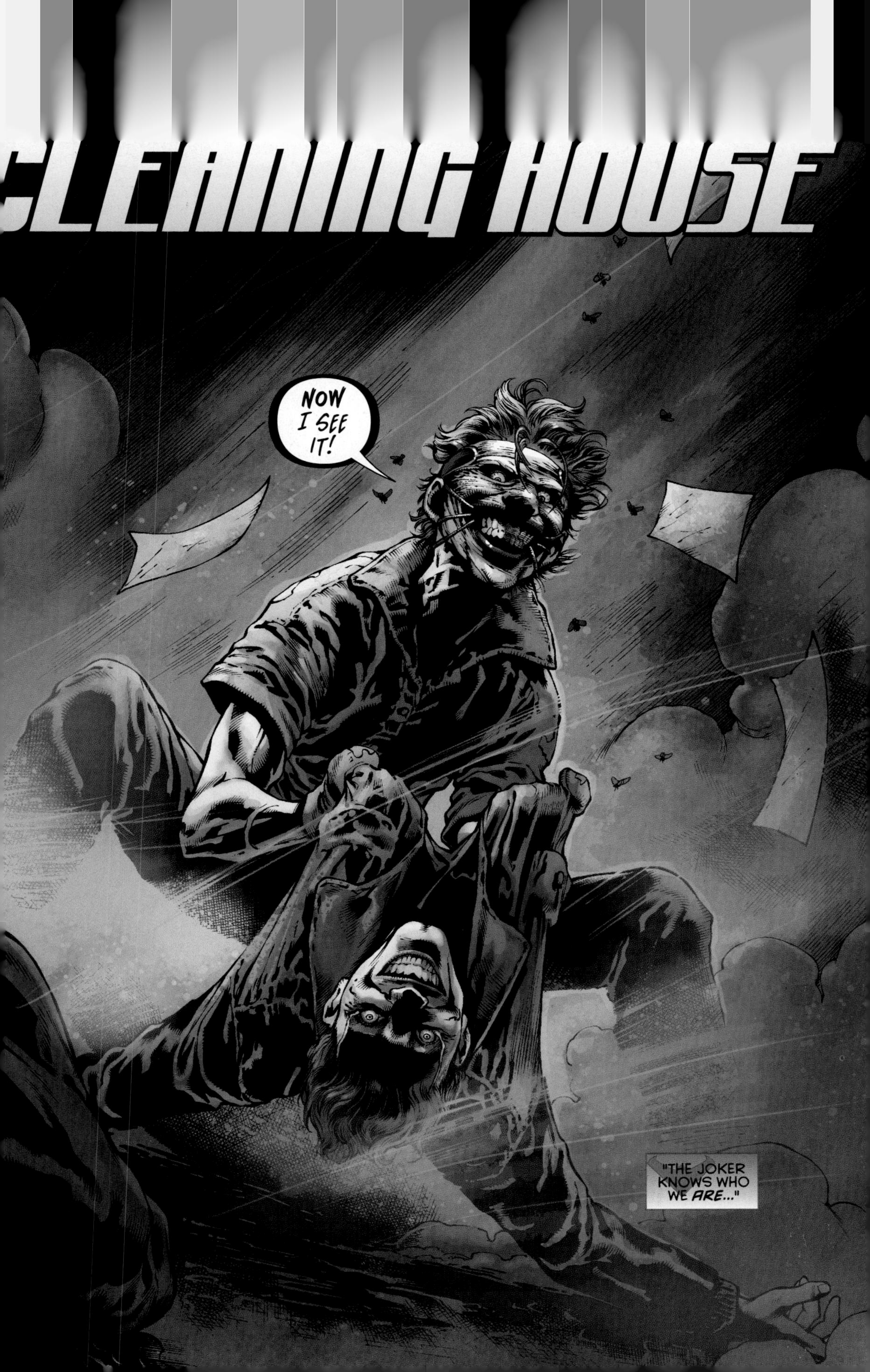
CLEANING HOUSE
NOW I SEE IT!
"THE JOKER KNOWS WHO WE ARE..."

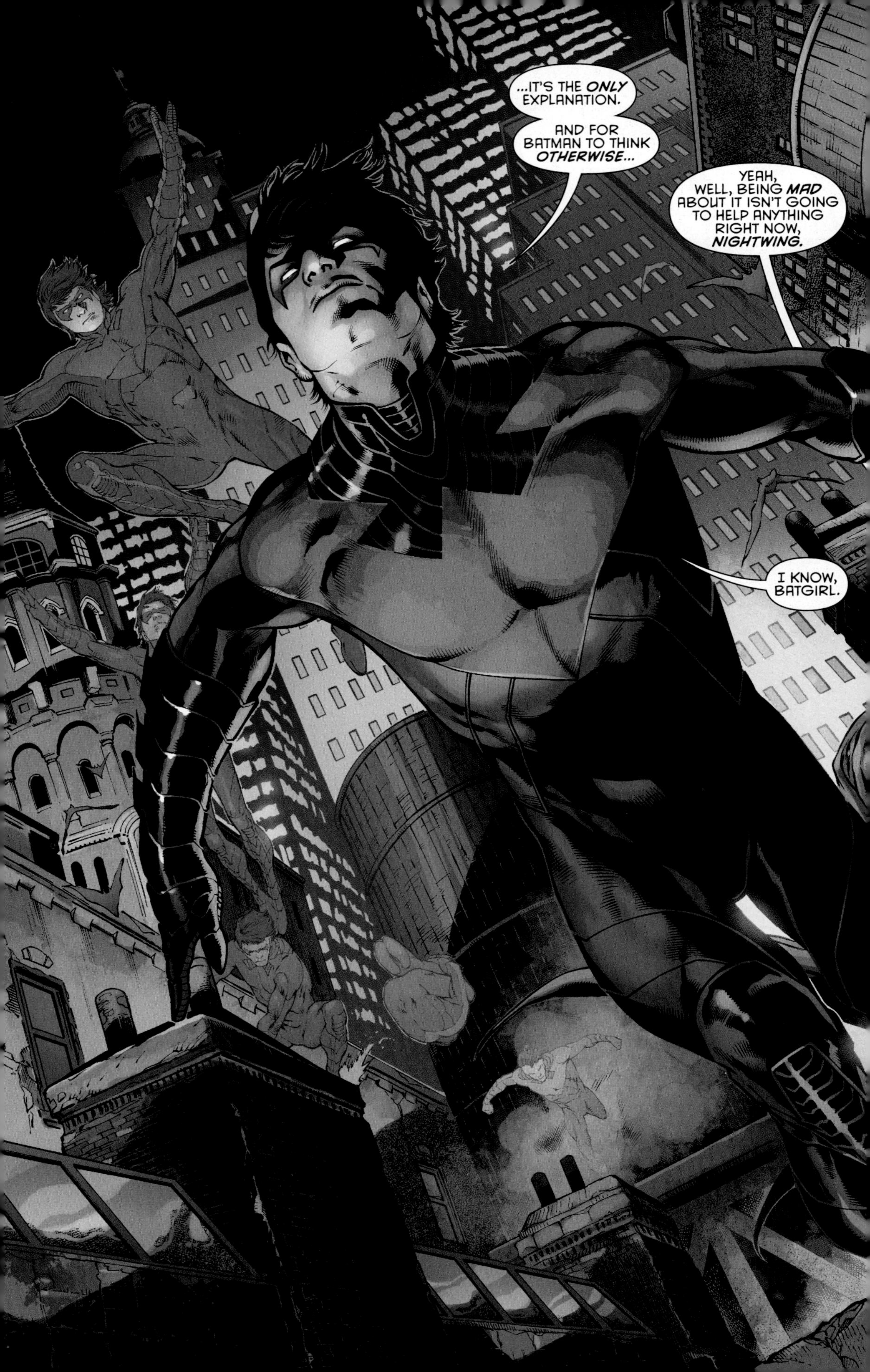
...IT'S THE ONLY EXPLANATION.
AND FOR BATMAN TO THINK OTHERWISE...
YEAH, WELL, BEING MAD ABOUT IT ISN'T GOING TO HELP ANYTHING RIGHT NOW, NIGHTWING.
I KNOW, BATGIRL.

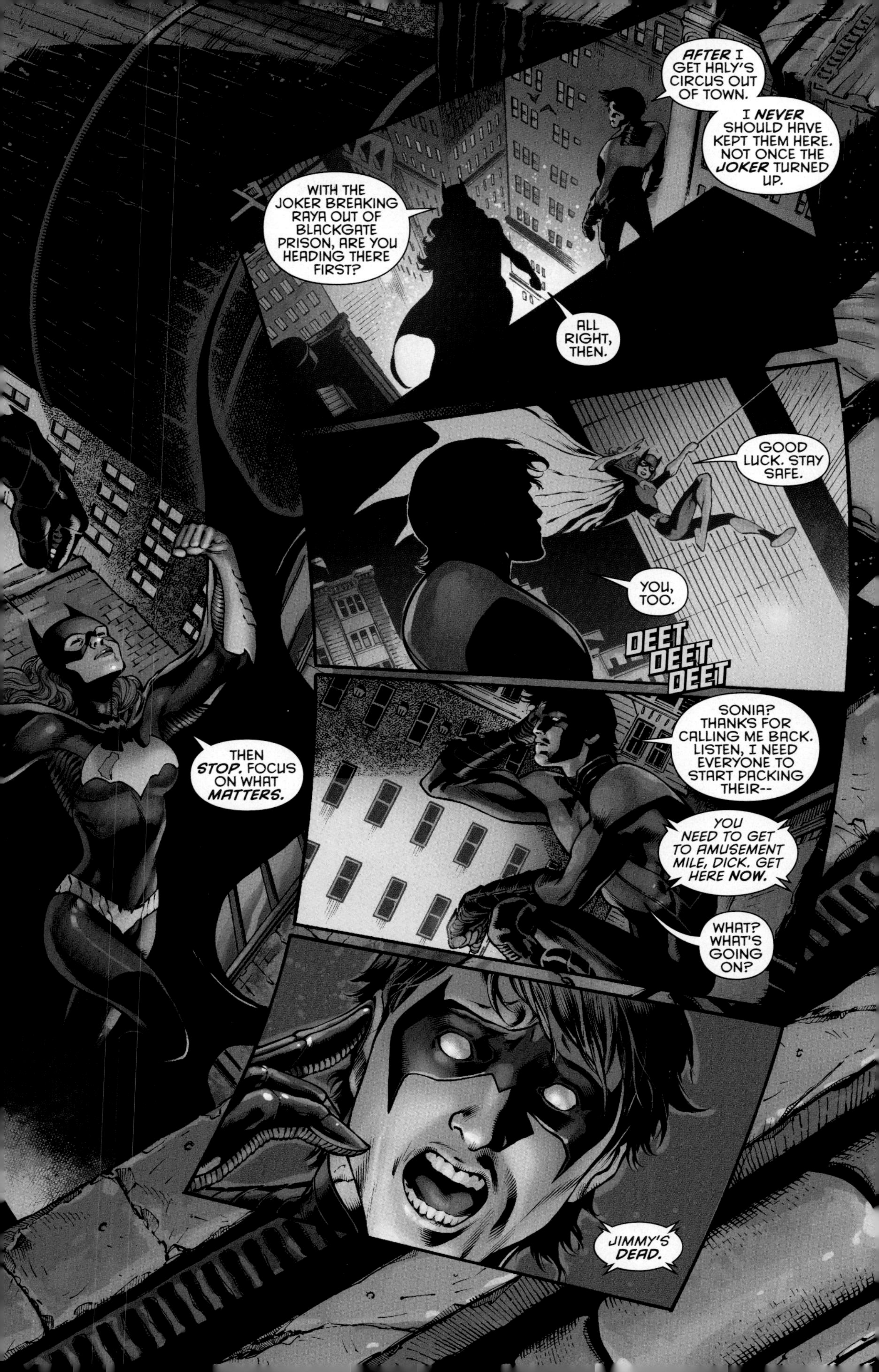
WITH THE JOKER BREAKING RAYA OUT OF BLACKGATE PRISON, ARE YOU HEADING THERE FIRST?
AFTER I GET HALY'S CIRCUS OUT OF TOWN.
I NEVER SHOULD HAVE KEPT THEM HERE. NOT ONCE THE JOKER TURNED UP.
ALL RIGHT, THEN.
THEN STOP. FOCUS ON WHAT MATTERS.
GOOD LUCK. STAY SAFE.
YOU, TOO.
DEET DEET DEET
SONIA? THANKS FOR CALLING ME BACK. LISTEN, I NEED EVERYONE TO START PACKING THEIR--
YOU NEED TO GET TO AMUSEMENT MILE, DICK. GET HERE NOW.
WHAT? WHAT'S GOING ON?
JIMMY'S DEAD.

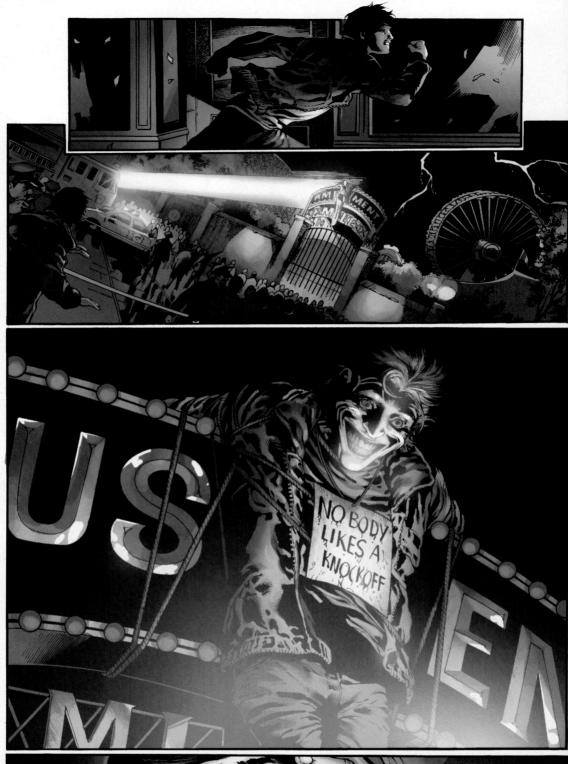

NO BODY LIKES A KNOCKOFF

OH GOD, NO...

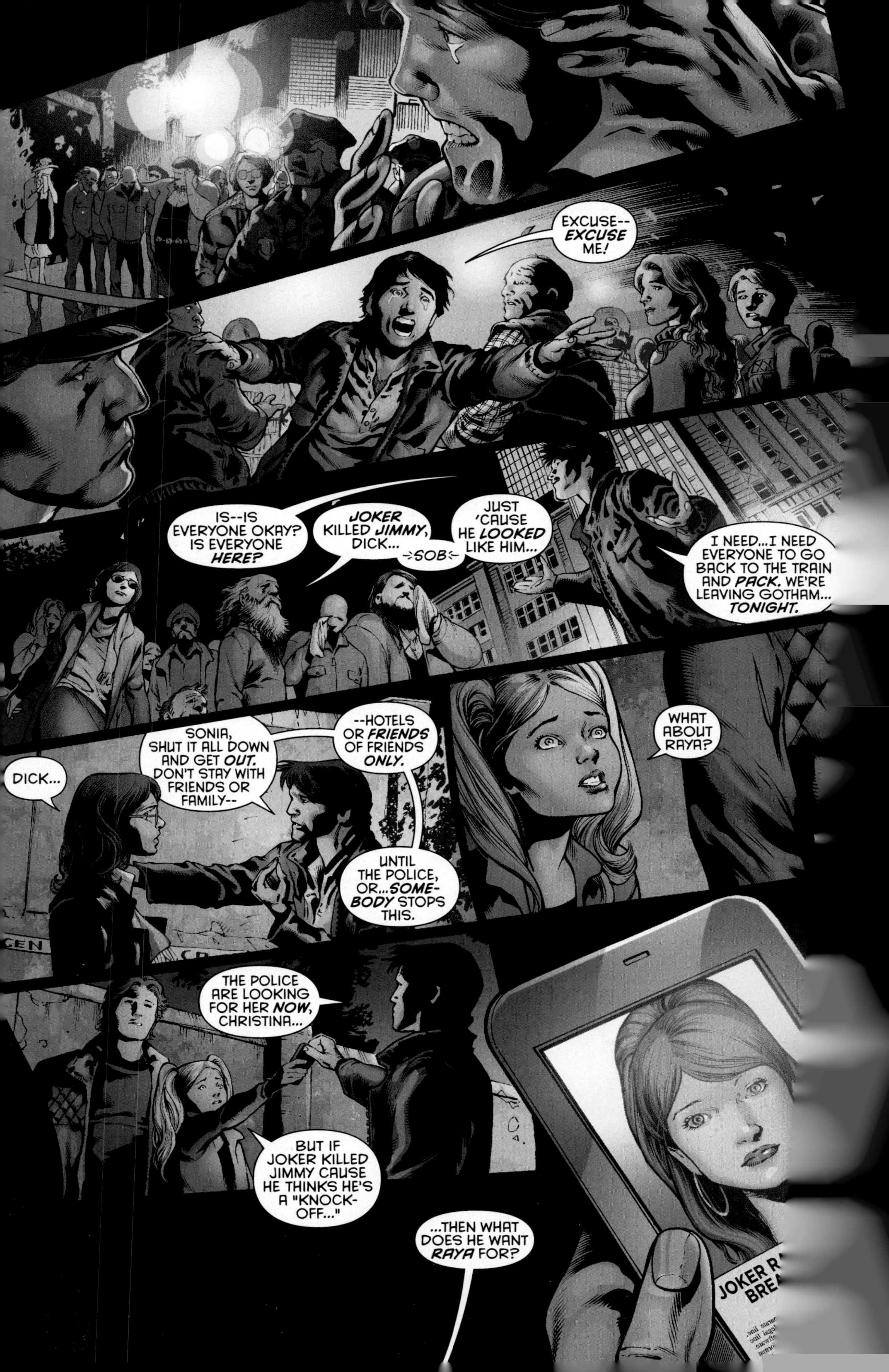
EXCUSE--
EXCUSE ME!
IS--IS EVERYONE OKAY? IS EVERYONE HERE?
JOKER KILLED JIMMY, DICK...
SOB
JUST 'CAUSE HE LOOKED LIKE HIM...
I NEED...I NEED EVERYONE TO GO BACK TO THE TRAIN AND PACK. WE'RE LEAVING GOTHAM... TONIGHT.
DICK...
SONIA, SHUT IT ALL DOWN AND GET OUT. DON'T STAY WITH FRIENDS OR FAMILY--
--HOTELS OR FRIENDS OF FRIENDS ONLY.
UNTIL THE POLICE, OR...SOMEBODY STOPS THIS.
WHAT ABOUT RAYA?
THE POLICE ARE LOOKING FOR HER NOW, CHRISTINA...
BUT IF JOKER KILLED JIMMY CAUSE HE THINKS HE'S A "KNOCK-OFF..."
...THEN WHAT DOES HE WANT RAYA FOR?
JOKER RA
BREA

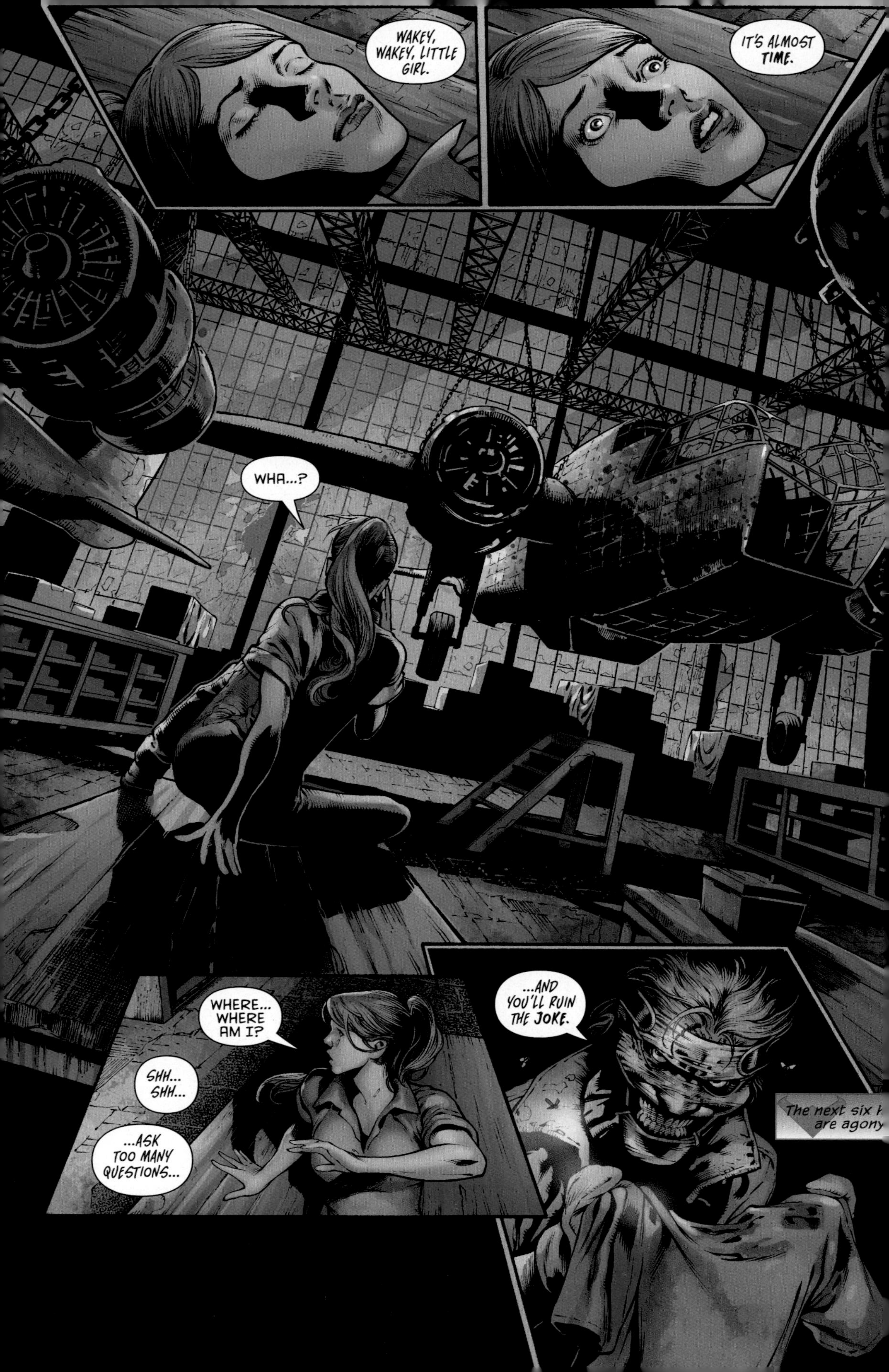
WAKEY, WAKEY, LITTLE GIRL.
IT'S ALMOST TIME.
WHA...?
WHERE... WHERE AM I?
SHH... SHH...
...ASK TOO MANY QUESTIONS...
...AND YOU'LL RUIN THE JOKE.
The next six
are agony

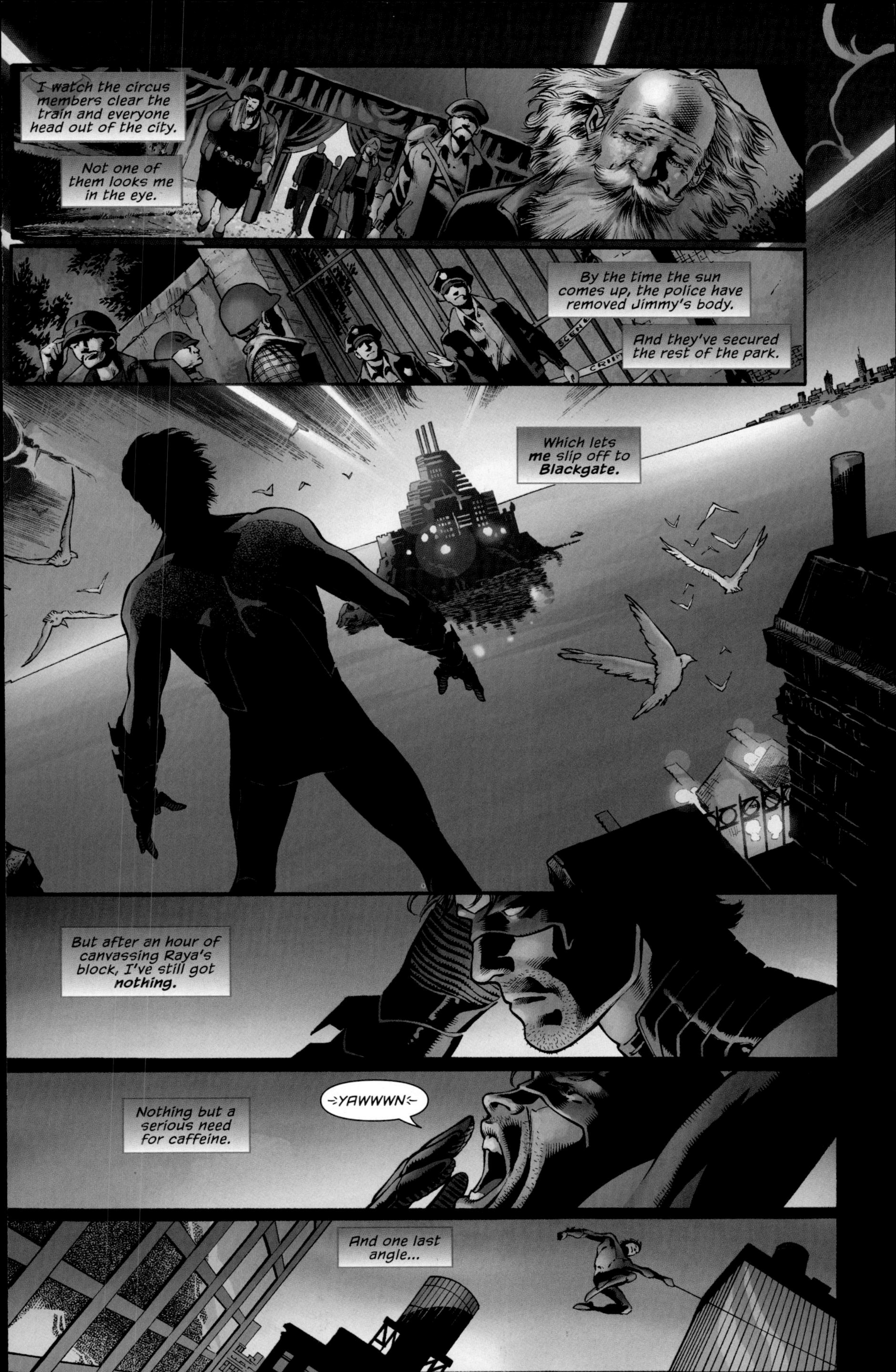
I watch the circus members clear the train and everyone head out of the city.
Not one of them looks me in the eye.
By the time the sun comes up, the police have removed Jimmy's body.
And they've secured the rest of the park.
SCENE
CRIM
Which lets me slip off to Blackgate.
But after an hour of canvassing Raya's block, I've still got nothing.
Nothing but a serious need for caffeine.
YAWWWN
And one last angle...

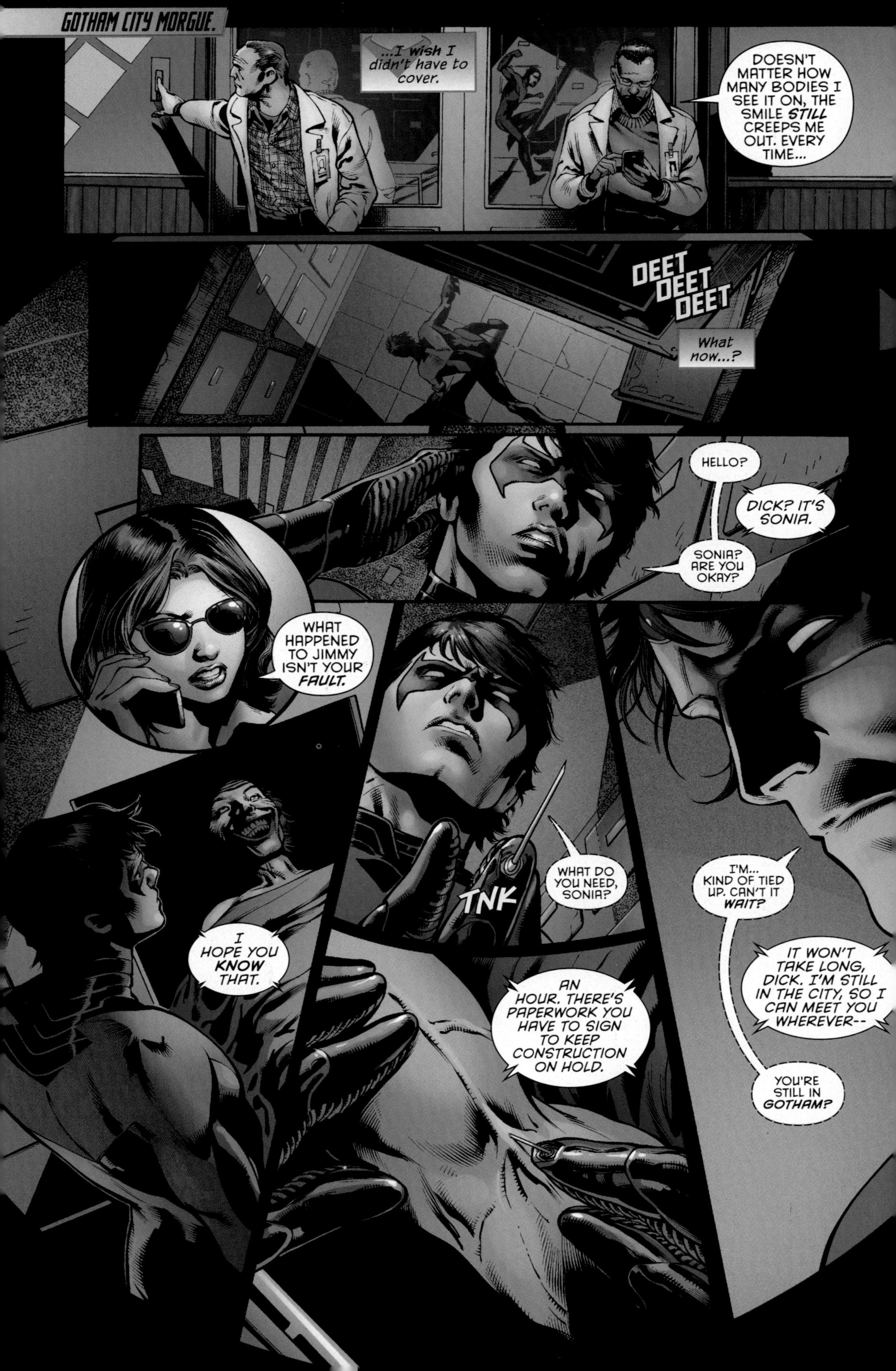
GOTHAM CITY MORGUE.
...I wish I didn't have to cover.
DOESN'T MATTER HOW MANY BODIES I SEE IT ON, THE SMILE STILL CREEPS ME OUT. EVERY TIME...
DEET DEET DEET
What now...?
HELLO?
DICK? IT'S SONIA.
SONIA? ARE YOU OKAY?
WHAT HAPPENED TO JIMMY ISN'T YOUR FAULT.
I HOPE YOU KNOW THAT.
TNK
WHAT DO YOU NEED, SONIA?
I'M... KIND OF TIED UP. CAN'T IT WAIT?
AN HOUR. THERE'S PAPERWORK YOU HAVE TO SIGN TO KEEP CONSTRUCTION ON HOLD.
IT WON'T TAKE LONG, DICK. I'M STILL IN THE CITY, SO I CAN MEET YOU WHEREVER--
YOU'RE STILL IN GOTHAM?

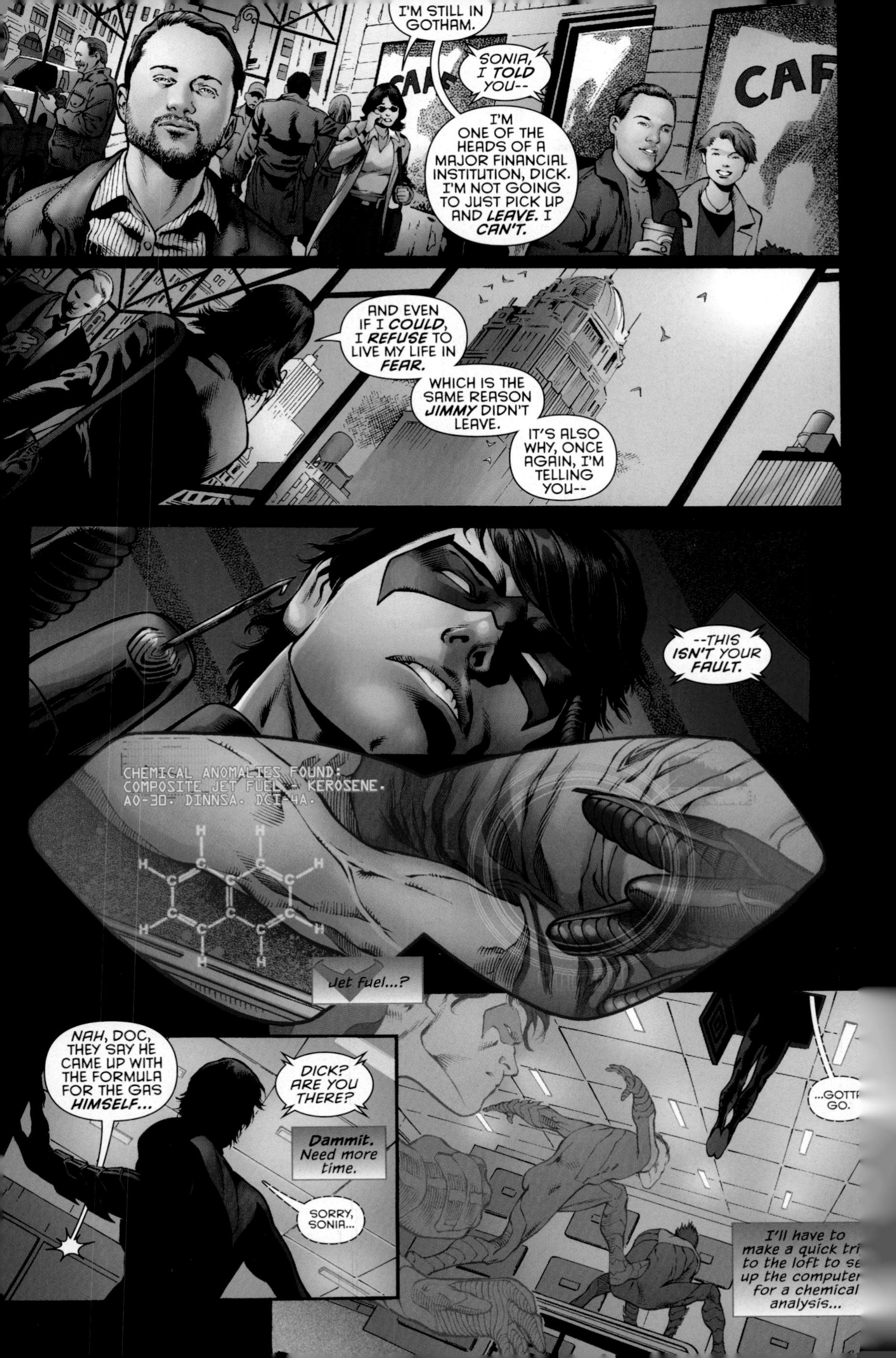

CAF
I'M STILL IN GOTHAM.
SONIA, I TOLD YOU--
I'M ONE OF THE HEADS OF A MAJOR FINANCIAL INSTITUTION, DICK. I'M NOT GOING TO JUST PICK UP AND LEAVE. I CAN'T.
AND EVEN IF I COULD, I REFUSE TO LIVE MY LIFE IN FEAR.
WHICH IS THE SAME REASON JIMMY DIDN'T LEAVE.
IT'S ALSO WHY, ONCE AGAIN, I'M TELLING YOU--
--THIS ISN'T YOUR FAULT.
CHEMICAL ANOMALIES FOUND:
COMPOSITE JET FUEL - KEROSENE.
AO-30. DINNSA. DCI-4A.
Jet fuel...?
NAH, DOC, THEY SAY HE CAME UP WITH THE FORMULA FOR THE GAS HIMSELF...
DICK? ARE YOU THERE?
Dammit. Need more time.
SORRY, SONIA...
...GOTT GO.
I'll have to make a quick tri to the loft to se up the compute for a chemical analysis...

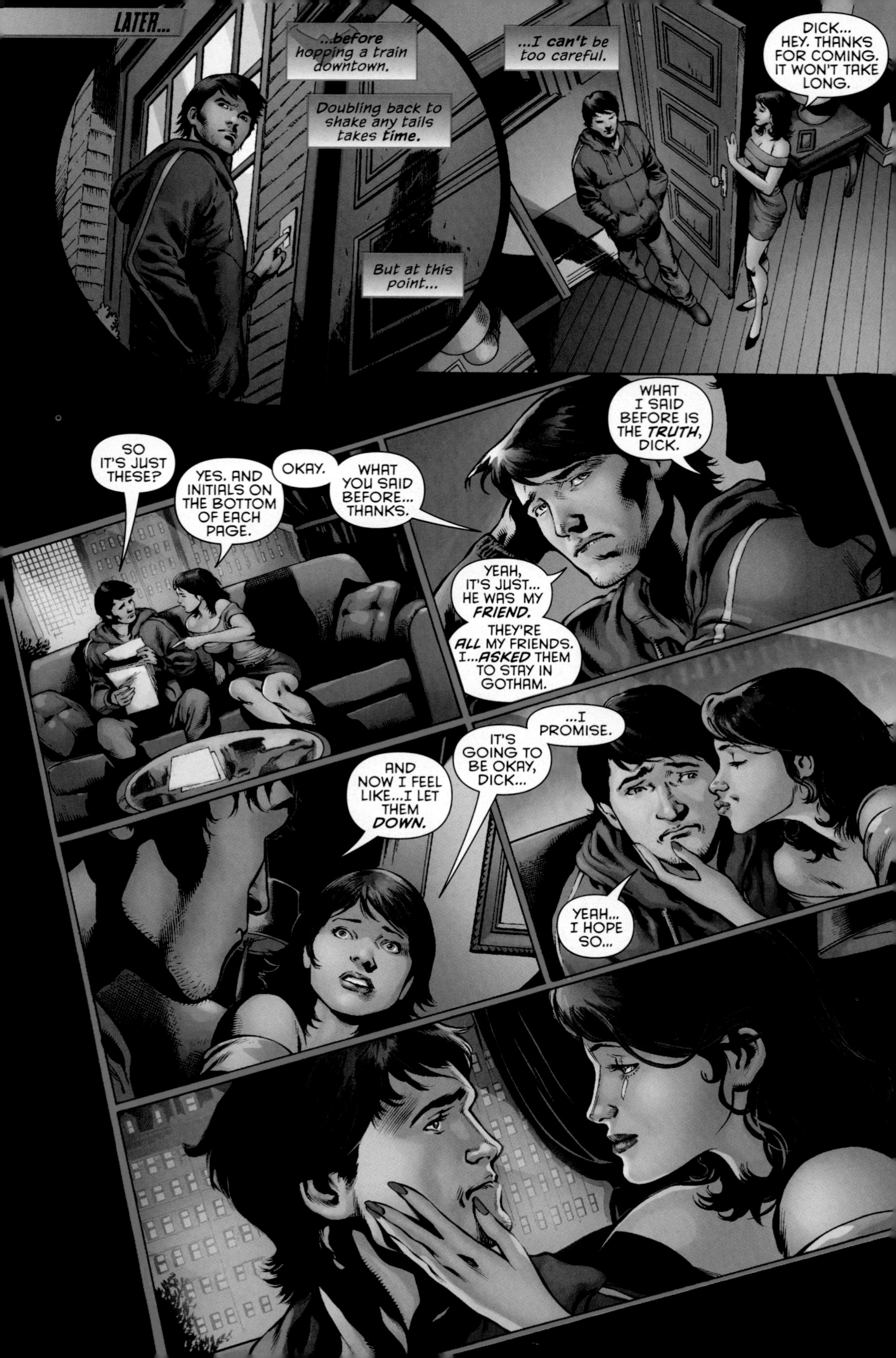
LATER...
...before hopping a train downtown.
Doubling back to shake any tails takes time.
But at this point...
...I can't be too careful.
DICK... HEY. THANKS FOR COMING. IT WON'T TAKE LONG.
SO IT'S JUST THESE?
YES. AND INITIALS ON THE BOTTOM OF EACH PAGE.
OKAY.
WHAT YOU SAID BEFORE... THANKS.
WHAT I SAID BEFORE IS THE TRUTH, DICK.
YEAH, IT'S JUST... HE WAS MY FRIEND.
THEY'RE ALL MY FRIENDS. I...ASKED THEM TO STAY IN GOTHAM.
AND NOW I FEEL LIKE...I LET THEM DOWN.
IT'S GOING TO BE OKAY, DICK...
...I PROMISE.
YEAH... I HOPE SO...

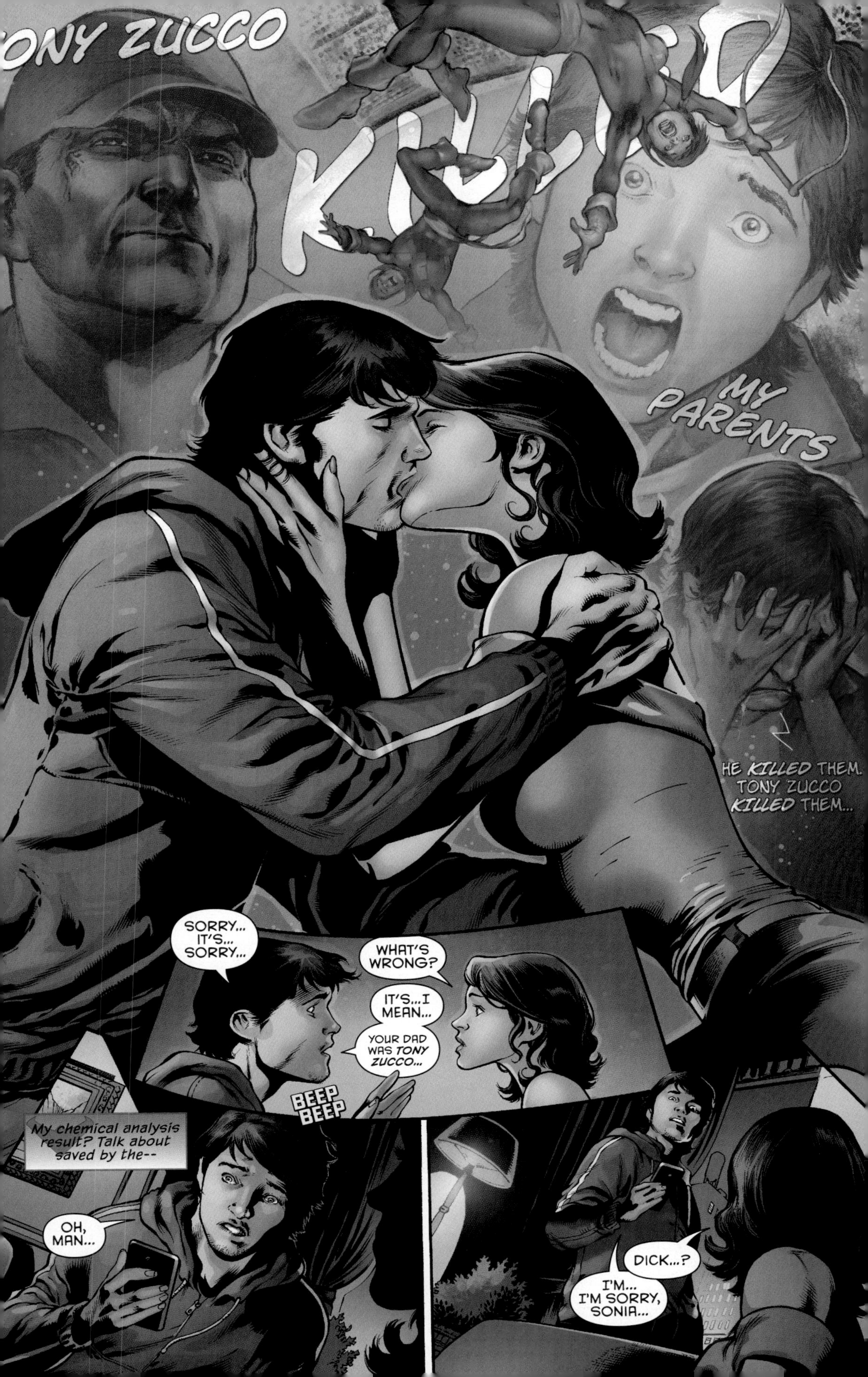
TONY ZUCCO
KILLED
MY PARENTS
HE KILLED THEM. TONY ZUCCO KILLED THEM...
SORRY... IT'S... SORRY...
WHAT'S WRONG?
IT'S...I MEAN...
YOUR DAD WAS TONY ZUCCO...
BEEP BEEP
My chemical analysis result? Talk about saved by the--
OH, MAN...
DICK...?
I'M... I'M SORRY, SONIA...

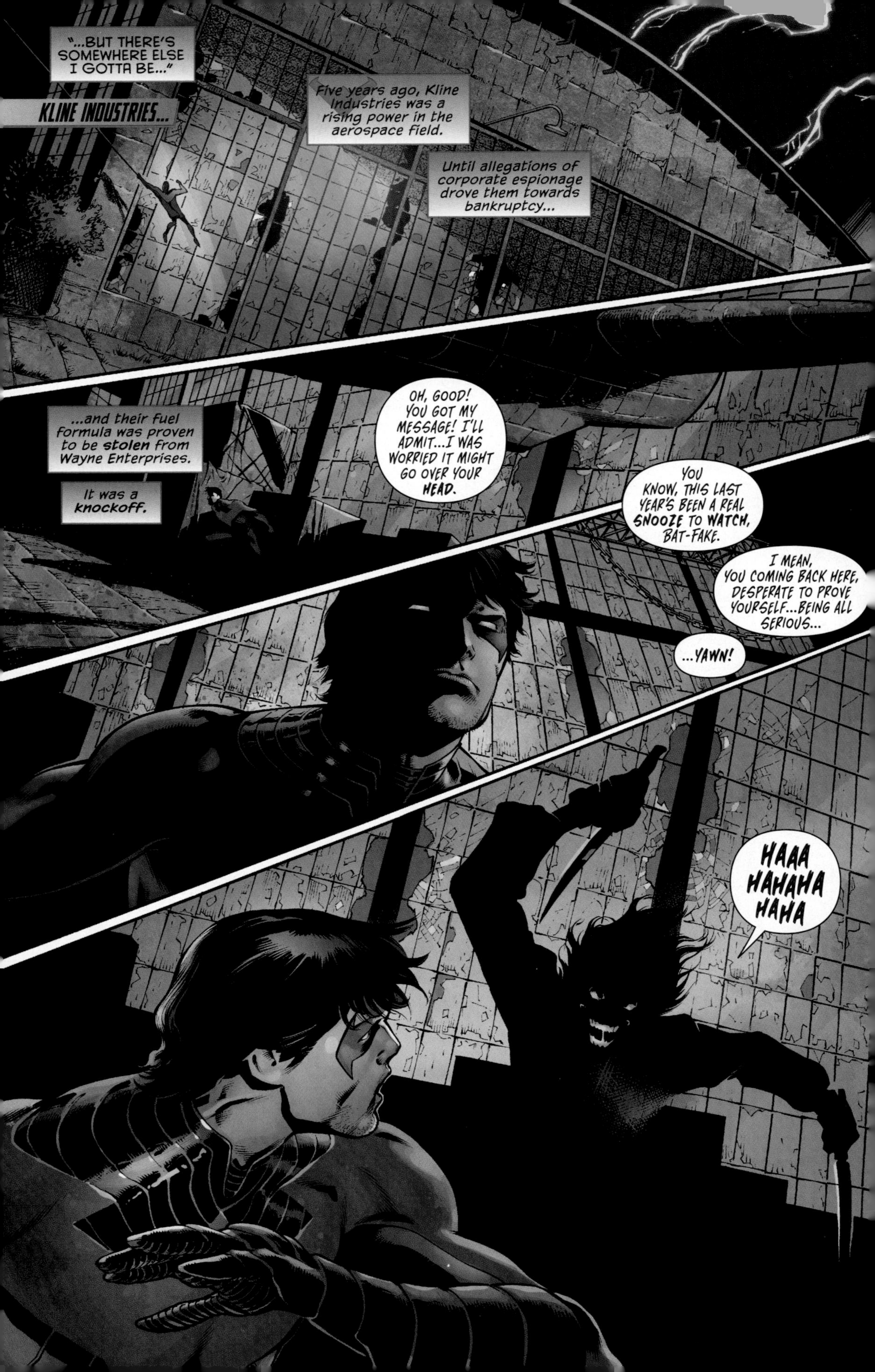
"...BUT THERE'S SOMEWHERE ELSE I GOTTA BE..."
KLINE INDUSTRIES...
Five years ago, Kline Industries was a rising power in the aerospace field.
Until allegations of corporate espionage drove them towards bankruptcy...
...and their fuel formula was proven to be stolen from Wayne Enterprises.
It was a knockoff.
OH, GOOD! YOU GOT MY MESSAGE! I'LL ADMIT...I WAS WORRIED IT MIGHT GO OVER YOUR HEAD.
YOU KNOW, THIS LAST YEAR'S BEEN A REAL SNOOZE TO WATCH, BAT-FAKE.
I MEAN, YOU COMING BACK HERE, DESPERATE TO PROVE YOURSELF...BEING ALL SERIOUS...
...YAWN!
HAAA HAHAHA HAHA

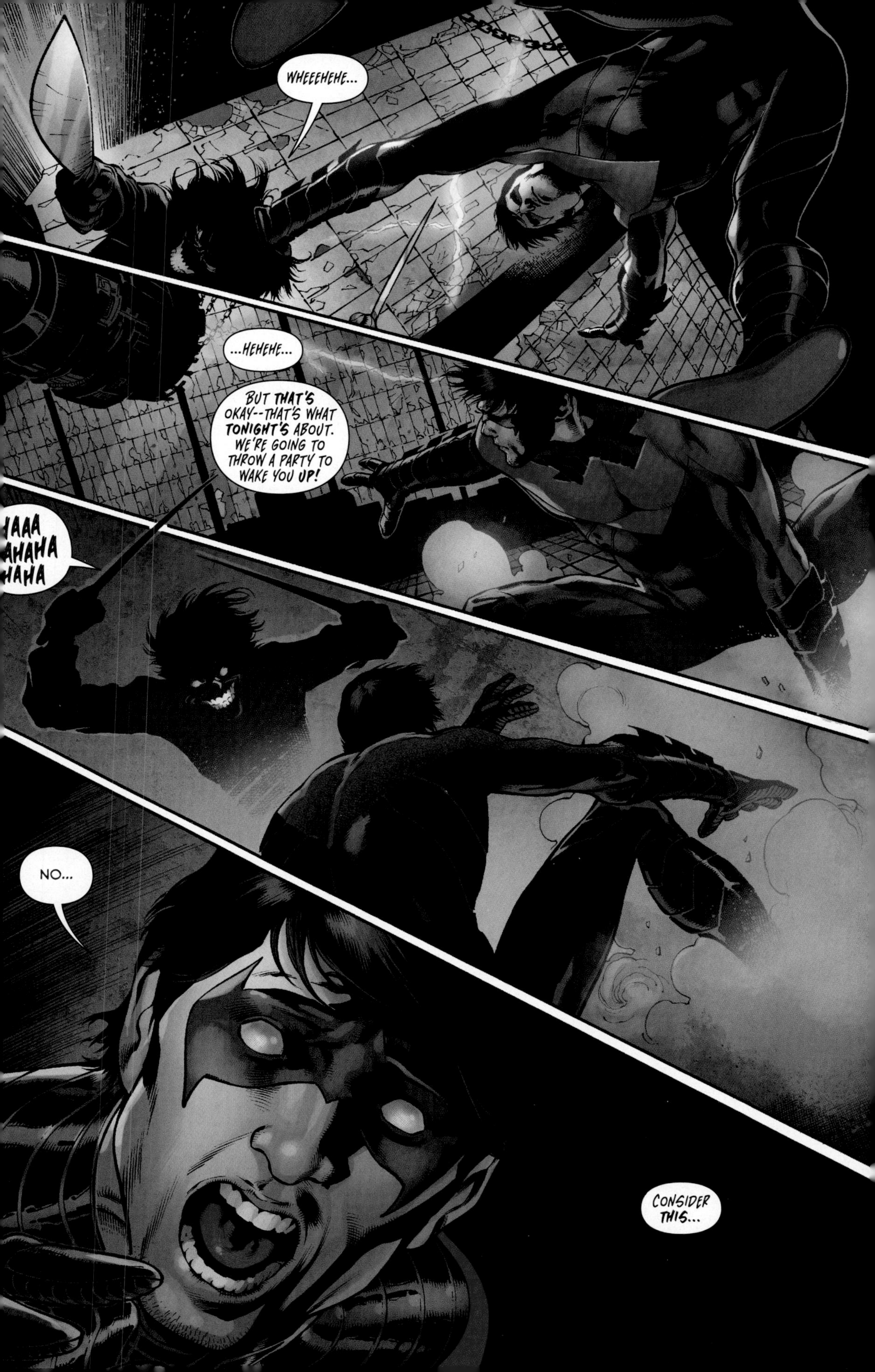
WHEEEHEHE...
...HEHEHE...
BUT THAT'S OKAY--THAT'S WHAT TONIGHT'S ABOUT. WE'RE GOING TO THROW A PARTY TO WAKE YOU UP!
HAAA AHAHA HAHA
NO...
CONSIDER THIS...

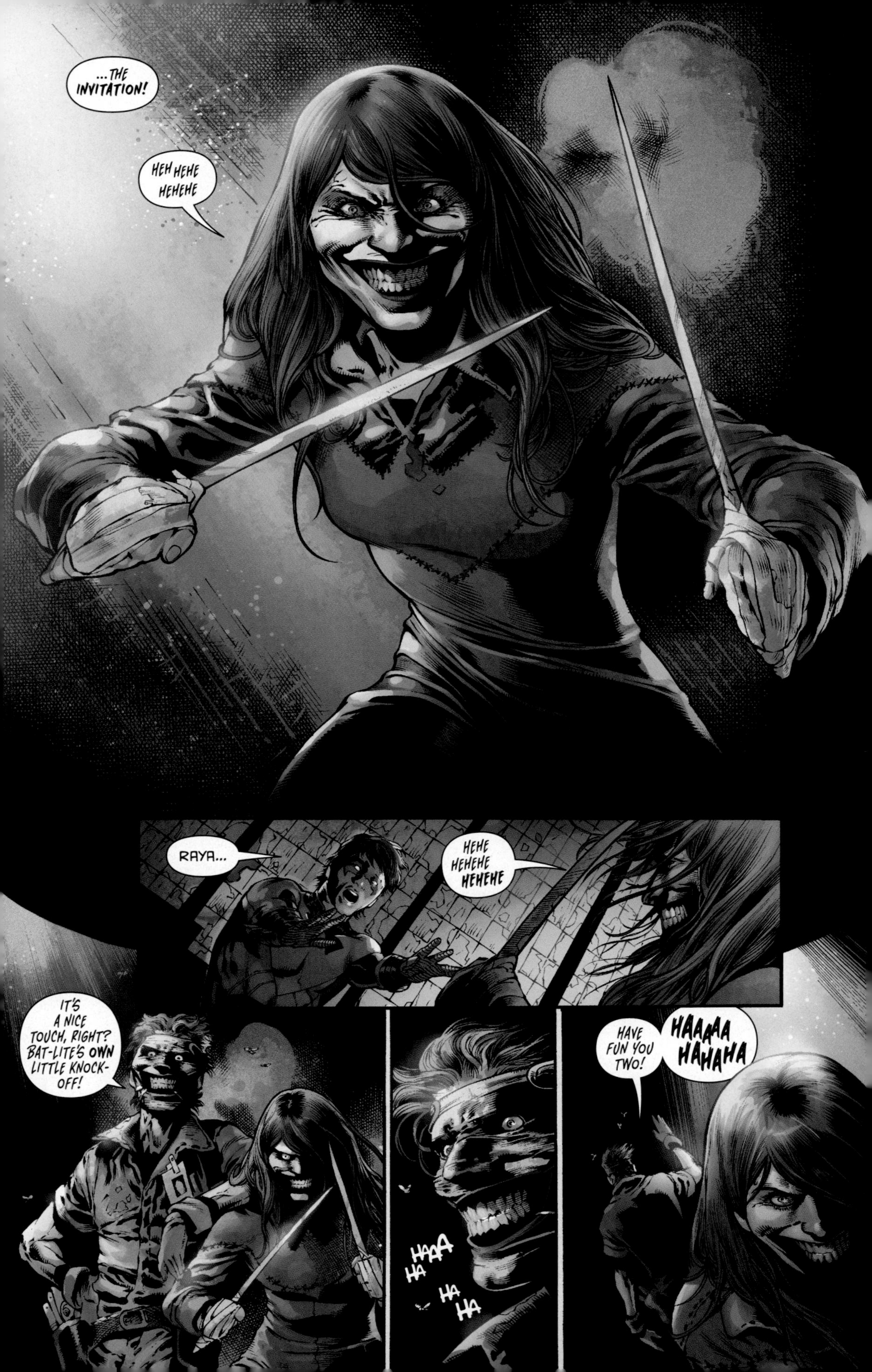
...THE INVITATION!
HEH HEHE HEHEHE
RAYA...
HEHE HEHEHE HEHEHE
IT'S A NICE TOUCH, RIGHT? BAT-LITE'S OWN LITTLE KNOCK-OFF!
HAAA HA HA HA
HAVE FUN YOU TWO!
HAAAAA HAHAHA

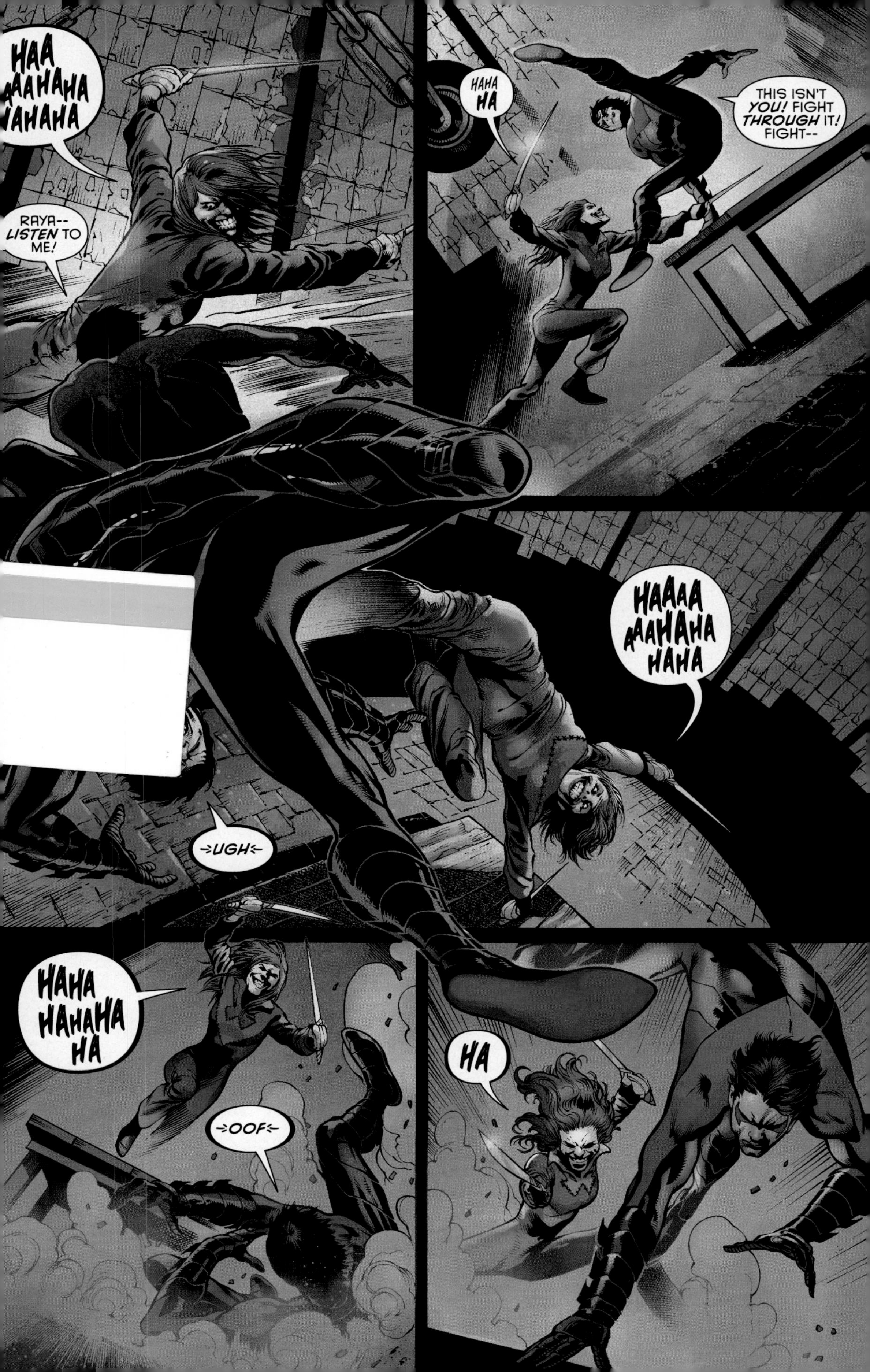
HAA
AAAHAHA
AHAHA
RAYA--
LISTEN TO
ME!
HAHA
HA
THIS ISN'T
YOU! FIGHT
THROUGH IT!
FIGHT--
HAAAA
AAAHAHA
HAHA
UGH
HAHA
HAHAHA
HA
OOF
HA

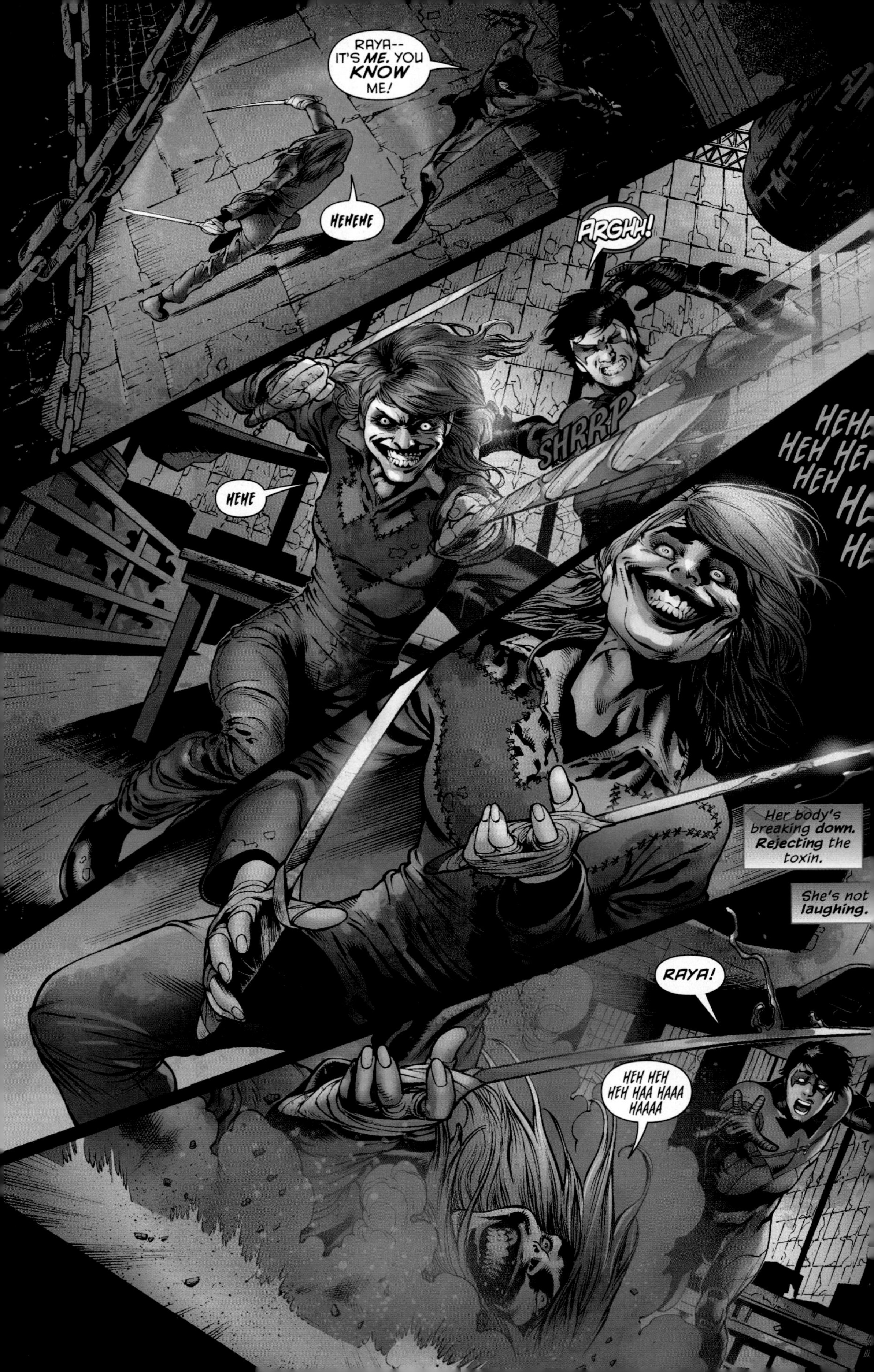
RAYA-- IT'S ME. YOU KNOW ME!
HEHEHE
ARGHH!
SHRRP
HEHE
HEHE HEH HEH HEH HE HE
Her body's breaking down. Rejecting the toxin.
She's not laughing.
RAYA!
HEH HEH HEH HAA HAAA HAAAA

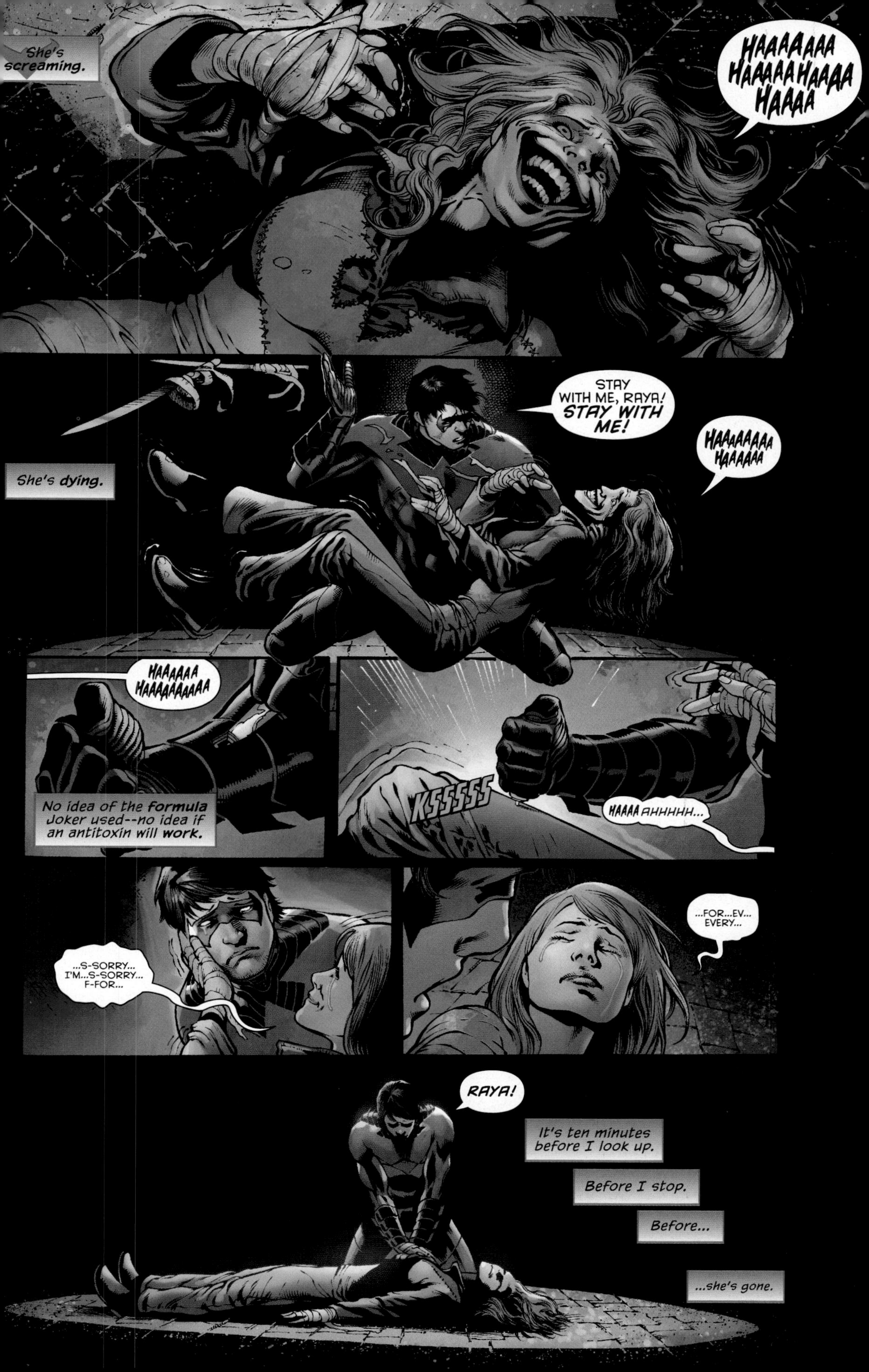
She's screaming.
HAAAAAAA HAAAAAHAAAA HAAAA
STAY WITH ME, RAYA! STAY WITH ME!
HAAAAAAAA HAAAAAA
She's dying.
HAAAAAA HAAAAAAAAAA
No idea of the formula Joker used--no idea if an antitoxin will work.
KSSSSS
HAAAA AHHHHH...
...S-SORRY... I'M...S-SORRY... F-FOR...
...FOR...EV... EVERY...
RAYA!
It's ten minutes before I look up.
Before I stop.
Before...
...she's gone.

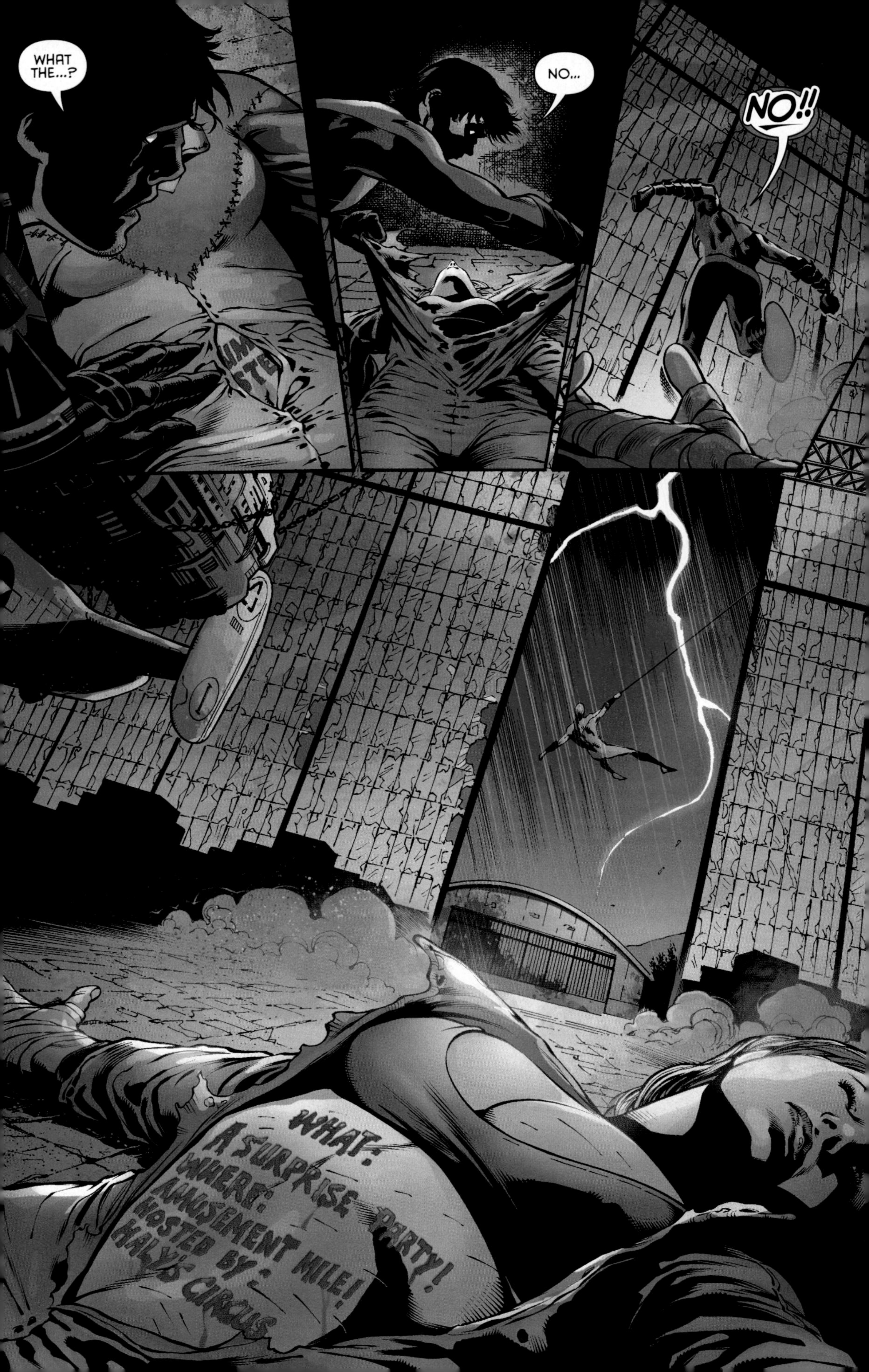
WHAT THE...?
NO...
NO!!
WHAT:
A SURPRISE PARTY!
WHERE:
AMUSEMENT MILE!
HOSTED BY:
HALY'S CIRCUS

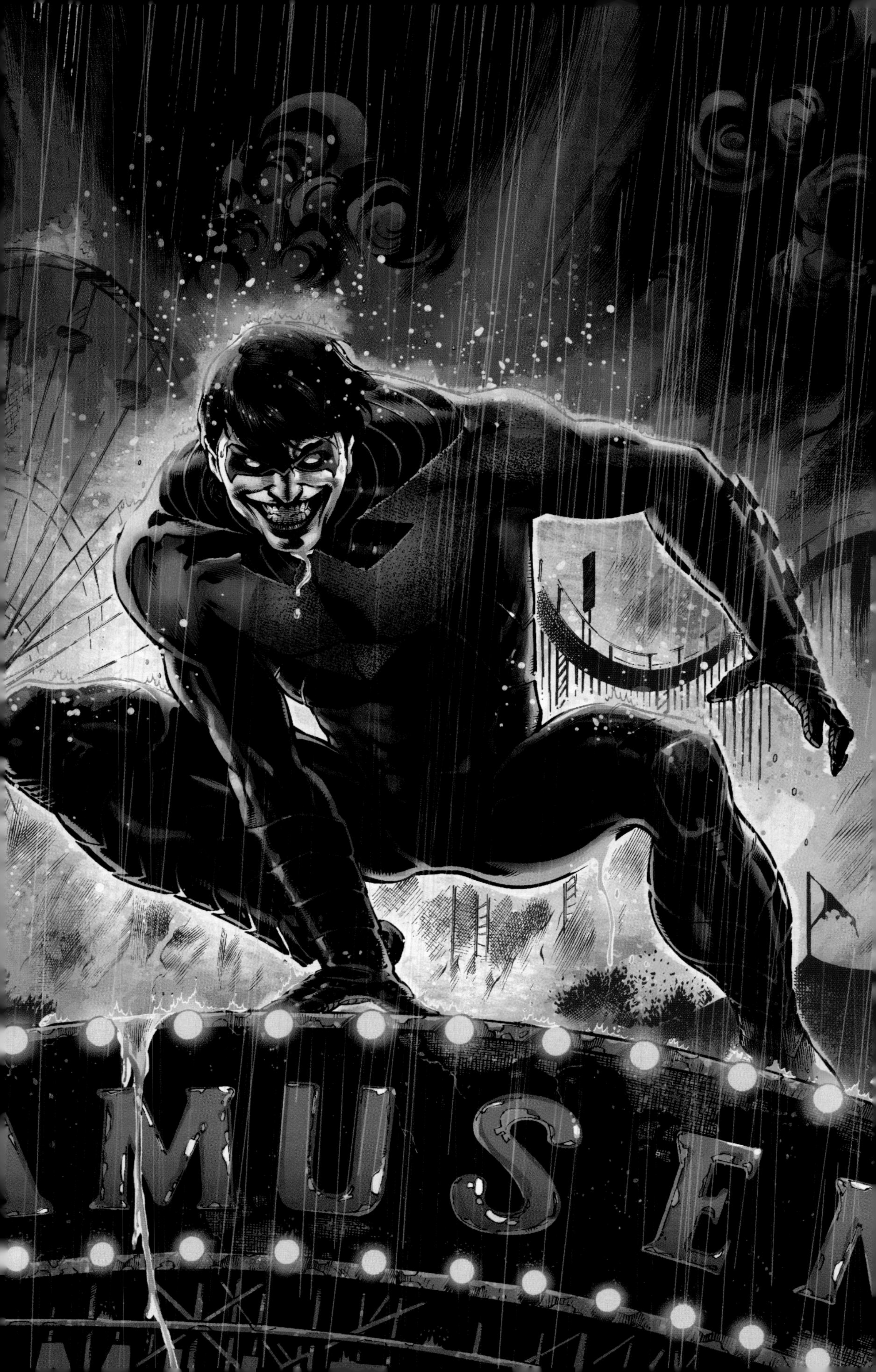
MUSE

CURTAIN CALL

KYLE HIGGINS writer **EDDY BARROWS** penciller **EBER FERREIRA** inker cover art by **EDDY BARROWS, EBER FERREIRA & ROD REIS**

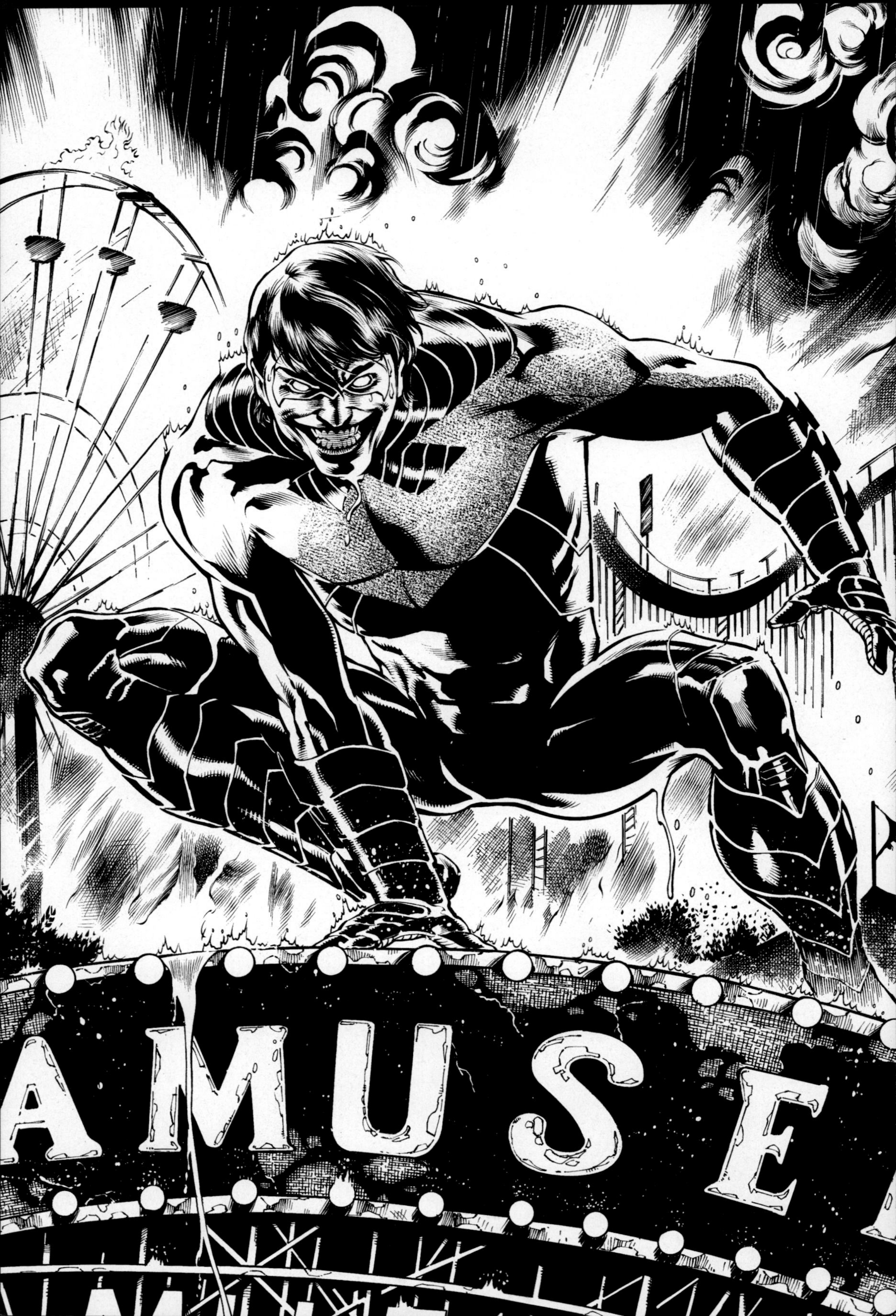
AMUSE

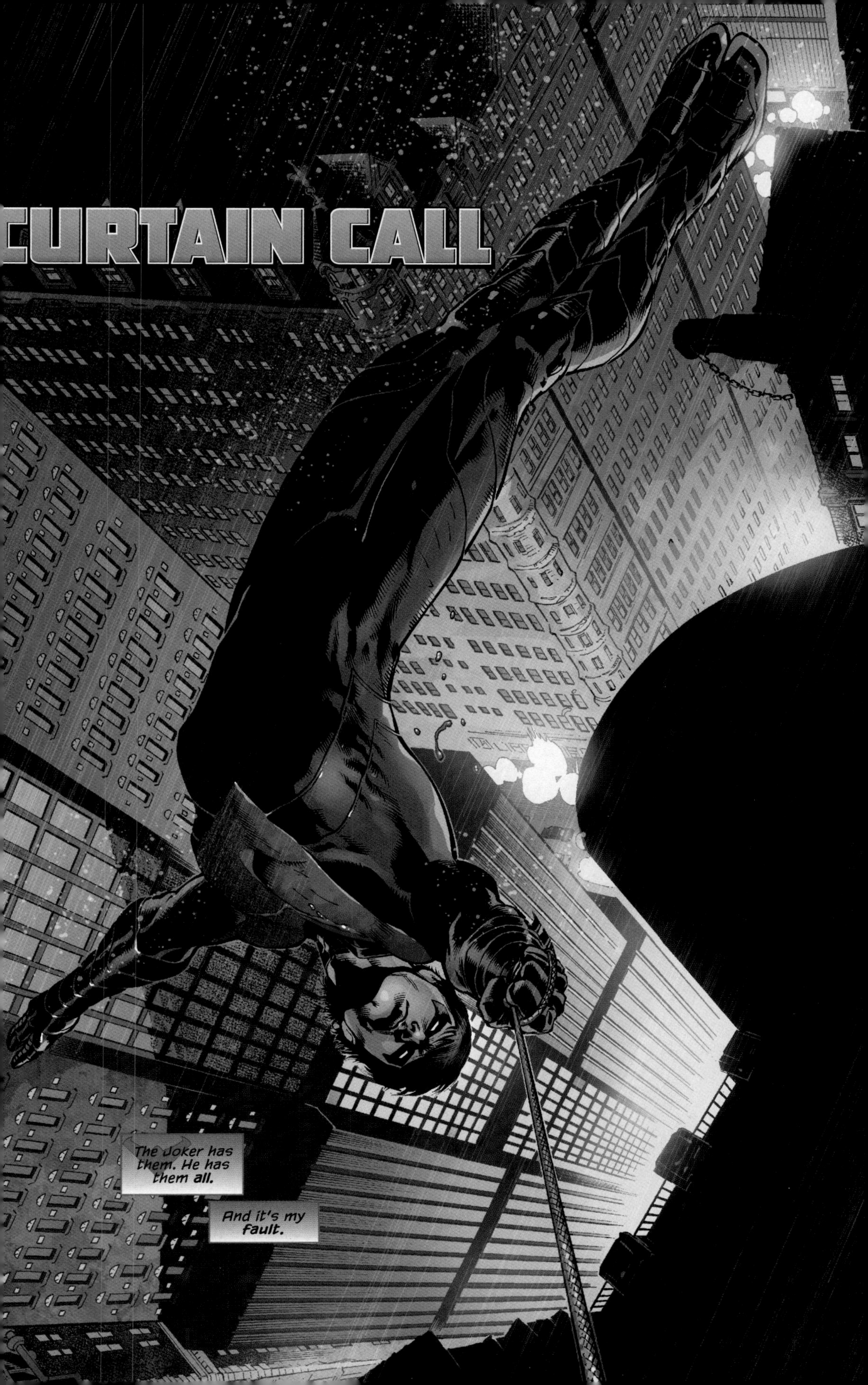
CURTAIN CALL
The Joker has them. He has them all.
And it's my fault.

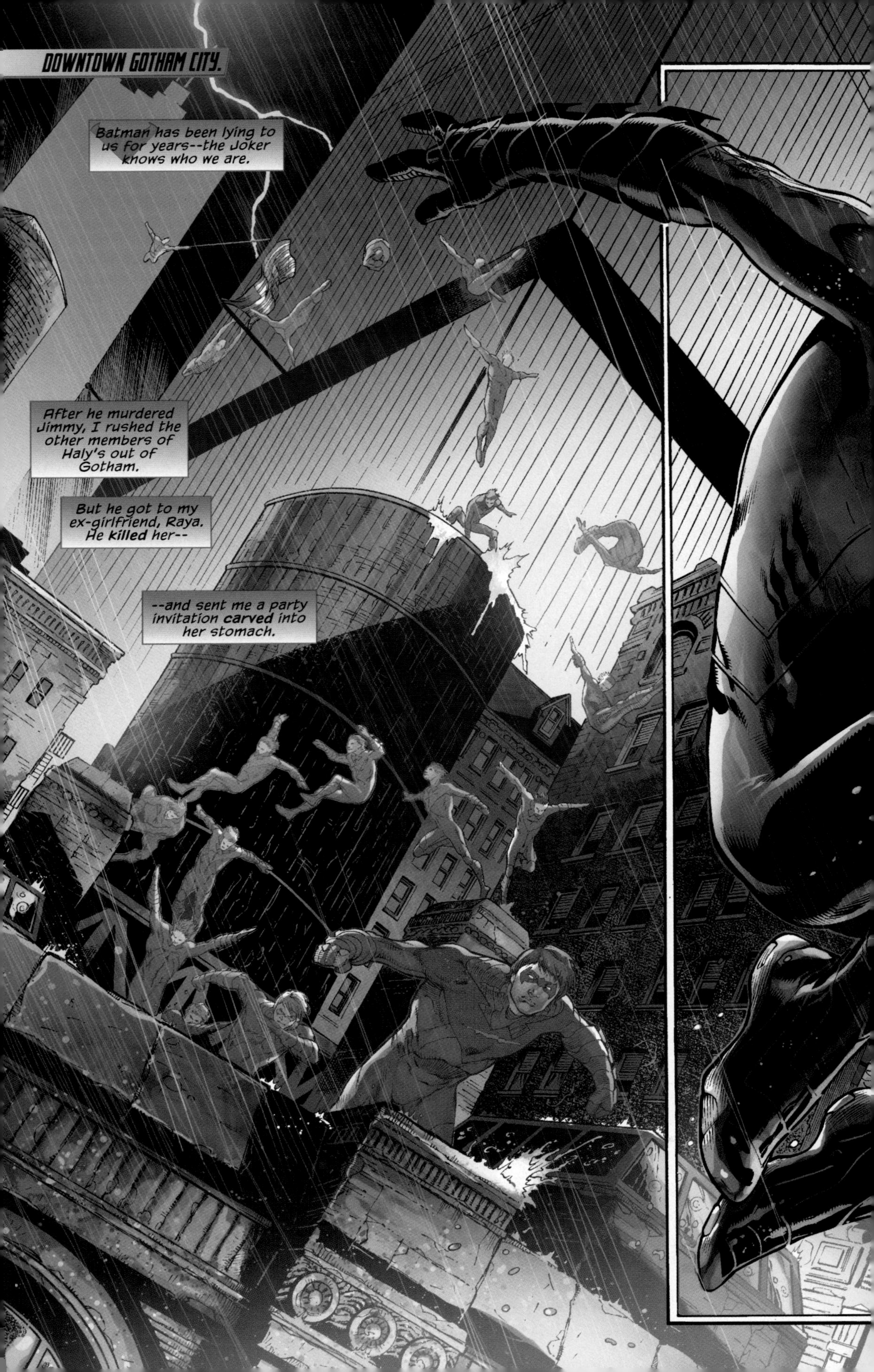
DOWNTOWN GOTHAM CITY.
Batman has been lying to us for years--the Joker knows who we are.
After he murdered Jimmy, I rushed the other members of Haly's out of Gotham.
But he got to my ex-girlfriend, Raya. He killed her--
--and sent me a party invitation carved into her stomach.

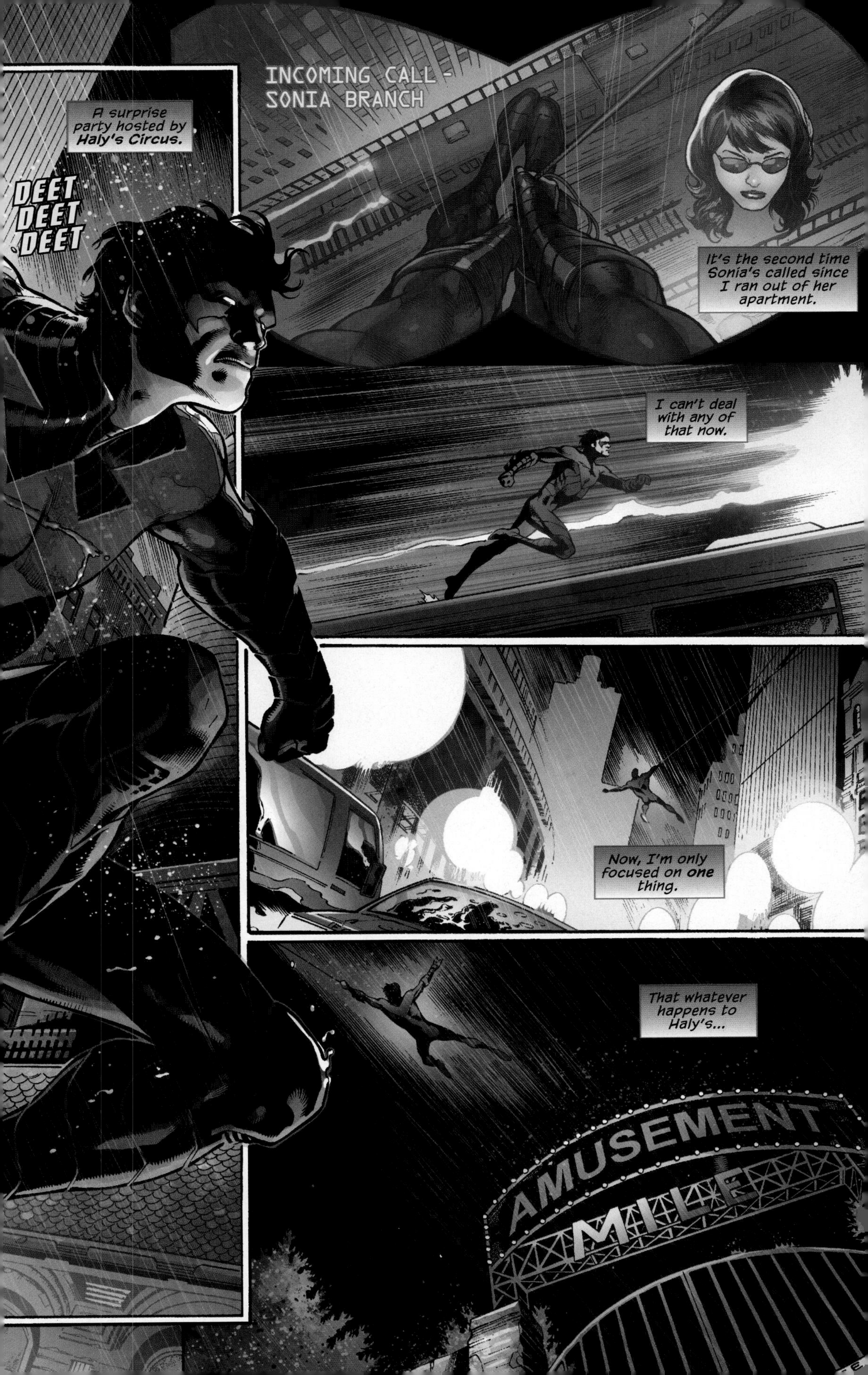
A surprise party hosted by Haly's Circus.
DEET DEET DEET
INCOMING CALL - SONIA BRANCH
It's the second time Sonia's called since I ran out of her apartment.
I can't deal with any of that now.
Now, I'm only focused on one thing.
That whatever happens to Haly's...
AMUSEMENT MILE

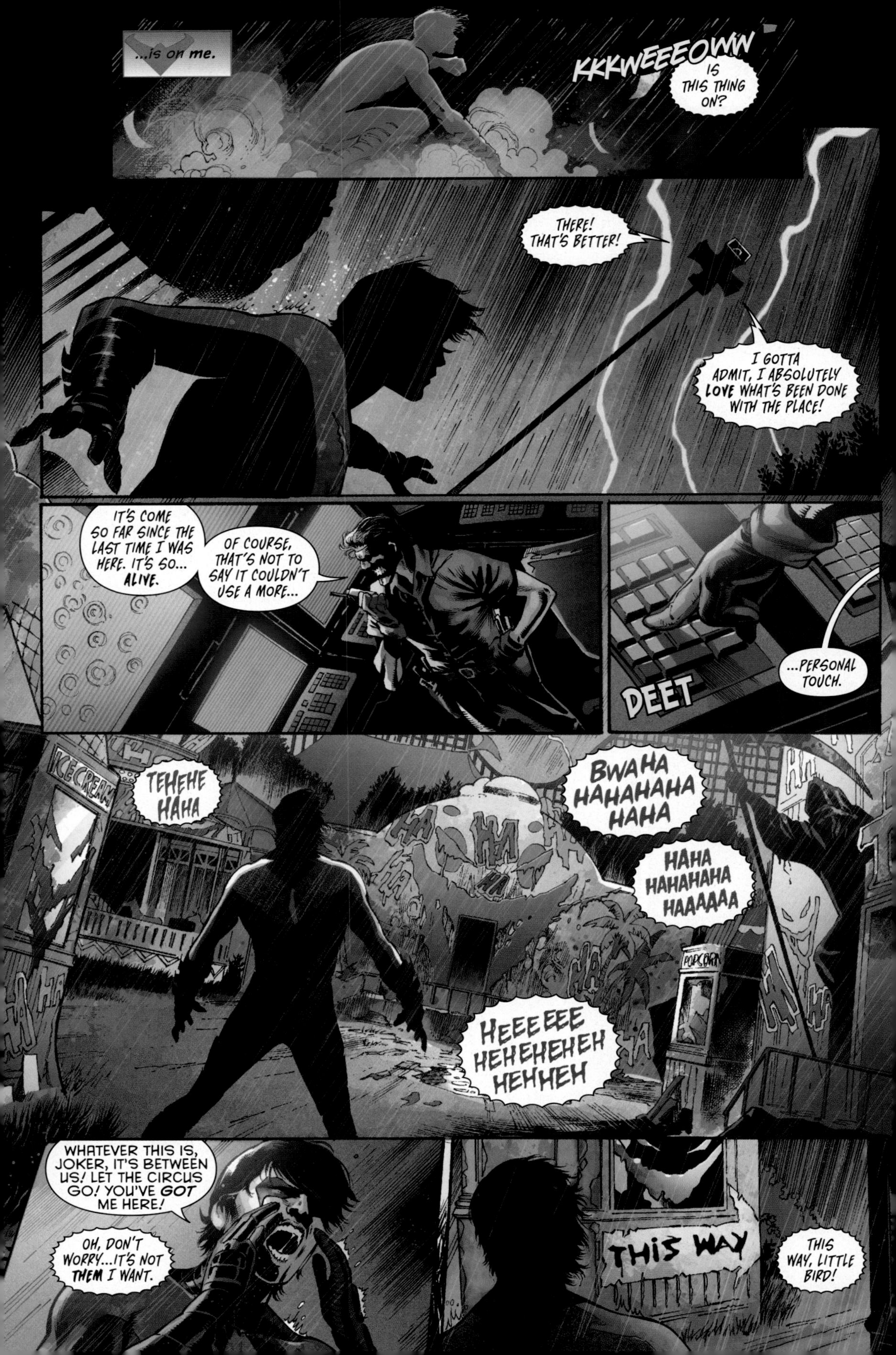
...is on me.
KKKWEEEOWN
IS THIS THING ON?
THERE! THAT'S BETTER!
I GOTTA ADMIT, I ABSOLUTELY LOVE WHAT'S BEEN DONE WITH THE PLACE!
IT'S COME SO FAR SINCE THE LAST TIME I WAS HERE. IT'S SO... ALIVE.
OF COURSE, THAT'S NOT TO SAY IT COULDN'T USE A MORE...
...PERSONAL TOUCH.
DEET
ICE CREAM
TEHEHE HAHA
BWAHA HAHAHAHA HAHA
HAHA HAHAHAHA HAAAAAA
POPCORN
HEEEEEE HEHEHEHEH HEHHEH
WHATEVER THIS IS, JOKER, IT'S BETWEEN US! LET THE CIRCUS GO! YOU'VE GOT ME HERE!
OH, DON'T WORRY...IT'S NOT THEM I WANT.
THIS WAY
THIS WAY, LITTLE BIRD!

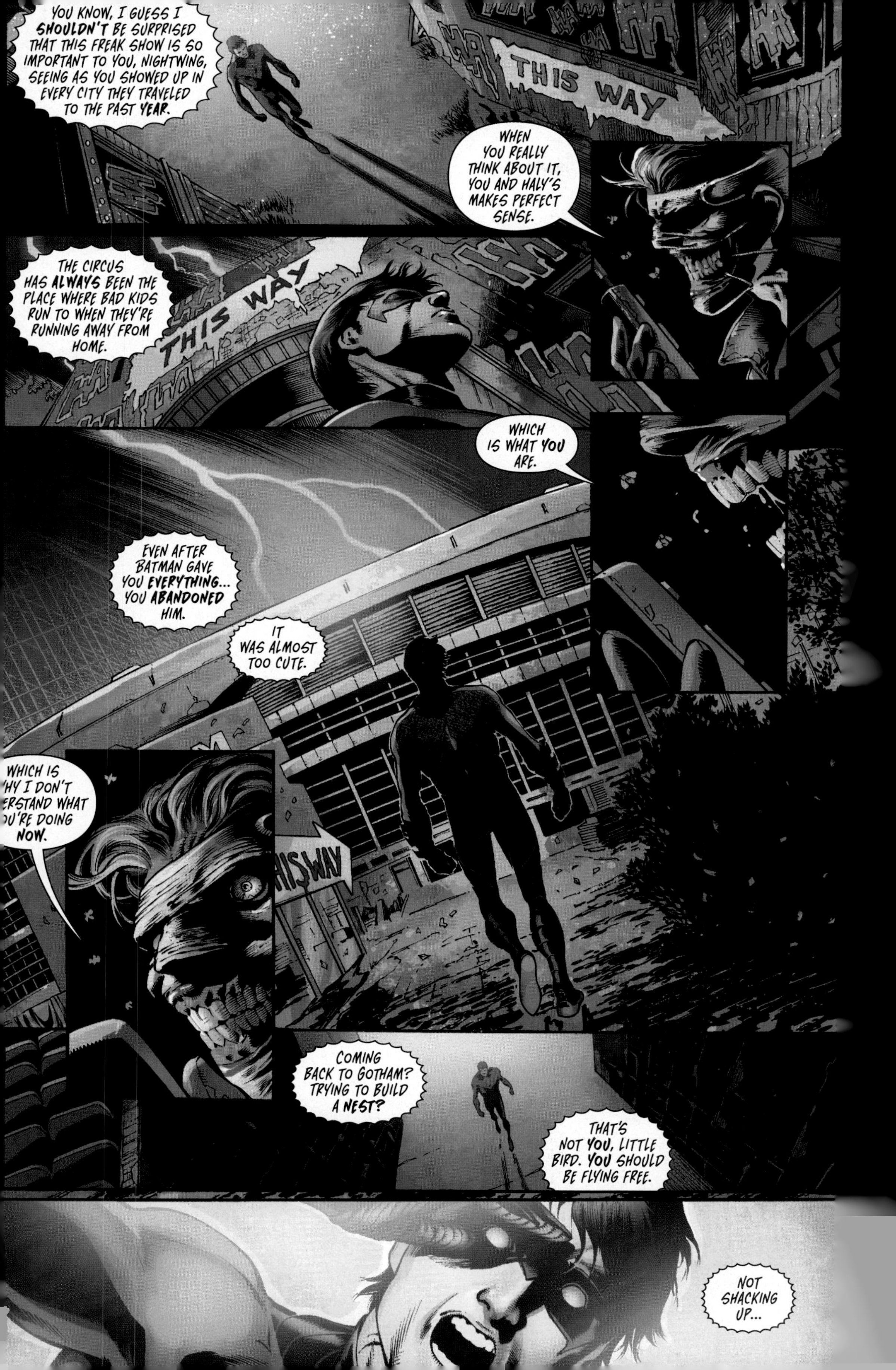

YOU KNOW, I GUESS I SHOULDN'T BE SURPRISED THAT THIS FREAK SHOW IS SO IMPORTANT TO YOU, NIGHTWING, SEEING AS YOU SHOWED UP IN EVERY CITY THEY TRAVELED TO THE PAST YEAR.
THIS WAY
WHEN YOU REALLY THINK ABOUT IT, YOU AND HALY'S MAKES PERFECT SENSE.
THE CIRCUS HAS ALWAYS BEEN THE PLACE WHERE BAD KIDS RUN TO WHEN THEY'RE RUNNING AWAY FROM HOME.
THIS WAY
WHICH IS WHAT YOU ARE.
EVEN AFTER BATMAN GAVE YOU EVERYTHING... YOU ABANDONED HIM.
IT WAS ALMOST TOO CUTE.
WHICH IS WHY I DON'T UNDERSTAND WHAT YOU'RE DOING NOW.
COMING BACK TO GOTHAM? TRYING TO BUILD A NEST?
THAT'S NOT YOU, LITTLE BIRD. YOU SHOULD BE FLYING FREE.
NOT SHACKING UP...

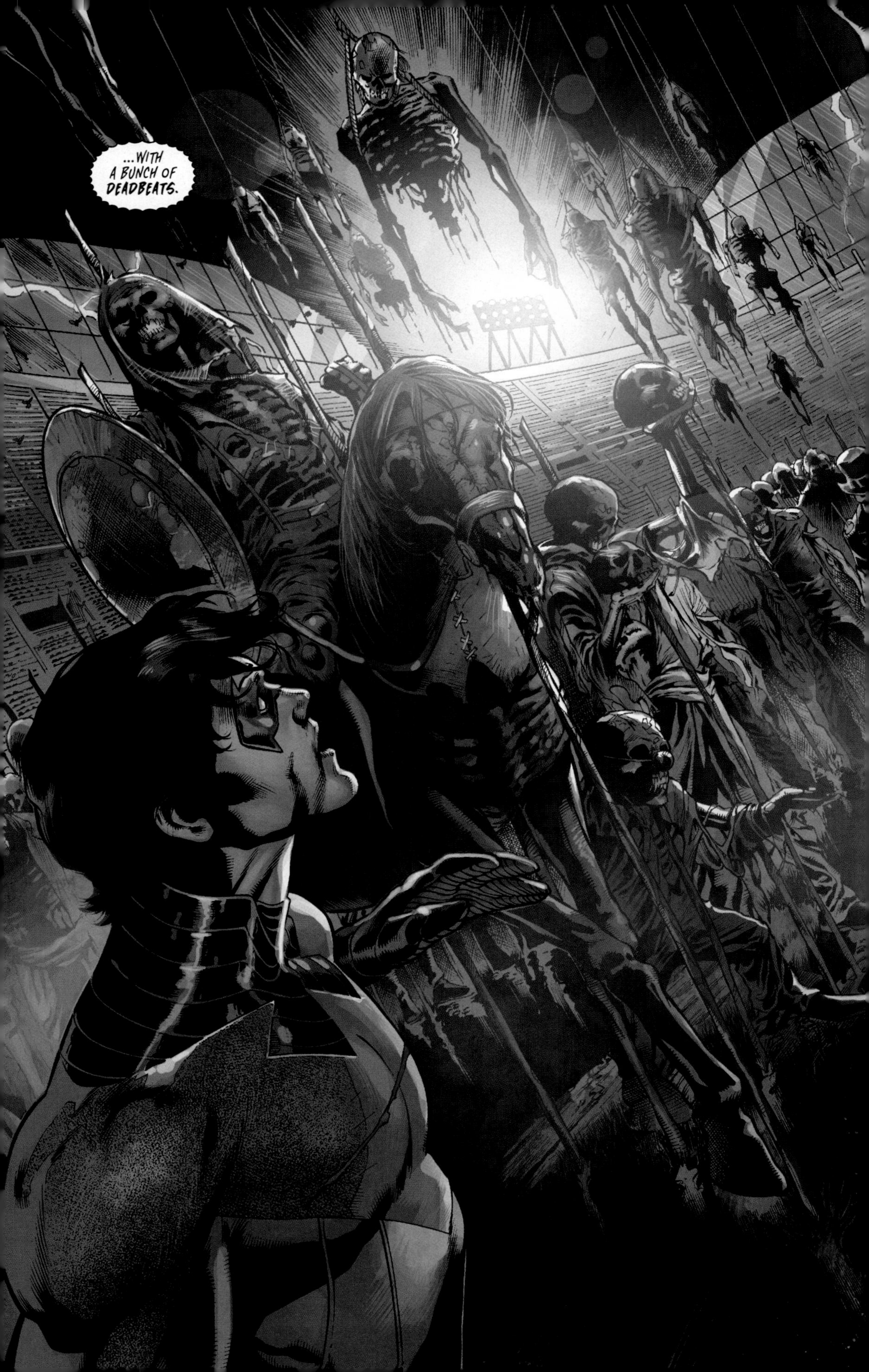
...WITH A BUNCH OF DEADBEATS.

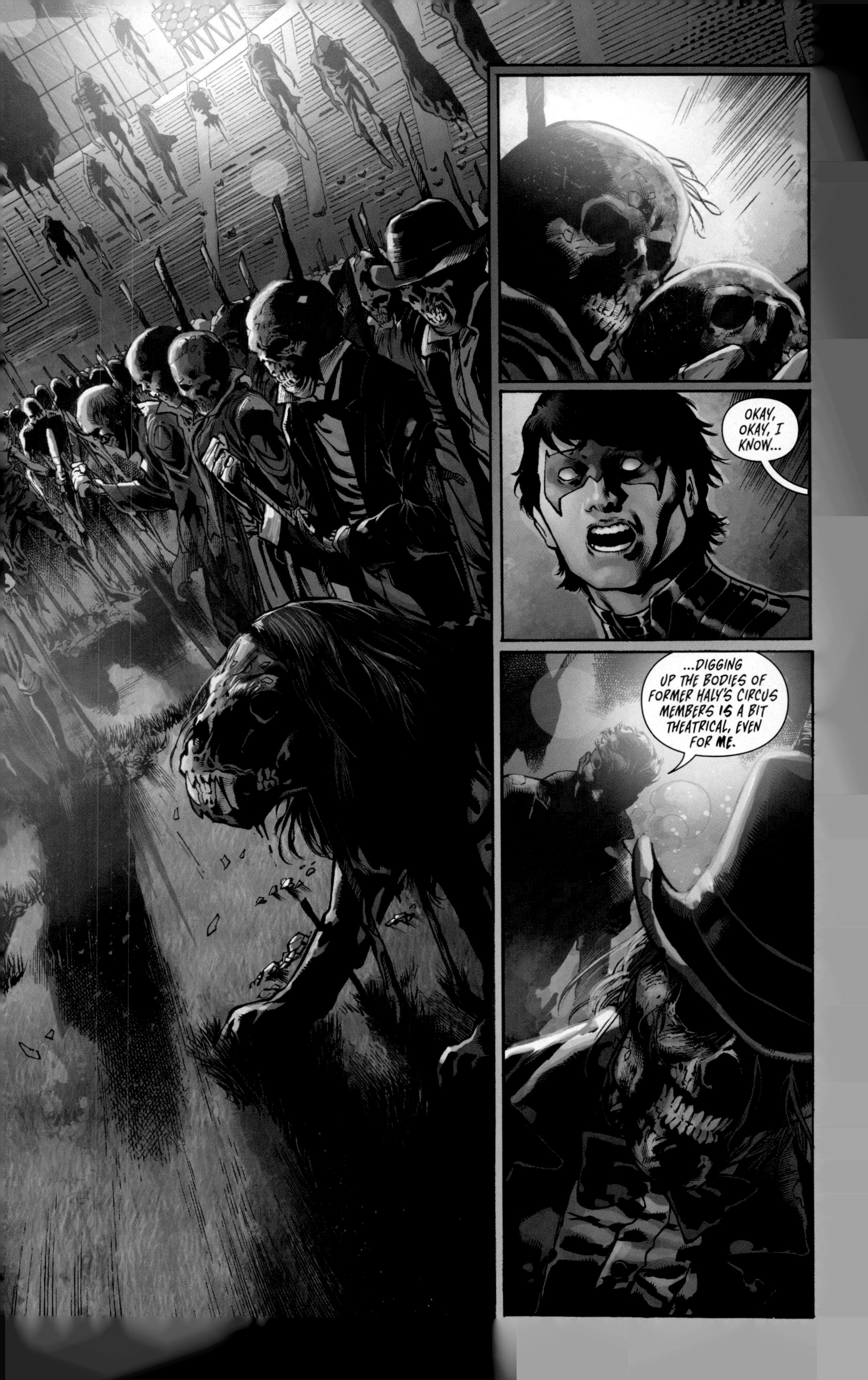
OKAY, OKAY, I KNOW...
...DIGGING UP THE BODIES OF FORMER HALY'S CIRCUS MEMBERS IS A BIT THEATRICAL, EVEN FOR ME.

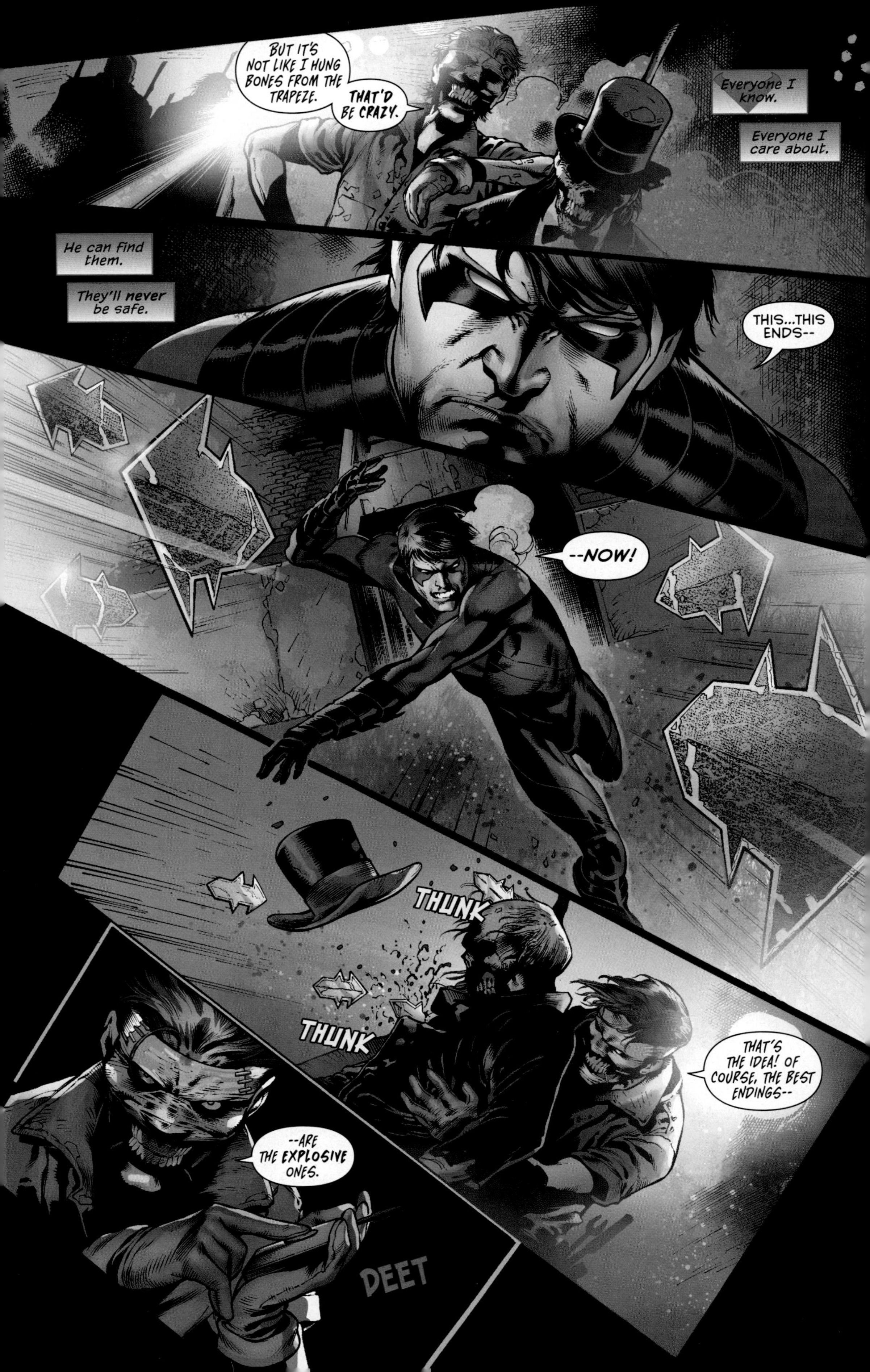
BUT IT'S NOT LIKE I HUNG BONES FROM THE TRAPEZE.
THAT'D BE CRAZY.
Everyone I know.
Everyone I care about.
He can find them.
They'll never be safe.
THIS...THIS ENDS--
--NOW!
THUNK
THUNK
THAT'S THE IDEA! OF COURSE, THE BEST ENDINGS--
--ARE THE EXPLOSIVE ONES.
DEET

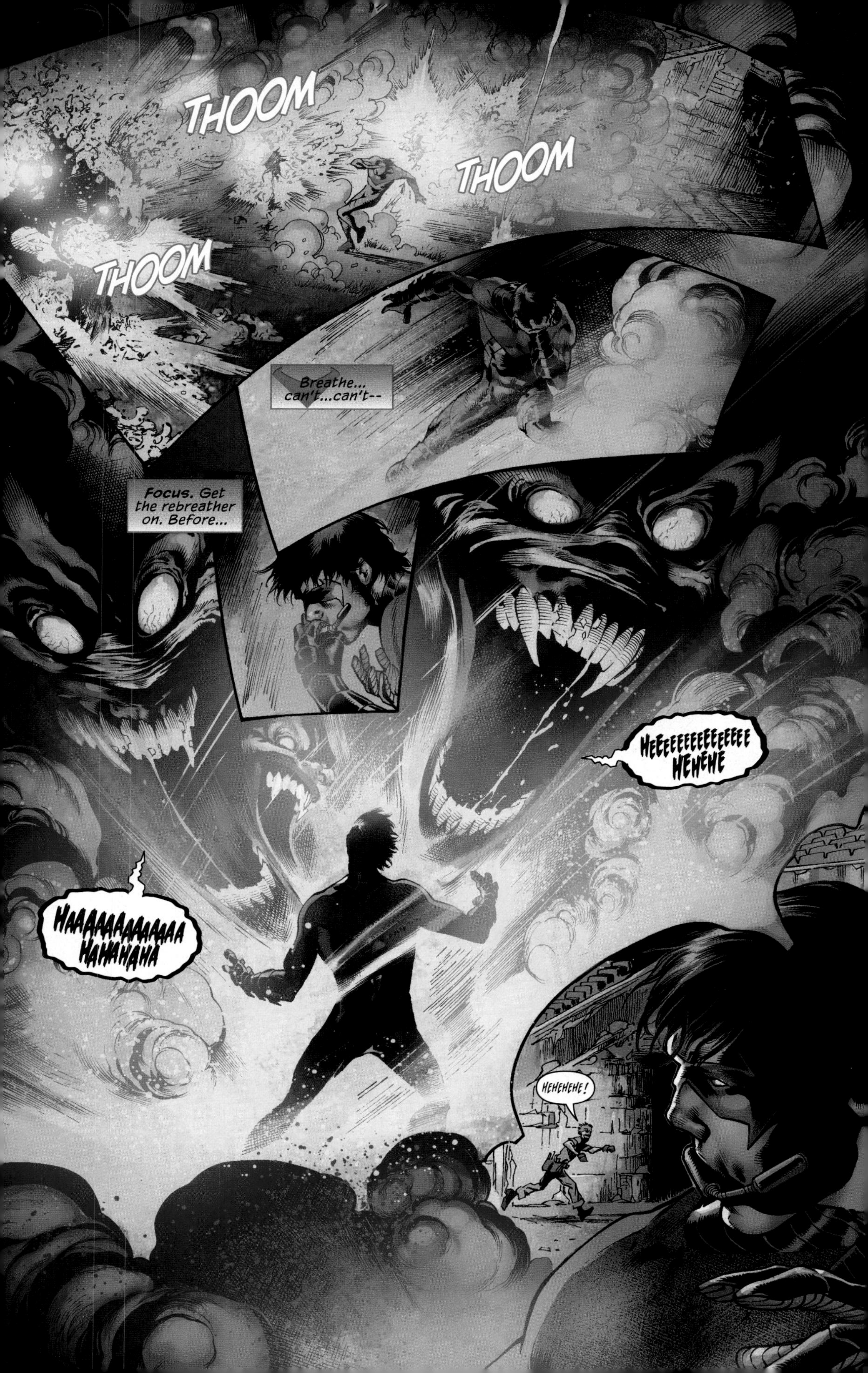
THOOM
THOOM
THOOM
Breathe... can't...can't--
Focus. Get the rebreather on. Before...
HEEEEEEEEEEEEEEE HEHEHE
HAAAAAAAAAAAAA HAHAHAHA
HEHEHEHE!

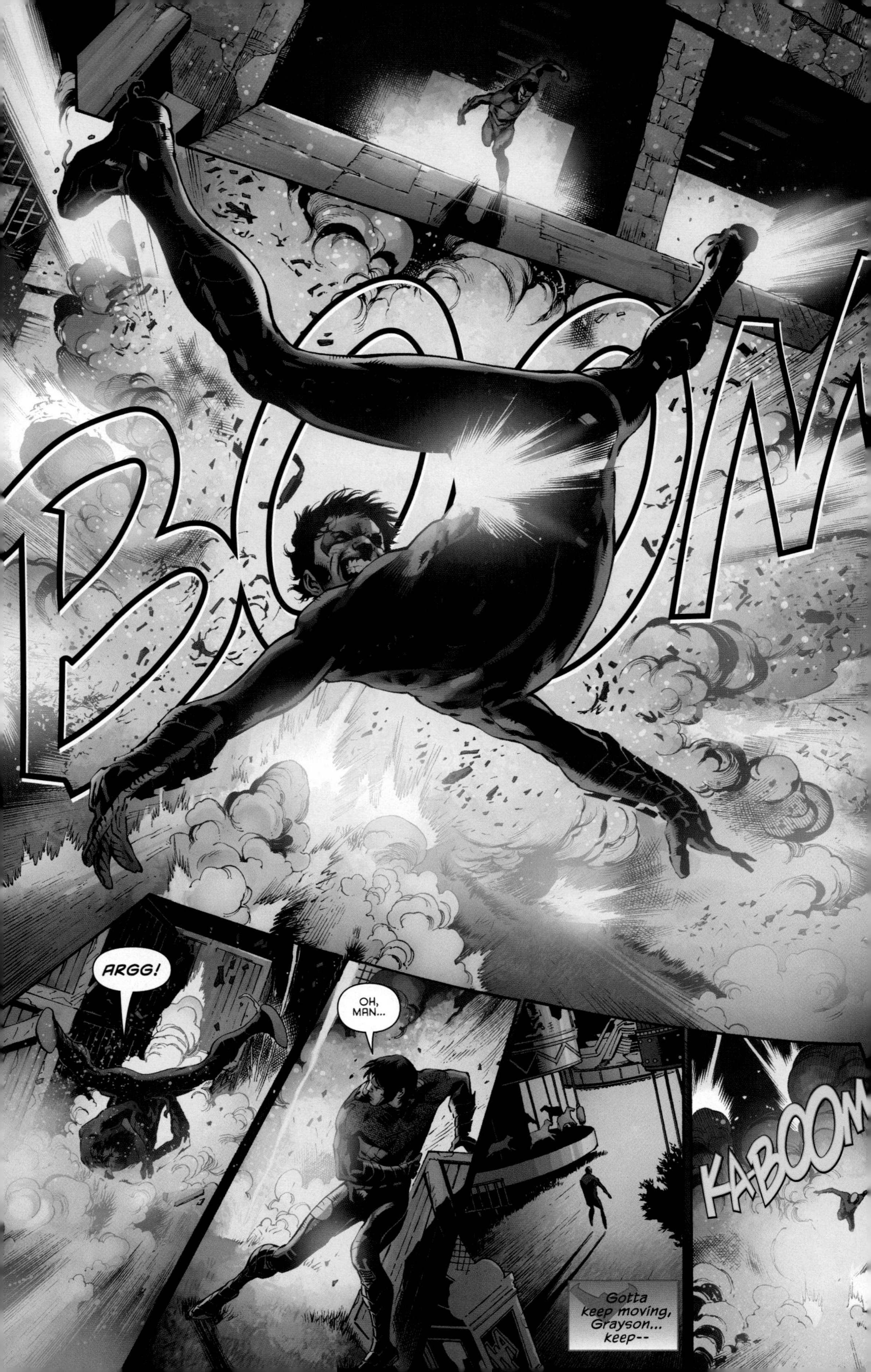
BOOM
ARGG!
OH, MAN...
KABOOM
Gotta keep moving, Grayson... keep--

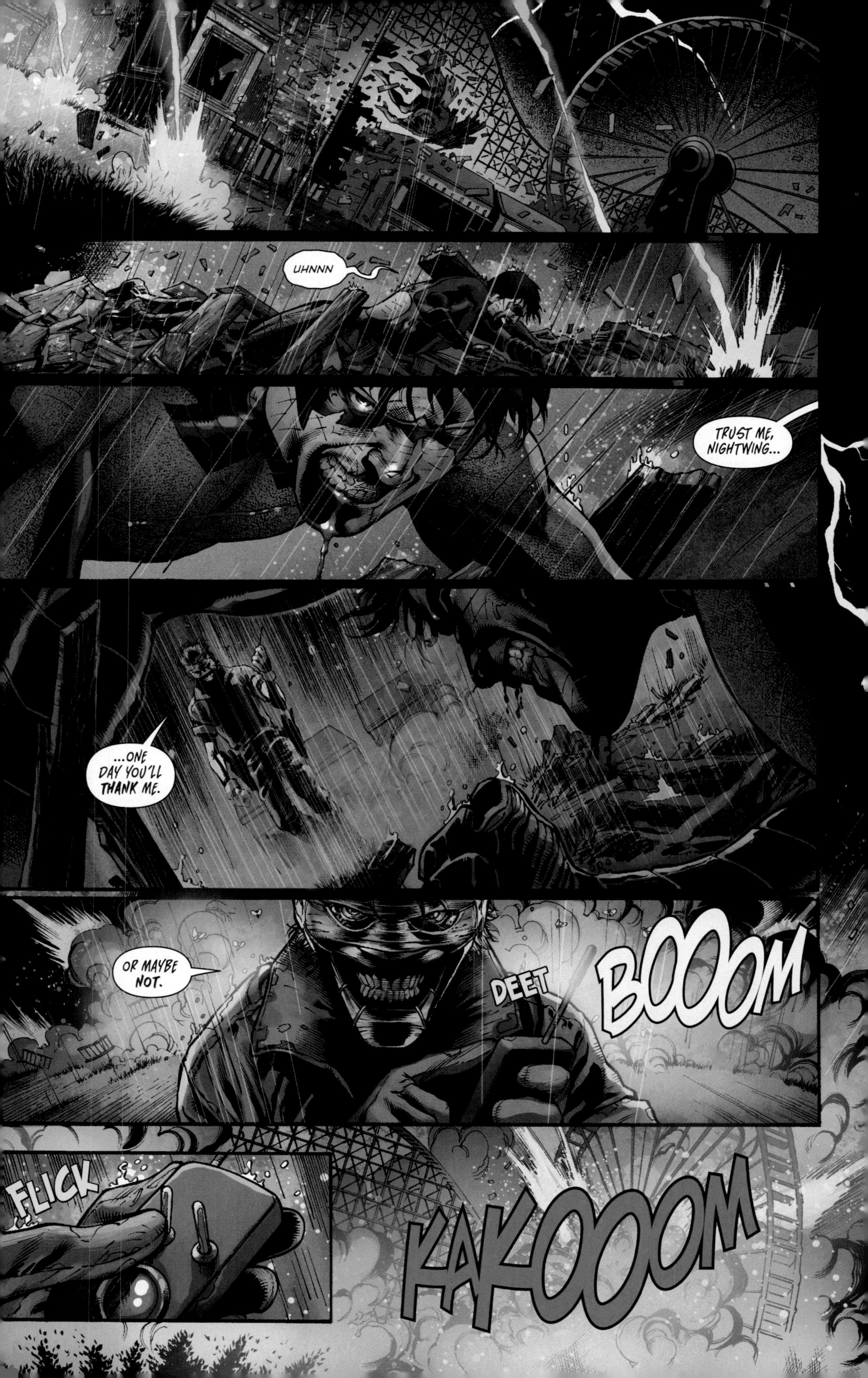
UHNNN
TRUST ME, NIGHTWING...
...ONE DAY YOU'LL THANK ME.
OR MAYBE NOT.
DEET
BOOOM
FLICK
KAKOOOM

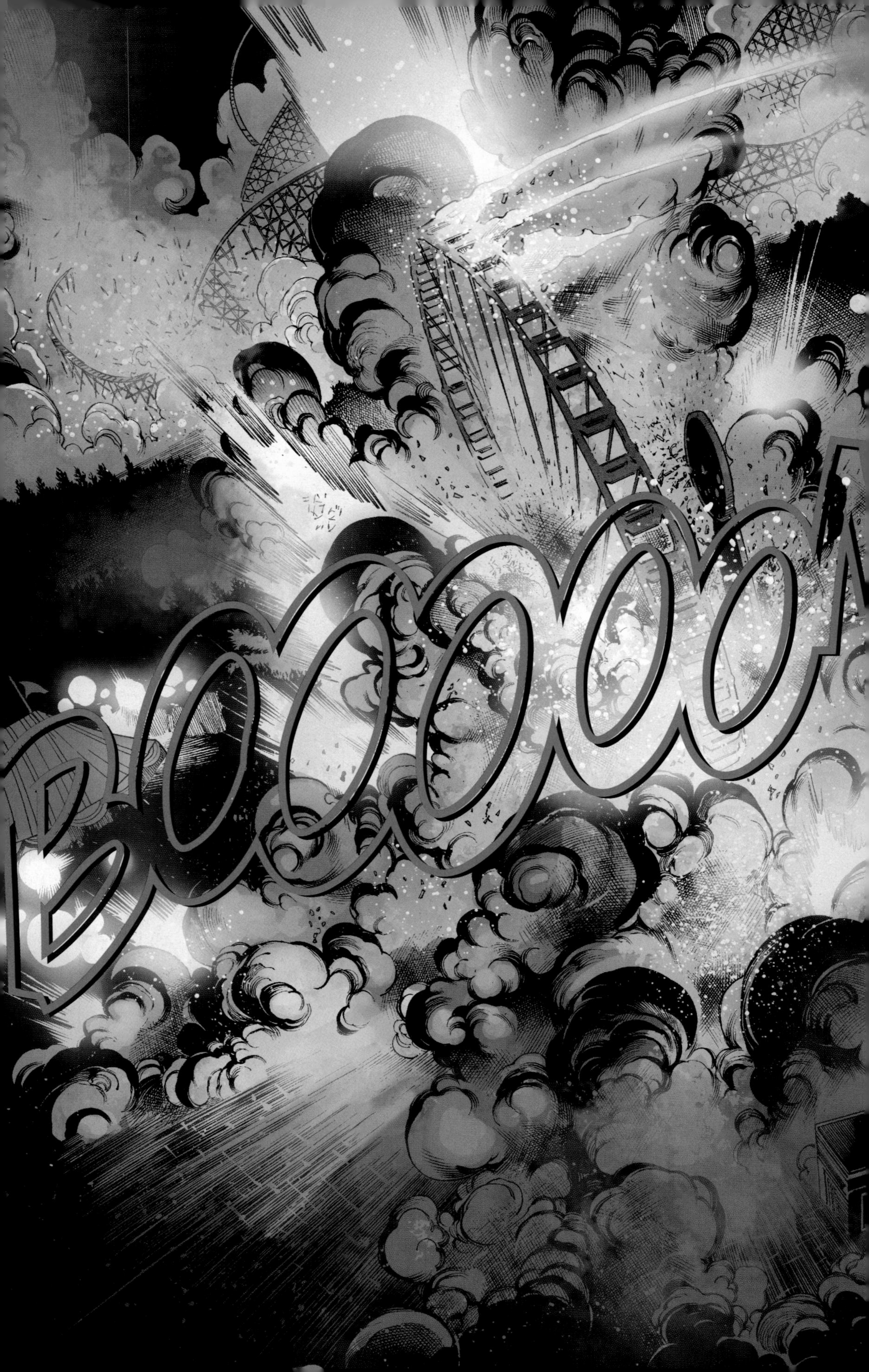
BOOOOOOOO

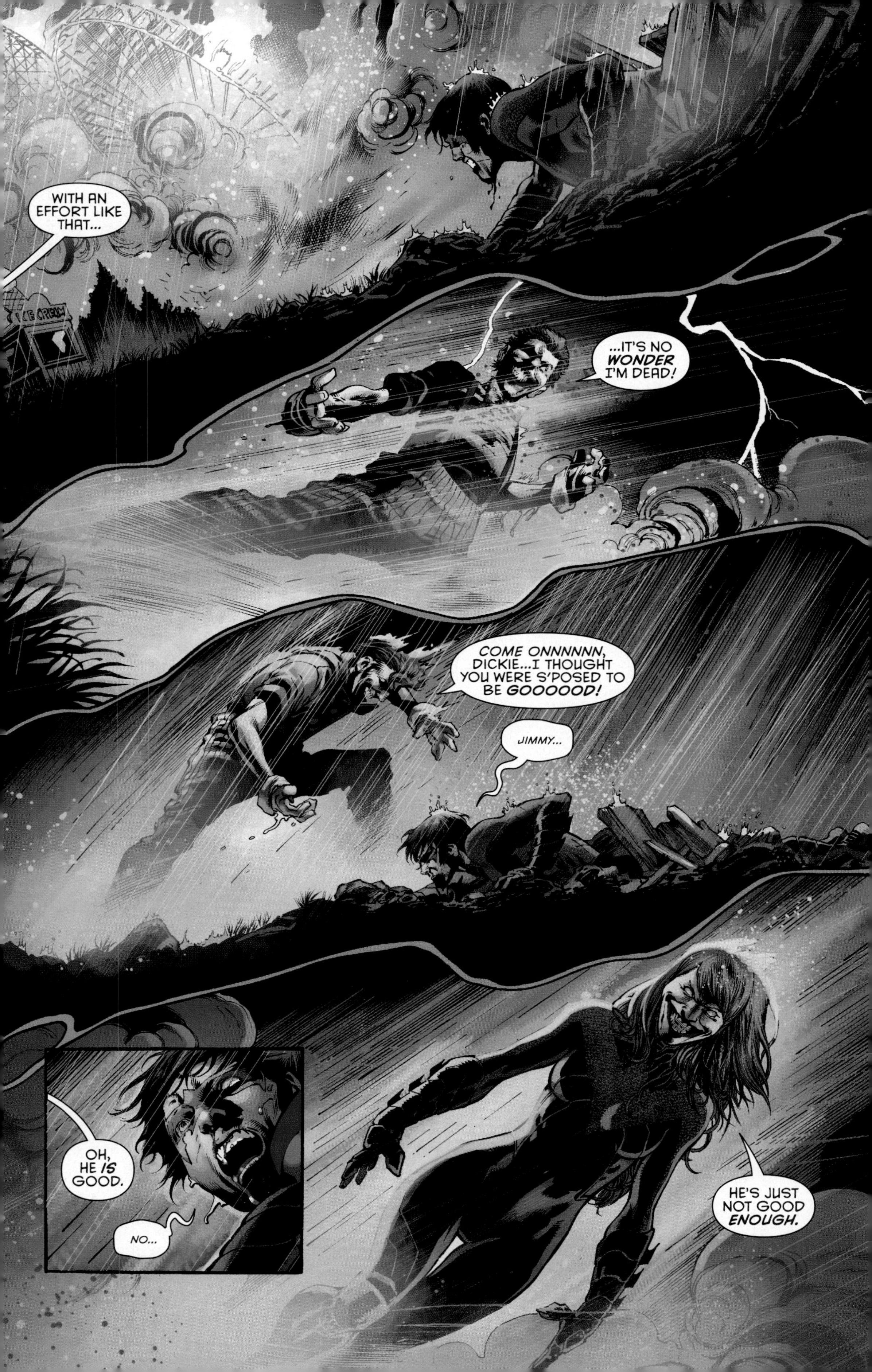
WITH AN EFFORT LIKE THAT...
...IT'S NO *WONDER* I'M DEAD!
COME ONNNNNN, DICKIE...I THOUGHT YOU WERE S'POSED TO BE *GOOOOOD!*
JIMMY...
OH, HE *IS* GOOD.
NO...
HE'S JUST NOT GOOD *ENOUGH.*

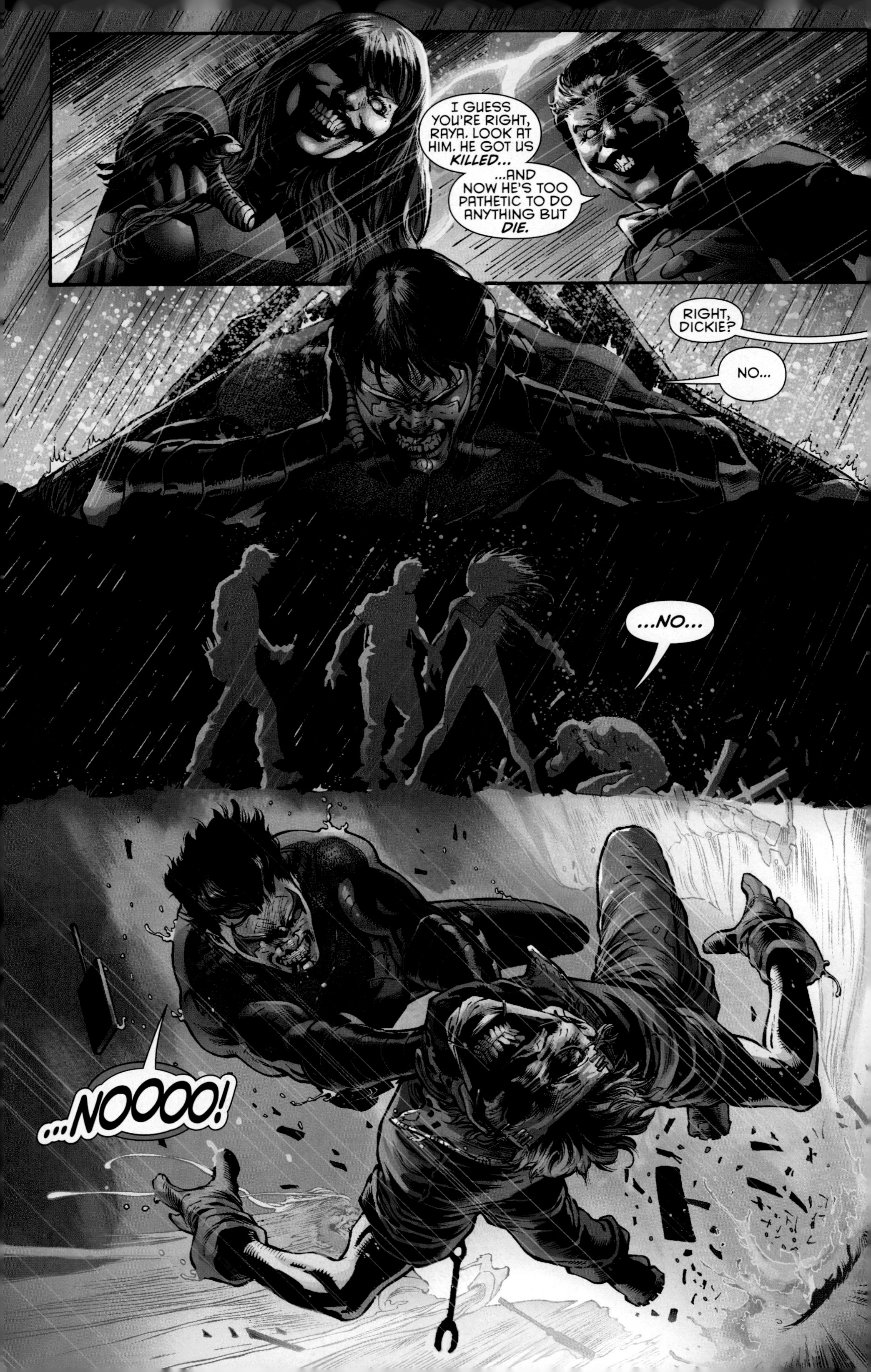
I GUESS YOU'RE RIGHT, RAYA. LOOK AT HIM. HE GOT US *KILLED*...
...AND NOW HE'S TOO PATHETIC TO DO ANYTHING BUT *DIE*.
RIGHT, DICKIE?
NO...
...NO...
...NOOOO!

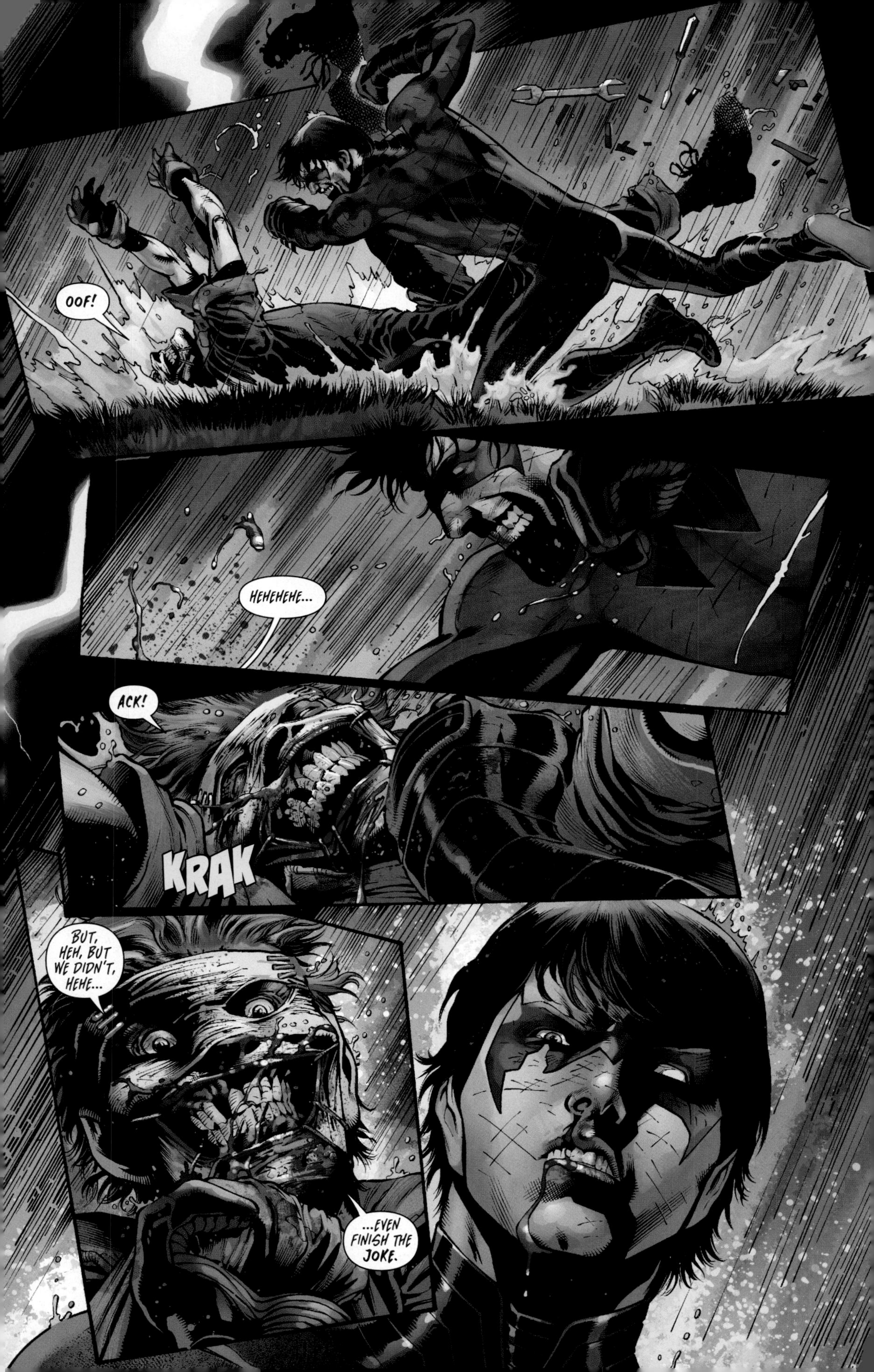
OOF!
HEHEHEHE...
ACK!
KRAK
BUT, HEH, BUT WE DIDN'T, HEHE...
...EVEN FINISH THE JOKE.

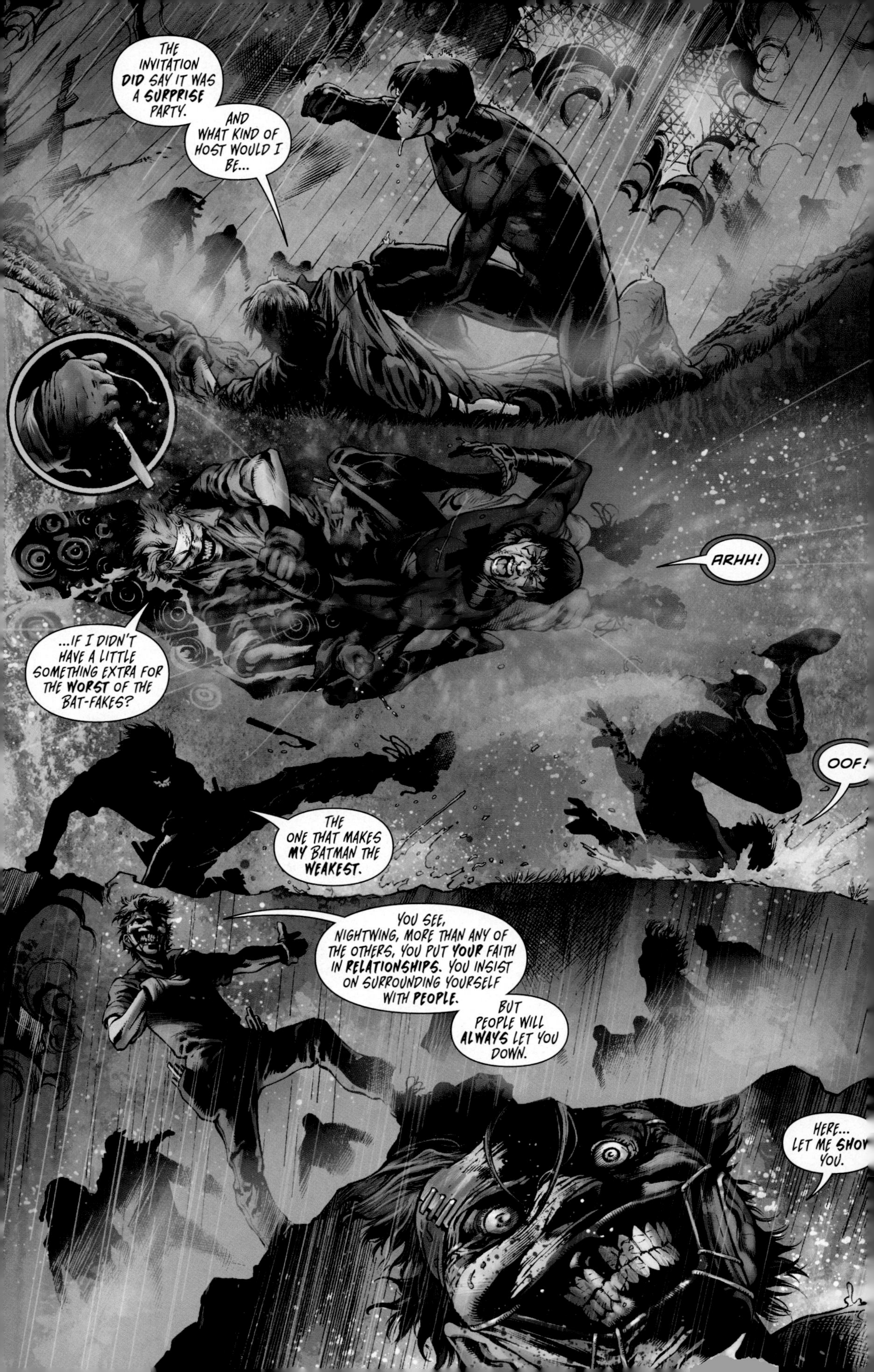
THE INVITATION DID SAY IT WAS A SURPRISE PARTY.
AND WHAT KIND OF HOST WOULD I BE...
ARHH!
...IF I DIDN'T HAVE A LITTLE SOMETHING EXTRA FOR THE WORST OF THE BAT-FAKES?
OOF!
THE ONE THAT MAKES MY BATMAN THE WEAKEST.
YOU SEE, NIGHTWING, MORE THAN ANY OF THE OTHERS, YOU PUT YOUR FAITH IN RELATIONSHIPS. YOU INSIST ON SURROUNDING YOURSELF WITH PEOPLE.
BUT PEOPLE WILL ALWAYS LET YOU DOWN.
HERE... LET ME SHOW YOU.

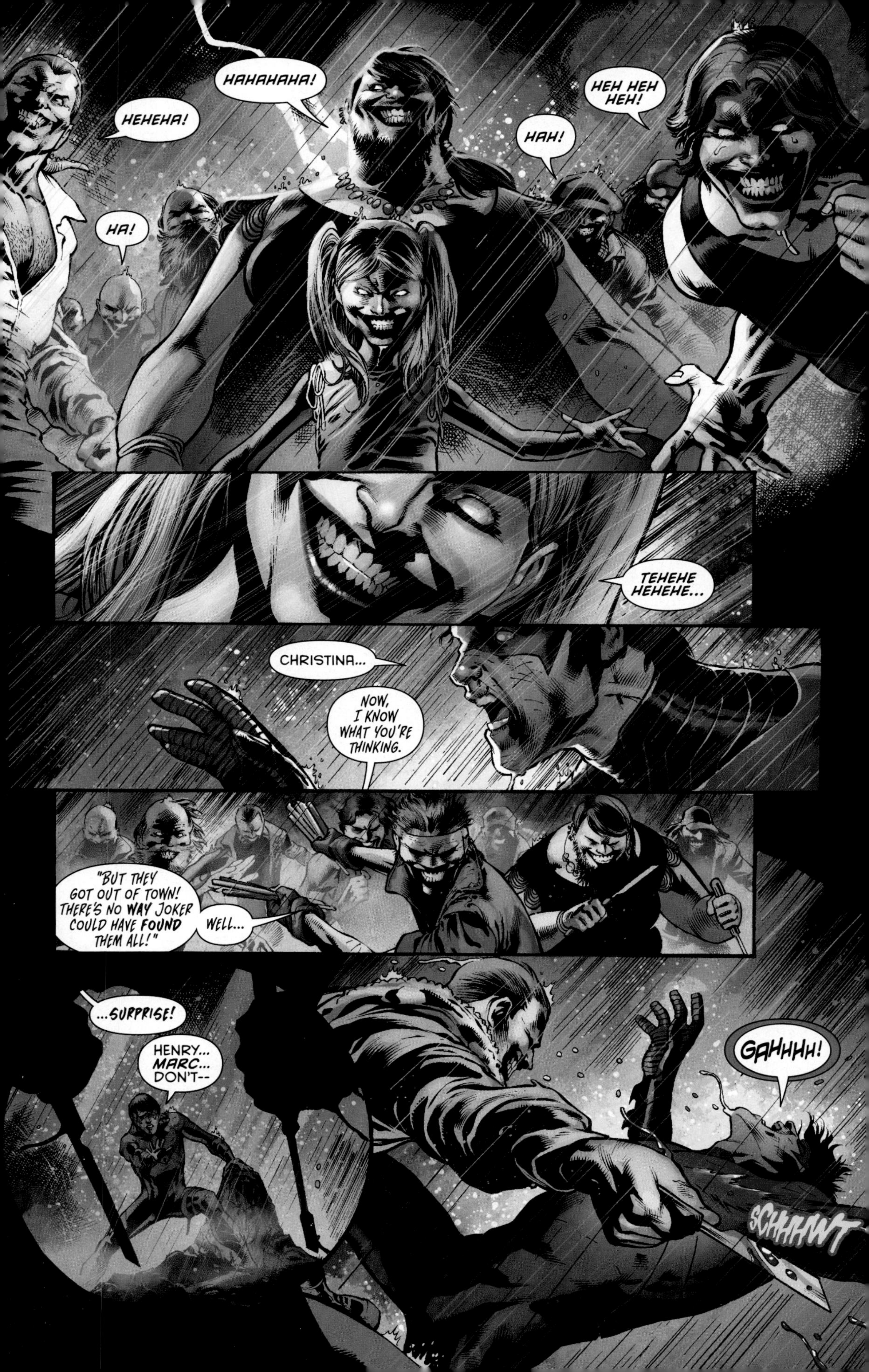
HEHEHA!
HAHAHAHA!
HA!
HAH!
HEH HEH HEH!
TEHEHE HEHEHE...
CHRISTINA...
NOW, I KNOW WHAT YOU'RE THINKING.
"BUT THEY GOT OUT OF TOWN! THERE'S NO WAY JOKER COULD HAVE FOUND THEM ALL!"
WELL...
...SURPRISE!
HENRY... MARC... DON'T--
GAHHHH!
SCHHHWT

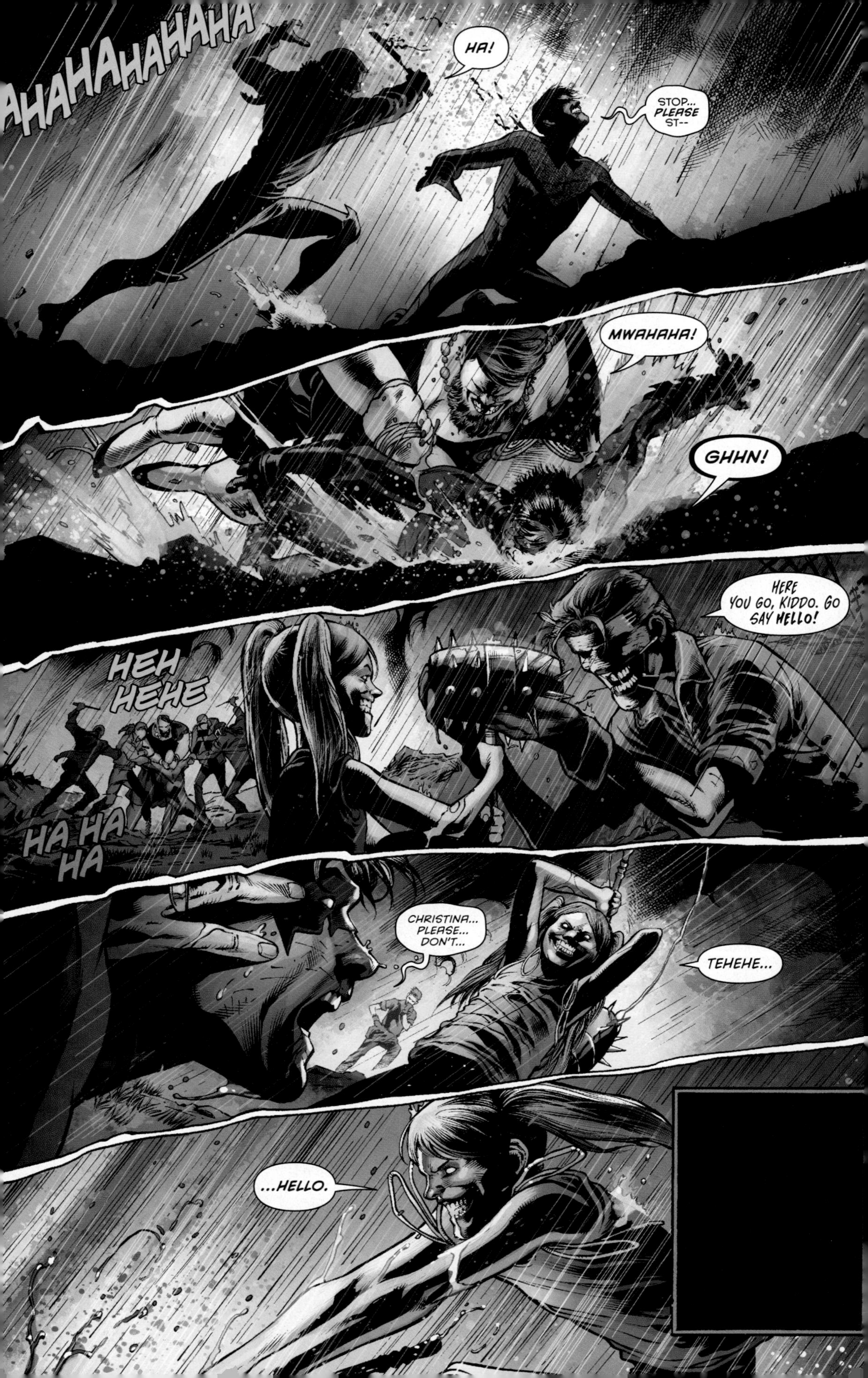
AHAHAHAHAHAHA
HA!
STOP... PLEASE ST--
MWAHAHA!
GHHN!
HERE YOU GO, KIDDO. GO SAY HELLO!
HEH HEHE
HA HA HA
CHRISTINA... PLEASE... DON'T...
TEHEHE...
...HELLO.

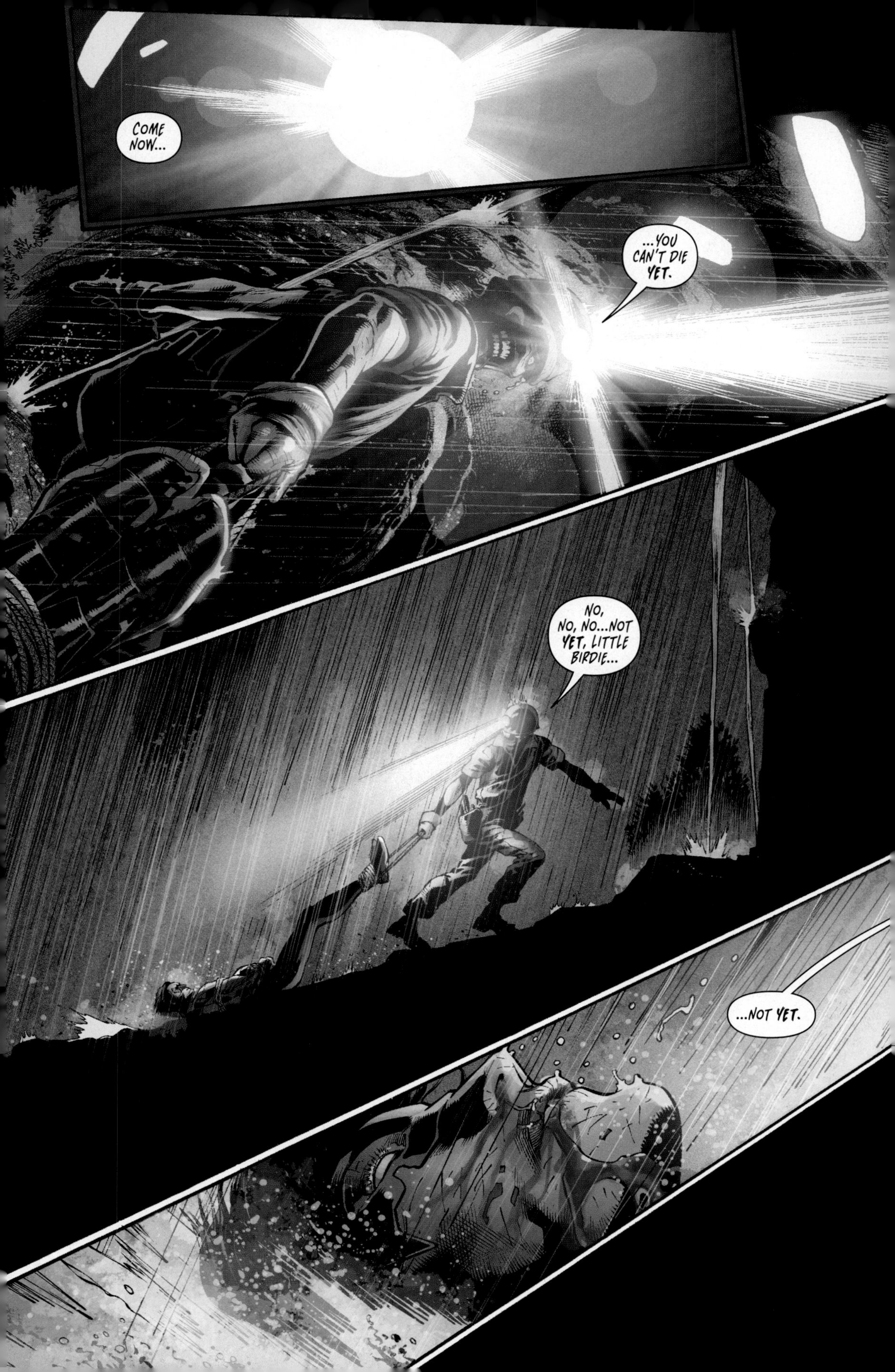
COME NOW...
...YOU CAN'T DIE YET.
NO, NO, NO...NOT YET, LITTLE BIRDIE...
...NOT YET.

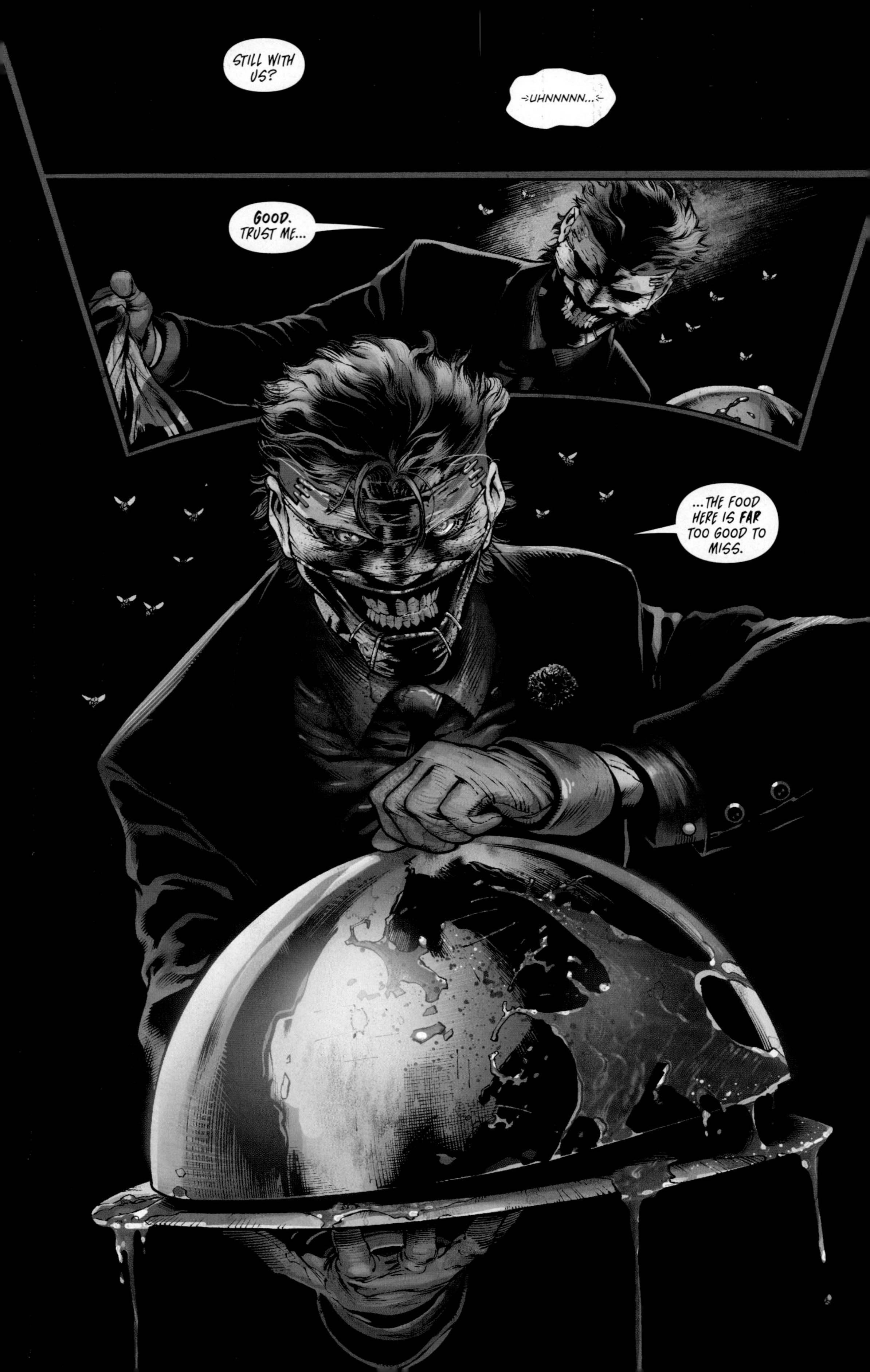
STILL WITH US?
=UHNNNNN...=
GOOD. TRUST ME...
...THE FOOD HERE IS **FAR** TOO GOOD TO MISS.

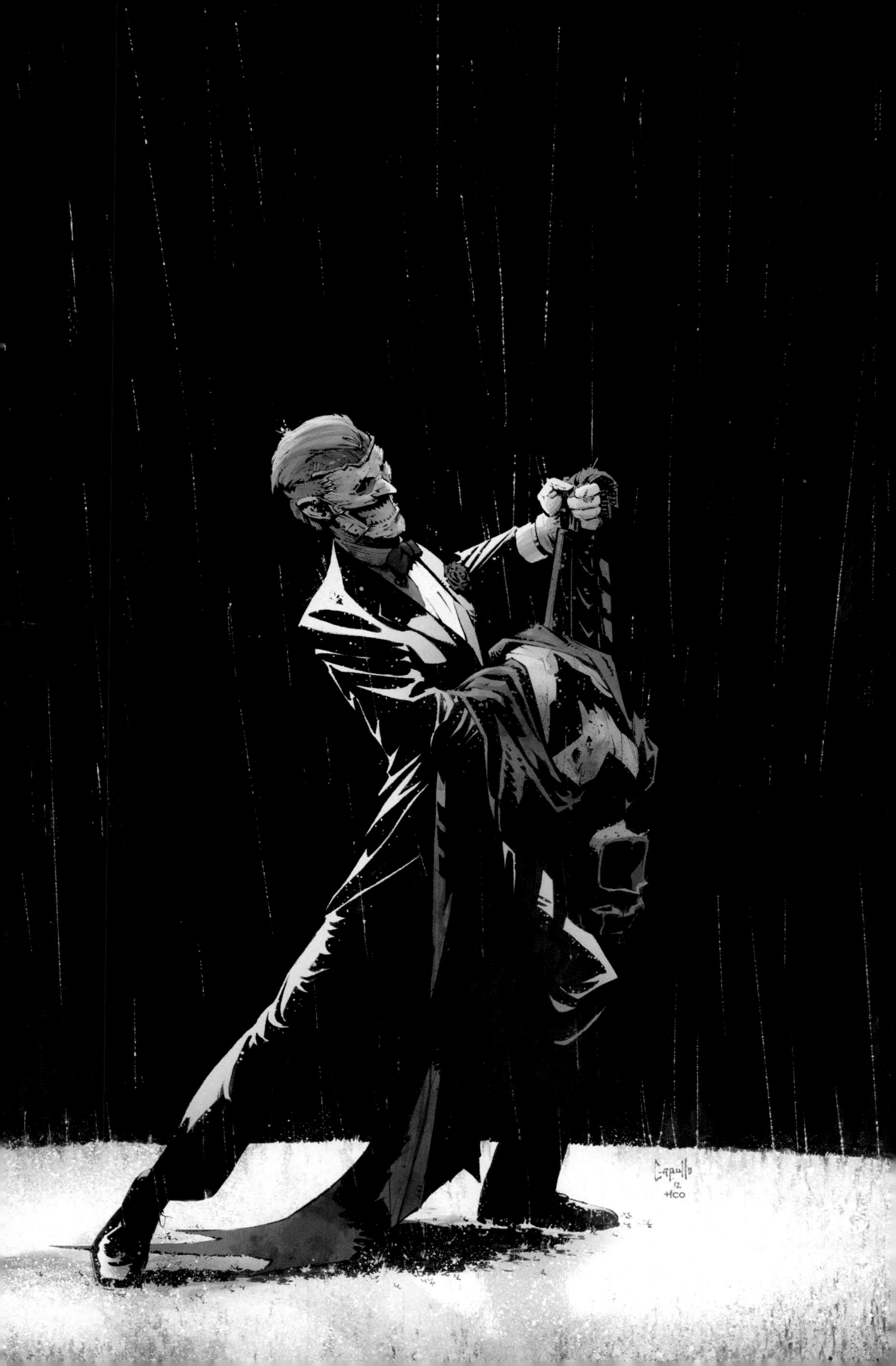

SCOTT SNYDER writer GREG CAPULLO penciller JONATHAN GLAPION inker cover art by GREG CAPULLO & FCO PLASCENCIA

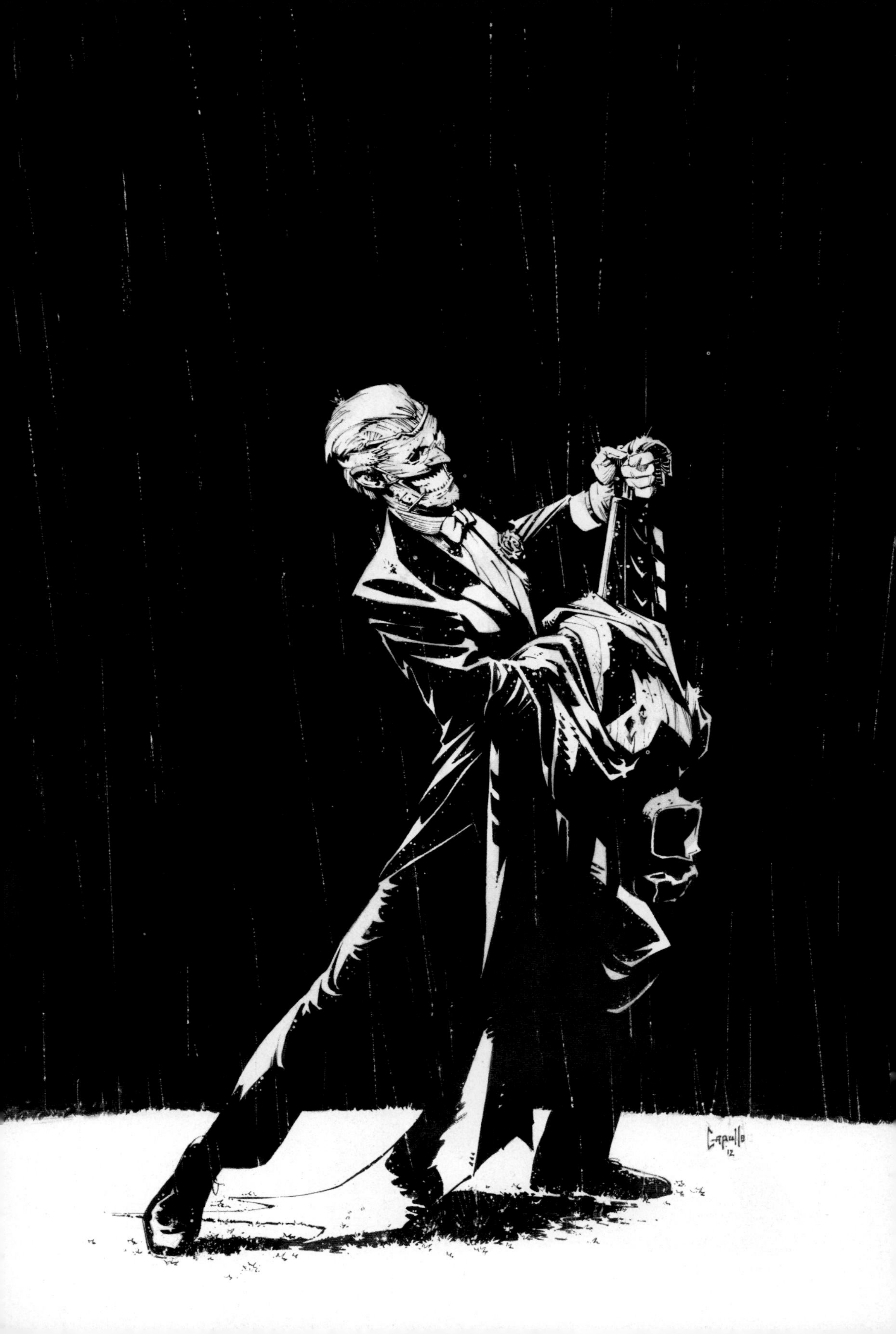

Capullo
12

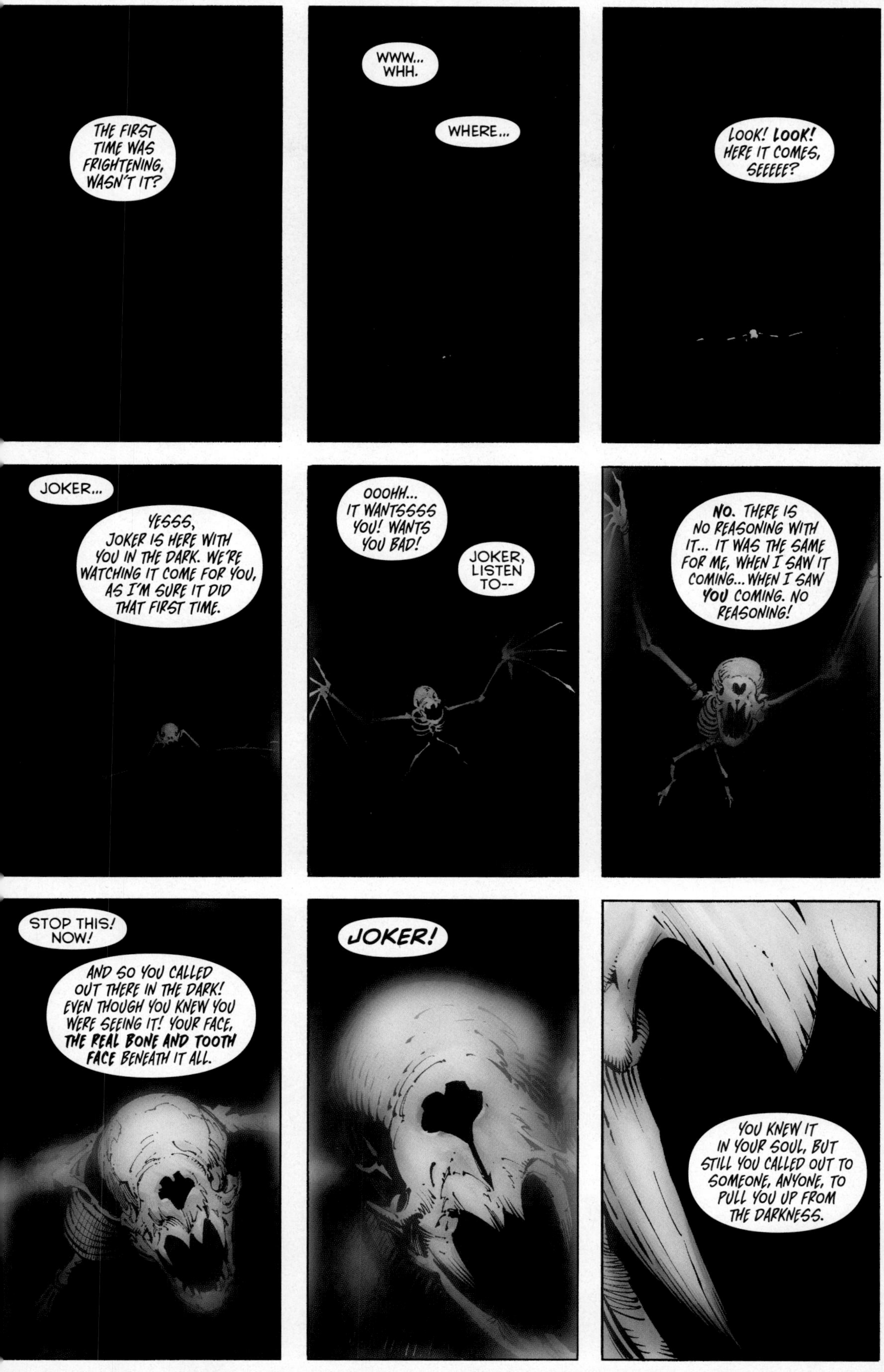
THE FIRST TIME WAS FRIGHTENING, WASN'T IT?
WWW... WHH.
WHERE...
LOOK! LOOK! HERE IT COMES, SEEEEE?
JOKER...
YESSS, JOKER IS HERE WITH YOU IN THE DARK. WE'RE WATCHING IT COME FOR YOU, AS I'M SURE IT DID THAT FIRST TIME.
OOOHH... IT WANTSSSS YOU! WANTS YOU BAD!
JOKER, LISTEN TO--
NO. THERE IS NO REASONING WITH IT... IT WAS THE SAME FOR ME, WHEN I SAW IT COMING... WHEN I SAW YOU COMING. NO REASONING!
STOP THIS! NOW!
AND SO YOU CALLED OUT THERE IN THE DARK! EVEN THOUGH YOU KNEW YOU WERE SEEING IT! YOUR FACE, THE REAL BONE AND TOOTH FACE BENEATH IT ALL.
JOKER!
YOU KNEW IT IN YOUR SOUL, BUT STILL YOU CALLED OUT TO SOMEONE, ANYONE, TO PULL YOU UP FROM THE DARKNESS.

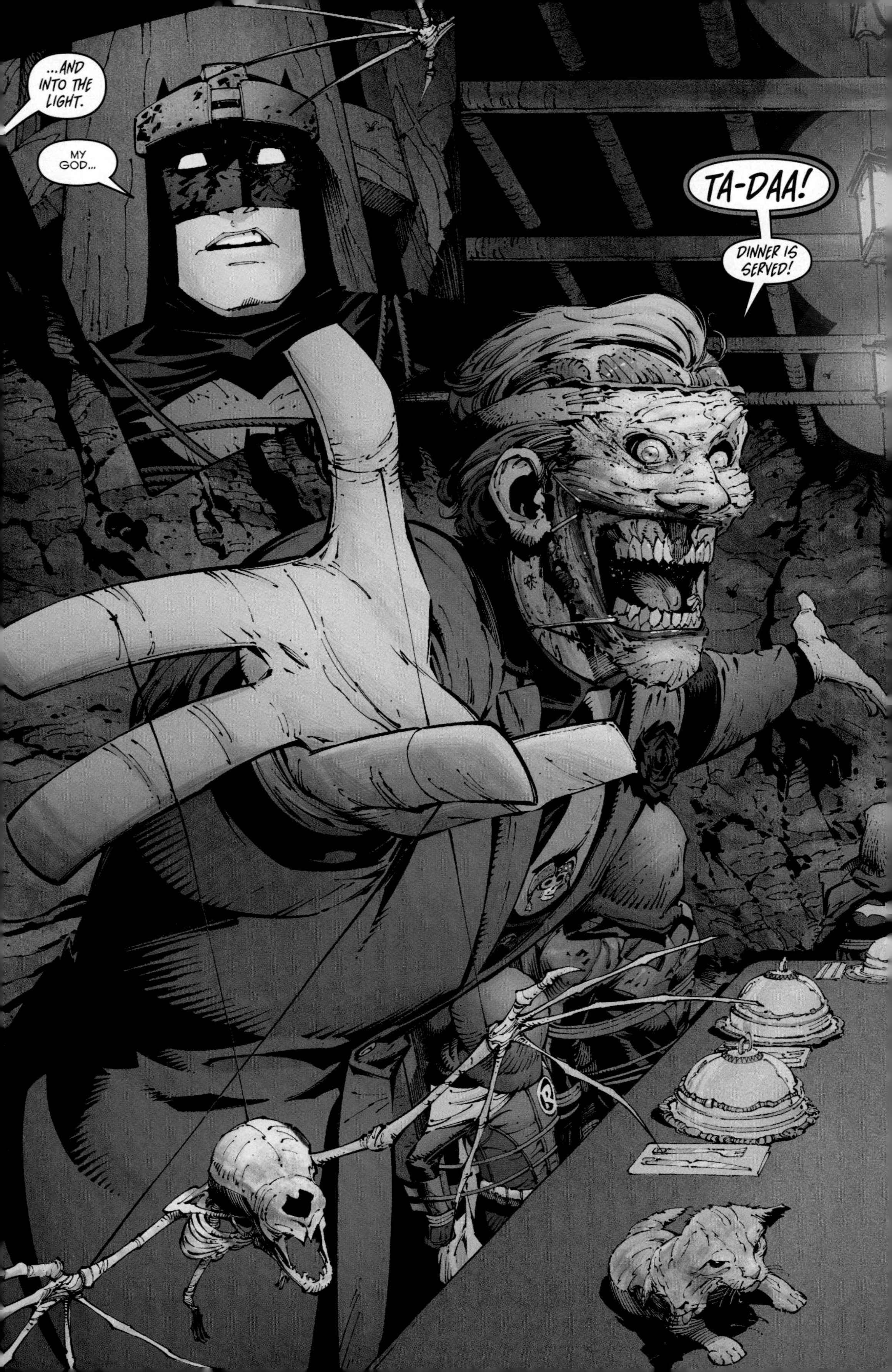
...AND INTO THE LIGHT.
MY GOD...
TA-DAA!
DINNER IS SERVED!

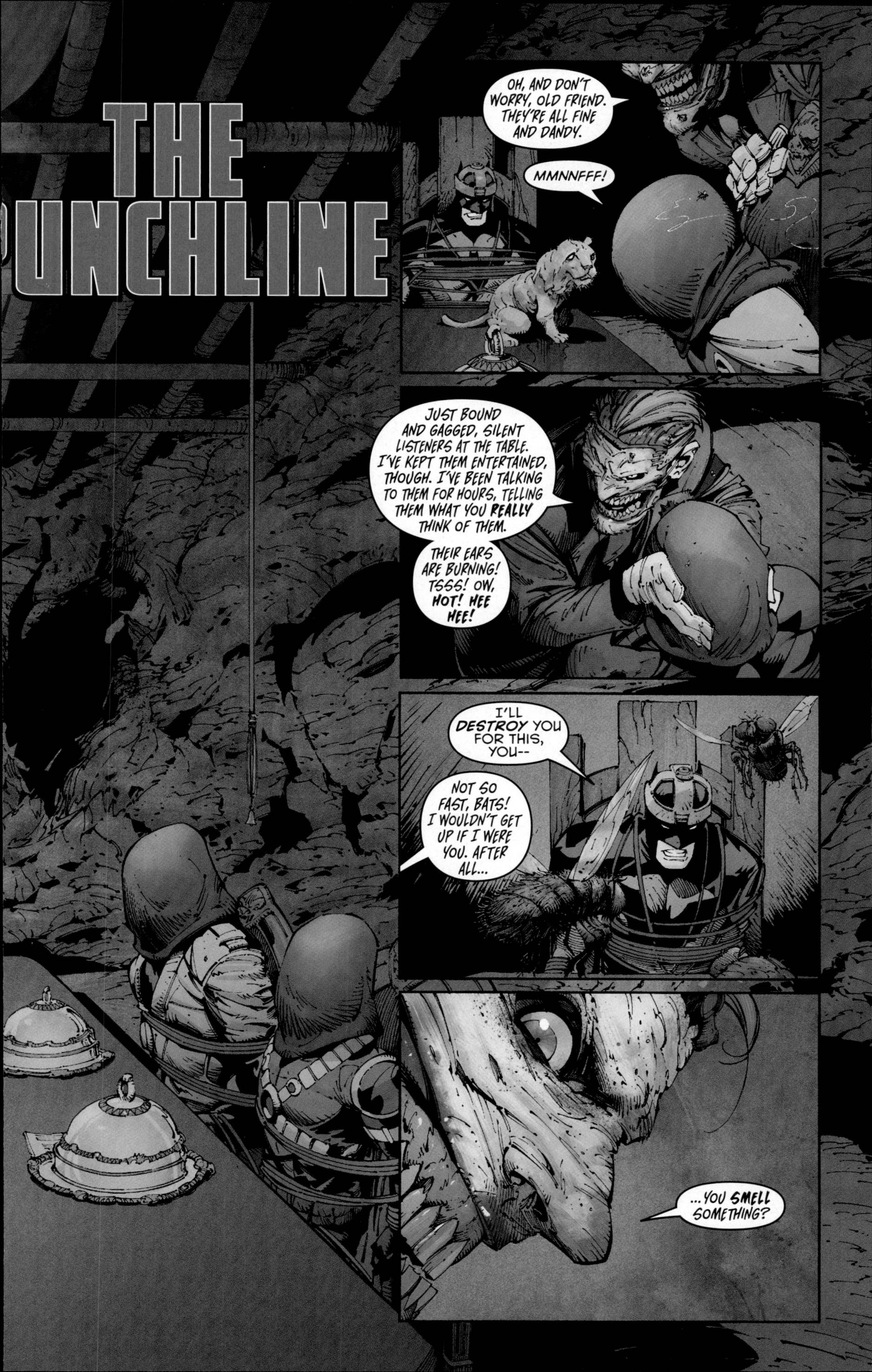
THE PUNCHLINE
OH, AND DON'T WORRY, OLD FRIEND. THEY'RE ALL FINE AND DANDY.
MMNNFFF!
JUST BOUND AND GAGGED, SILENT LISTENERS AT THE TABLE. I'VE KEPT THEM ENTERTAINED, THOUGH. I'VE BEEN TALKING TO THEM FOR HOURS, TELLING THEM WHAT YOU REALLY THINK OF THEM.
THEIR EARS ARE BURNING! TSSS! OW, HOT! HEE HEE!
I'LL DESTROY YOU FOR THIS, YOU--
NOT SO FAST, BATS! I WOULDN'T GET UP IF I WERE YOU. AFTER ALL...
...YOU SMELL SOMETHING?

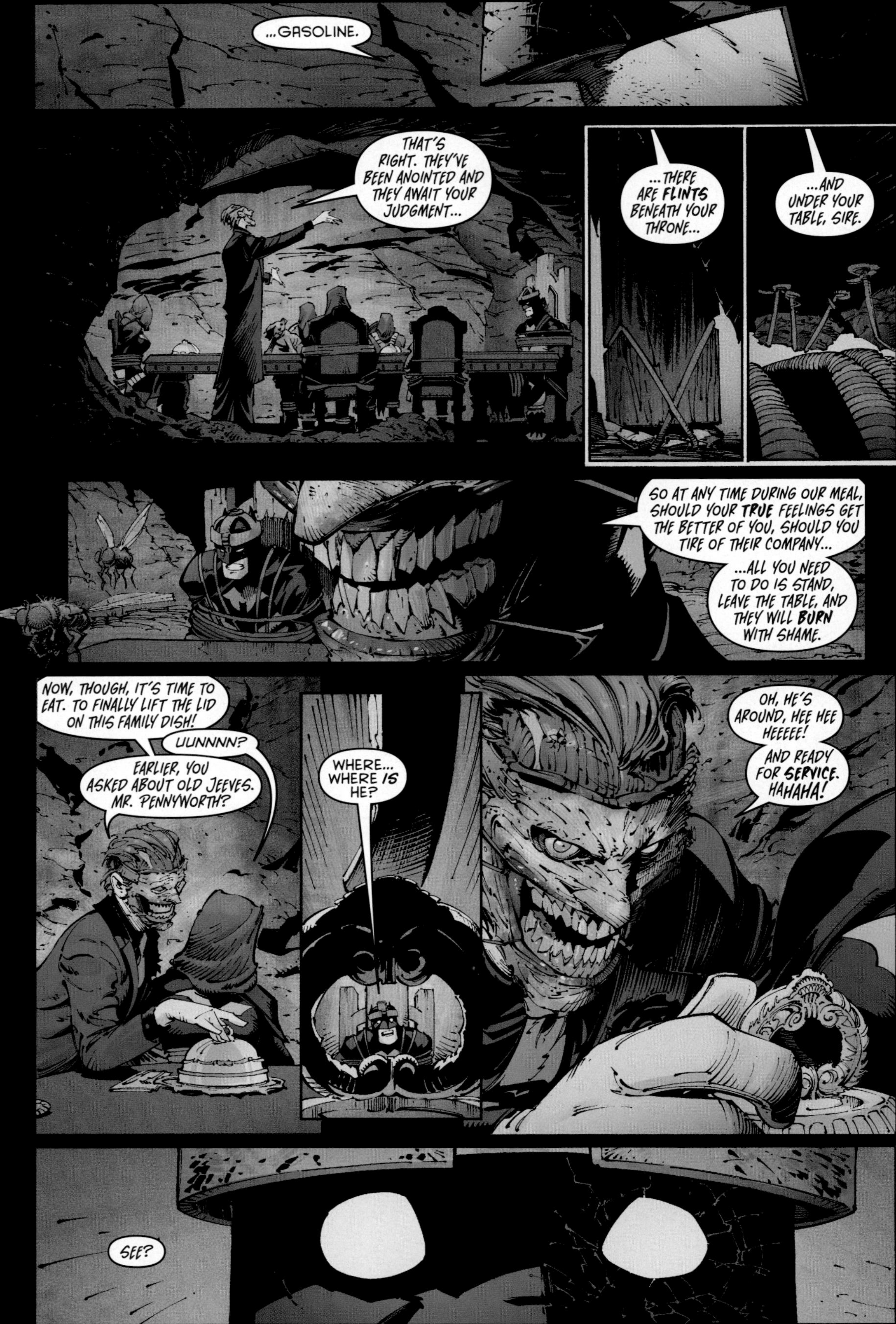
...GASOLINE.
THAT'S RIGHT. THEY'VE BEEN ANOINTED AND THEY AWAIT YOUR JUDGMENT...
...THERE ARE FLINTS BENEATH YOUR THRONE...
...AND UNDER YOUR TABLE, SIRE.
SO AT ANY TIME DURING OUR MEAL, SHOULD YOUR TRUE FEELINGS GET THE BETTER OF YOU, SHOULD YOU TIRE OF THEIR COMPANY...
...ALL YOU NEED TO DO IS STAND, LEAVE THE TABLE, AND THEY WILL BURN WITH SHAME.
NOW, THOUGH, IT'S TIME TO EAT. TO FINALLY LIFT THE LID ON THIS FAMILY DISH!
UUNNNN?
EARLIER, YOU ASKED ABOUT OLD JEEVES. MR. PENNYWORTH?
WHERE... WHERE IS HE?
OH, HE'S AROUND, HEE HEE HEEEEE!
AND READY FOR SERVICE. HAHAHA!
SEE?

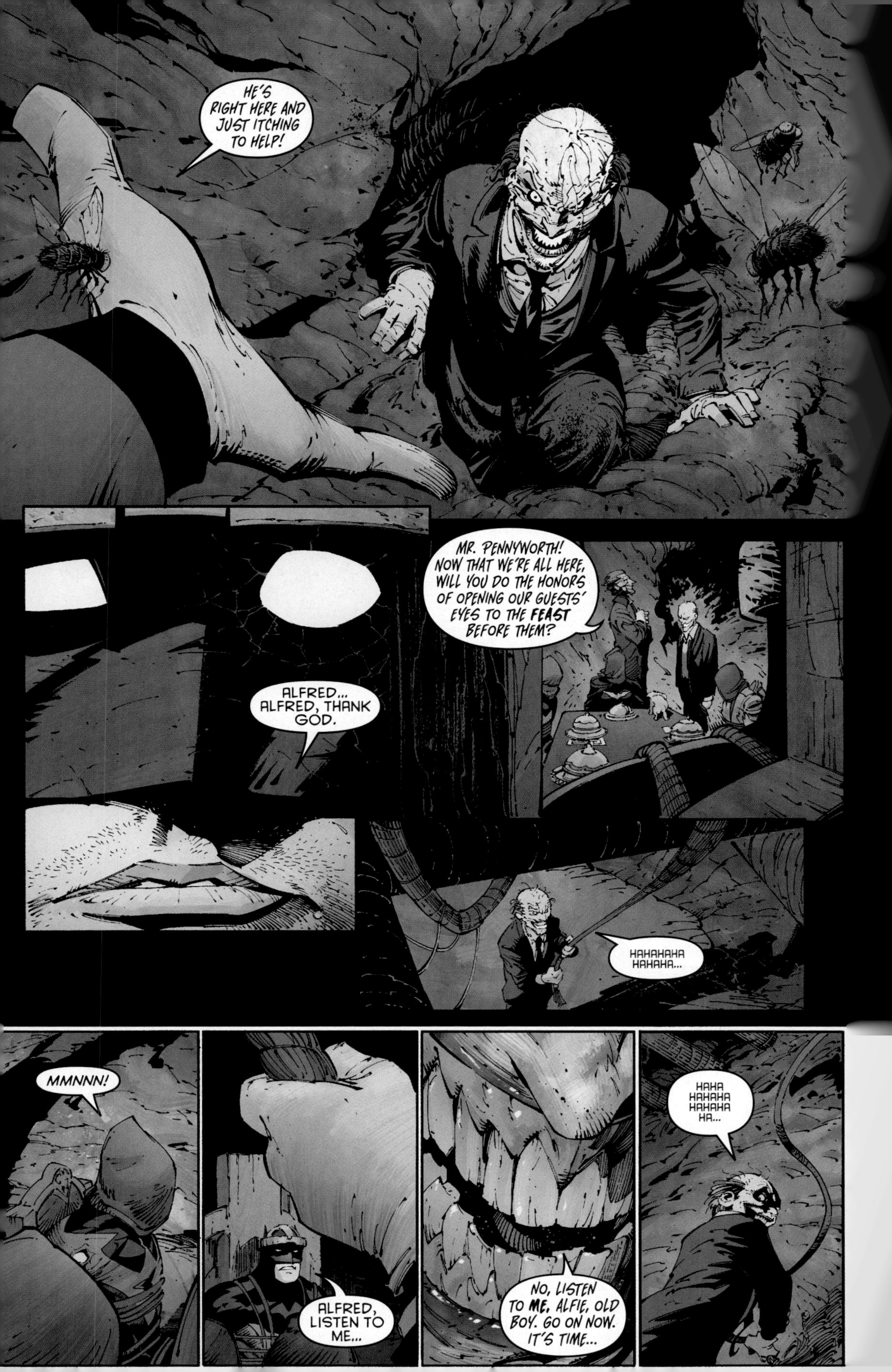
HE'S RIGHT HERE AND JUST ITCHING TO HELP!
MR. PENNYWORTH! NOW THAT WE'RE ALL HERE, WILL YOU DO THE HONORS OF OPENING OUR GUESTS' EYES TO THE FEAST BEFORE THEM?
ALFRED... ALFRED, THANK GOD.
HAHAHAHA HAHAHA...
MMNNN!
ALFRED, LISTEN TO ME...
NO, LISTEN TO ME, ALFIE, OLD BOY. GO ON NOW. IT'S TIME...
HAHA HAHAHA HAHAHA HA...

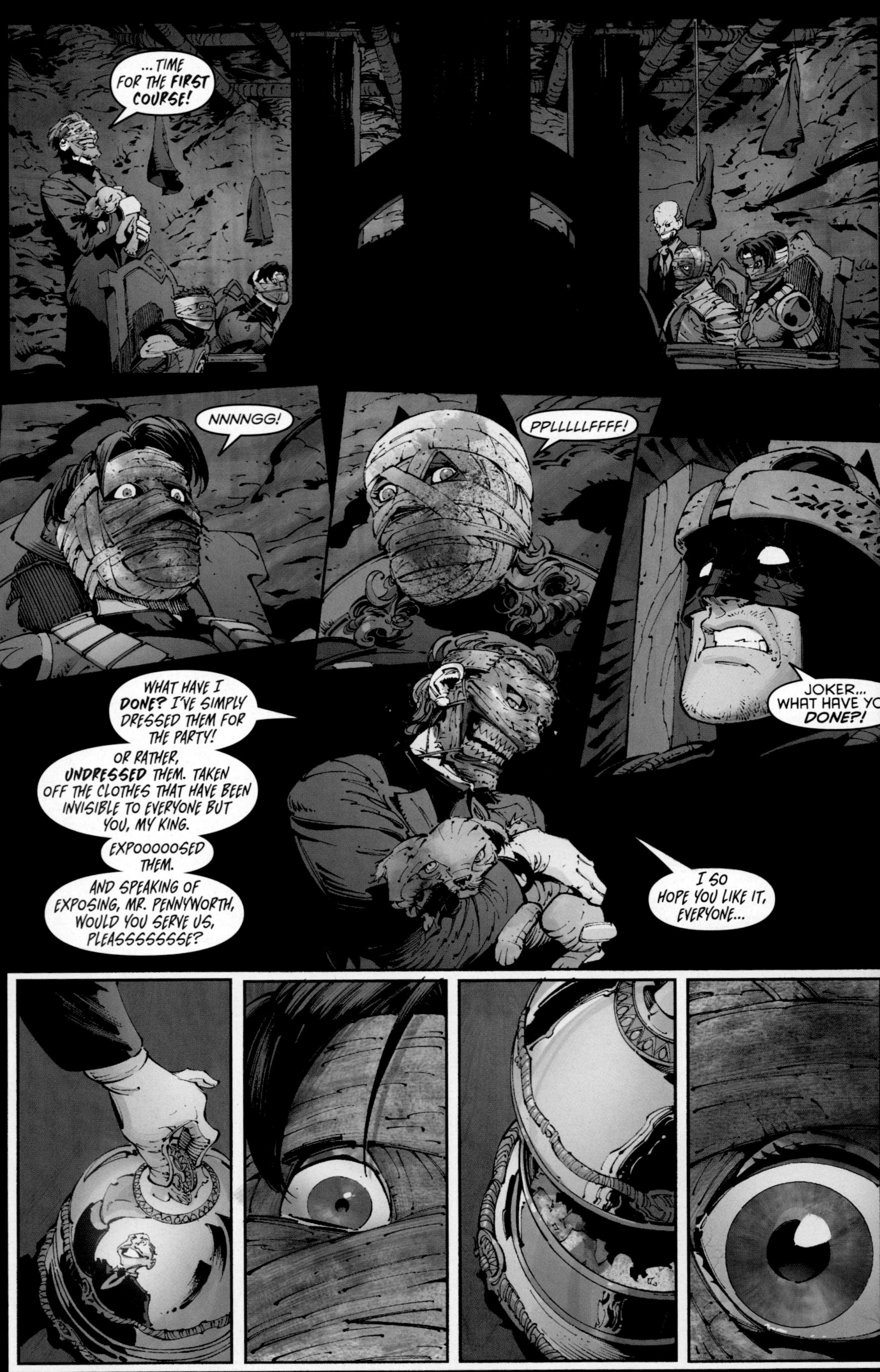
...TIME FOR THE FIRST COURSE!
NNNNGG!
PPLLLLLLFFFF!
JOKER... WHAT HAVE YO DONE?!
WHAT HAVE I DONE? I'VE SIMPLY DRESSED THEM FOR THE PARTY!
OR RATHER, UNDRESSED THEM. TAKEN OFF THE CLOTHES THAT HAVE BEEN INVISIBLE TO EVERYONE BUT YOU, MY KING.
EXPOOOOOSED THEM.
AND SPEAKING OF EXPOSING, MR. PENNYWORTH, WOULD YOU SERVE US, PLEASSSSSSSSE?
I SO HOPE YOU LIKE IT, EVERYONE...

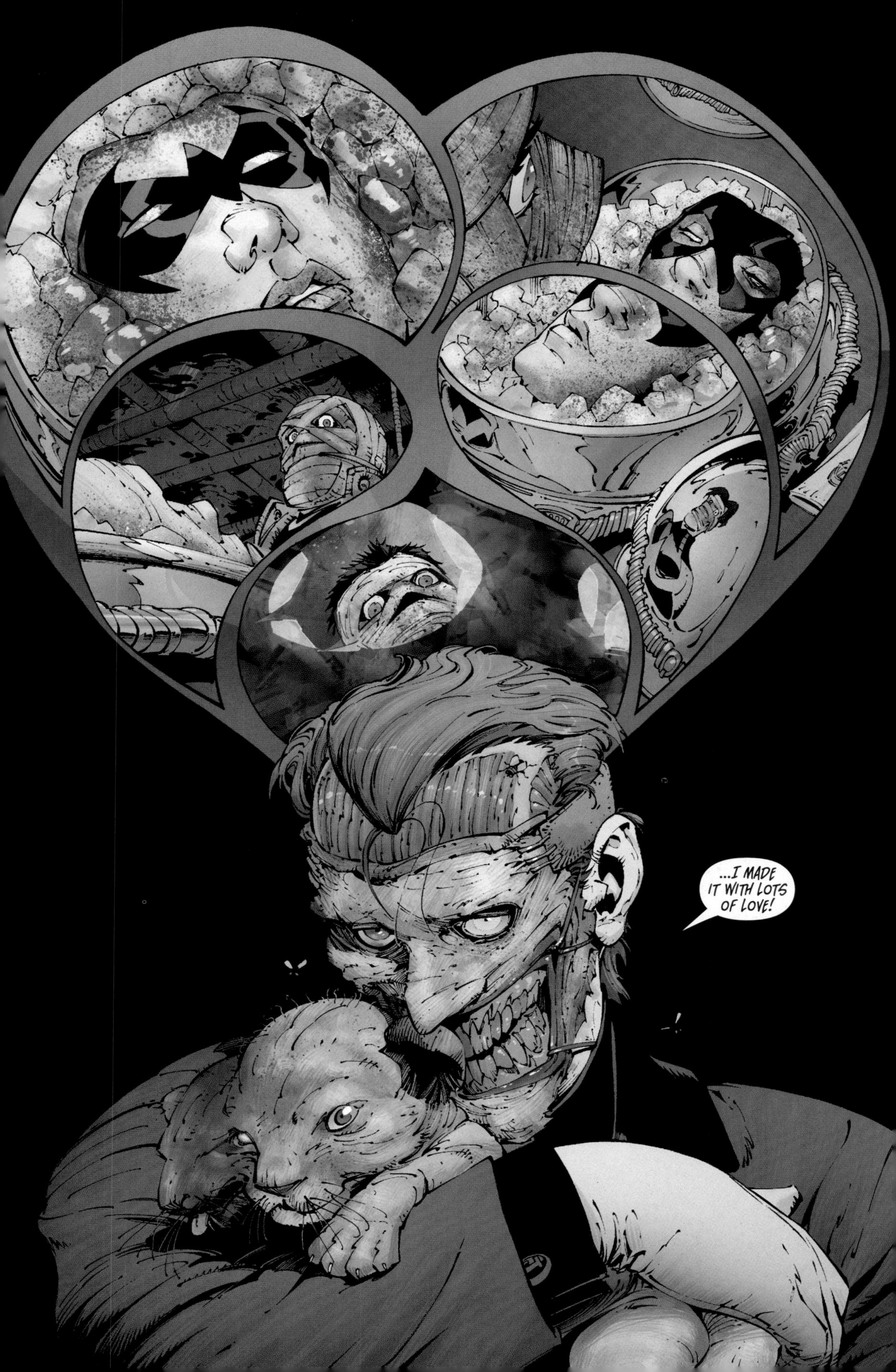
...I MADE IT WITH LOTS OF LOVE!

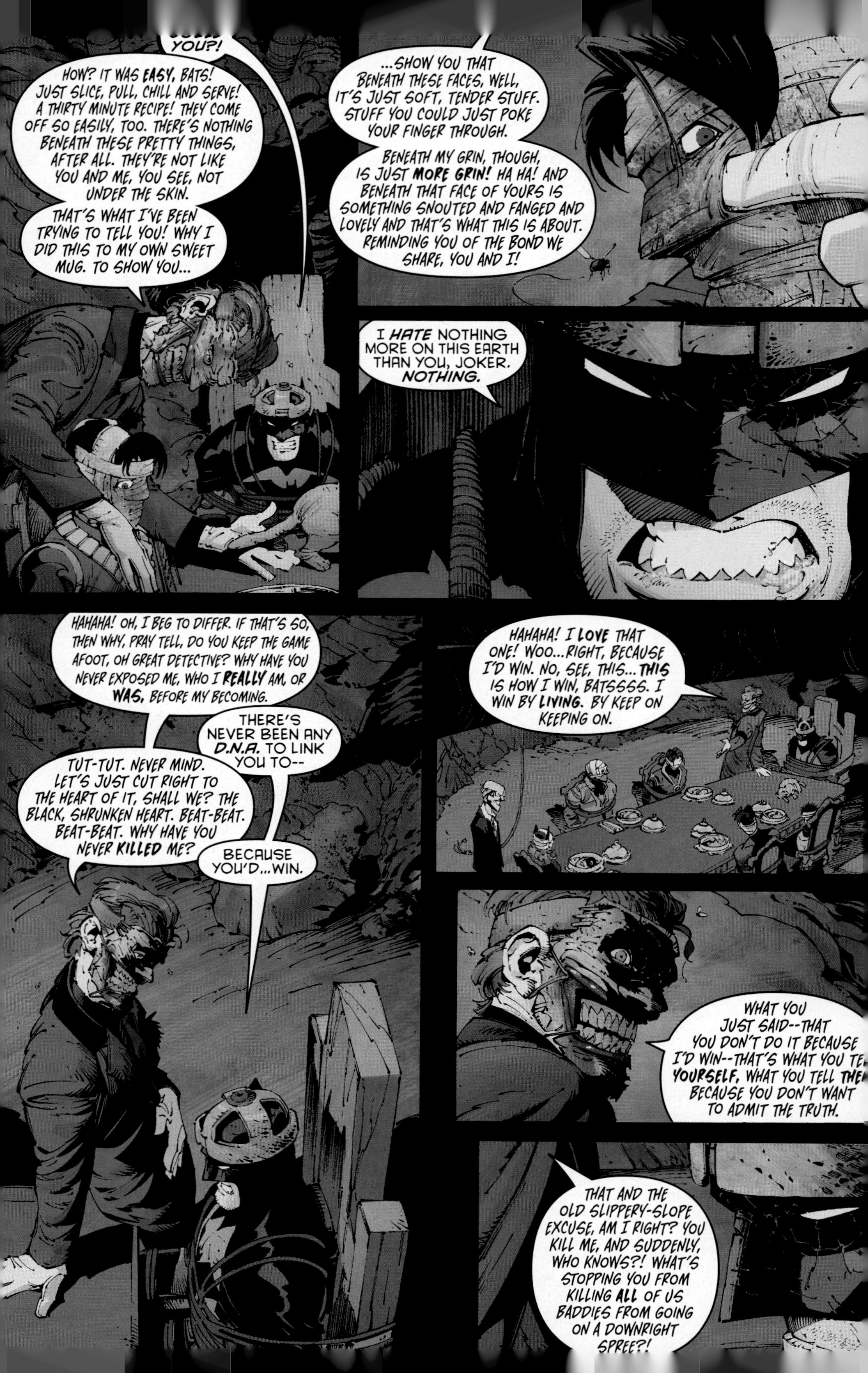
YOU?!
HOW? IT WAS EASY, BATS! JUST SLICE, PULL, CHILL AND SERVE! A THIRTY MINUTE RECIPE! THEY COME OFF SO EASILY, TOO. THERE'S NOTHING BENEATH THESE PRETTY THINGS, AFTER ALL. THEY'RE NOT LIKE YOU AND ME, YOU SEE, NOT UNDER THE SKIN.
THAT'S WHAT I'VE BEEN TRYING TO TELL YOU! WHY I DID THIS TO MY OWN SWEET MUG. TO SHOW YOU...
...SHOW YOU THAT BENEATH THESE FACES, WELL, IT'S JUST SOFT, TENDER STUFF. STUFF YOU COULD JUST POKE YOUR FINGER THROUGH.
BENEATH MY GRIN, THOUGH, IS JUST MORE GRIN! HA HA! AND BENEATH THAT FACE OF YOURS IS SOMETHING SNOUTED AND FANGED AND LOVELY AND THAT'S WHAT THIS IS ABOUT. REMINDING YOU OF THE BOND WE SHARE, YOU AND I!
I HATE NOTHING MORE ON THIS EARTH THAN YOU, JOKER. NOTHING.
HAHAHA! OH, I BEG TO DIFFER. IF THAT'S SO, THEN WHY, PRAY TELL, DO YOU KEEP THE GAME AFOOT, OH GREAT DETECTIVE? WHY HAVE YOU NEVER EXPOSED ME, WHO I REALLY AM, OR WAS, BEFORE MY BECOMING.
THERE'S NEVER BEEN ANY D.N.A. TO LINK YOU TO--
TUT-TUT. NEVER MIND. LET'S JUST CUT RIGHT TO THE HEART OF IT, SHALL WE? THE BLACK, SHRUNKEN HEART. BEAT-BEAT. BEAT-BEAT. WHY HAVE YOU NEVER KILLED ME?
BECAUSE YOU'D...WIN.
HAHAHA! I LOVE THAT ONE! WOO...RIGHT, BECAUSE I'D WIN. NO, SEE, THIS... THIS IS HOW I WIN, BATSSSS. I WIN BY LIVING. BY KEEP ON KEEPING ON.
WHAT YOU JUST SAID--THAT YOU DON'T DO IT BECAUSE I'D WIN--THAT'S WHAT YOU TE YOURSELF, WHAT YOU TELL THE BECAUSE YOU DON'T WANT TO ADMIT THE TRUTH.
THAT AND THE OLD SLIPPERY-SLOPE EXCUSE, AM I RIGHT? YOU KILL ME, AND SUDDENLY, WHO KNOWS?! WHAT'S STOPPING YOU FROM KILLING ALL OF US BADDIES FROM GOING ON A DOWNRIGHT SPREE?!

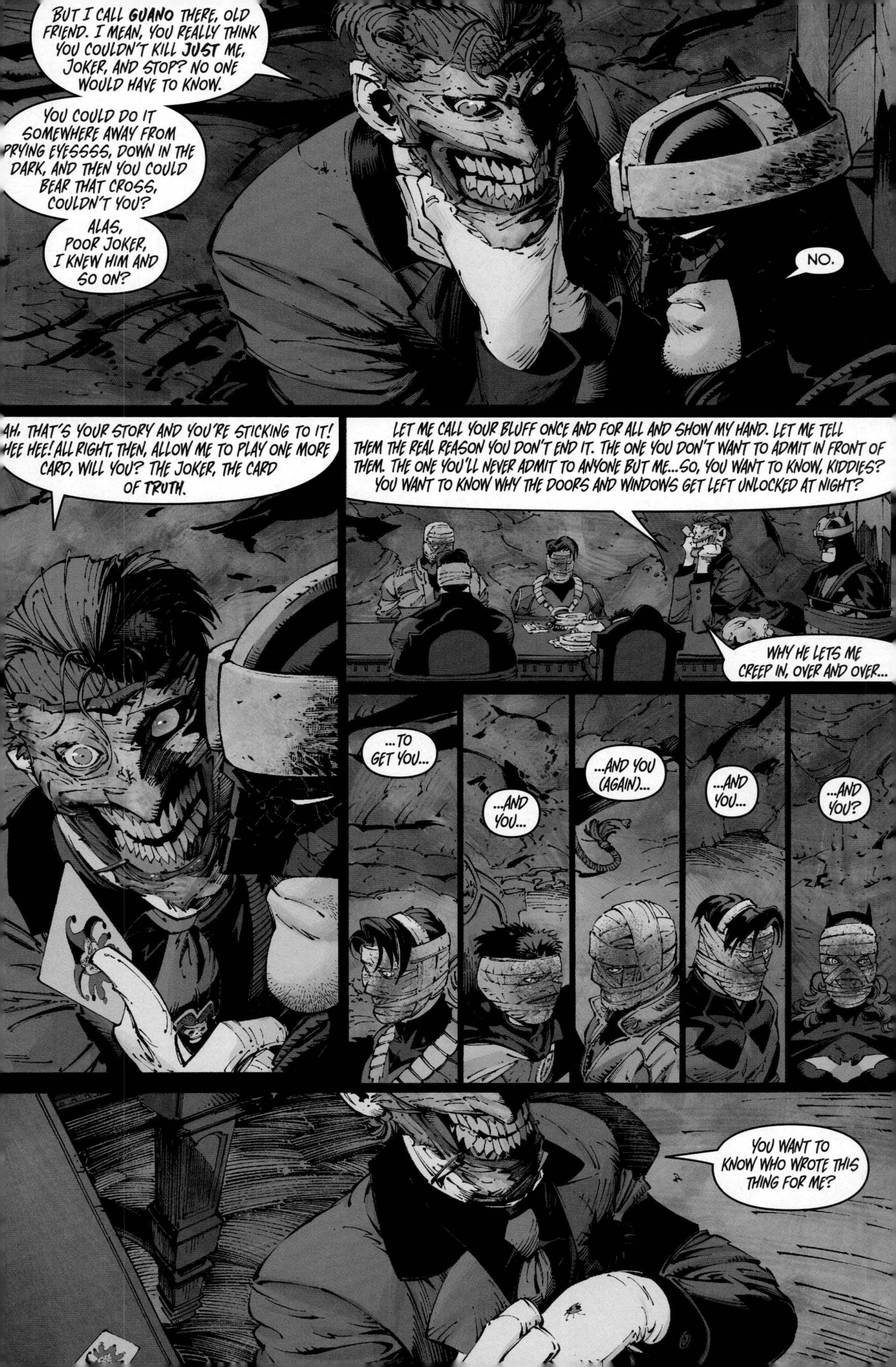
BUT I CALL GUANO THERE, OLD FRIEND. I MEAN, YOU REALLY THINK YOU COULDN'T KILL JUST ME, JOKER, AND STOP? NO ONE WOULD HAVE TO KNOW.
YOU COULD DO IT SOMEWHERE AWAY FROM PRYING EYESSSS, DOWN IN THE DARK, AND THEN YOU COULD BEAR THAT CROSS, COULDN'T YOU?
ALAS, POOR JOKER, I KNEW HIM AND SO ON?
NO.
AH, THAT'S YOUR STORY AND YOU'RE STICKING TO IT! HEE HEE! ALL RIGHT, THEN, ALLOW ME TO PLAY ONE MORE CARD, WILL YOU? THE JOKER, THE CARD OF TRUTH.
LET ME CALL YOUR BLUFF ONCE AND FOR ALL AND SHOW MY HAND. LET ME TELL THEM THE REAL REASON YOU DON'T END IT. THE ONE YOU DON'T WANT TO ADMIT IN FRONT OF THEM. THE ONE YOU'LL NEVER ADMIT TO ANYONE BUT ME...SO, YOU WANT TO KNOW, KIDDIES? YOU WANT TO KNOW WHY THE DOORS AND WINDOWS GET LEFT UNLOCKED AT NIGHT?
WHY HE LETS ME CREEP IN, OVER AND OVER...
...TO GET YOU...
...AND YOU...
...AND YOU (AGAIN)...
...AND YOU...
...AND YOU?
YOU WANT TO KNOW WHO WROTE THIS THING FOR ME?

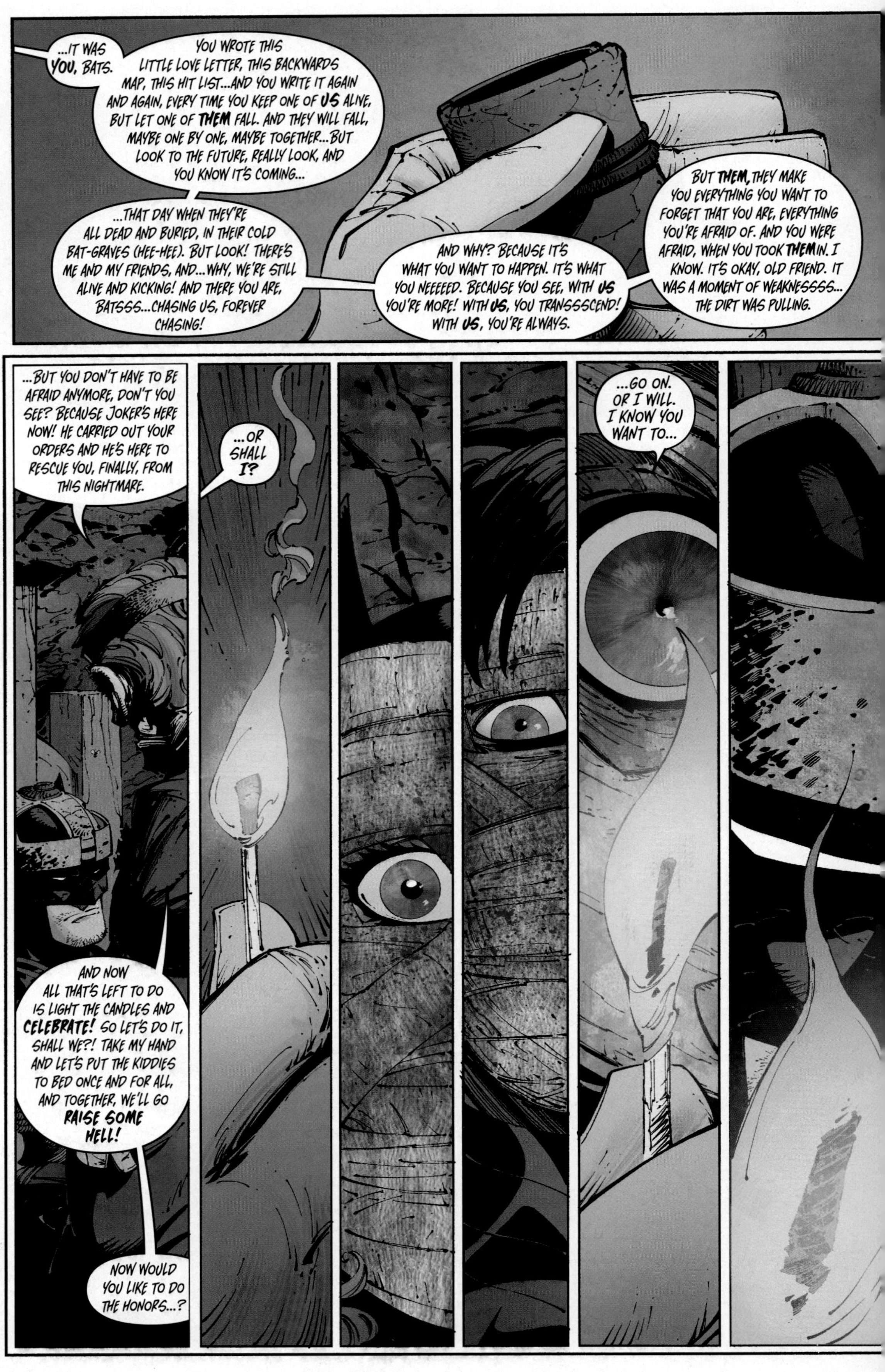
...IT WAS YOU, BATS.
YOU WROTE THIS LITTLE LOVE LETTER, THIS BACKWARDS MAP, THIS HIT LIST...AND YOU WRITE IT AGAIN AND AGAIN, EVERY TIME YOU KEEP ONE OF US ALIVE, BUT LET ONE OF THEM FALL. AND THEY WILL FALL, MAYBE ONE BY ONE, MAYBE TOGETHER...BUT LOOK TO THE FUTURE, REALLY LOOK, AND YOU KNOW IT'S COMING...
...THAT DAY WHEN THEY'RE ALL DEAD AND BURIED, IN THEIR COLD BAT-GRAVES (HEE-HEE). BUT LOOK! THERE'S ME AND MY FRIENDS, AND...WHY, WE'RE STILL ALIVE AND KICKING! AND THERE YOU ARE, BATSSS...CHASING US, FOREVER CHASING!
AND WHY? BECAUSE IT'S WHAT YOU WANT TO HAPPEN. IT'S WHAT YOU NEEEEED. BECAUSE YOU SEE, WITH US YOU'RE MORE! WITH US, YOU TRANSSSCEND! WITH US, YOU'RE ALWAYS.
BUT THEM, THEY MAKE YOU EVERYTHING YOU WANT TO FORGET THAT YOU ARE, EVERYTHING YOU'RE AFRAID OF. AND YOU WERE AFRAID, WHEN YOU TOOK THEM IN. I KNOW. IT'S OKAY, OLD FRIEND. IT WAS A MOMENT OF WEAKNESSSS... THE DIRT WAS PULLING.
...BUT YOU DON'T HAVE TO BE AFRAID ANYMORE, DON'T YOU SEE? BECAUSE JOKER'S HERE NOW! HE CARRIED OUT YOUR ORDERS AND HE'S HERE TO RESCUE YOU, FINALLY, FROM THIS NIGHTMARE.
AND NOW ALL THAT'S LEFT TO DO IS LIGHT THE CANDLES AND CELEBRATE! SO LET'S DO IT, SHALL WE?! TAKE MY HAND AND LET'S PUT THE KIDDIES TO BED ONCE AND FOR ALL, AND TOGETHER, WE'LL GO RAISE SOME HELL!
NOW WOULD YOU LIKE TO DO THE HONORS...?
...OR SHALL I?
...GO ON. OR I WILL. I KNOW YOU WANT TO...

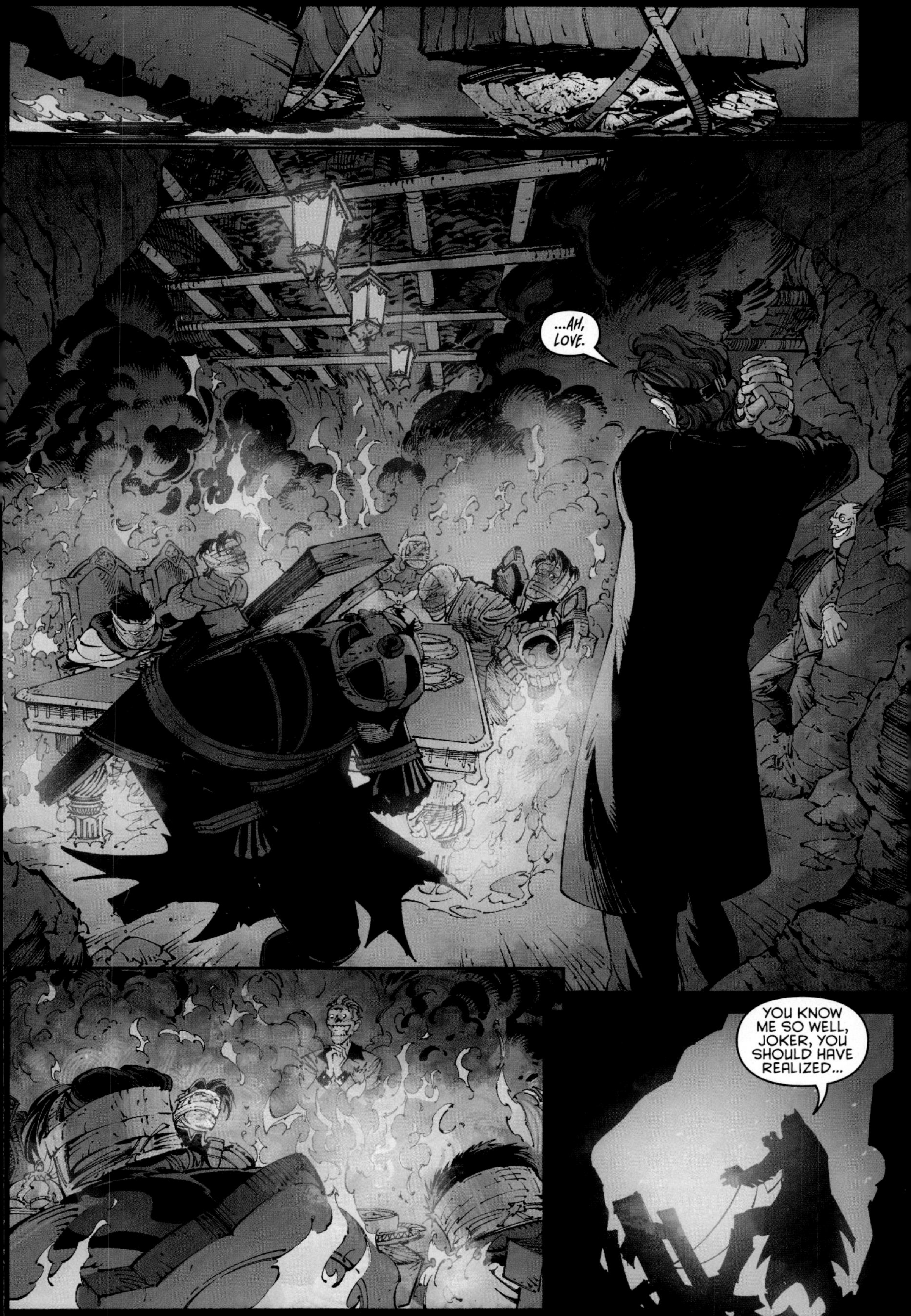
...AH, LOVE.
YOU KNOW ME SO WELL, JOKER, YOU SHOULD HAVE REALIZED...

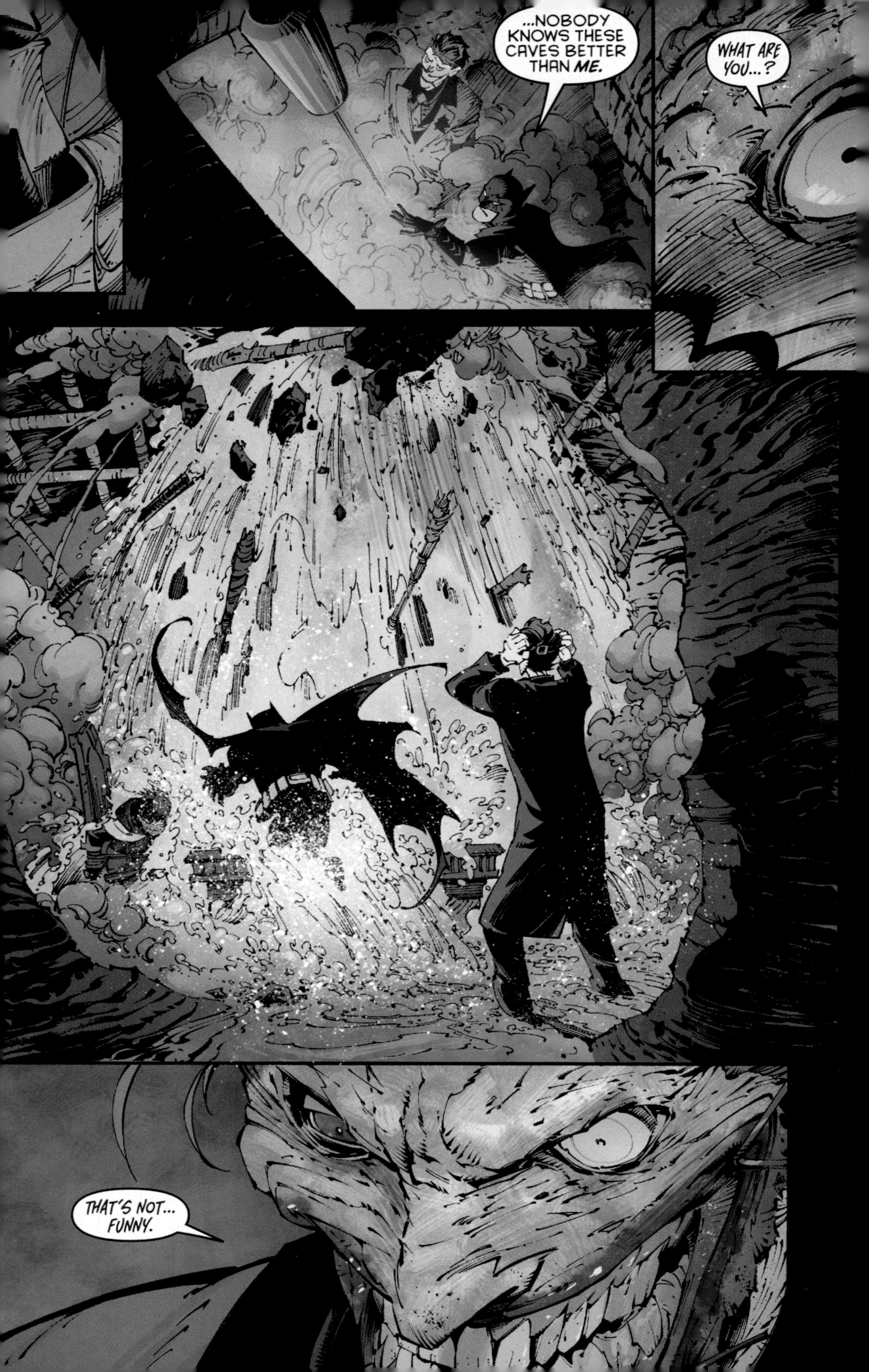
...NOBODY KNOWS THESE CAVES BETTER THAN ME.
WHAT ARE YOU...?
THAT'S NOT... FUNNY.

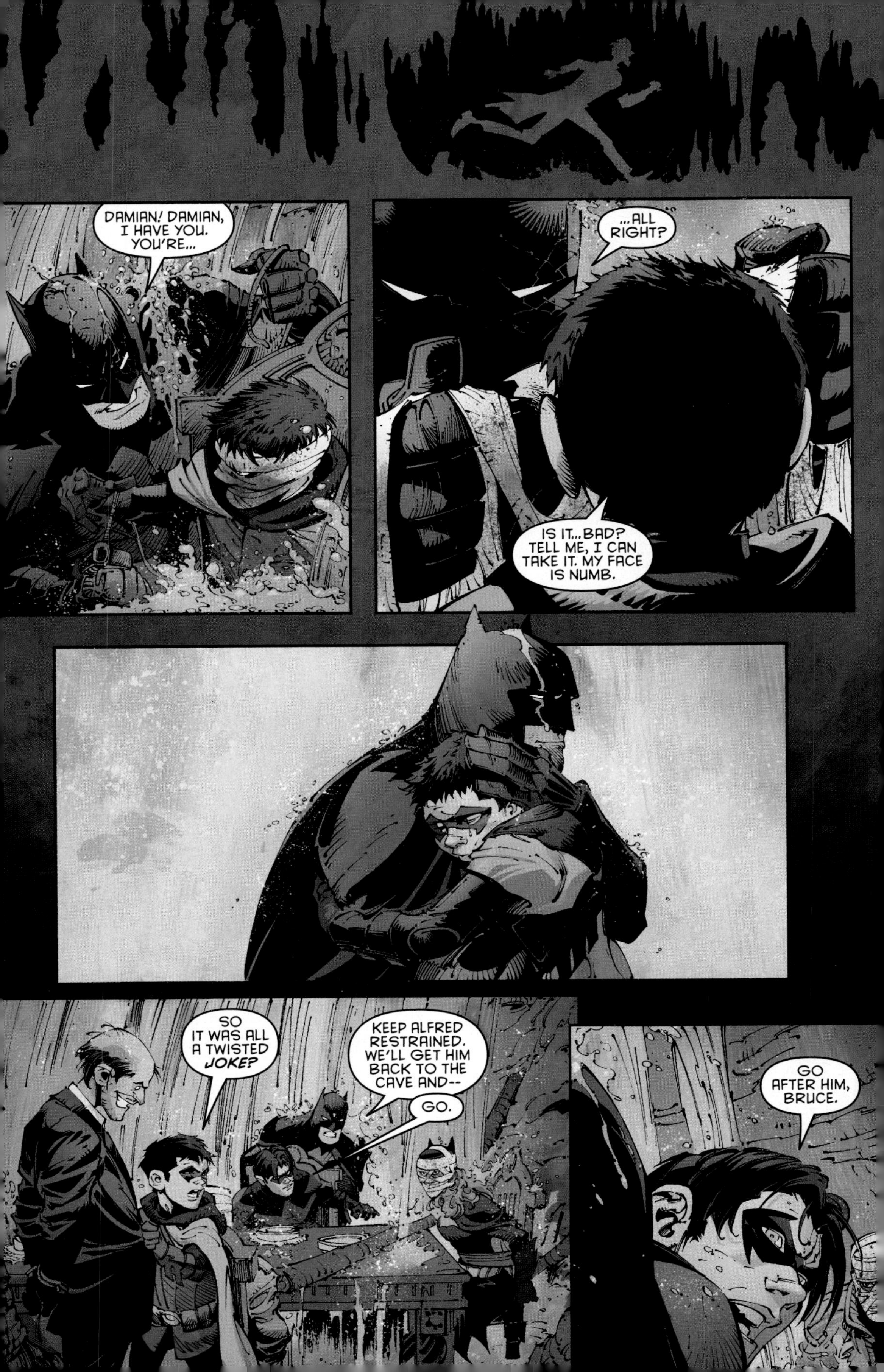
DAMIAN! DAMIAN, I HAVE YOU. YOU'RE...
...ALL RIGHT?
IS IT...BAD? TELL ME, I CAN TAKE IT. MY FACE IS NUMB.
SO IT WAS ALL A TWISTED JOKE?
KEEP ALFRED RESTRAINED. WE'LL GET HIM BACK TO THE CAVE AND--
GO.
GO AFTER HIM, BRUCE.

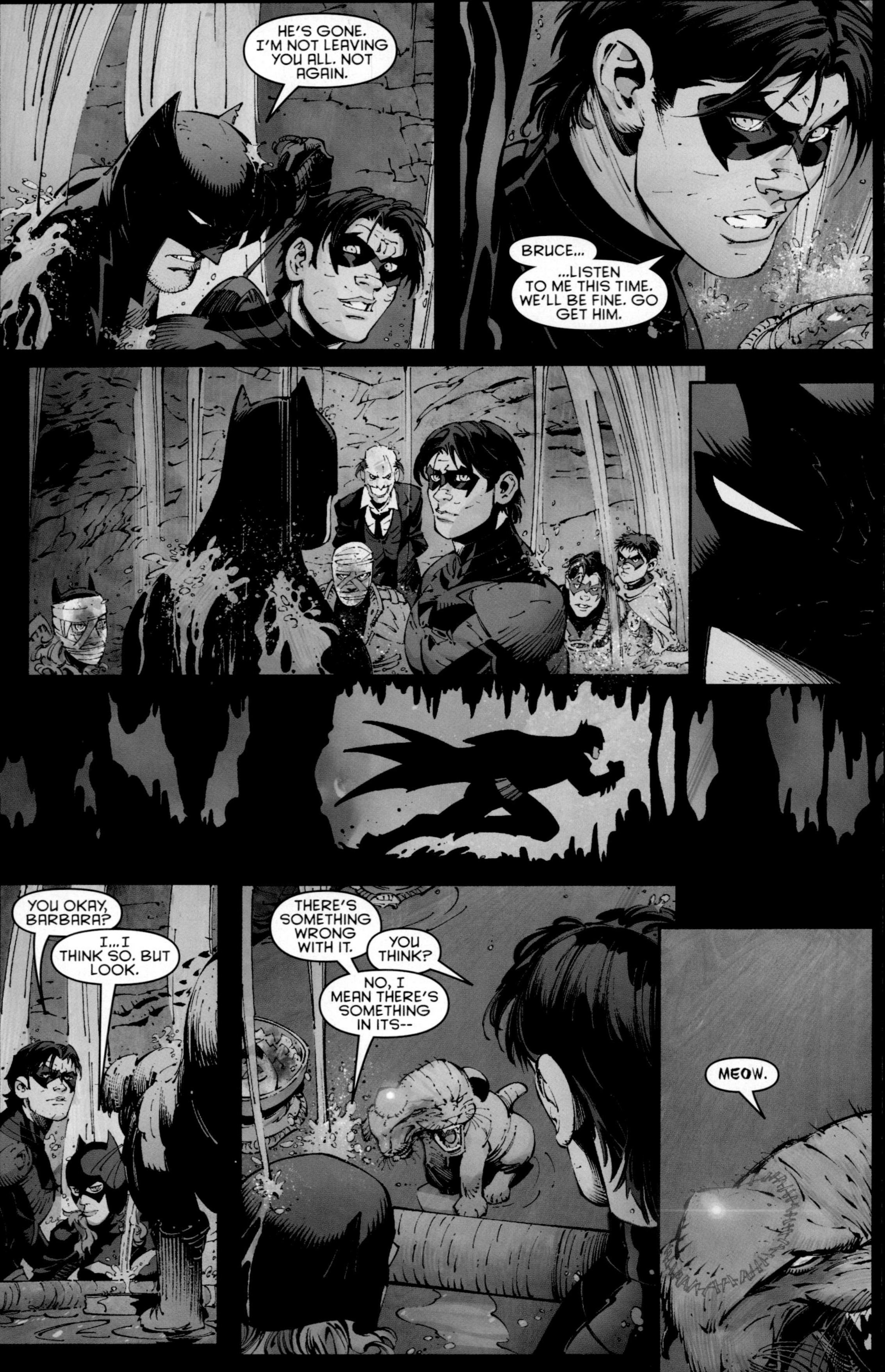
HE'S GONE. I'M NOT LEAVING YOU ALL. NOT AGAIN.
BRUCE...
...LISTEN TO ME THIS TIME. WE'LL BE FINE. GO GET HIM.
YOU OKAY, BARBARA?
I...I THINK SO. BUT LOOK.
THERE'S SOMETHING WRONG WITH IT.
YOU THINK?
NO, I MEAN THERE'S SOMETHING IN ITS--
MEOW.

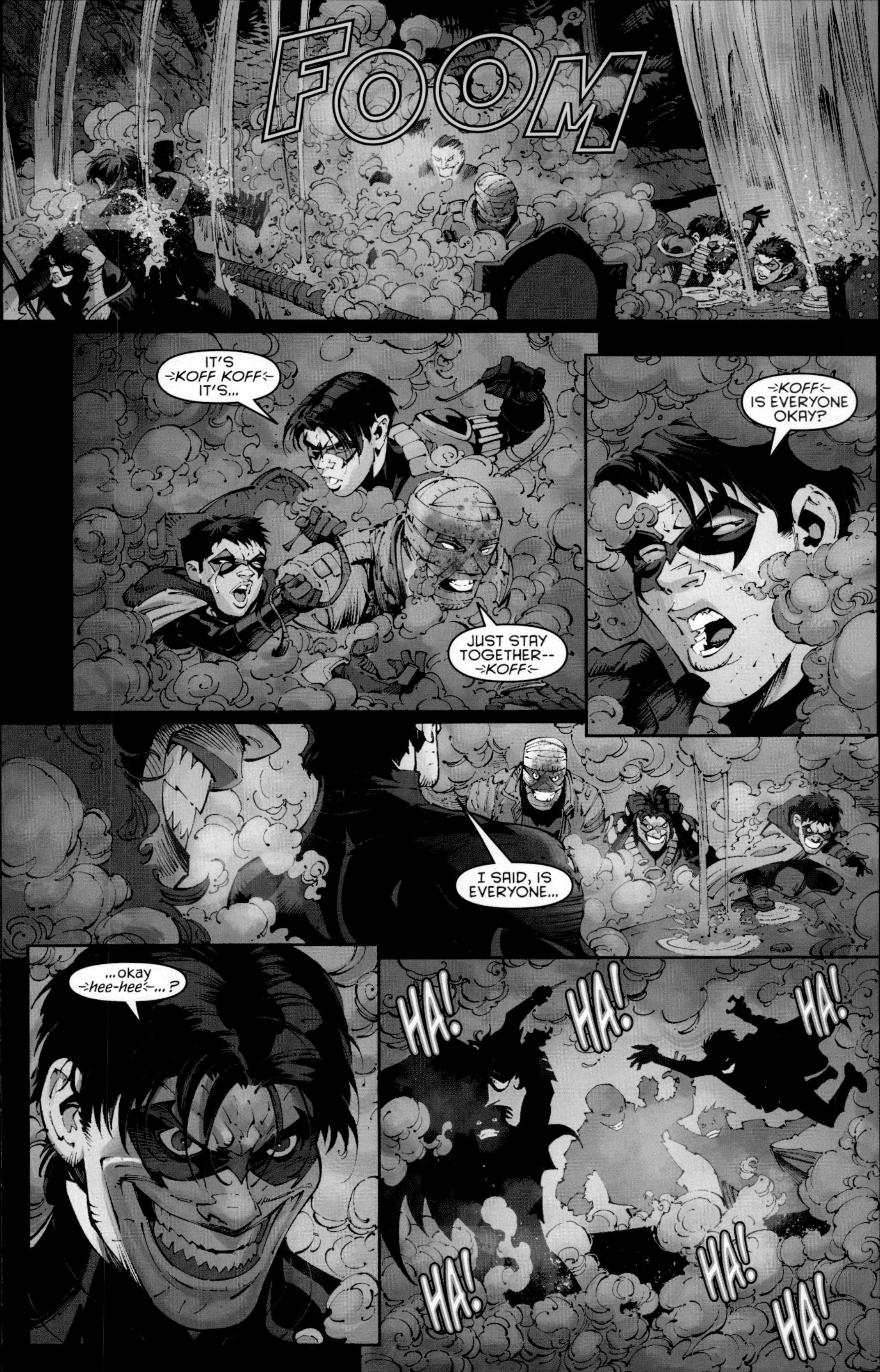
FOOM
IT'S -KOFF KOFF- IT'S...
JUST STAY TOGETHER-- -KOFF-
-KOFF- IS EVERYONE OKAY?
I SAID, IS EVERYONE...
...okay -hee-hee-...?
HA! HA! HA!
HA! HA! HA!

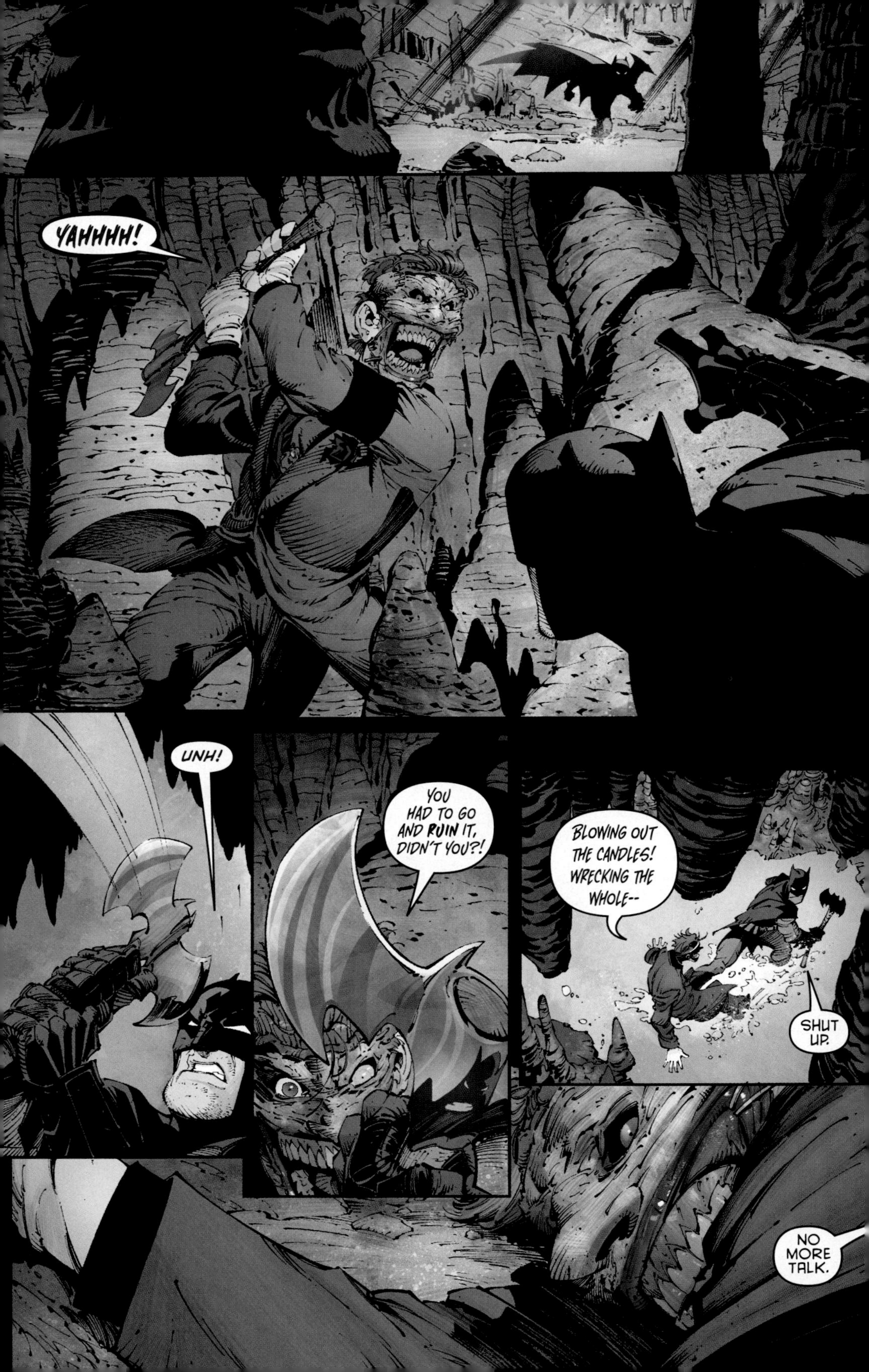
YAHHHH!
UNH!
YOU HAD TO GO AND RUIN IT, DIDN'T YOU?!
BLOWING OUT THE CANDLES! WRECKING THE WHOLE--
SHUT UP.
NO MORE TALK.

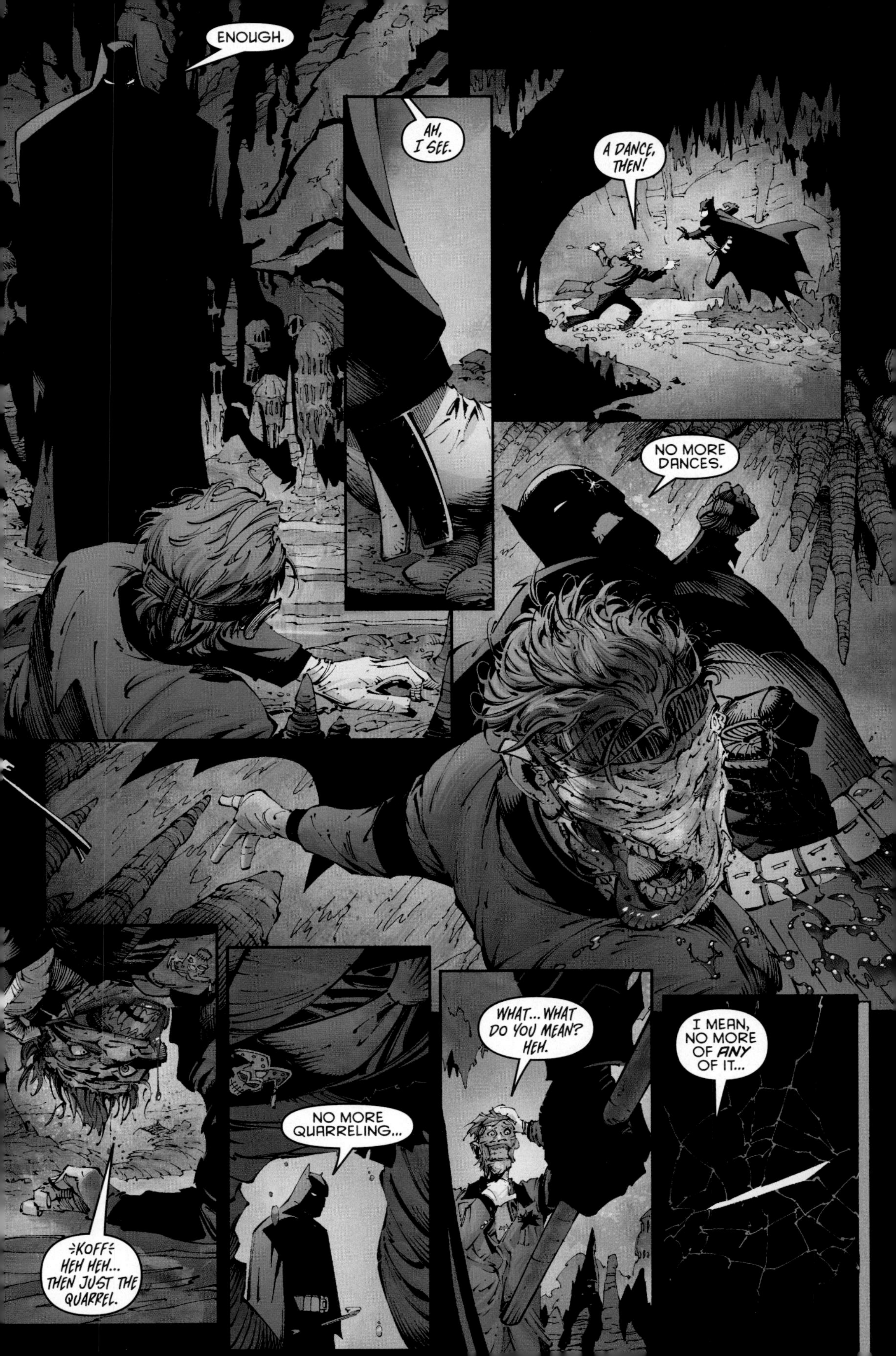
ENOUGH.
AH, I SEE.
A DANCE, THEN!
NO MORE DANCES.
⚡KOFF⚡ HEH HEH... THEN JUST THE QUARREL.
NO MORE QUARRELING...
WHAT... WHAT DO YOU MEAN? HEH.
I MEAN, NO MORE OF *ANY* OF IT...

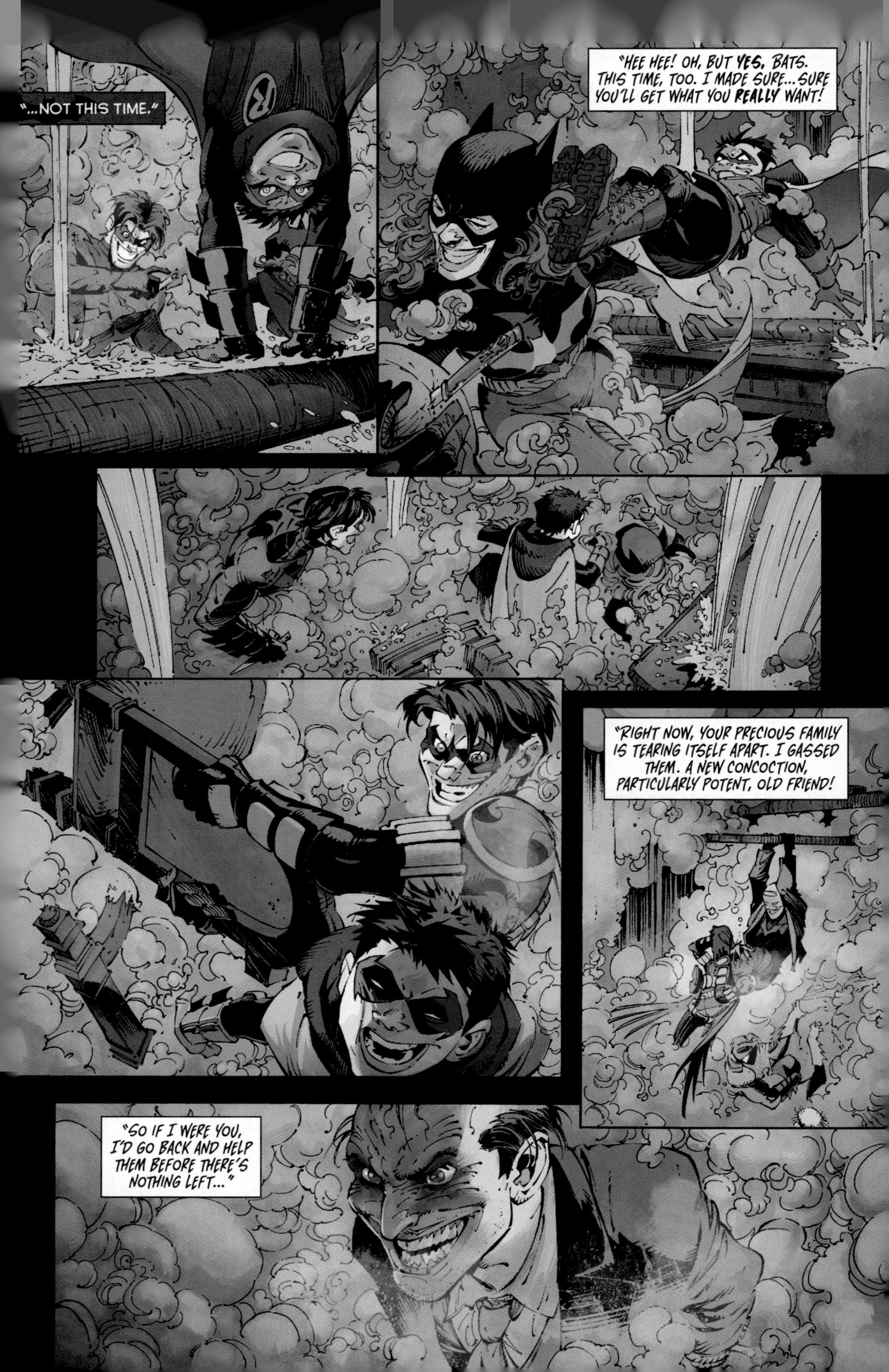
"...NOT THIS TIME."
"HEE HEE! OH, BUT YES, BATS. THIS TIME, TOO. I MADE SURE... SURE YOU'LL GET WHAT YOU REALLY WANT!
"RIGHT NOW, YOUR PRECIOUS FAMILY IS TEARING ITSELF APART. I GASSED THEM. A NEW CONCOCTION, PARTICULARLY POTENT, OLD FRIEND!
"SO IF I WERE YOU, I'D GO BACK AND HELP THEM BEFORE THERE'S NOTHING LEFT..."

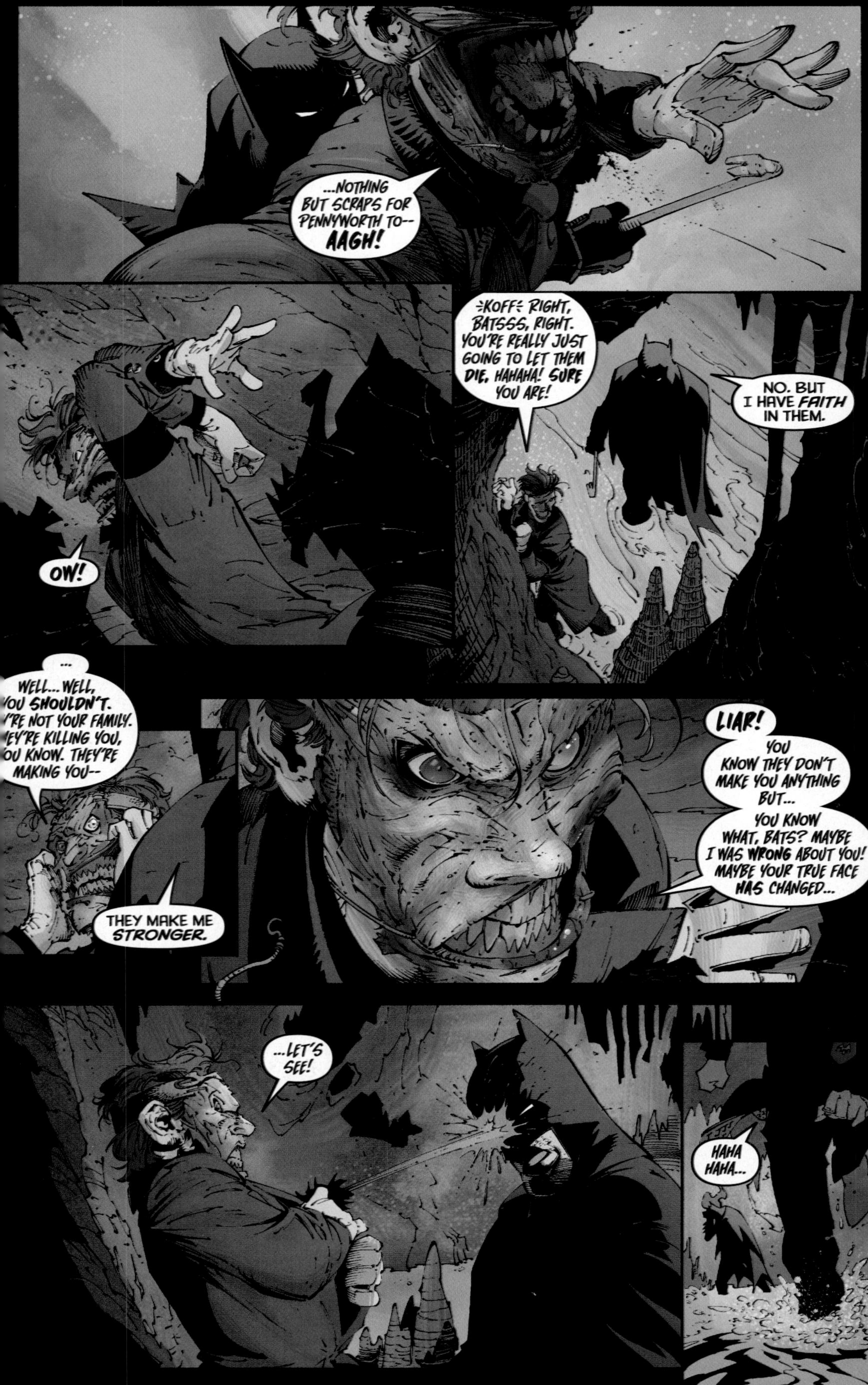

...NOTHING BUT SCRAPS FOR PENNYWORTH TO-- AAGH!
OW!
≡KOFF≡ RIGHT, BATSSS, RIGHT. YOU'RE REALLY JUST GOING TO LET THEM DIE, HAHAHA! SURE YOU ARE!
NO. BUT I HAVE FAITH IN THEM.
...
WELL... WELL, YOU SHOULDN'T. 'Y'RE NOT YOUR FAMILY. 'EY'RE KILLING YOU, YOU KNOW. THEY'RE MAKING YOU--
THEY MAKE ME STRONGER.
LIAR!
YOU KNOW THEY DON'T MAKE YOU ANYTHING BUT...
YOU KNOW WHAT, BATS? MAYBE I WAS WRONG ABOUT YOU! MAYBE YOUR TRUE FACE HAS CHANGED...
...LET'S SEE!
HAHA HAHA...

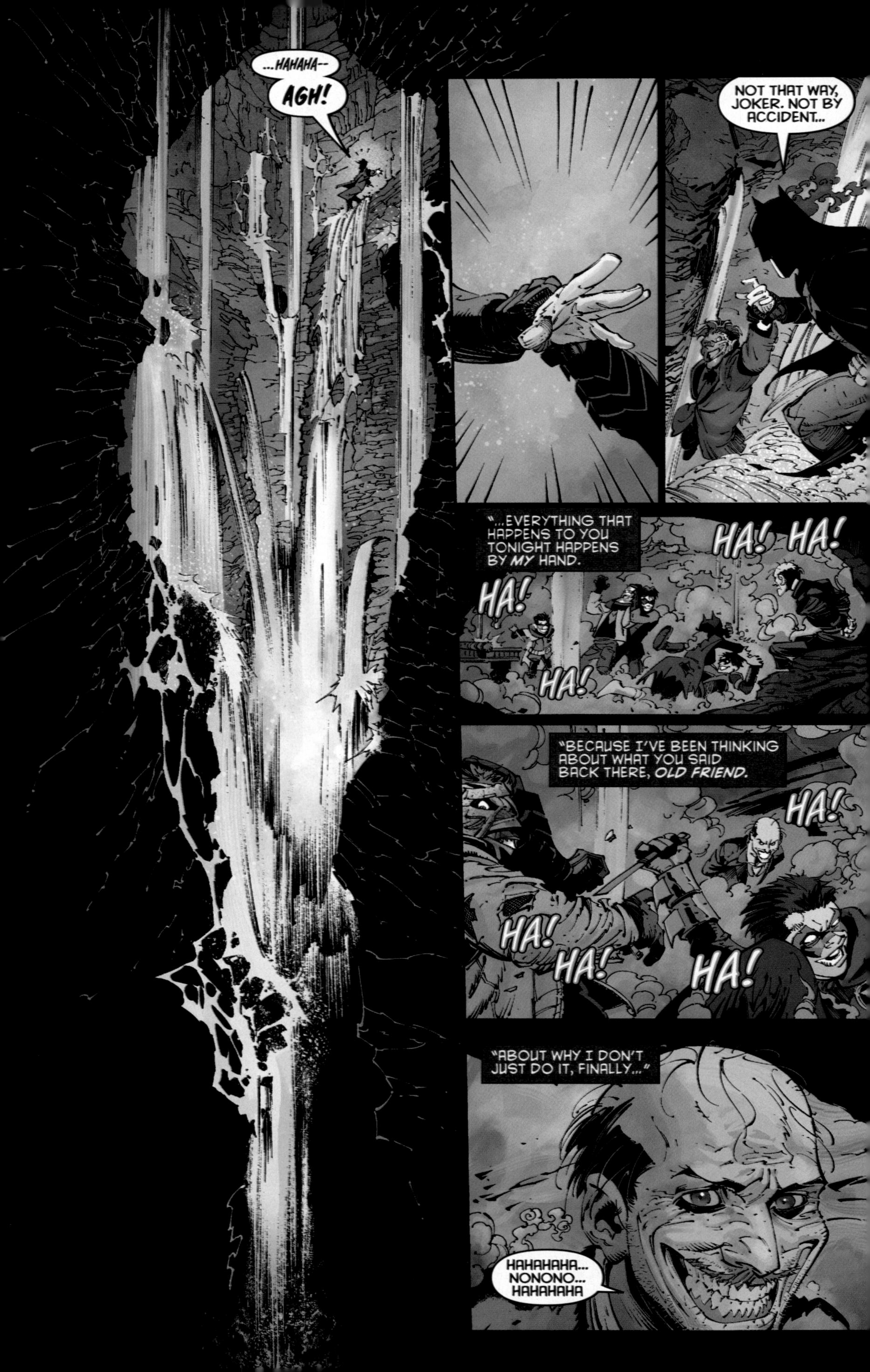
...HAHAHA--
AGH!
NOT THAT WAY, JOKER. NOT BY ACCIDENT...
"...EVERYTHING THAT HAPPENS TO YOU TONIGHT HAPPENS BY MY HAND.
HA! HA!
HA!
HA!
"BECAUSE I'VE BEEN THINKING ABOUT WHAT YOU SAID BACK THERE, OLD FRIEND.
HA!
HA!
HA!
HA!
"ABOUT WHY I DON'T JUST DO IT, FINALLY..."
HAHAHAHA... NONONO... HAHAHAHA

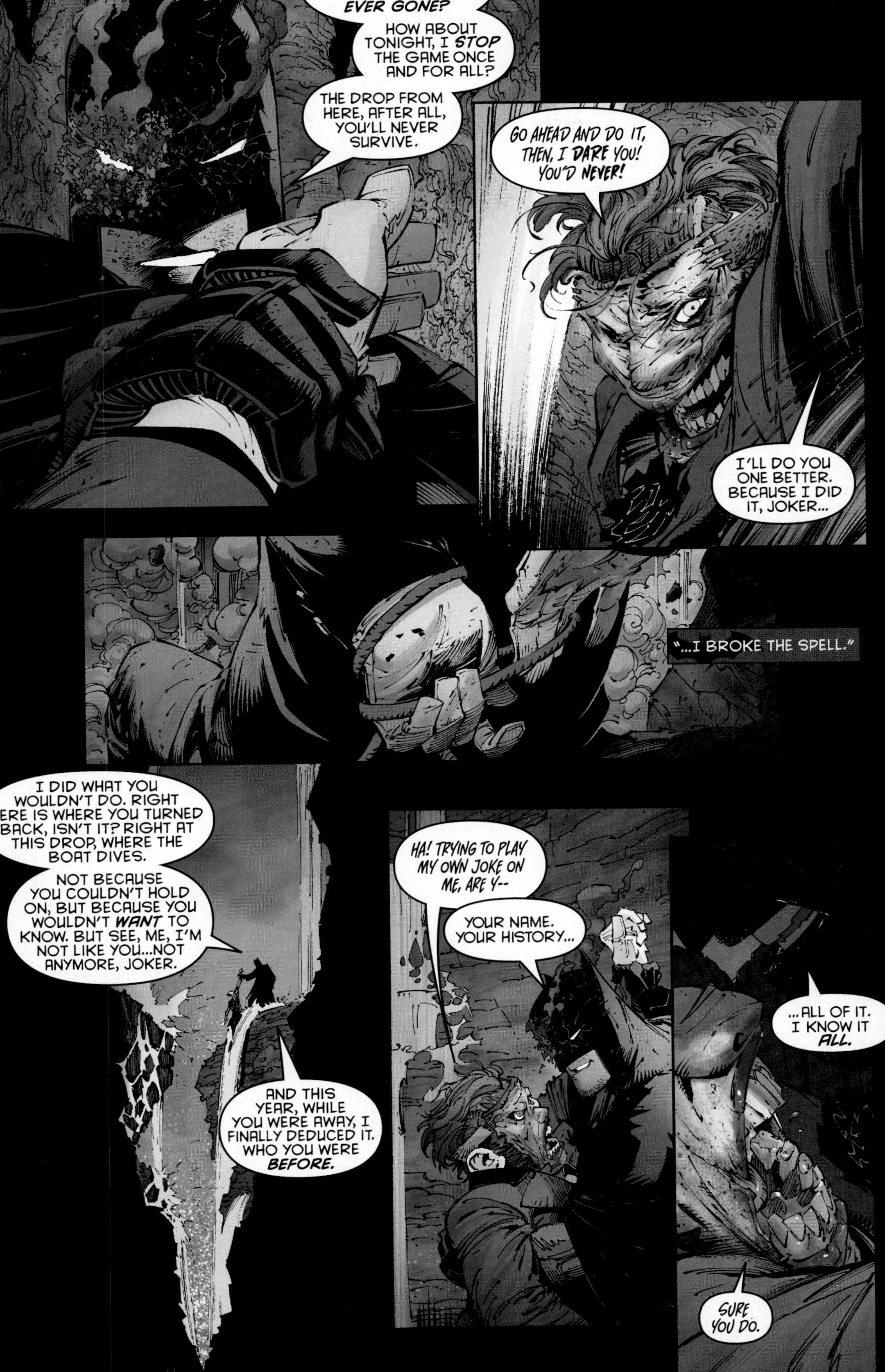
EVER GONE?
HOW ABOUT TONIGHT, I STOP THE GAME ONCE AND FOR ALL?
THE DROP FROM HERE, AFTER ALL, YOU'LL NEVER SURVIVE.
GO AHEAD AND DO IT, THEN, I DARE YOU! YOU'D NEVER!
I'LL DO YOU ONE BETTER. BECAUSE I DID IT, JOKER...
"...I BROKE THE SPELL."
I DID WHAT YOU WOULDN'T DO. RIGHT ERE IS WHERE YOU TURNED BACK, ISN'T IT? RIGHT AT THIS DROP, WHERE THE BOAT DIVES.
NOT BECAUSE YOU COULDN'T HOLD ON, BUT BECAUSE YOU WOULDN'T WANT TO KNOW. BUT SEE, ME, I'M NOT LIKE YOU...NOT ANYMORE, JOKER.
AND THIS YEAR, WHILE YOU WERE AWAY, I FINALLY DEDUCED IT. WHO YOU WERE BEFORE.
HA! TRYING TO PLAY MY OWN JOKE ON ME, ARE Y--
YOUR NAME. YOUR HISTORY...
...ALL OF IT. I KNOW IT ALL.
SURE YOU DO.

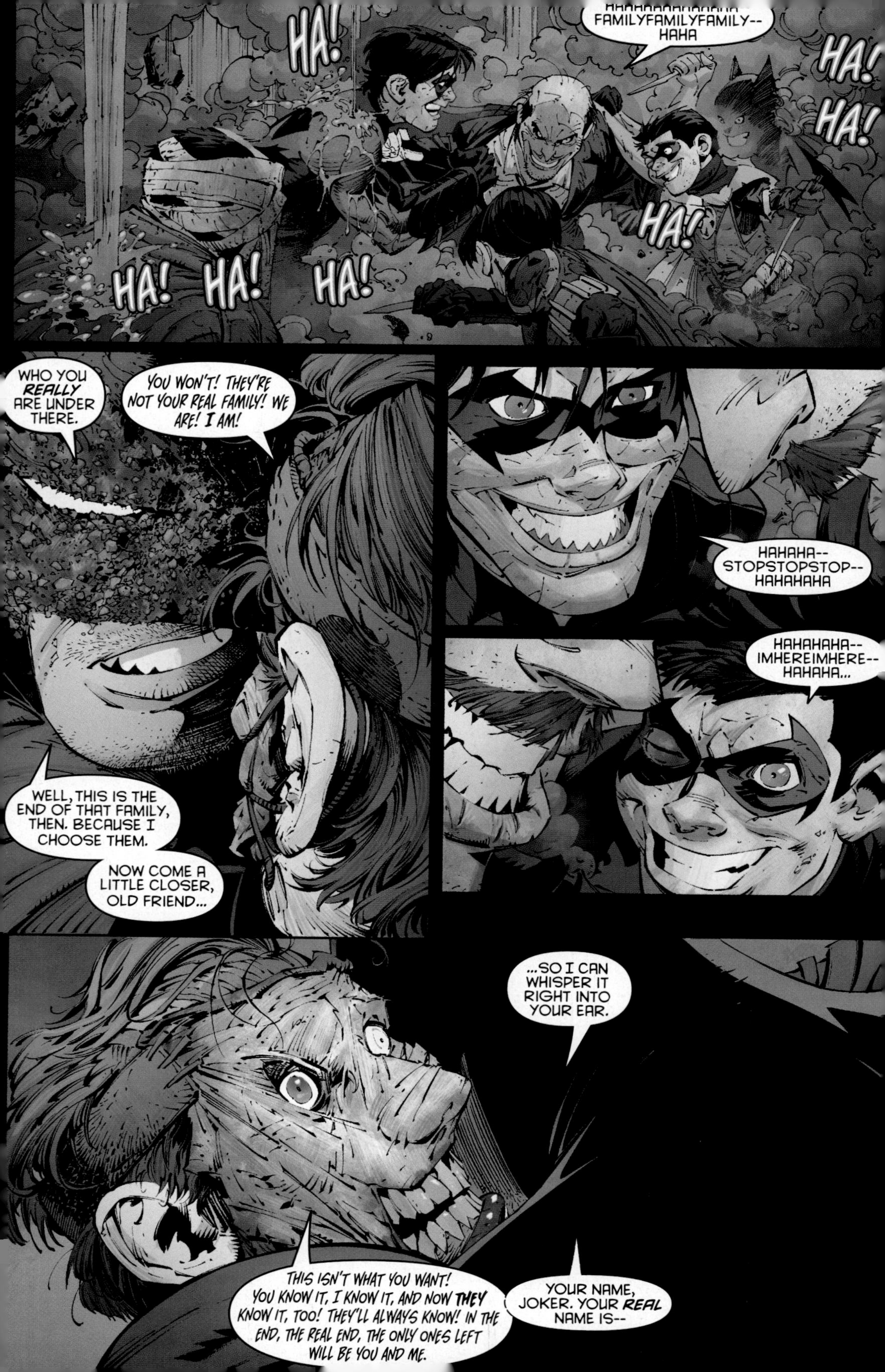

HA!
FAMILYFAMILYFAMILY-- HAHA
HA! HA!
HA!
HA! HA! HA!
WHO YOU REALLY ARE UNDER THERE.
YOU WON'T! THEY'RE NOT YOUR REAL FAMILY! WE ARE! I AM!
HAHAHA-- STOPSTOPSTOP-- HAHAHAHA
HAHAHAHA-- IMHEREIMHERE-- HAHAHA...
WELL, THIS IS THE END OF THAT FAMILY, THEN. BECAUSE I CHOOSE THEM.
NOW COME A LITTLE CLOSER, OLD FRIEND...
...SO I CAN WHISPER IT RIGHT INTO YOUR EAR.
THIS ISN'T WHAT YOU WANT! YOU KNOW IT, I KNOW IT, AND NOW THEY KNOW IT, TOO! THEY'LL ALWAYS KNOW! IN THE END, THE REAL END, THE ONLY ONES LEFT WILL BE YOU AND ME.
YOUR NAME, JOKER. YOUR REAL NAME IS--

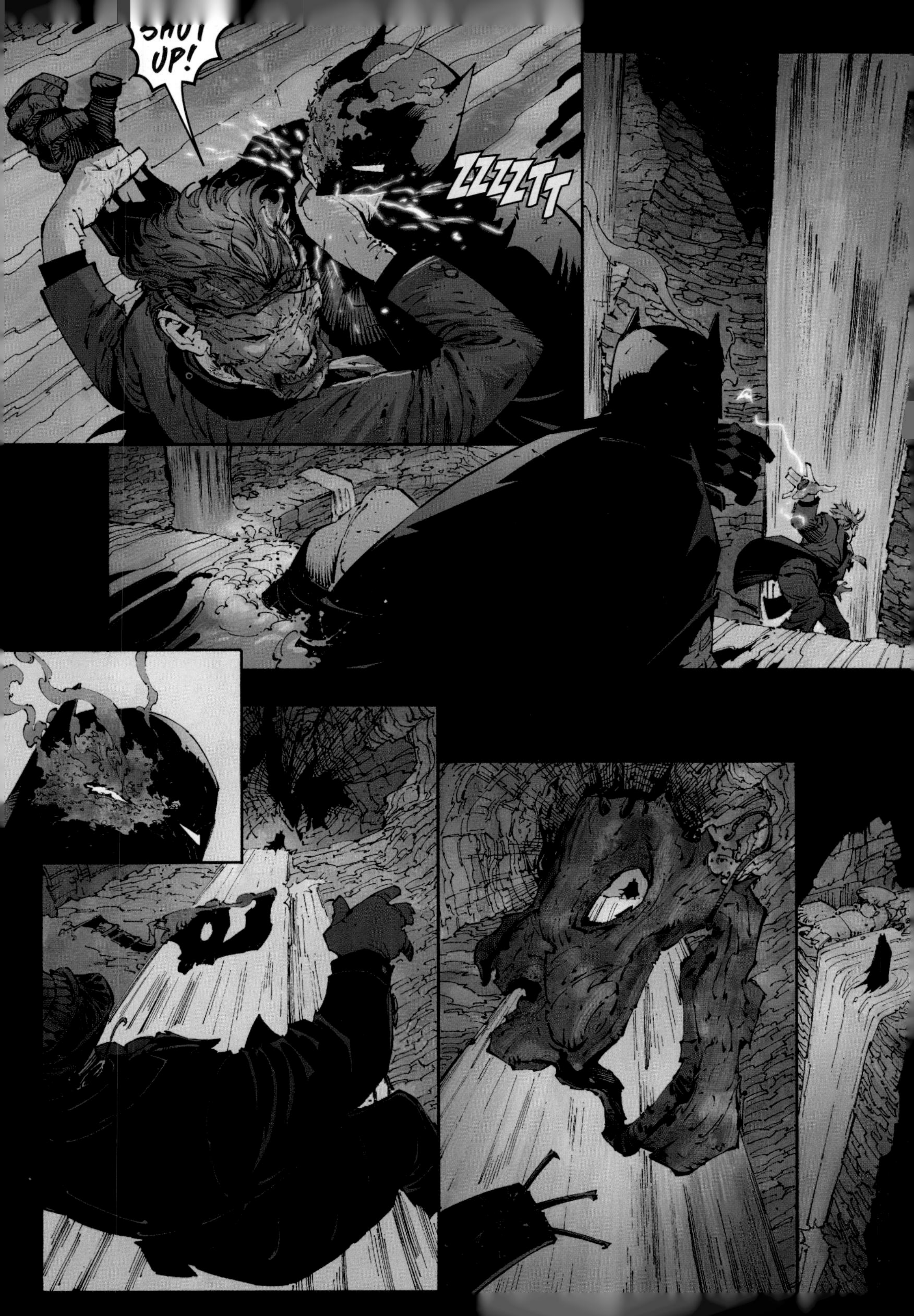
SHUT UP!
ZZZZTT

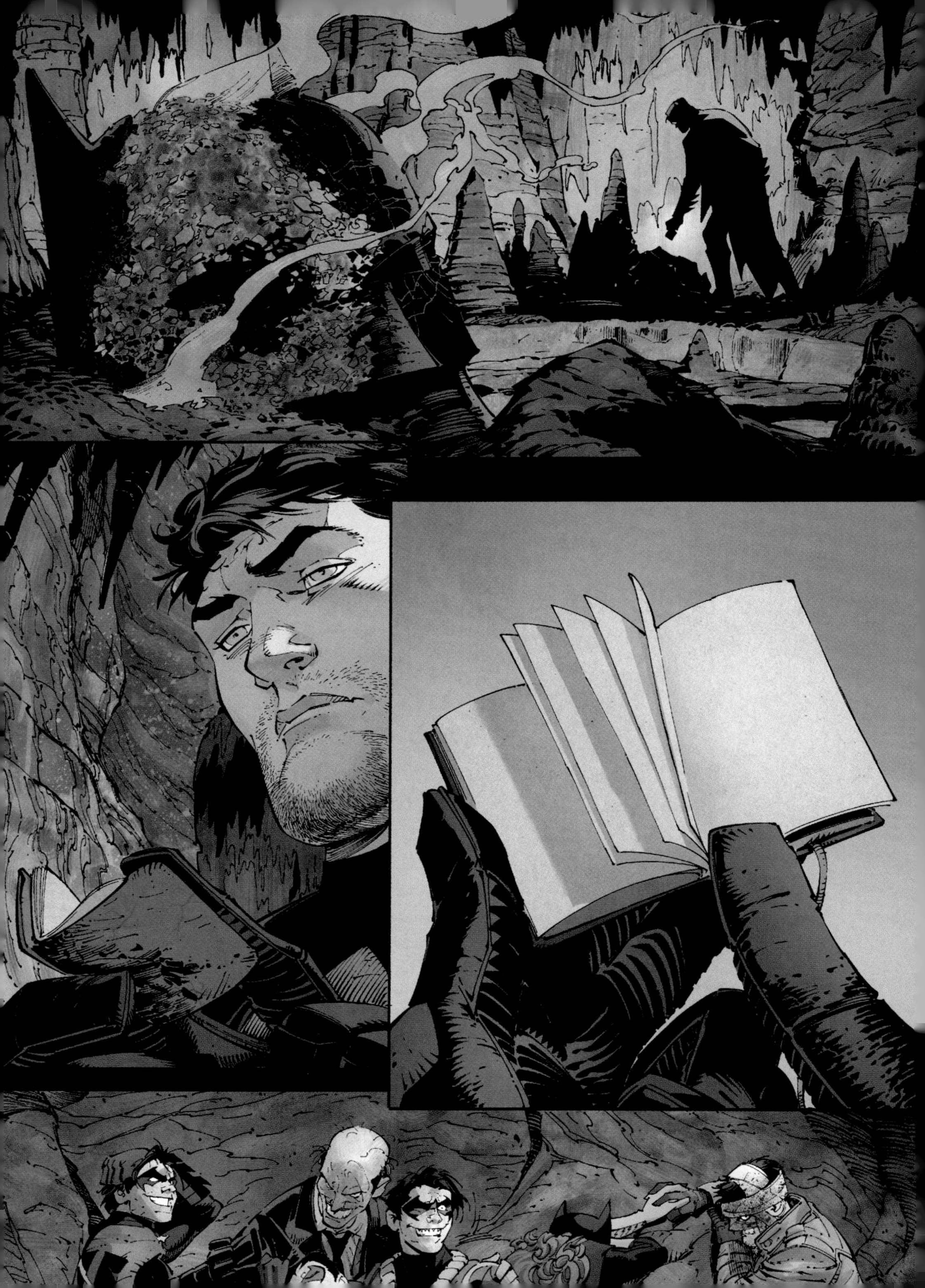

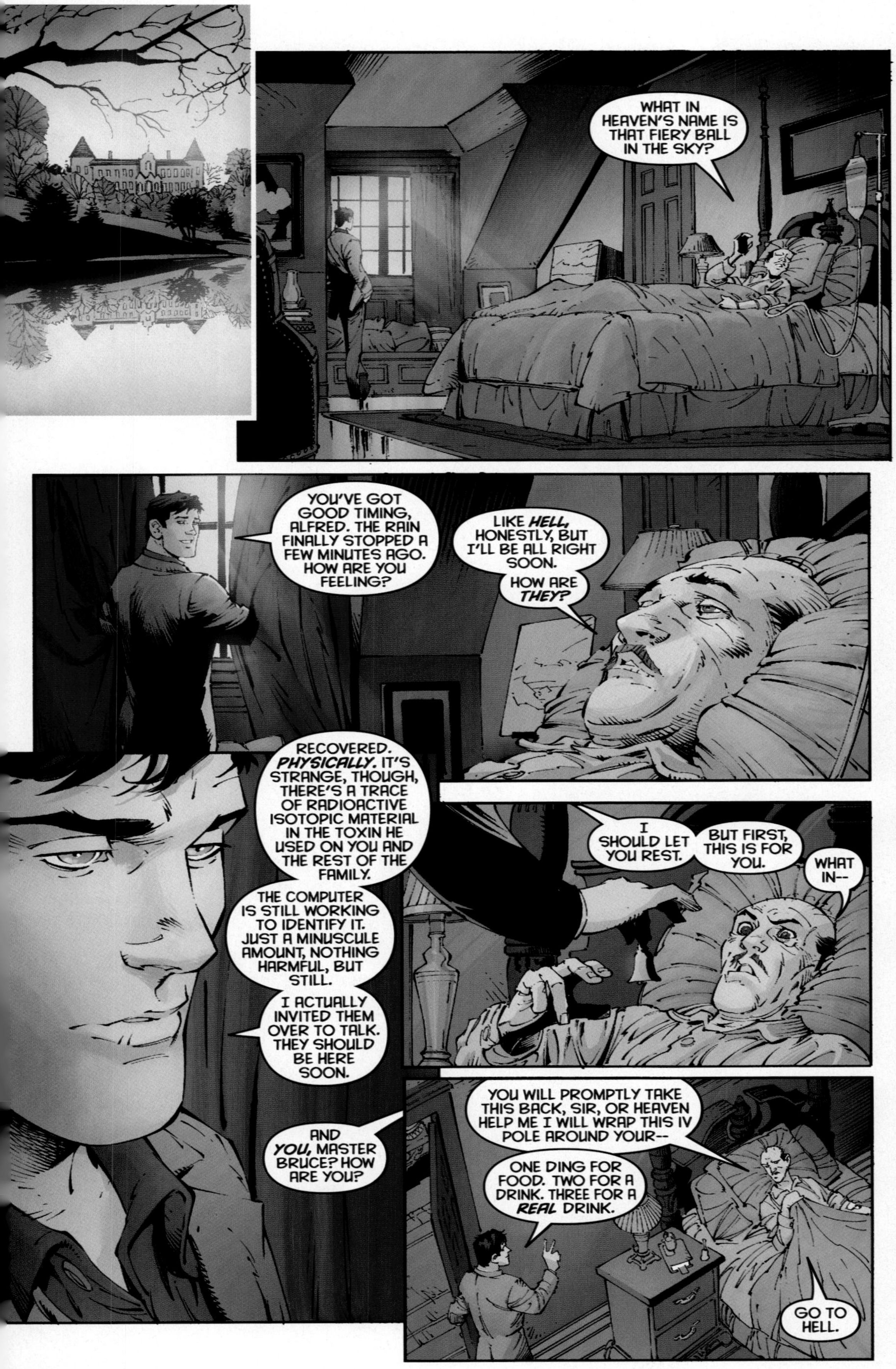
WHAT IN HEAVEN'S NAME IS THAT FIERY BALL IN THE SKY?
YOU'VE GOT GOOD TIMING, ALFRED. THE RAIN FINALLY STOPPED A FEW MINUTES AGO. HOW ARE YOU FEELING?
LIKE HELL, HONESTLY, BUT I'LL BE ALL RIGHT SOON.
HOW ARE THEY?
RECOVERED. PHYSICALLY. IT'S STRANGE, THOUGH, THERE'S A TRACE OF RADIOACTIVE ISOTOPIC MATERIAL IN THE TOXIN HE USED ON YOU AND THE REST OF THE FAMILY.
THE COMPUTER IS STILL WORKING TO IDENTIFY IT. JUST A MINUSCULE AMOUNT, NOTHING HARMFUL, BUT STILL.
I ACTUALLY INVITED THEM OVER TO TALK. THEY SHOULD BE HERE SOON.
AND YOU, MASTER BRUCE? HOW ARE YOU?
I SHOULD LET YOU REST.
BUT FIRST, THIS IS FOR YOU.
WHAT IN--
YOU WILL PROMPTLY TAKE THIS BACK, SIR, OR HEAVEN HELP ME I WILL WRAP THIS IV POLE AROUND YOUR--
ONE DING FOR FOOD. TWO FOR A DRINK. THREE FOR A REAL DRINK.
GO TO HELL.

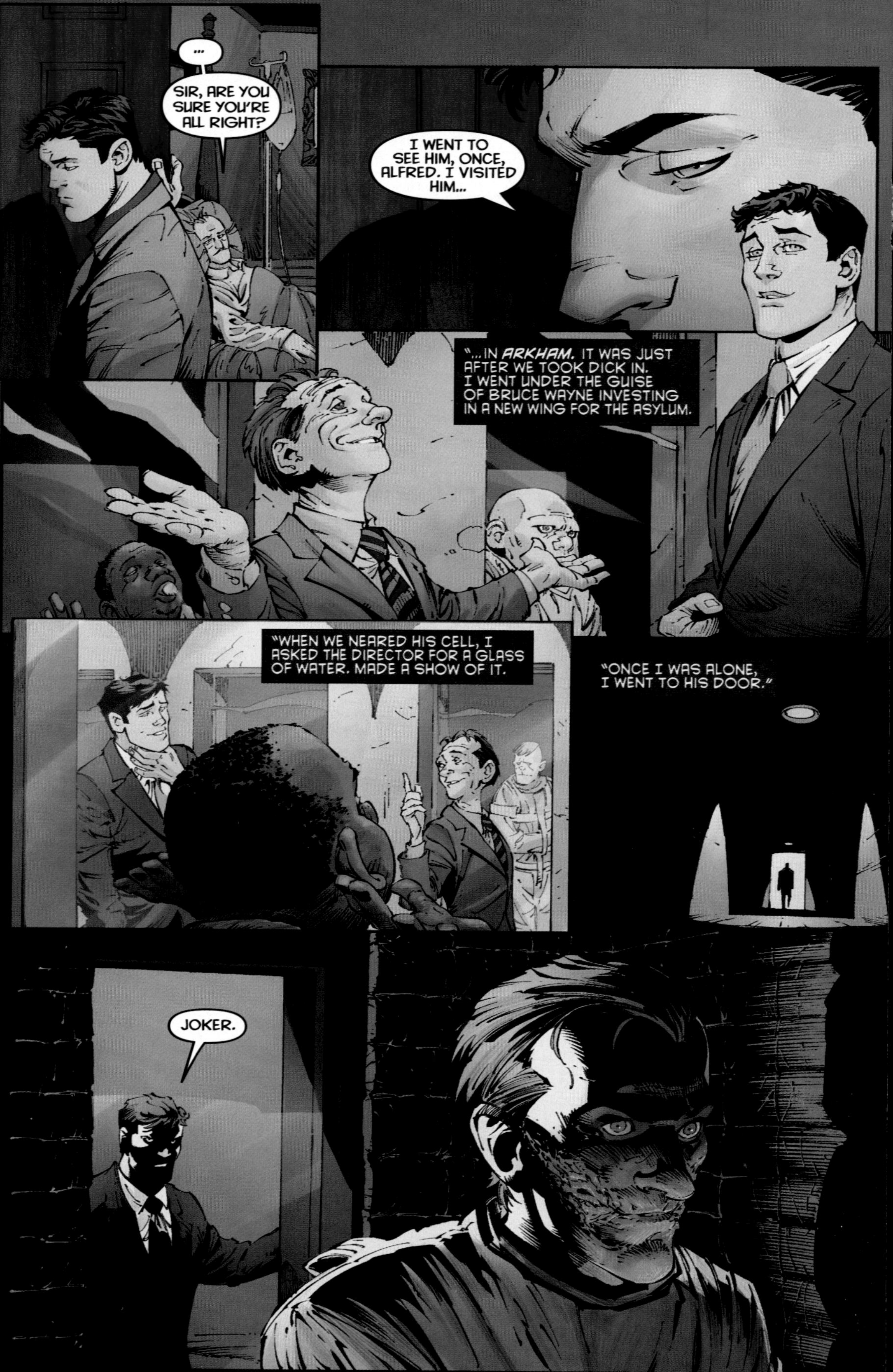
...
SIR, ARE YOU SURE YOU'RE ALL RIGHT?
I WENT TO SEE HIM, ONCE, ALFRED. I VISITED HIM...
"...IN ARKHAM. IT WAS JUST AFTER WE TOOK DICK IN. I WENT UNDER THE GUISE OF BRUCE WAYNE INVESTING IN A NEW WING FOR THE ASYLUM.
"WHEN WE NEARED HIS CELL, I ASKED THE DIRECTOR FOR A GLASS OF WATER. MADE A SHOW OF IT.
"ONCE I WAS ALONE, I WENT TO HIS DOOR."
JOKER.

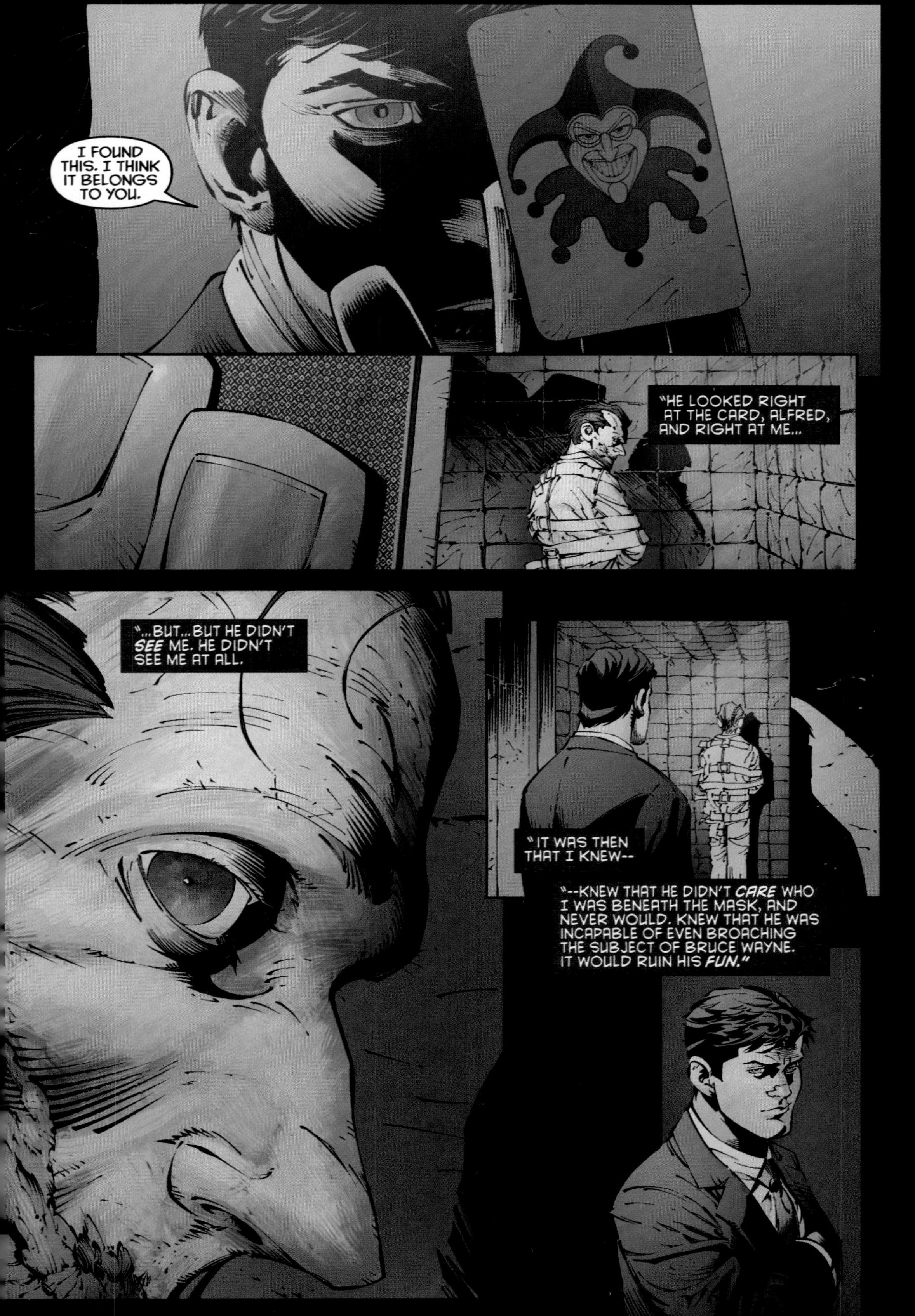
I FOUND THIS. I THINK IT BELONGS TO YOU.
"HE LOOKED RIGHT AT THE CARD, ALFRED, AND RIGHT AT ME...
"...BUT...BUT HE DIDN'T *SEE* ME. HE DIDN'T SEE ME AT ALL.
"IT WAS THEN THAT I KNEW--
"--KNEW THAT HE DIDN'T *CARE* WHO I WAS BENEATH THE MASK, AND NEVER WOULD. KNEW THAT HE WAS INCAPABLE OF EVEN BROACHING THE SUBJECT OF BRUCE WAYNE. IT WOULD RUIN HIS *FUN*."

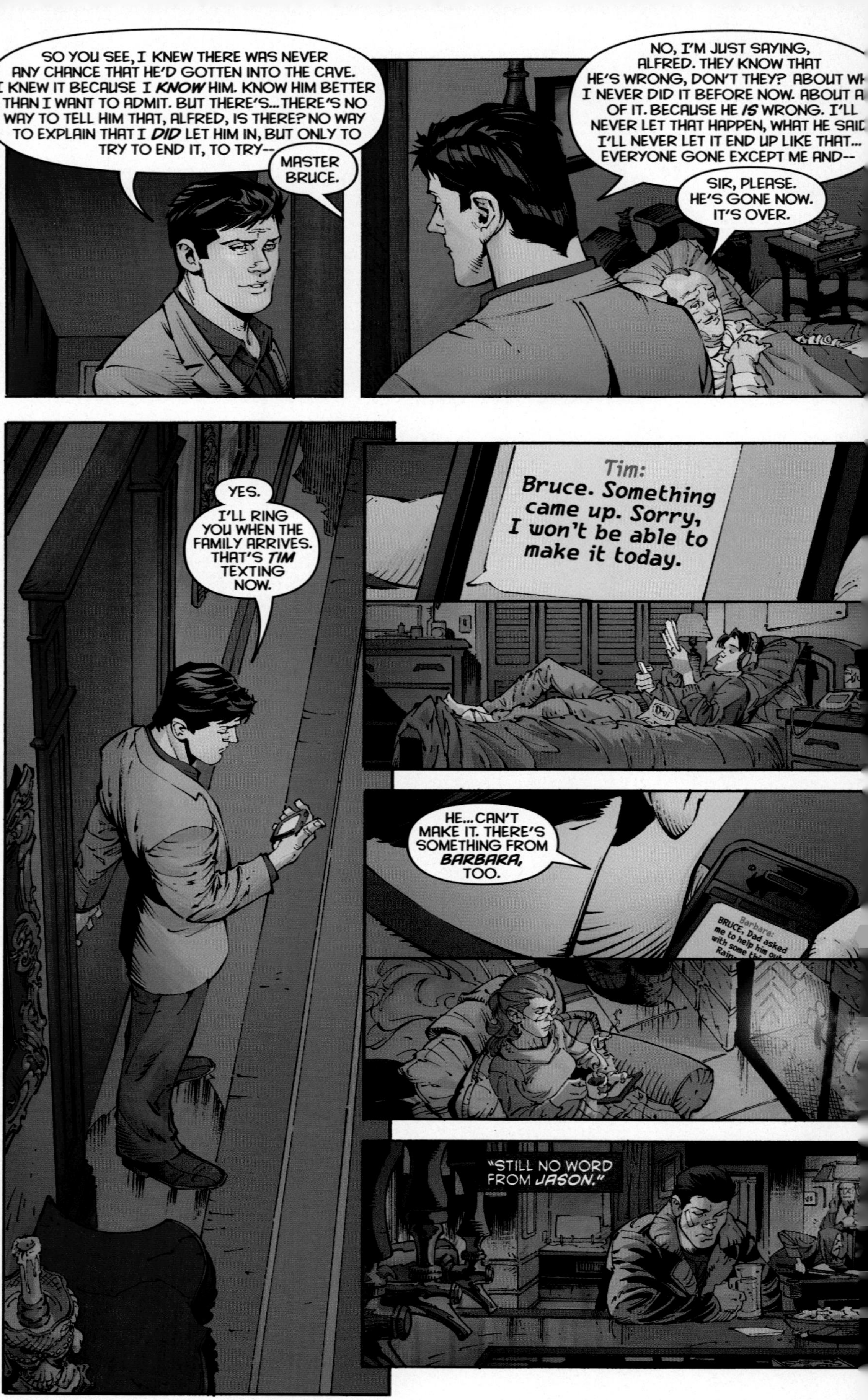

SO YOU SEE, I KNEW THERE WAS NEVER ANY CHANCE THAT HE'D GOTTEN INTO THE CAVE. I KNEW IT BECAUSE I **KNOW** HIM. KNOW HIM BETTER THAN I WANT TO ADMIT. BUT THERE'S...THERE'S NO WAY TO TELL HIM THAT, ALFRED, IS THERE? NO WAY TO EXPLAIN THAT I **DID** LET HIM IN, BUT ONLY TO TRY TO END IT, TO TRY--
MASTER BRUCE.
NO, I'M JUST SAYING, ALFRED. THEY KNOW THAT HE'S WRONG, DON'T THEY? ABOUT WH I NEVER DID IT BEFORE NOW. ABOUT A OF IT. BECAUSE HE **IS** WRONG. I'LL NEVER LET THAT HAPPEN, WHAT HE SAID I'LL NEVER LET IT END UP LIKE THAT... EVERYONE GONE EXCEPT ME AND--
SIR, PLEASE. HE'S GONE NOW. IT'S OVER.
YES.
I'LL RING YOU WHEN THE FAMILY ARRIVES. THAT'S **TIM** TEXTING NOW.
Tim:
Bruce. Something came up. Sorry, I won't be able to make it today.
HE...CAN'T MAKE IT. THERE'S SOMETHING FROM **BARBARA,** TOO.
Barbara:
BRUCE, Dad asked me to help him out
"STILL NO WORD FROM **JASON.**"

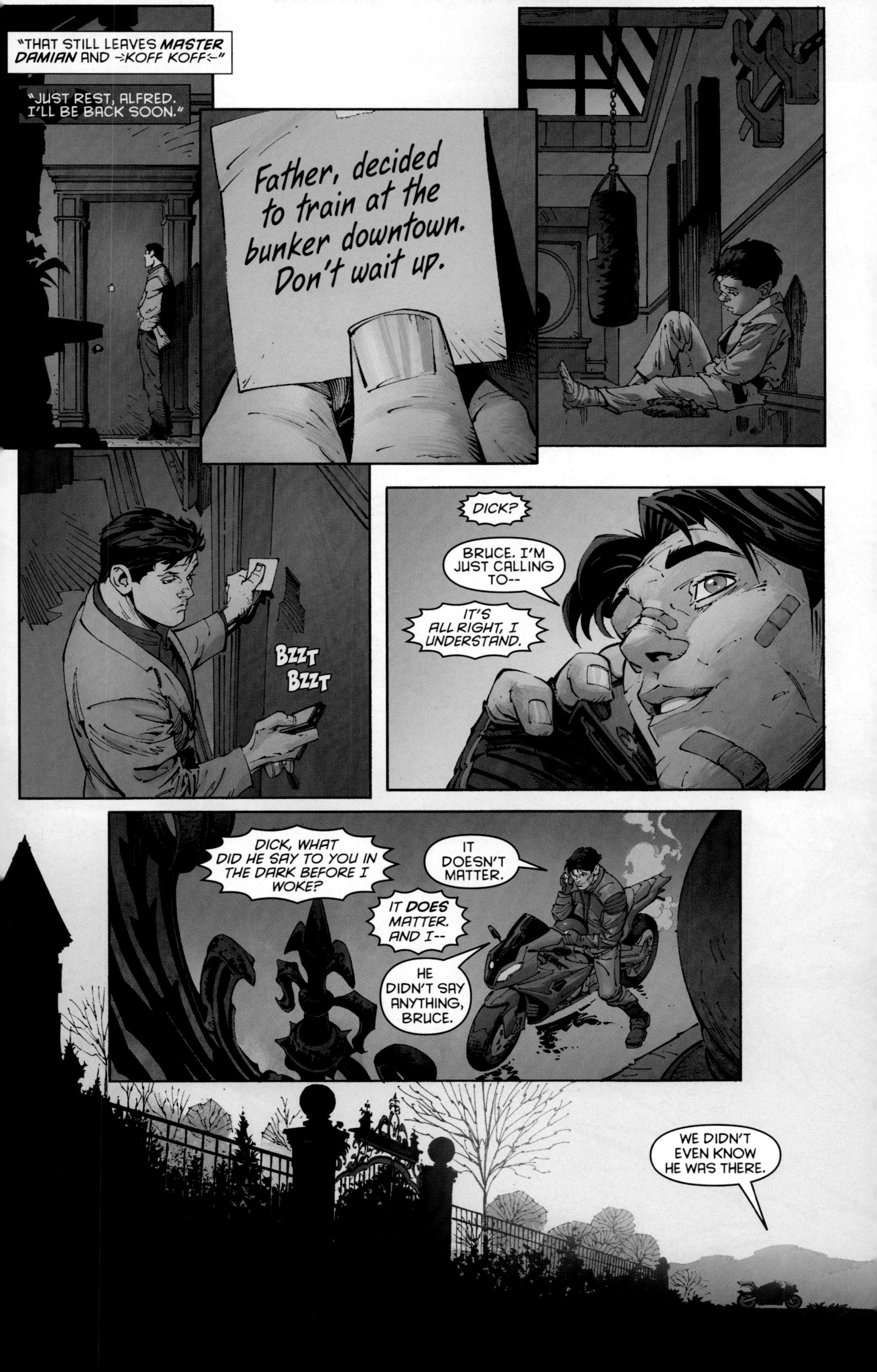

"THAT STILL LEAVES MASTER DAMIAN AND →KOFF KOFF←"
"JUST REST, ALFRED. I'LL BE BACK SOON."
Father, decided to train at the bunker downtown. Don't wait up.
BZZT BZZT
DICK?
BRUCE. I'M JUST CALLING TO--
IT'S ALL RIGHT, I UNDERSTAND.
DICK, WHAT DID HE SAY TO YOU IN THE DARK BEFORE I WOKE?
IT DOESN'T MATTER.
IT DOES MATTER. AND I--
HE DIDN'T SAY ANYTHING, BRUCE.
WE DIDN'T EVEN KNOW HE WAS THERE.

KYLE HIGGINS writer **SANFORD GREENE** artist

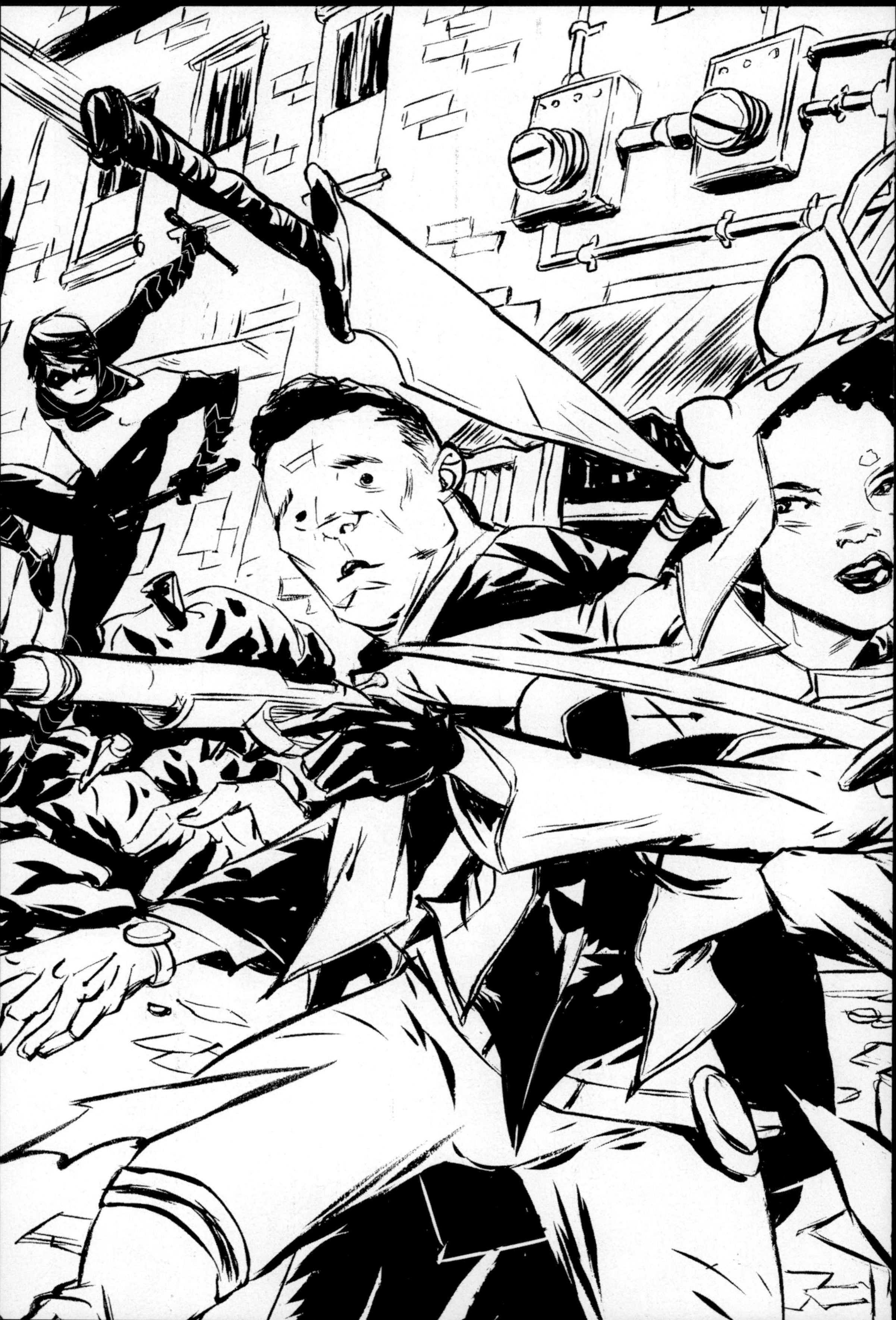

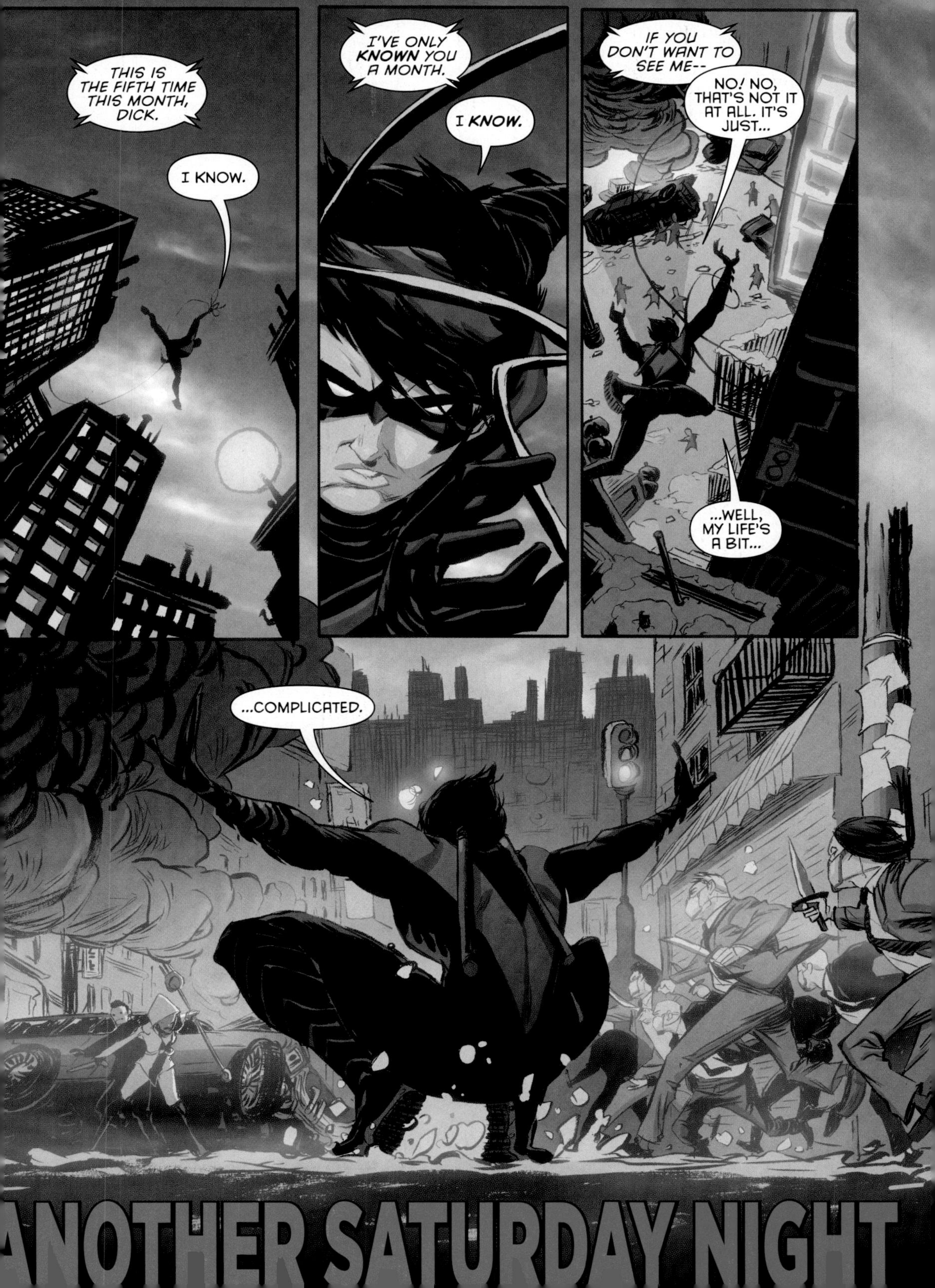
THIS IS THE FIFTH TIME THIS MONTH, DICK.
I KNOW.
I'VE ONLY KNOWN YOU A MONTH.
I KNOW.
IF YOU DON'T WANT TO SEE ME--
NO! NO, THAT'S NOT IT AT ALL. IT'S JUST...
...WELL, MY LIFE'S A BIT...
...COMPLICATED.
ANOTHER SATURDAY NIGHT

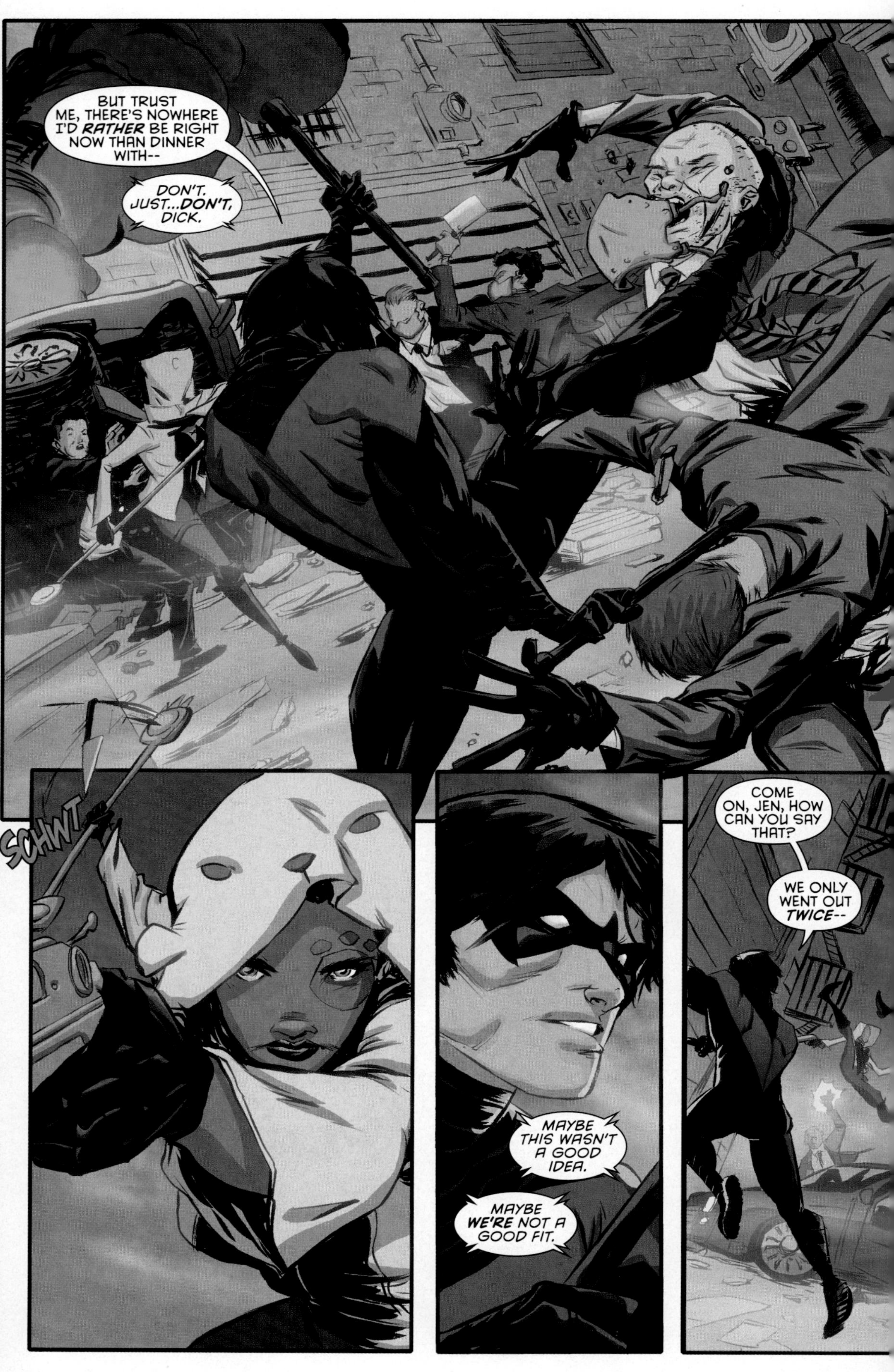
BUT TRUST ME, THERE'S NOWHERE I'D *RATHER* BE RIGHT NOW THAN DINNER WITH--
DON'T. JUST...*DON'T,* DICK.
SCHWT
MAYBE THIS WASN'T A GOOD IDEA.
MAYBE *WE'RE* NOT A GOOD FIT.
COME ON, JEN, HOW CAN YOU SAY THAT?
WE ONLY WENT OUT *TWICE*--

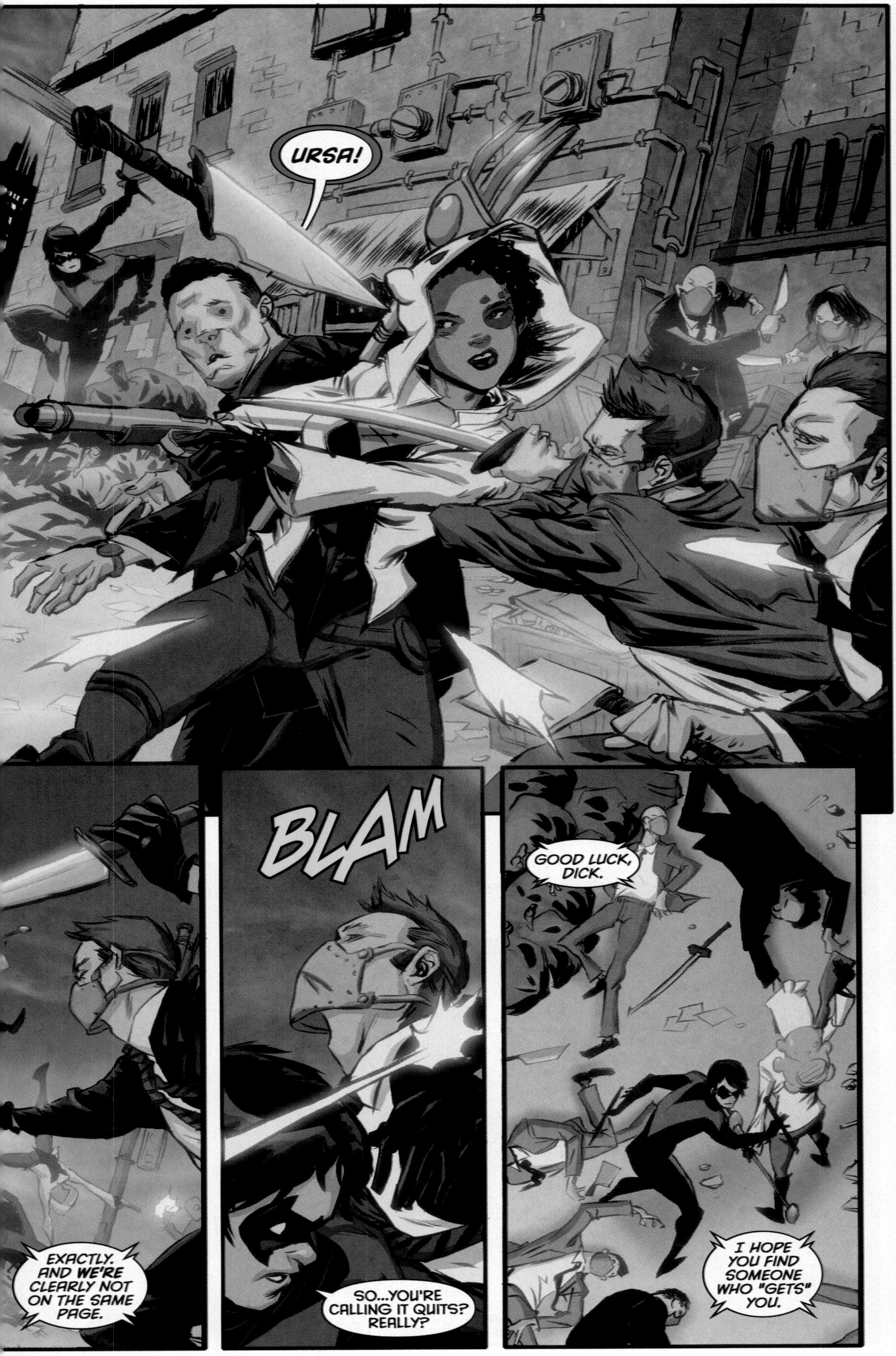
URSA!
BLAM
EXACTLY. AND WE'RE CLEARLY NOT ON THE SAME PAGE.
SO...YOU'RE CALLING IT QUITS? REALLY?
GOOD LUCK, DICK.
I HOPE YOU FIND SOMEONE WHO "GETS" YOU.

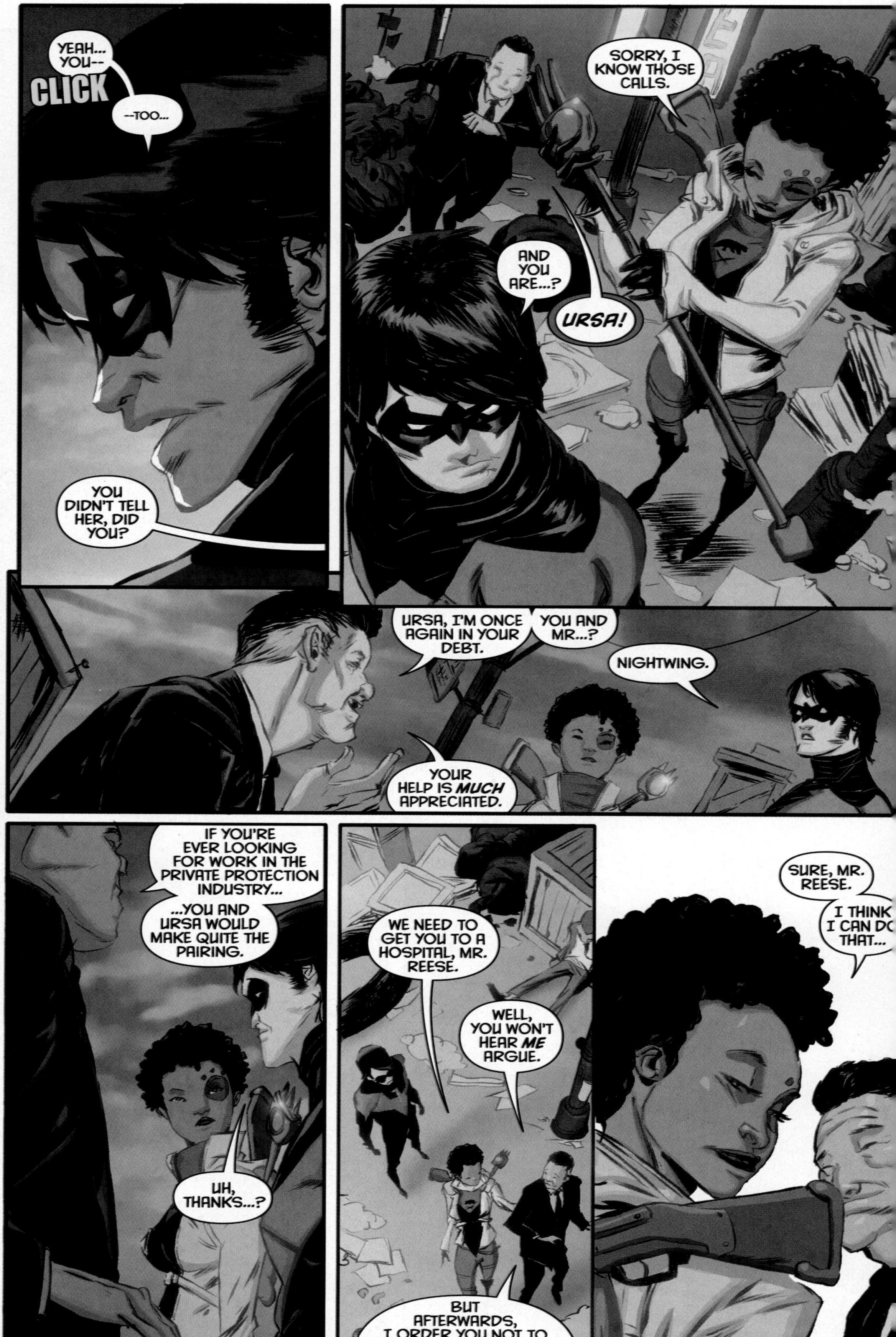
YEAH... YOU--
CLICK
--TOO...
YOU DIDN'T TELL HER, DID YOU?
SORRY, I KNOW THOSE CALLS.
AND YOU ARE...?
URSA!
URSA, I'M ONCE AGAIN IN YOUR DEBT.
YOUR HELP IS MUCH APPRECIATED.
YOU AND MR...?
NIGHTWING.
IF YOU'RE EVER LOOKING FOR WORK IN THE PRIVATE PROTECTION INDUSTRY...
...YOU AND URSA WOULD MAKE QUITE THE PAIRING.
UH, THANKS...?
WE NEED TO GET YOU TO A HOSPITAL, MR. REESE.
WELL, YOU WON'T HEAR ME ARGUE.
BUT AFTERWARDS, I ORDER YOU NOT TO LET THE NIGHT BE A TOTAL WASTE, OKAY? I KNOW YOU DON'T GET OUT MUCH.
SURE, MR. REESE.
I THINK I CAN DO THAT...

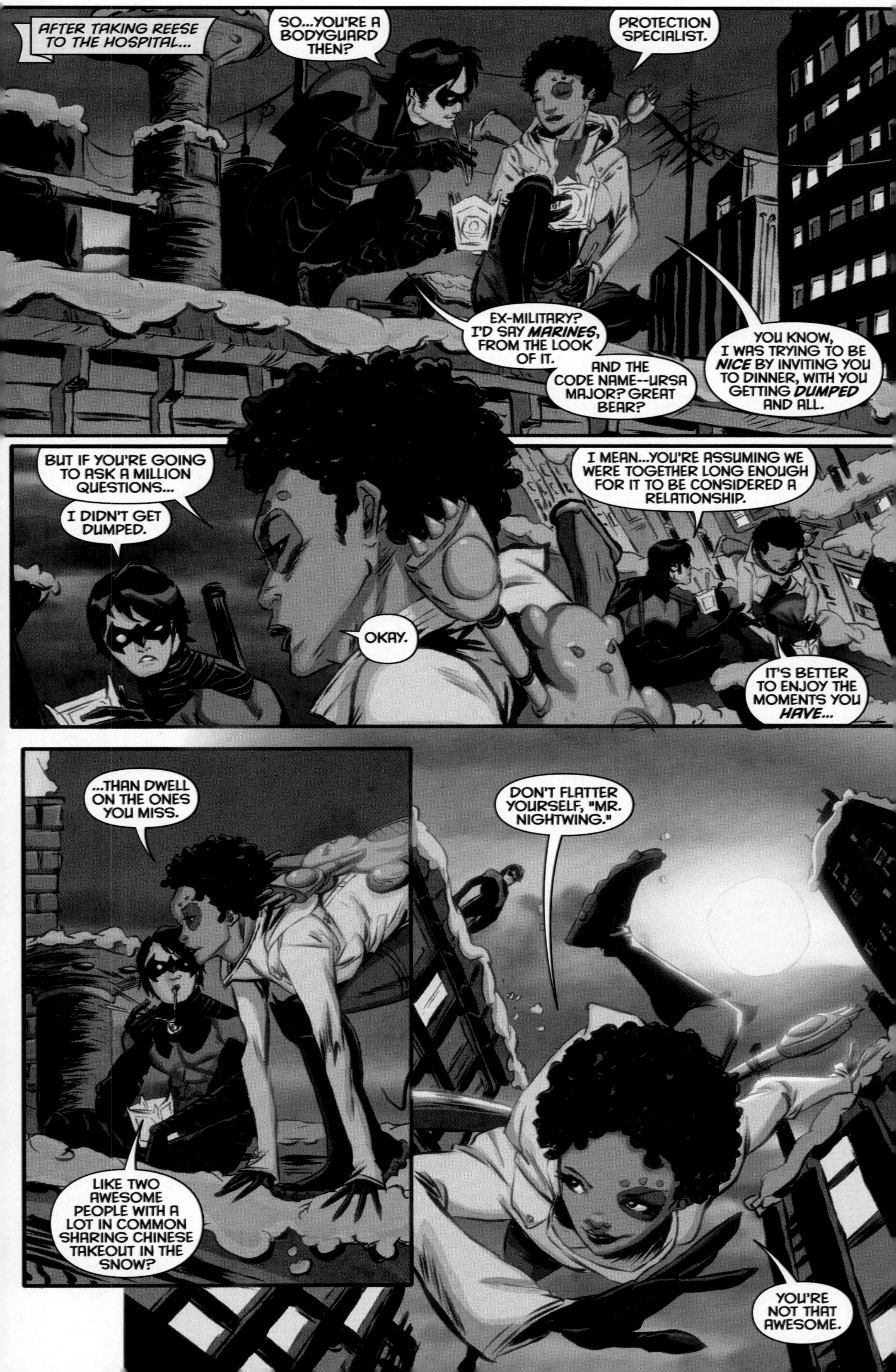

AFTER TAKING REESE TO THE HOSPITAL...
SO...YOU'RE A BODYGUARD THEN?
PROTECTION SPECIALIST.
EX-MILITARY? I'D SAY MARINES, FROM THE LOOK OF IT.
AND THE CODE NAME--URSA MAJOR? GREAT BEAR?
YOU KNOW, I WAS TRYING TO BE NICE BY INVITING YOU TO DINNER, WITH YOU GETTING DUMPED AND ALL.
BUT IF YOU'RE GOING TO ASK A MILLION QUESTIONS...
I DIDN'T GET DUMPED.
OKAY.
I MEAN...YOU'RE ASSUMING WE WERE TOGETHER LONG ENOUGH FOR IT TO BE CONSIDERED A RELATIONSHIP.
IT'S BETTER TO ENJOY THE MOMENTS YOU HAVE...
...THAN DWELL ON THE ONES YOU MISS.
LIKE TWO AWESOME PEOPLE WITH A LOT IN COMMON SHARING CHINESE TAKEOUT IN THE SNOW?
DON'T FLATTER YOURSELF, "MR. NIGHTWING."
YOU'RE NOT THAT AWESOME.

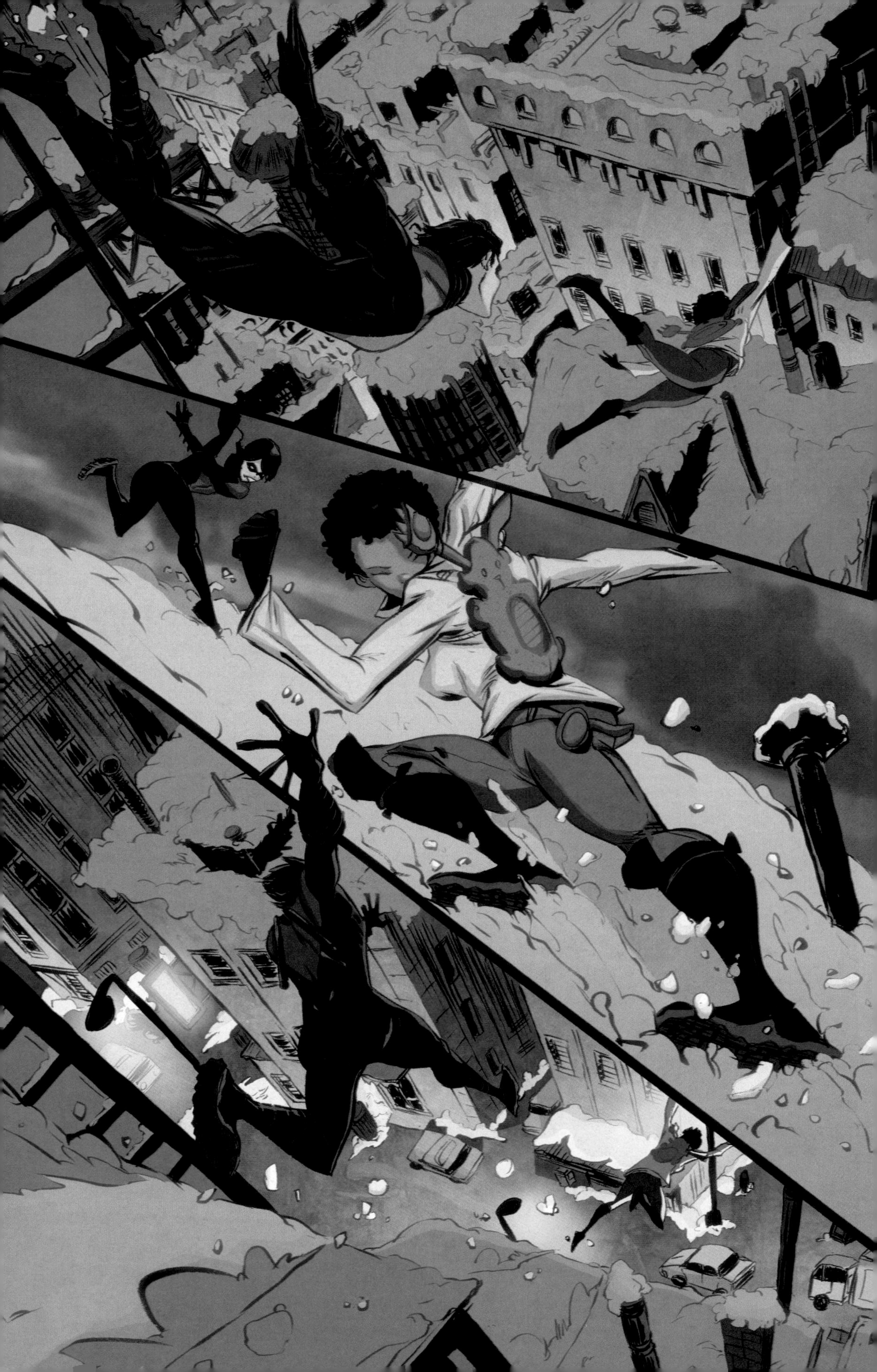

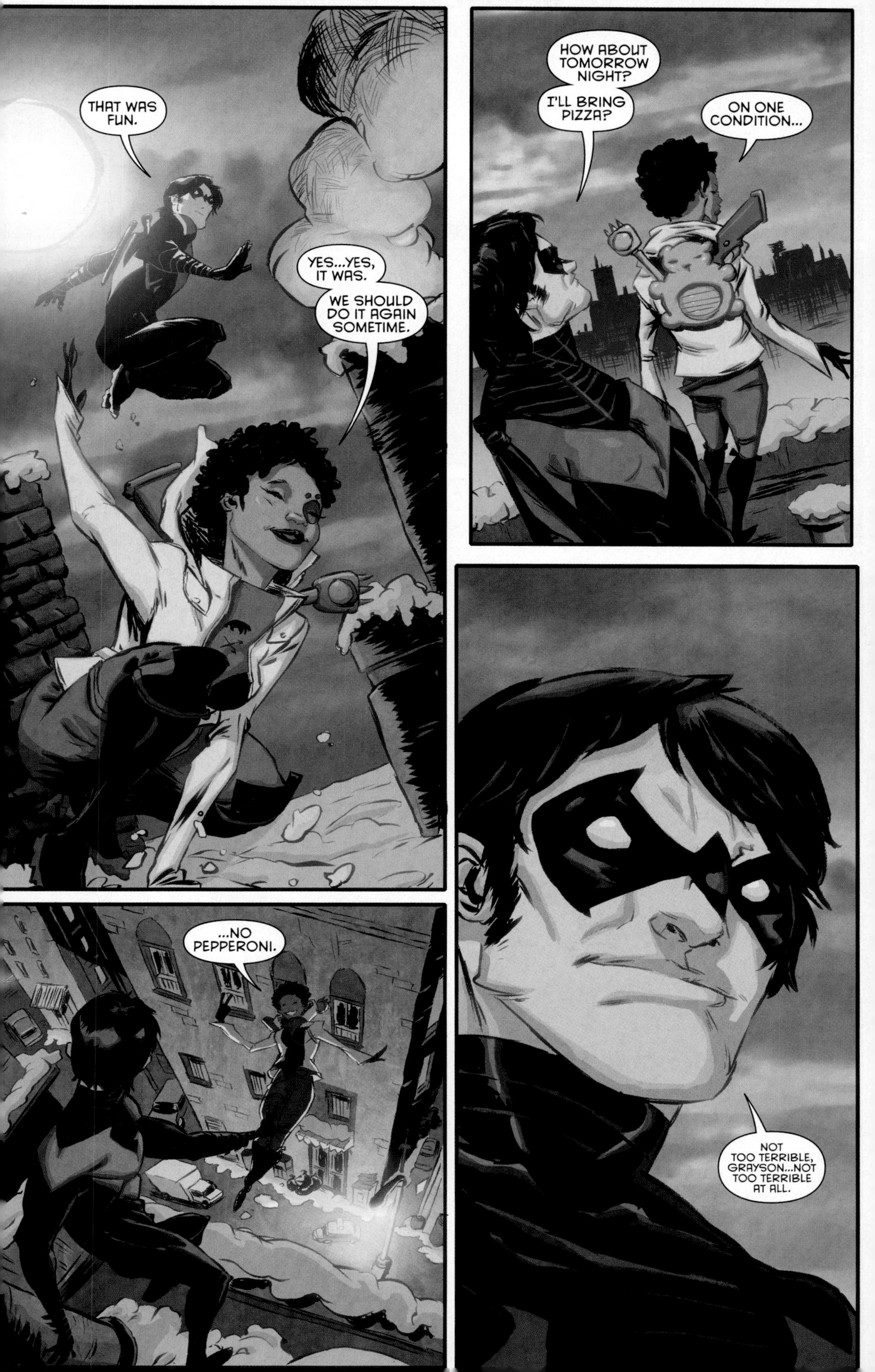
THAT WAS FUN.
YES...YES, IT WAS.
WE SHOULD DO IT AGAIN SOMETIME.
HOW ABOUT TOMORROW NIGHT?
I'LL BRING PIZZA?
ON ONE CONDITION...
...NO PEPPERONI.
NOT TOO TERRIBLE, GRAYSON...NOT TOO TERRIBLE AT ALL.

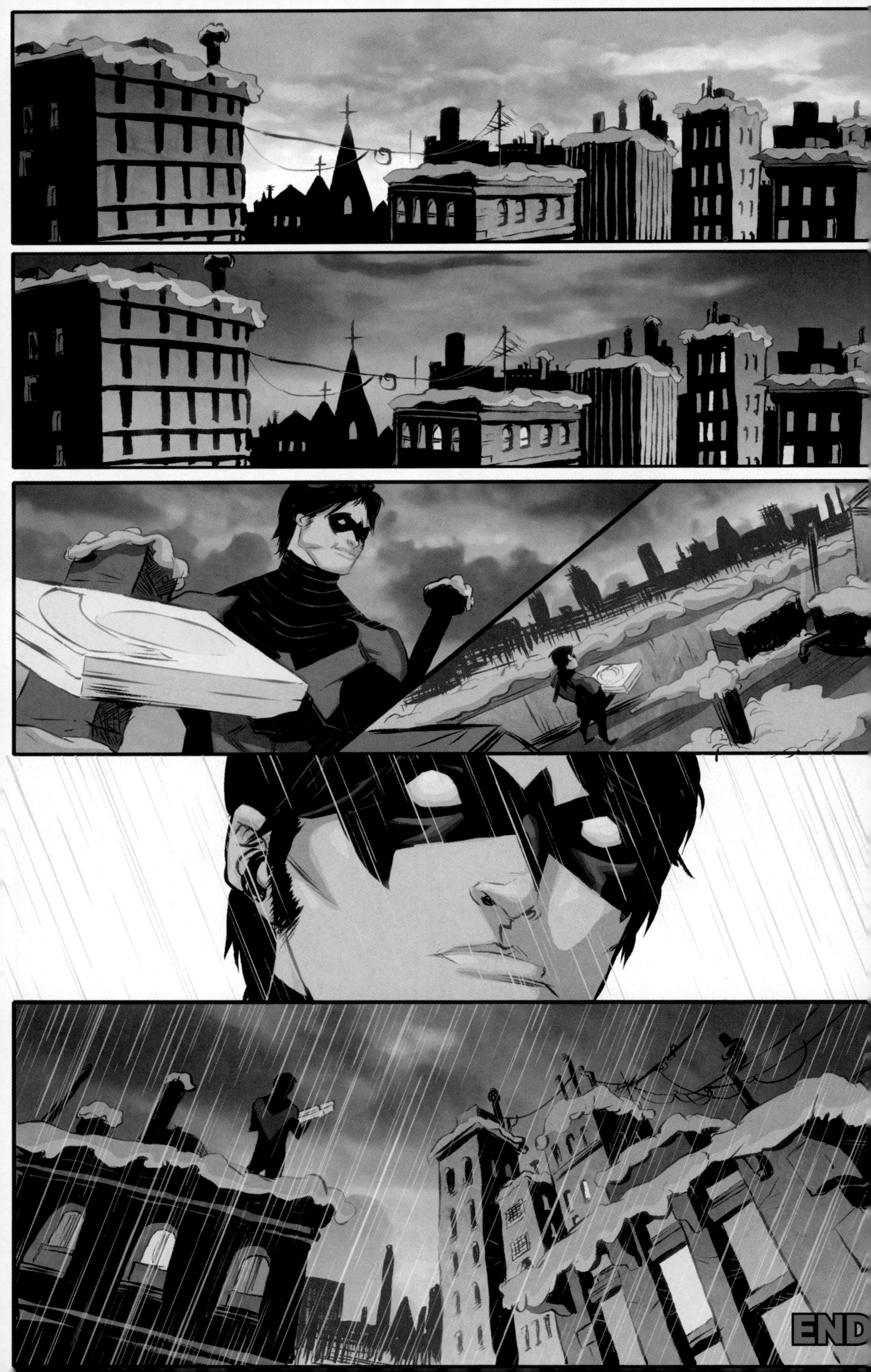
END

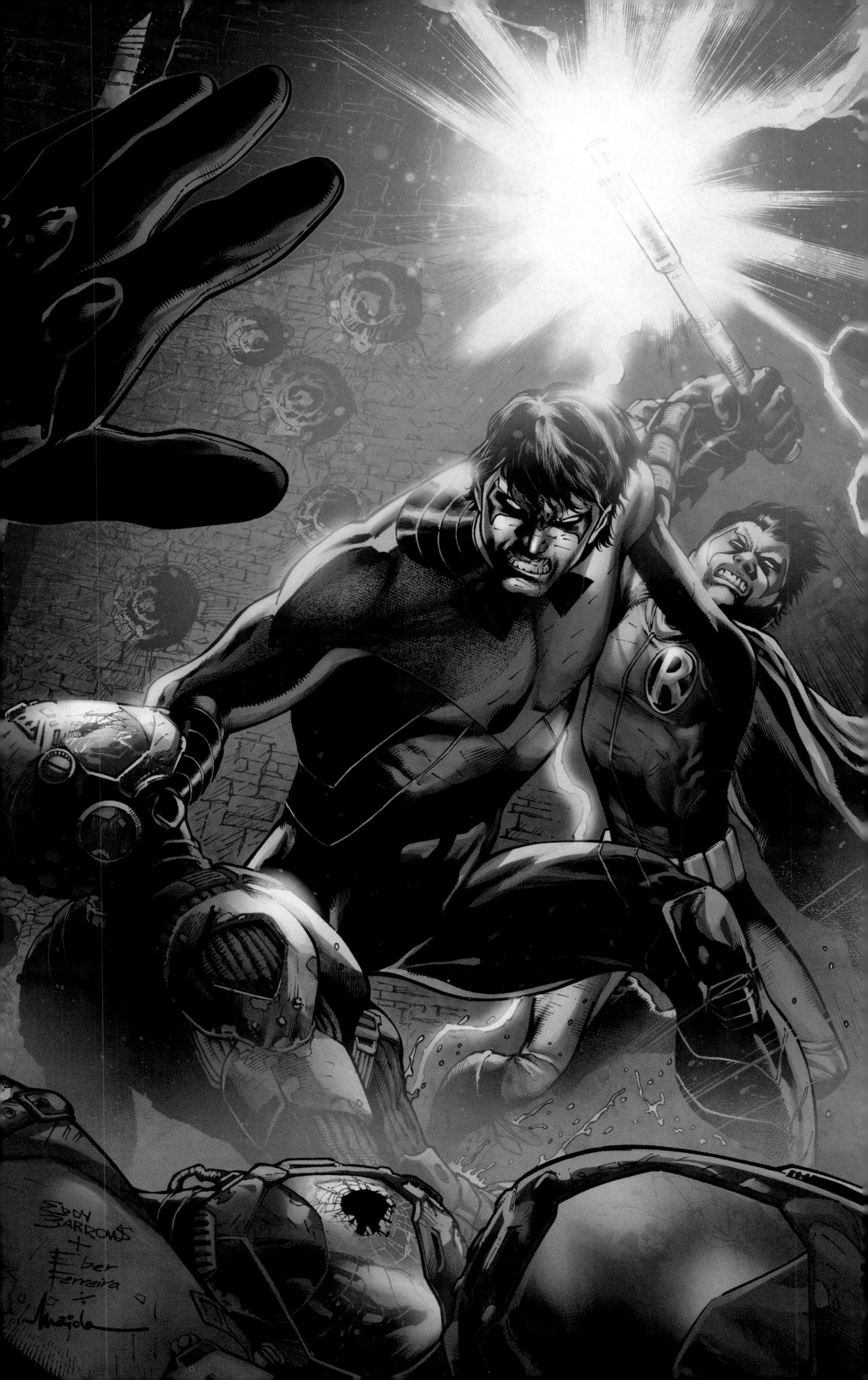
EDDY BARROWS
+
Eber Ferreira

KYLE HIGGINS writer JUAN JOSE RYP penciller ROGER BONET inker cover art by EDDY BARROWS, EBER FERREIRA & MARCELO MAIO

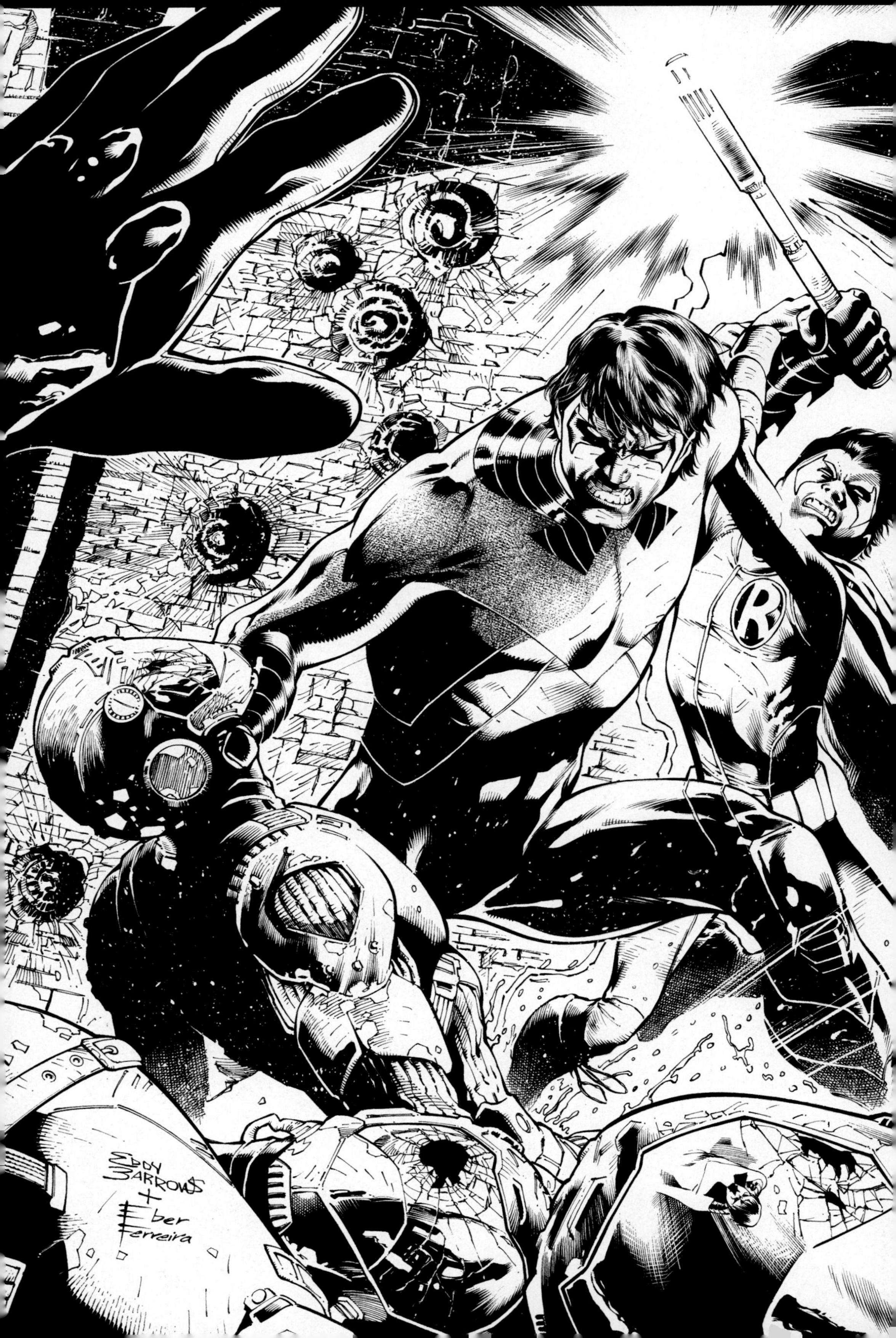
EDDY BARROWS
+
EBER
FERREIRA

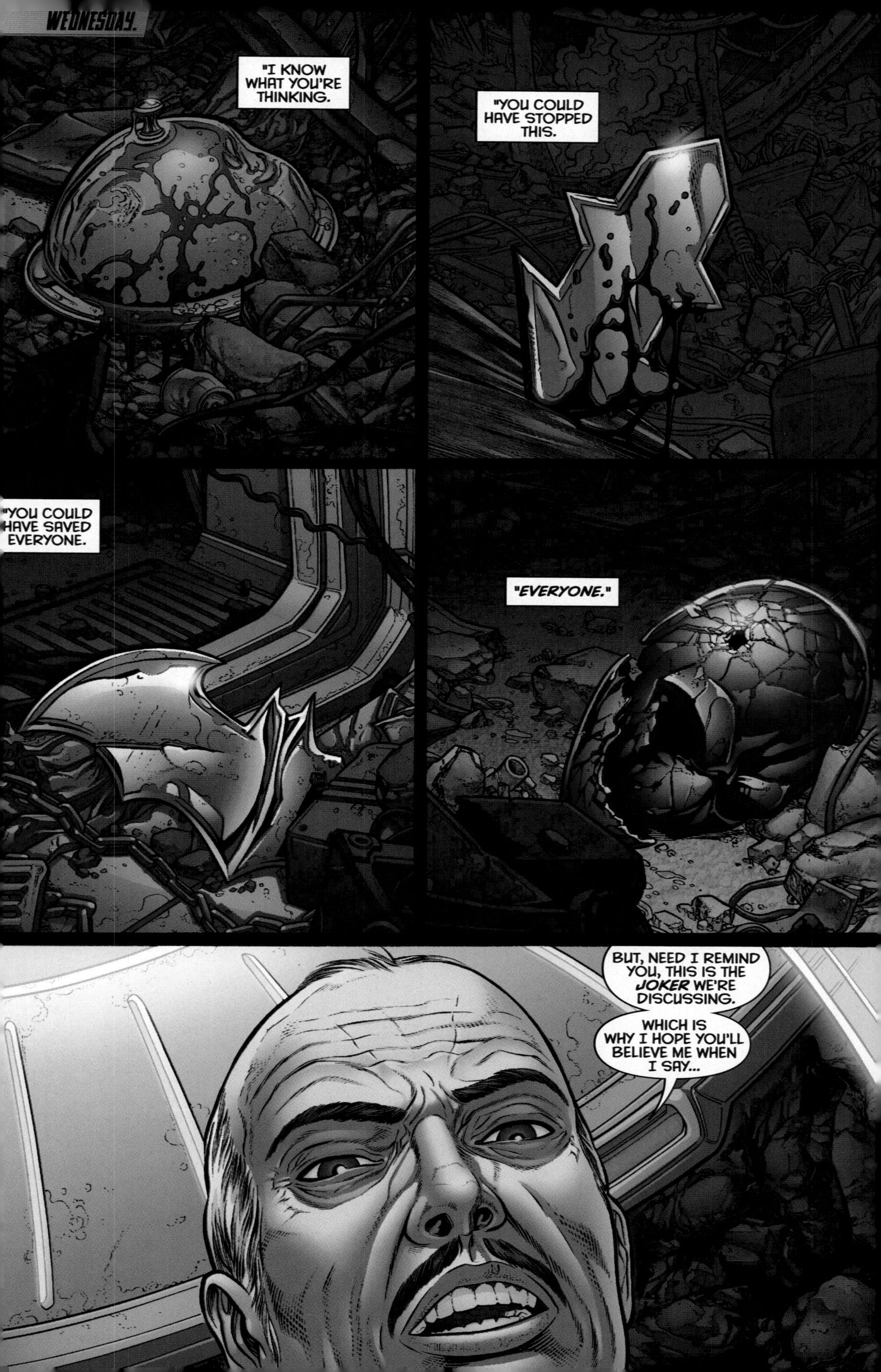
WEDNESDAY.
"I KNOW WHAT YOU'RE THINKING.
"YOU COULD HAVE STOPPED THIS.
"YOU COULD HAVE SAVED EVERYONE.
"EVERYONE."
BUT, NEED I REMIND YOU, THIS IS THE JOKER WE'RE DISCUSSING.
WHICH IS WHY I HOPE YOU'LL BELIEVE ME WHEN I SAY...

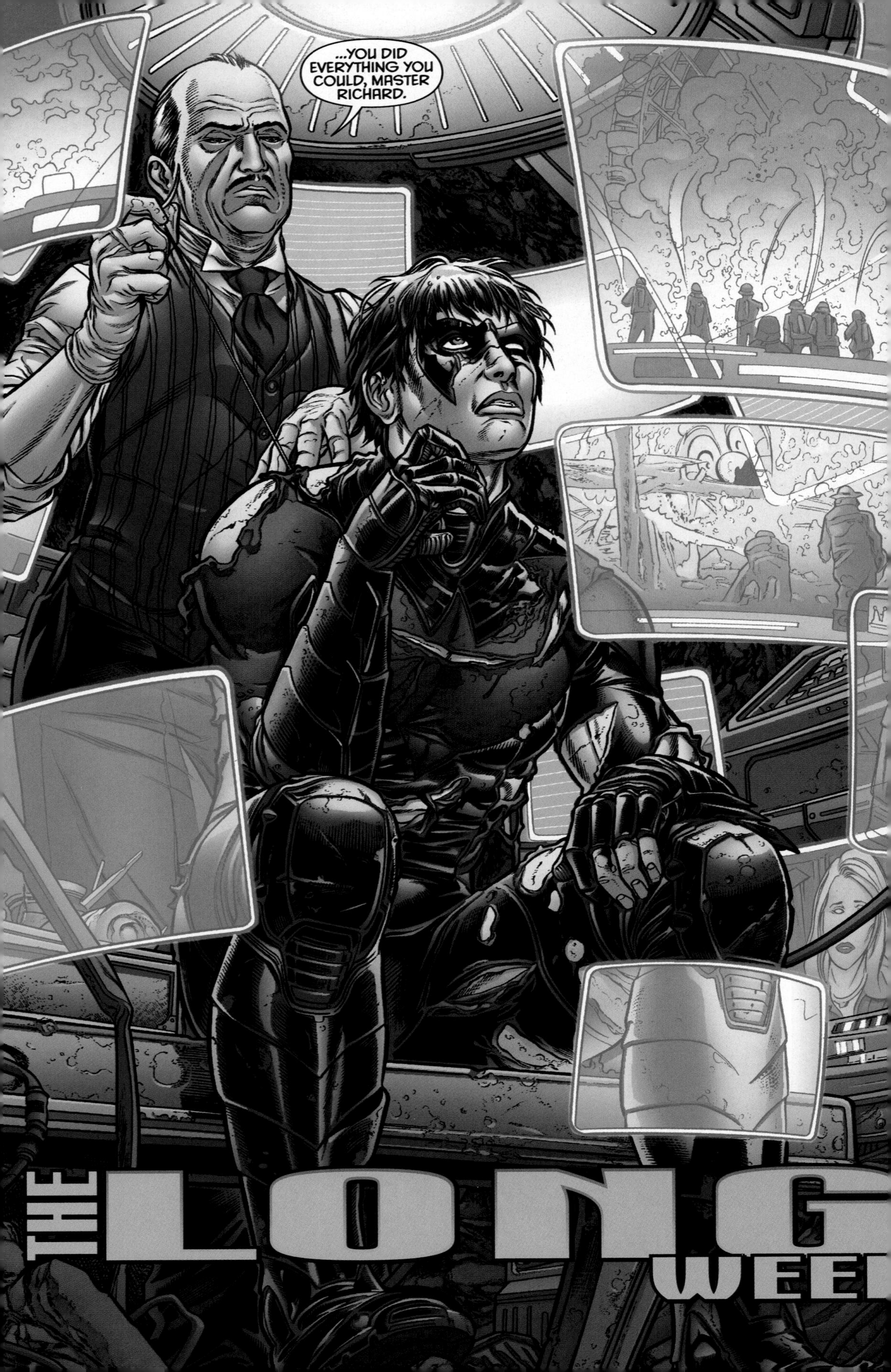
...YOU DID EVERYTHING YOU COULD, MASTER RICHARD.
THE LONG WEE

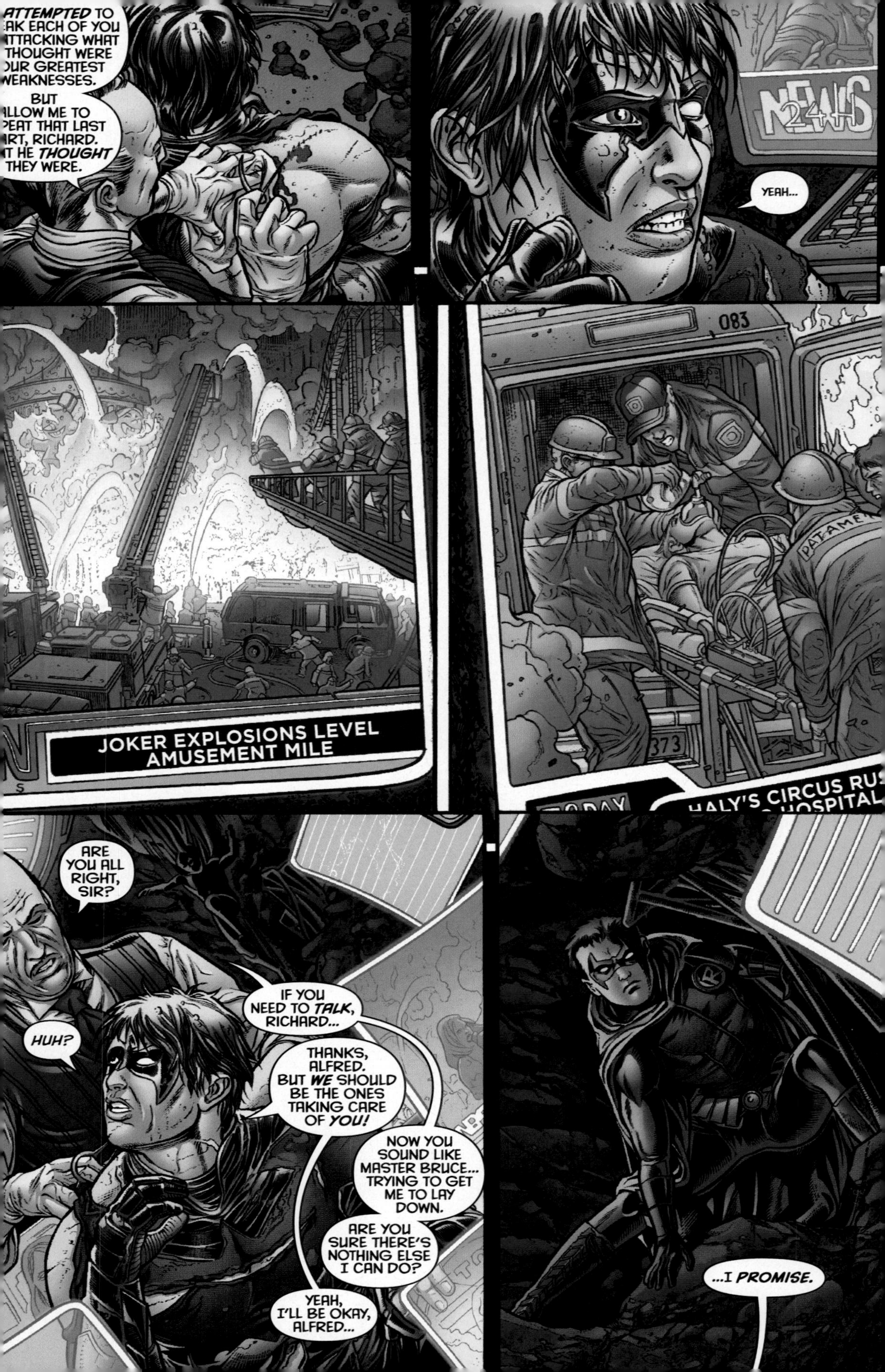

ATTEMPTED TO AK EACH OF YOU TTACKING WHAT THOUGHT WERE UR GREATEST WEAKNESSES.
BUT LLOW ME TO PEAT THAT LAST RT, RICHARD. T HE THOUGHT THEY WERE.
NEWS 24H
YEAH...
JOKER EXPLOSIONS LEVEL AMUSEMENT MILE
083
373
HALY'S CIRCUS RU HOSPITAL
ARE YOU ALL RIGHT, SIR?
HUH?
IF YOU NEED TO TALK, RICHARD...
THANKS, ALFRED. BUT WE SHOULD BE THE ONES TAKING CARE OF YOU!
NOW YOU SOUND LIKE MASTER BRUCE... TRYING TO GET ME TO LAY DOWN.
ARE YOU SURE THERE'S NOTHING ELSE I CAN DO?
YEAH, I'LL BE OKAY, ALFRED...
...I PROMISE.

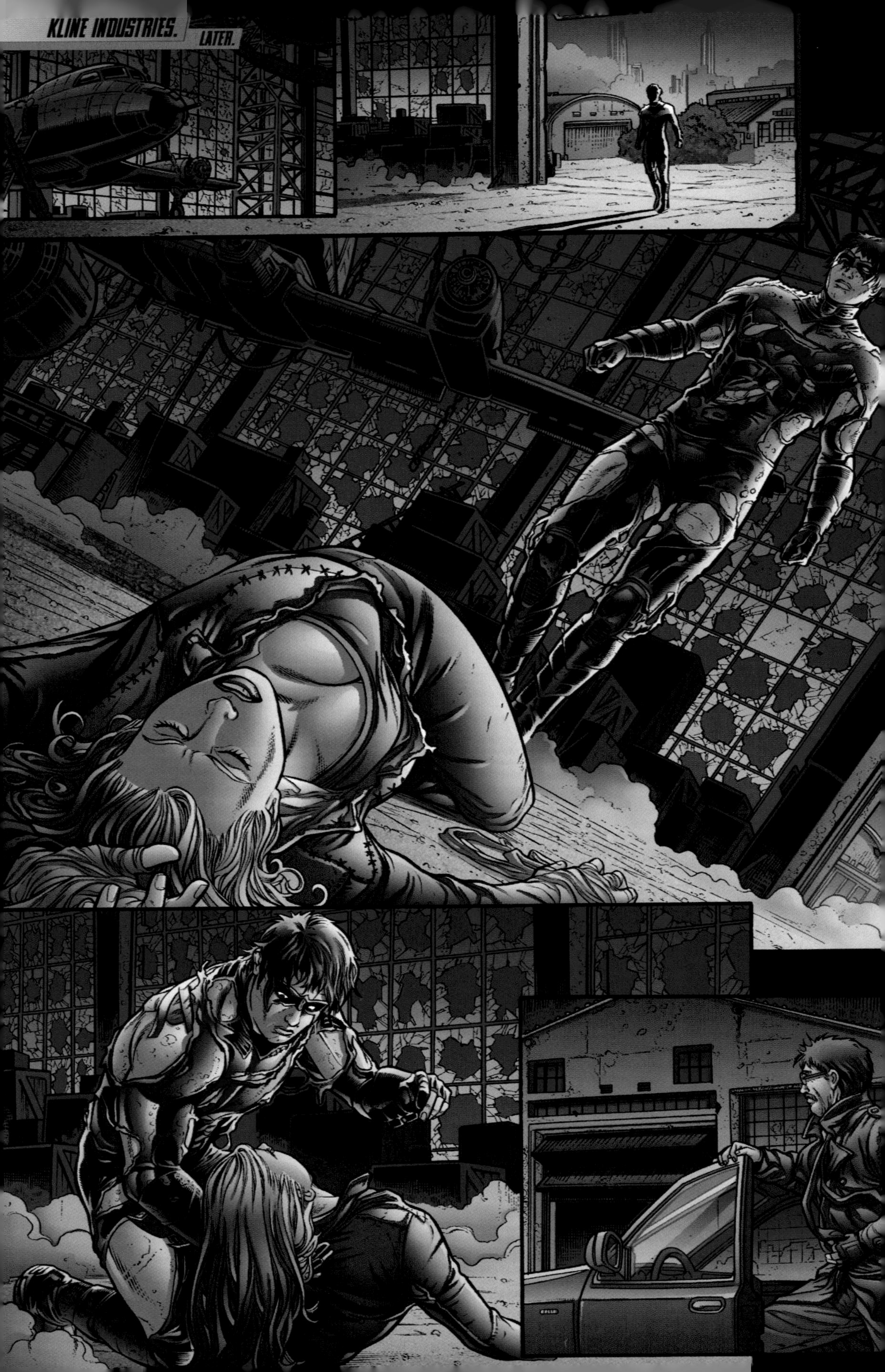
KLINE INDUSTRIES.
LATER.

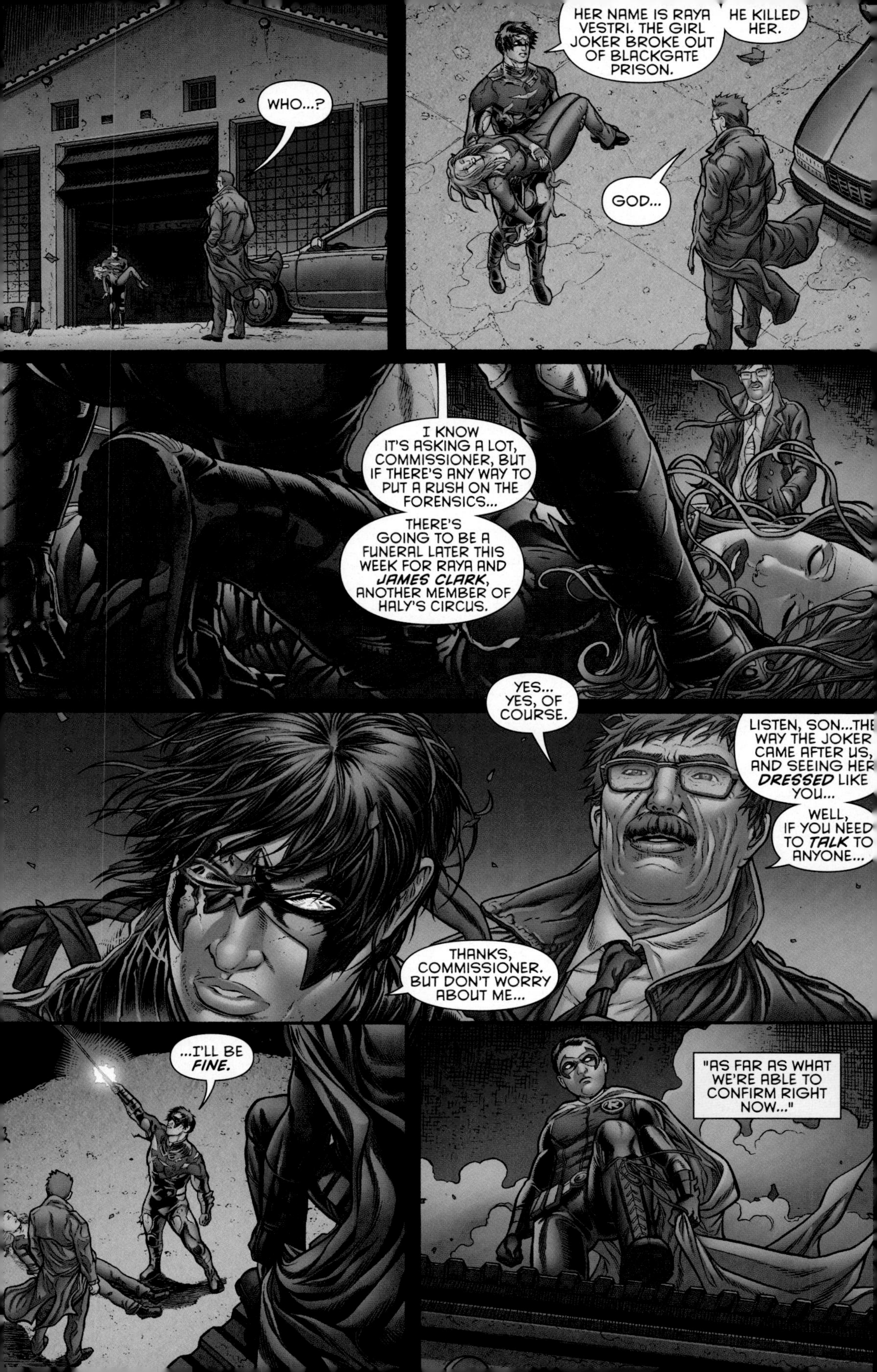
WHO...?
HER NAME IS RAYA VESTRI. THE GIRL JOKER BROKE OUT OF BLACKGATE PRISON.
HE KILLED HER.
GOD...
I KNOW IT'S ASKING A LOT, COMMISSIONER, BUT IF THERE'S ANY WAY TO PUT A RUSH ON THE FORENSICS...
THERE'S GOING TO BE A FUNERAL LATER THIS WEEK FOR RAYA AND JAMES CLARK, ANOTHER MEMBER OF HALY'S CIRCUS.
YES... YES, OF COURSE.
LISTEN, SON...THE WAY THE JOKER CAME AFTER US, AND SEEING HER DRESSED LIKE YOU...
WELL, IF YOU NEED TO TALK TO ANYONE...
THANKS, COMMISSIONER. BUT DON'T WORRY ABOUT ME...
...I'LL BE FINE.
"AS FAR AS WHAT WE'RE ABLE TO CONFIRM RIGHT NOW..."

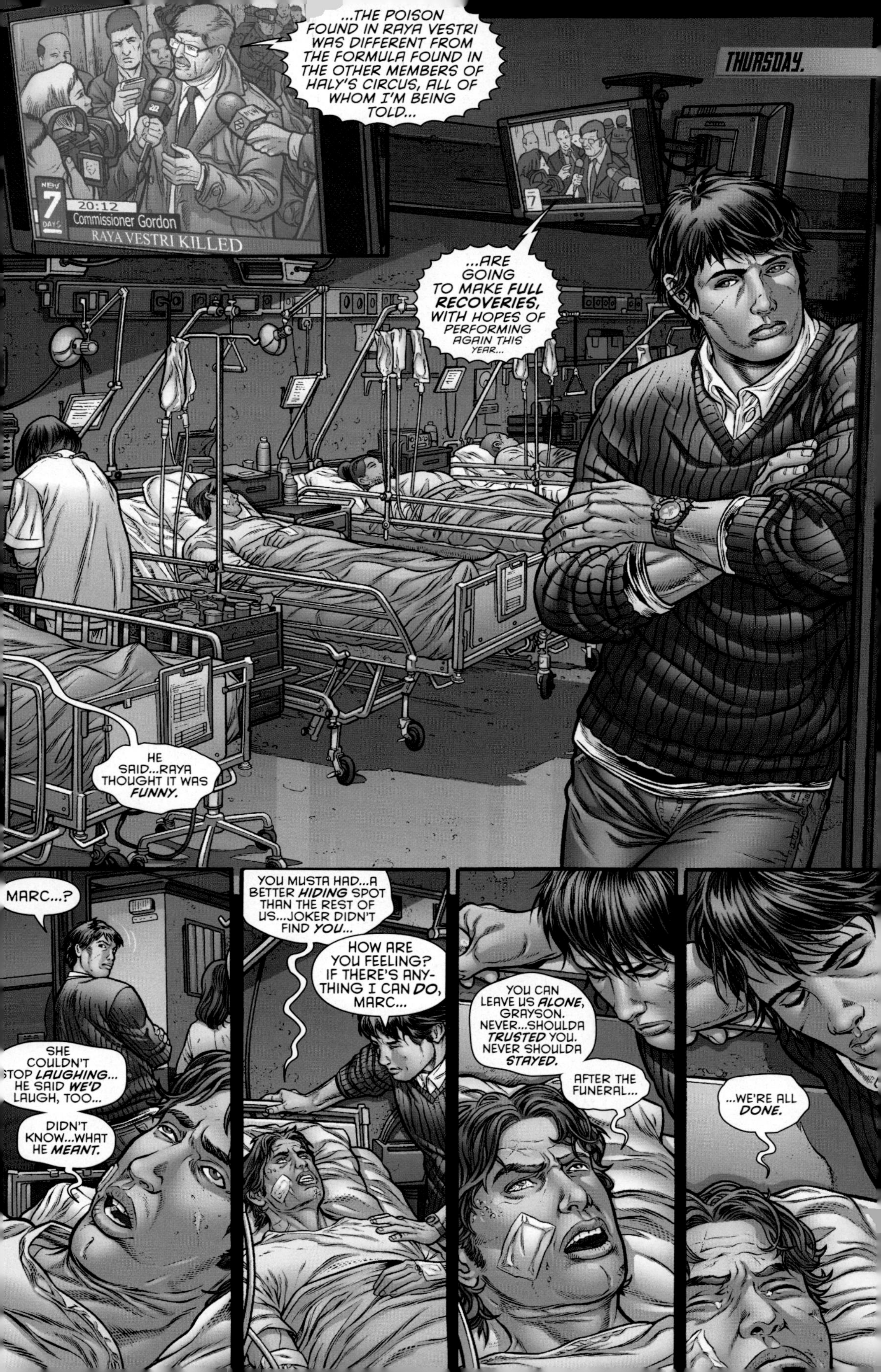
THURSDAY.
...THE POISON FOUND IN RAYA VESTRI WAS DIFFERENT FROM THE FORMULA FOUND IN THE OTHER MEMBERS OF HALY'S CIRCUS, ALL OF WHOM I'M BEING TOLD...
NEWS 7 DAYS
20:12
Commissioner Gordon
RAYA VESTRI KILLED
...ARE GOING TO MAKE FULL RECOVERIES, WITH HOPES OF PERFORMING AGAIN THIS YEAR...
HE SAID...RAYA THOUGHT IT WAS FUNNY.
MARC...?
SHE COULDN'T STOP LAUGHING... HE SAID WE'D LAUGH, TOO...
DIDN'T KNOW...WHAT HE MEANT.
YOU MUSTA HAD...A BETTER HIDING SPOT THAN THE REST OF US...JOKER DIDN'T FIND YOU...
HOW ARE YOU FEELING? IF THERE'S ANYTHING I CAN DO, MARC...
YOU CAN LEAVE US ALONE, GRAYSON. NEVER...SHOULDA TRUSTED YOU. NEVER SHOULDA STAYED.
AFTER THE FUNERAL...
...WE'RE ALL DONE.

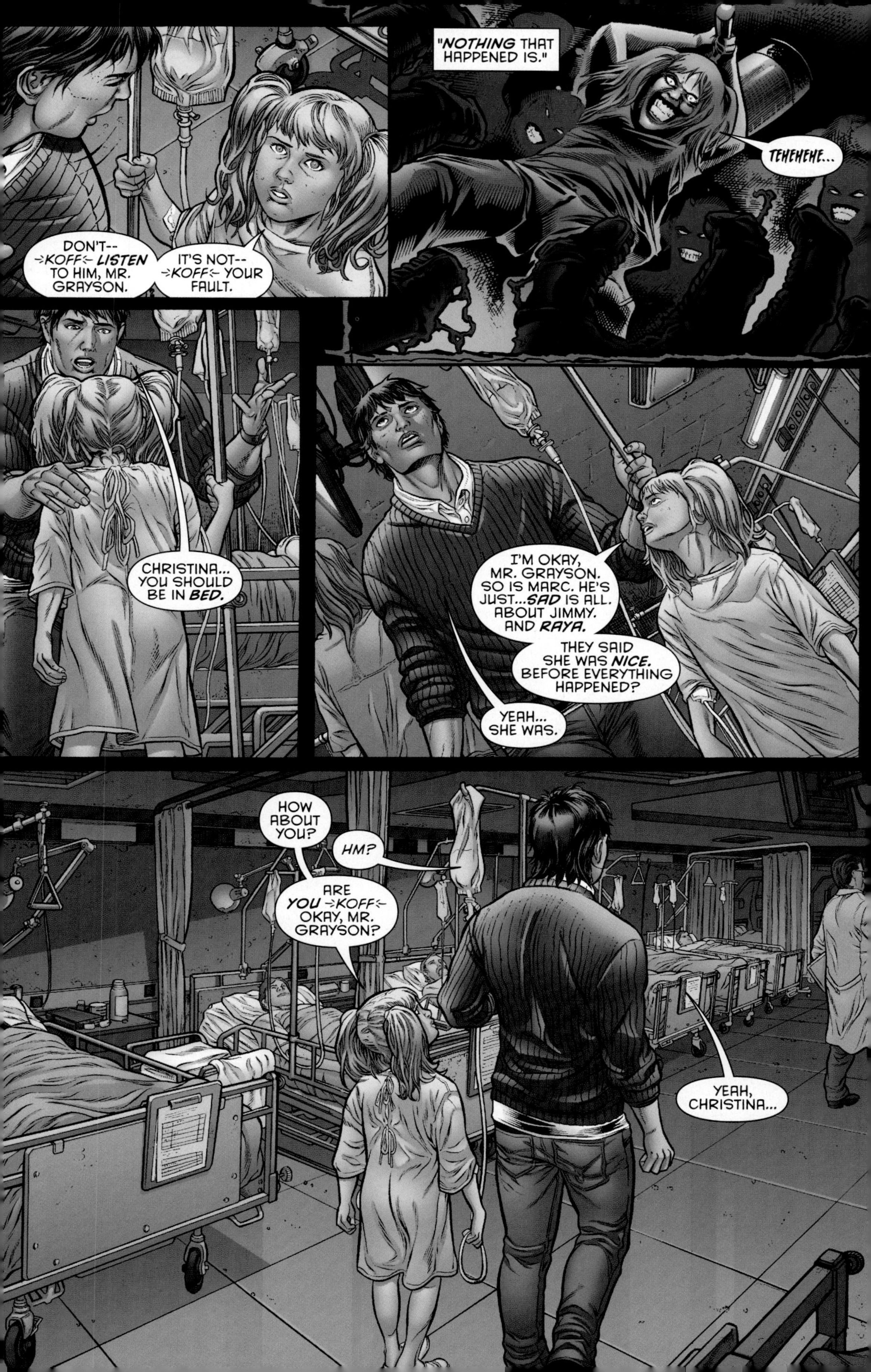
DON'T-- ⇒KOFF⇐ LISTEN TO HIM, MR. GRAYSON.
IT'S NOT-- ⇒KOFF⇐ YOUR FAULT.
"NOTHING THAT HAPPENED IS."
TEHEHEHE...
CHRISTINA... YOU SHOULD BE IN BED.
I'M OKAY, MR. GRAYSON. SO IS MARC. HE'S JUST...SAD IS ALL. ABOUT JIMMY. AND RAYA.
THEY SAID SHE WAS NICE. BEFORE EVERYTHING HAPPENED?
YEAH... SHE WAS.
HOW ABOUT YOU?
HM?
ARE YOU ⇒KOFF⇐ OKAY, MR. GRAYSON?
YEAH, CHRISTINA...

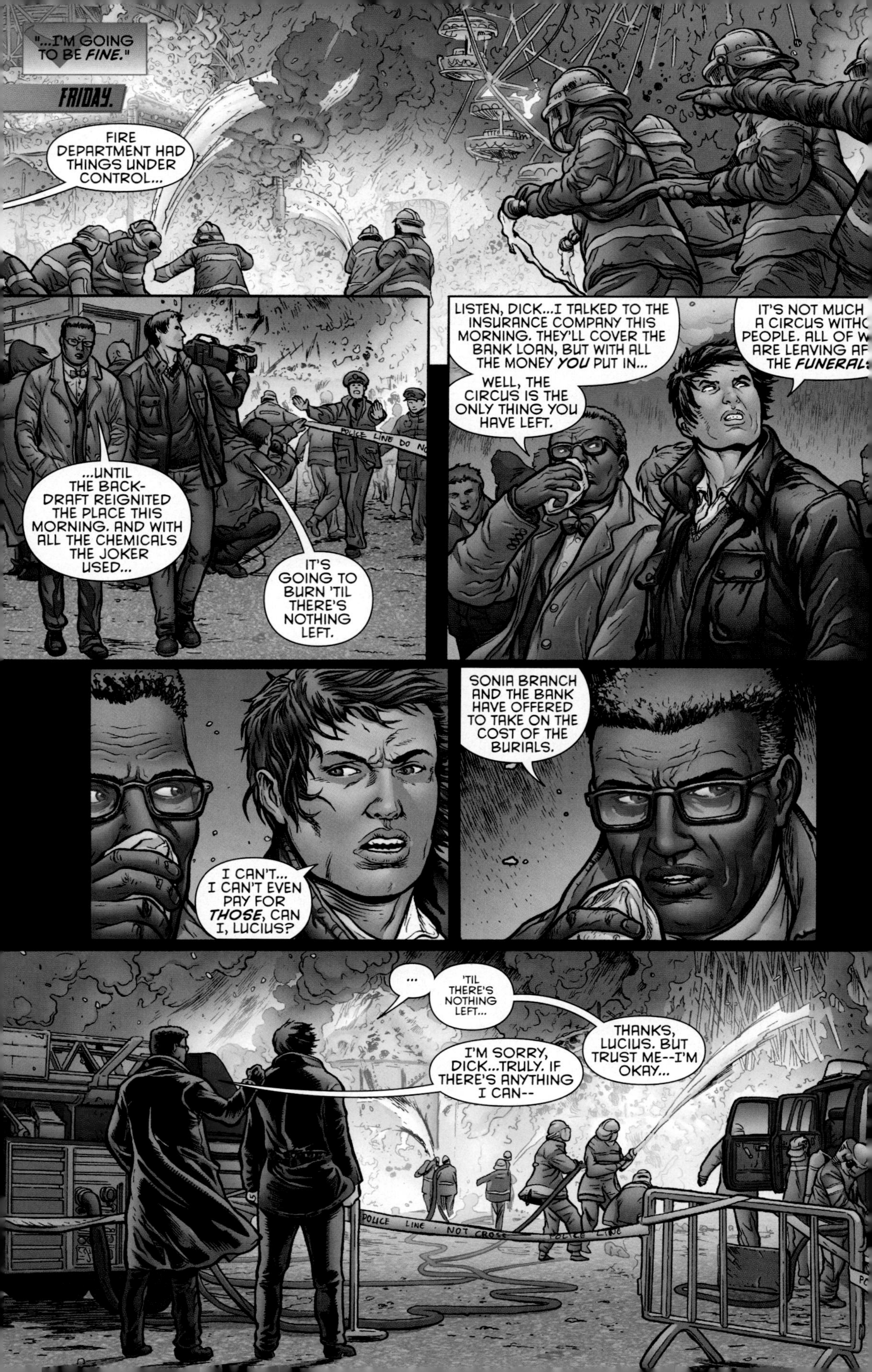
"...I'M GOING TO BE FINE."
FRIDAY.
FIRE DEPARTMENT HAD THINGS UNDER CONTROL...
...UNTIL THE BACK-DRAFT REIGNITED THE PLACE THIS MORNING. AND WITH ALL THE CHEMICALS THE JOKER USED...
IT'S GOING TO BURN 'TIL THERE'S NOTHING LEFT.
POLICE LINE DO NO
LISTEN, DICK...I TALKED TO THE INSURANCE COMPANY THIS MORNING. THEY'LL COVER THE BANK LOAN, BUT WITH ALL THE MONEY YOU PUT IN...
WELL, THE CIRCUS IS THE ONLY THING YOU HAVE LEFT.
IT'S NOT MUCH A CIRCUS WITHO PEOPLE. ALL OF W ARE LEAVING AF THE FUNERAL
SONIA BRANCH AND THE BANK HAVE OFFERED TO TAKE ON THE COST OF THE BURIALS.
I CAN'T... I CAN'T EVEN PAY FOR THOSE, CAN I, LUCIUS?
...
'TIL THERE'S NOTHING LEFT...
I'M SORRY, DICK...TRULY. IF THERE'S ANYTHING I CAN--
THANKS, LUCIUS. BUT TRUST ME--I'M OKAY...
POLICE LINE NOT CROSS POLICE LINE

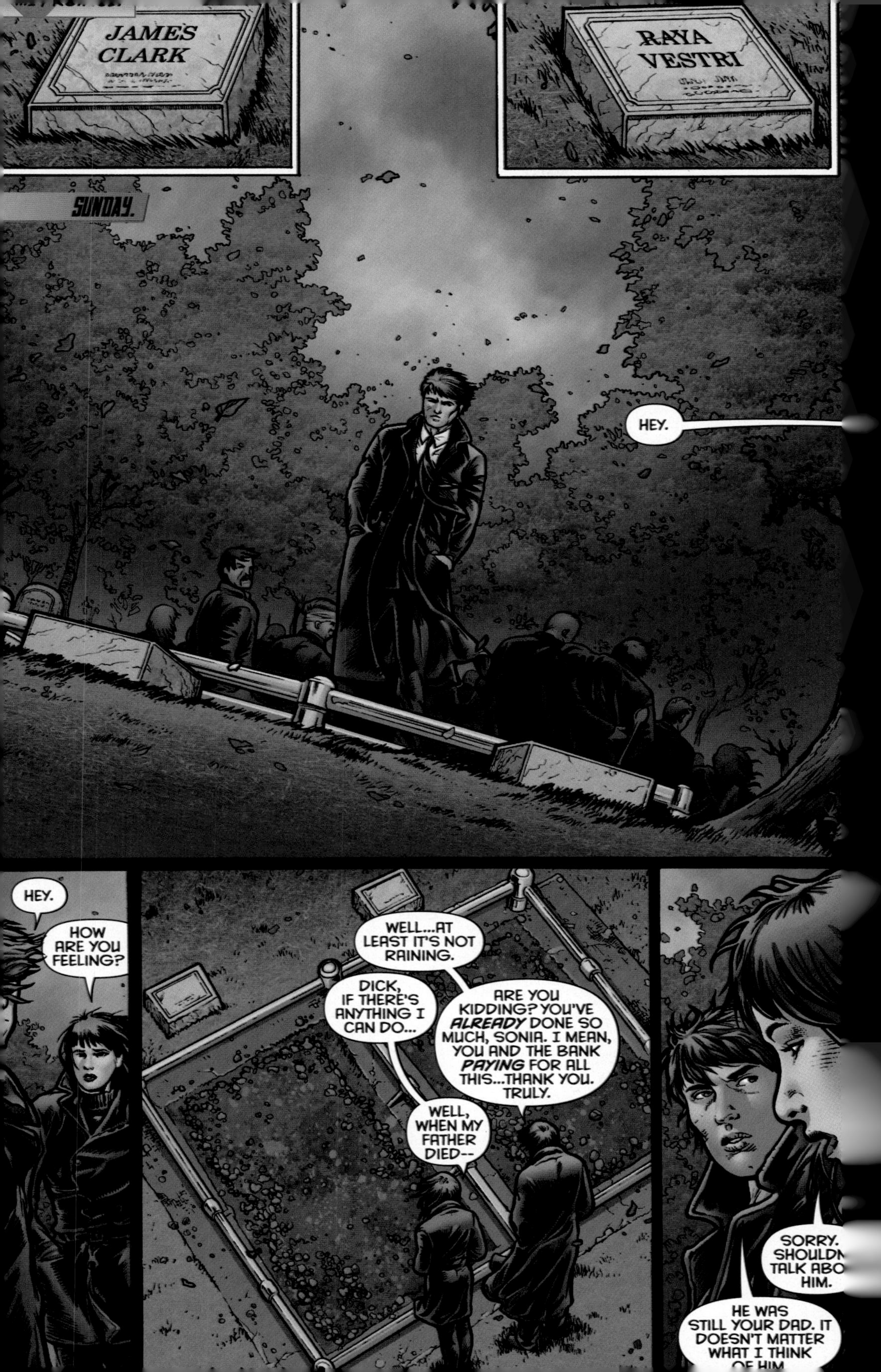
JAMES CLARK
RAYA VESTRI
SUNDAY.
HEY.
HEY.
HOW ARE YOU FEELING?
WELL...AT LEAST IT'S NOT RAINING.
DICK, IF THERE'S ANYTHING I CAN DO...
ARE YOU KIDDING? YOU'VE ALREADY DONE SO MUCH, SONIA. I MEAN, YOU AND THE BANK PAYING FOR ALL THIS...THANK YOU. TRULY.
WELL, WHEN MY FATHER DIED--
SORRY. SHOULDN TALK ABO HIM.
HE WAS STILL YOUR DAD. IT DOESN'T MATTER WHAT I THINK

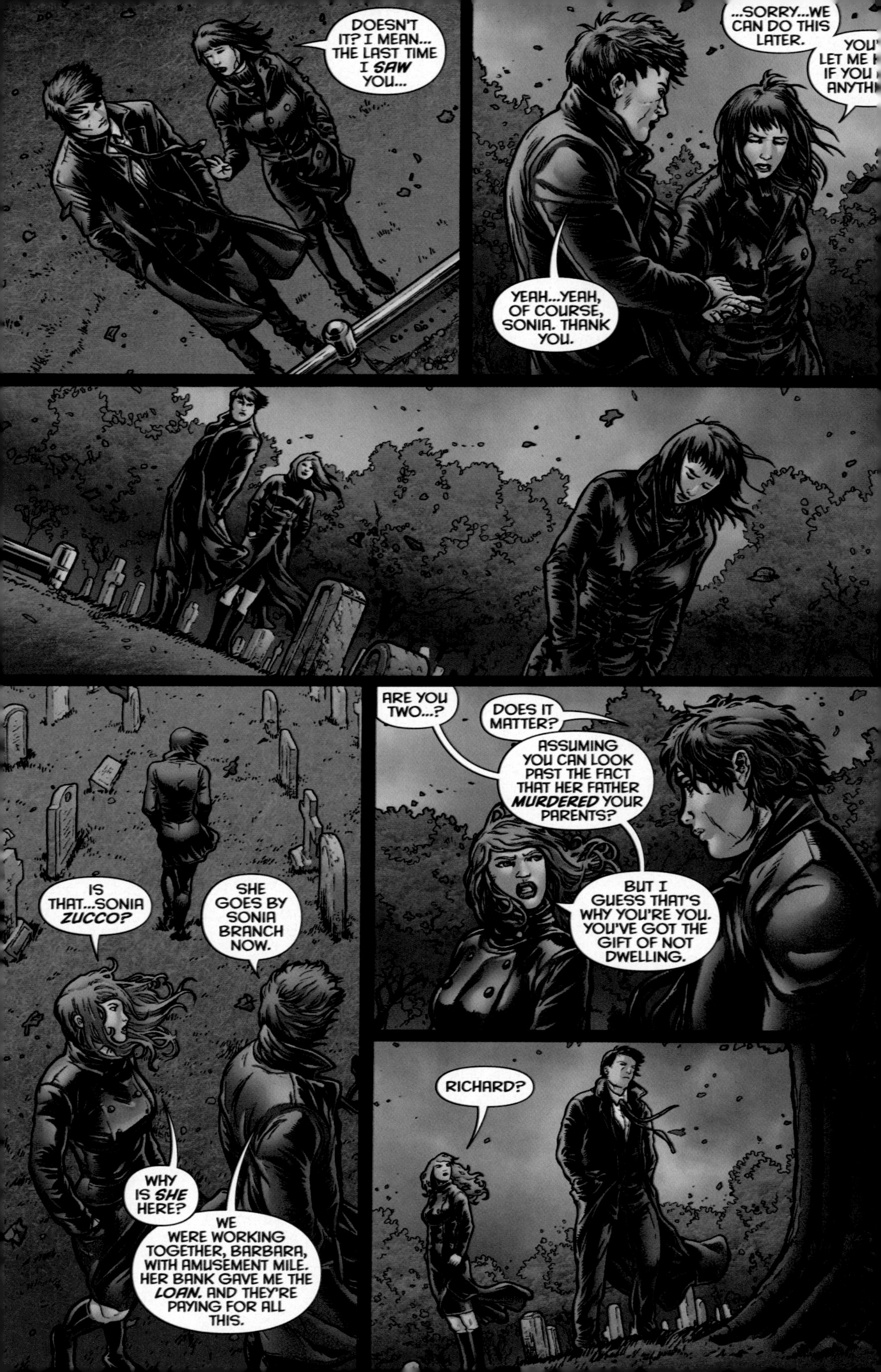
DOESN'T IT? I MEAN... THE LAST TIME I SAW YOU...
...SORRY...WE CAN DO THIS LATER.
YEAH...YEAH, OF COURSE, SONIA. THANK YOU.
IS THAT...SONIA ZUCCO?
SHE GOES BY SONIA BRANCH NOW.
WHY IS SHE HERE?
WE WERE WORKING TOGETHER, BARBARA, WITH AMUSEMENT MILE. HER BANK GAVE ME THE LOAN. AND THEY'RE PAYING FOR ALL THIS.
ARE YOU TWO...?
DOES IT MATTER?
ASSUMING YOU CAN LOOK PAST THE FACT THAT HER FATHER MURDERED YOUR PARENTS?
BUT I GUESS THAT'S WHY YOU'RE YOU. YOU'VE GOT THE GIFT OF NOT DWELLING.
RICHARD?

"YOU PUT YOUR TRUST IN PEOPLE, AND PEOPLE WILL ALWAYS LET YOU DOWN."

IT'S WHAT THE JOKER SAID ABOUT ME. ABOUT WHAT MADE ME *WEAK*.

YOU KNOW, WHEN I SAW THE NEWS REPORT THAT THE CIRCUS WAS STILL ALIVE...I DIDN'T BELIEVE IT.

IT DIDN'T MAKE ANY *SENSE*.

WHY WOULD HE LET THEM *LIVE*?

IS IT SELFISH TO THINK IT COULD HAVE BEEN FOR *THIS*?

SO IN CASE *I* MADE IT OUT ALIVE... I COULD SEE THEM *LEAVE* ME?

IT'S [GO]ING TO [B]E OKAY, [RI]CHARD...

I *AM* OKAY, BABS...

...I *AM* OKAY.

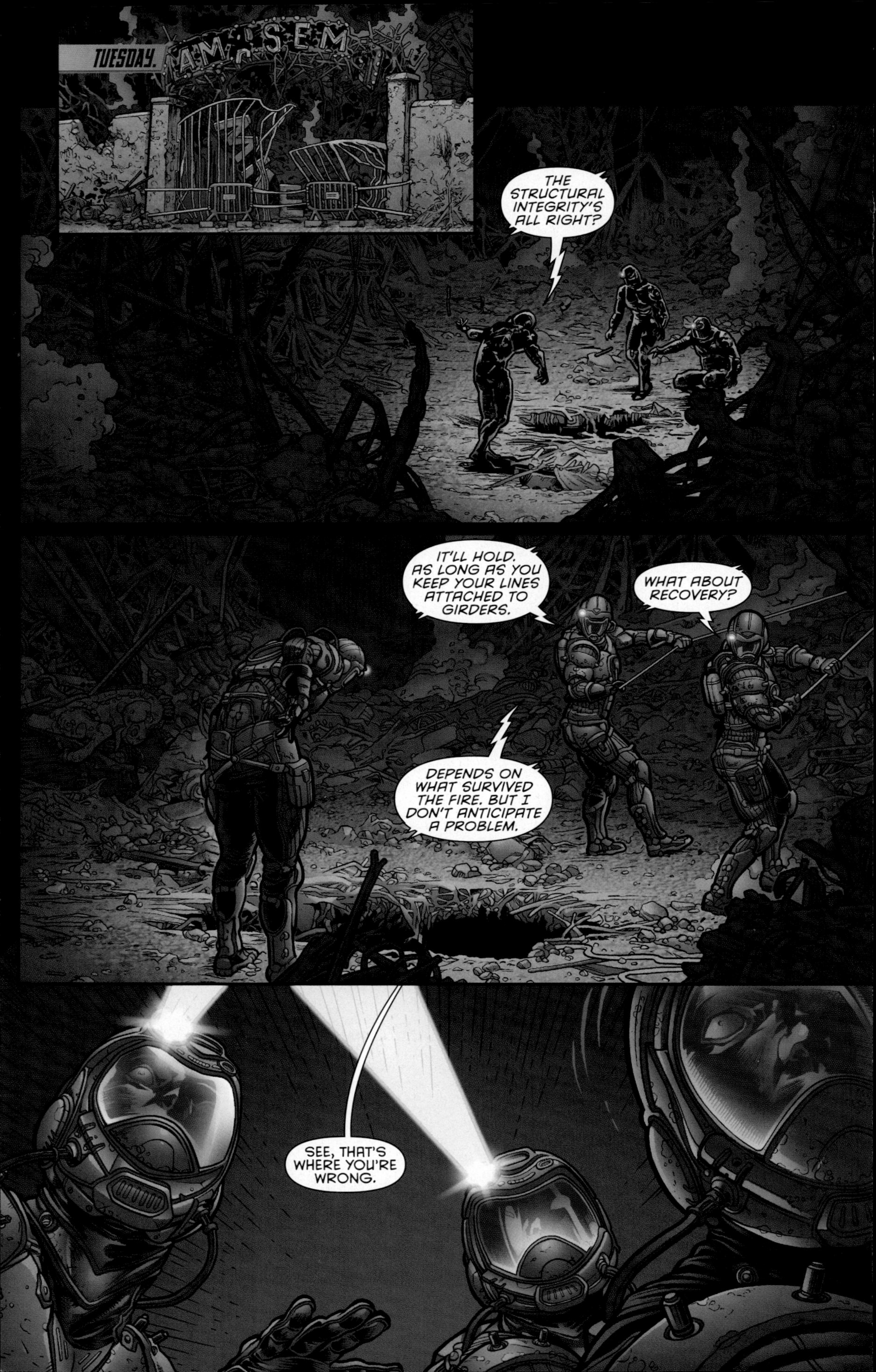
TUESDAY.
THE STRUCTURAL INTEGRITY'S ALL RIGHT?
IT'LL HOLD. AS LONG AS YOU KEEP YOUR LINES ATTACHED TO GIRDERS.
WHAT ABOUT RECOVERY?
DEPENDS ON WHAT SURVIVED THE FIRE. BUT I DON'T ANTICIPATE A PROBLEM.
SEE, THAT'S WHERE YOU'RE WRONG.

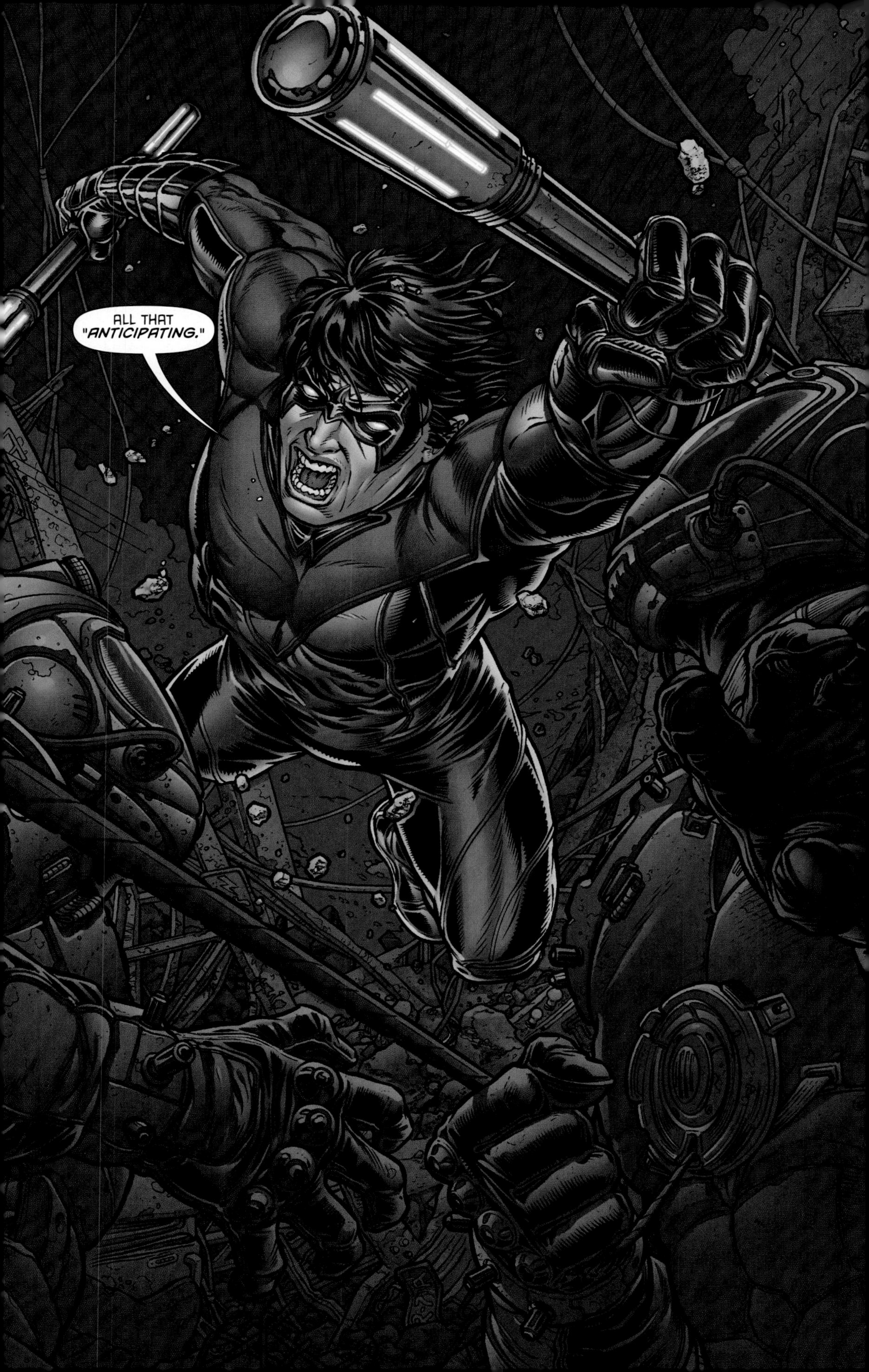
ALL THAT "ANTICIPATING."

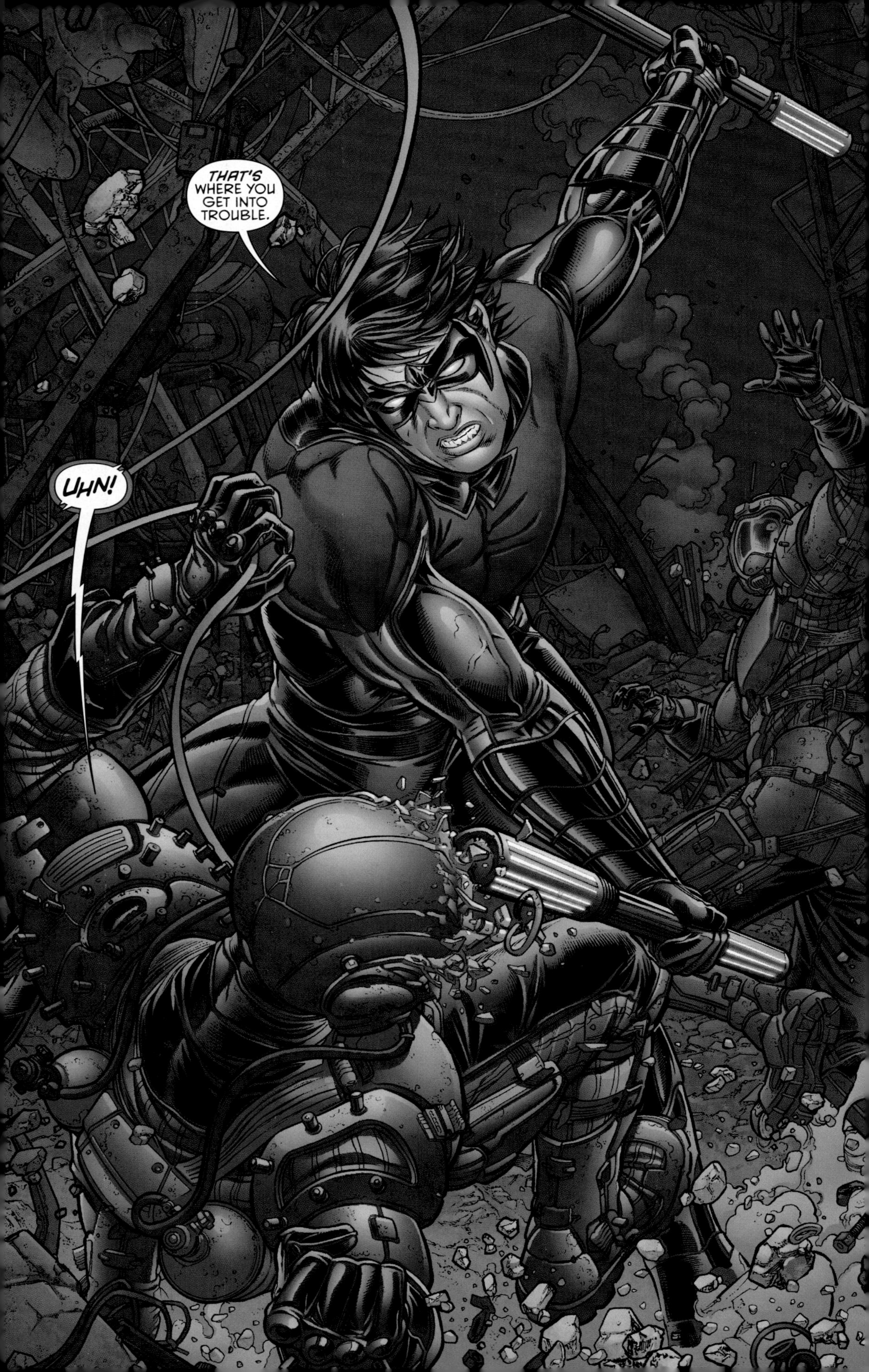
THAT'S WHERE YOU GET INTO TROUBLE.
UHN!

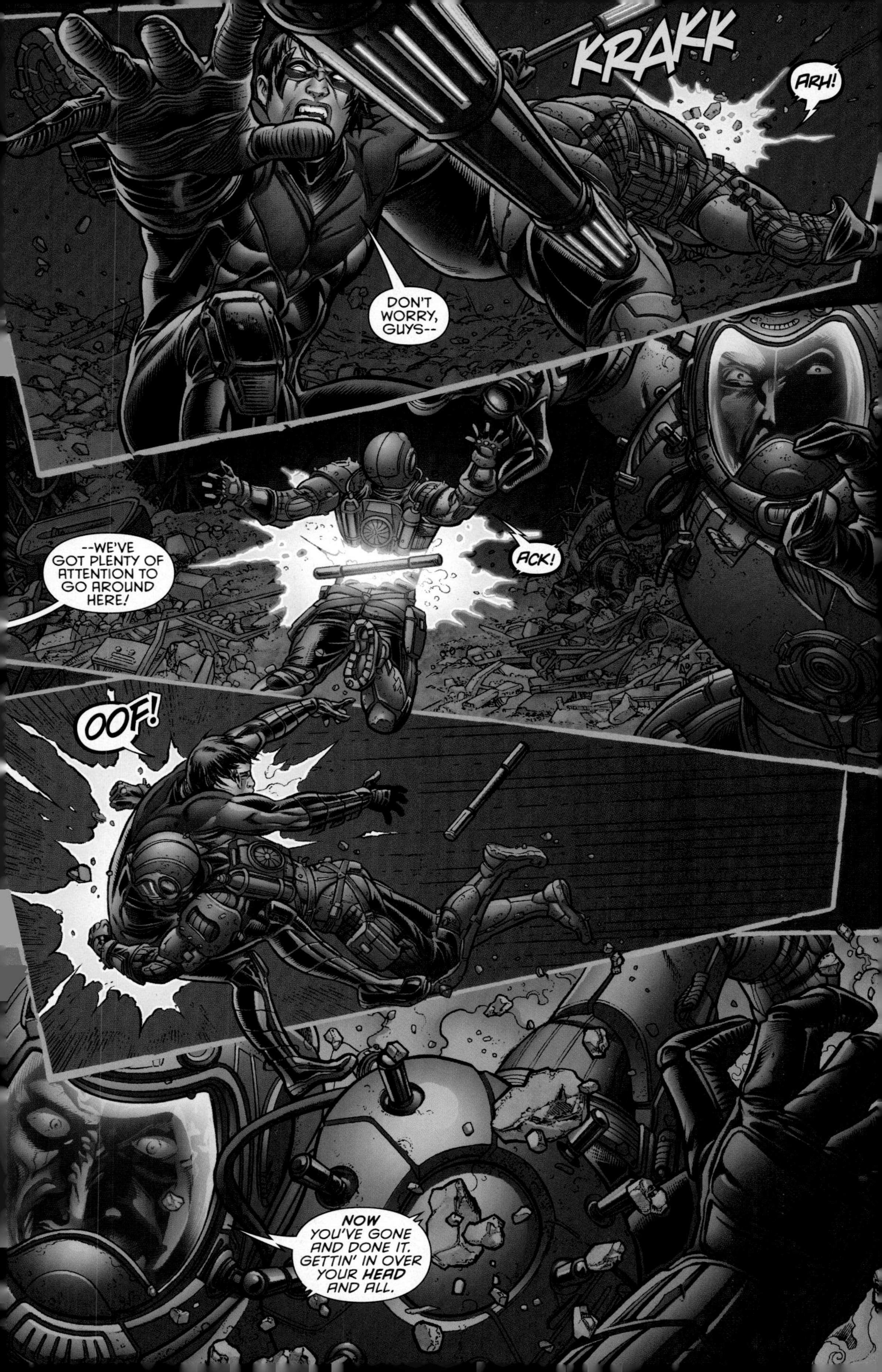
KRAKK
ARH!
DON'T WORRY, GUYS--
--WE'VE GOT PLENTY OF ATTENTION TO GO AROUND HERE!
ACK!
OOF!
NOW YOU'VE GONE AND DONE IT. GETTIN' IN OVER YOUR HEAD AND ALL.

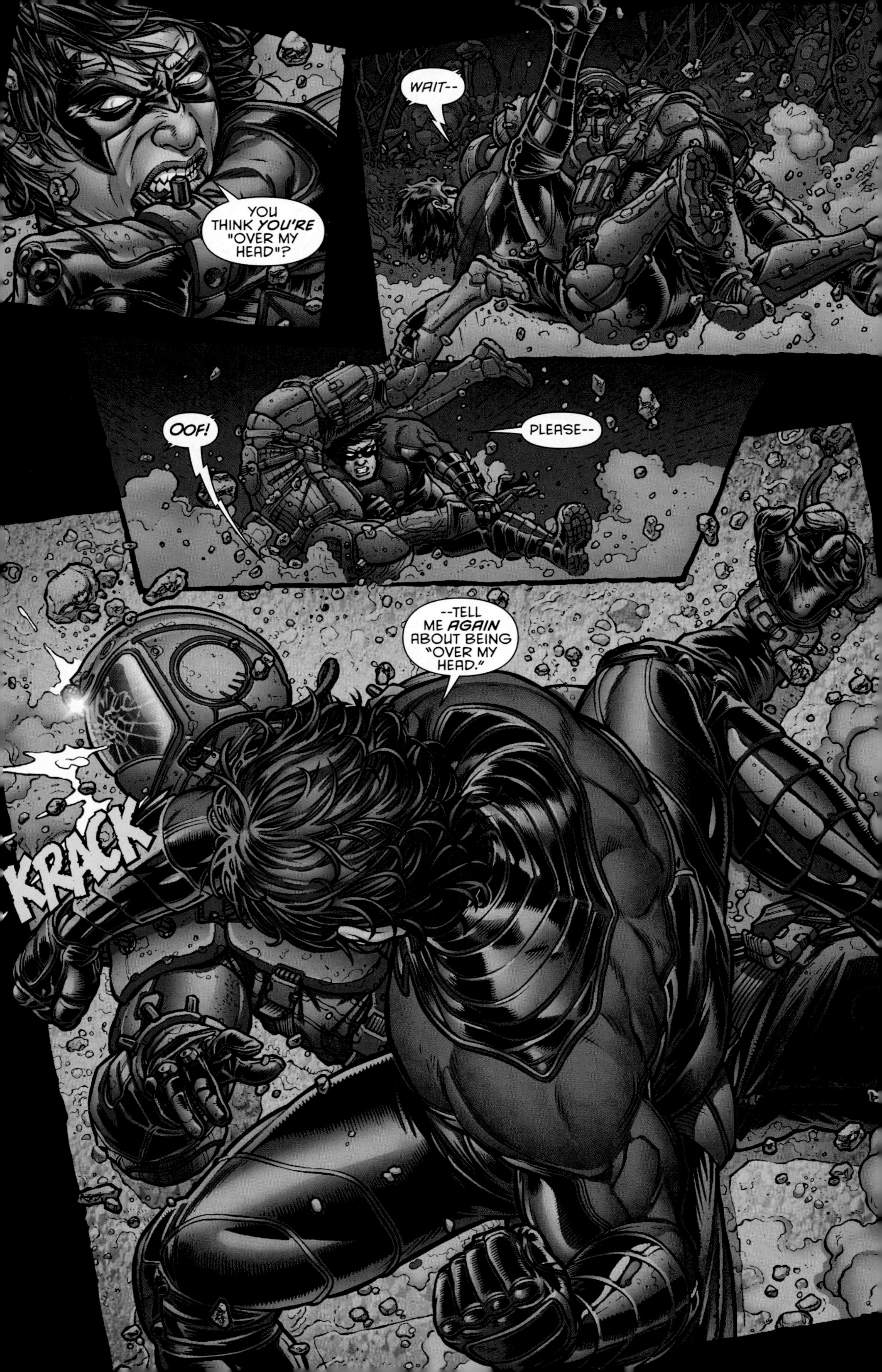
YOU THINK YOU'RE "OVER MY HEAD"?
WAIT--
OOF!
PLEASE--
--TELL ME AGAIN ABOUT BEING "OVER MY HEAD."
KRACK

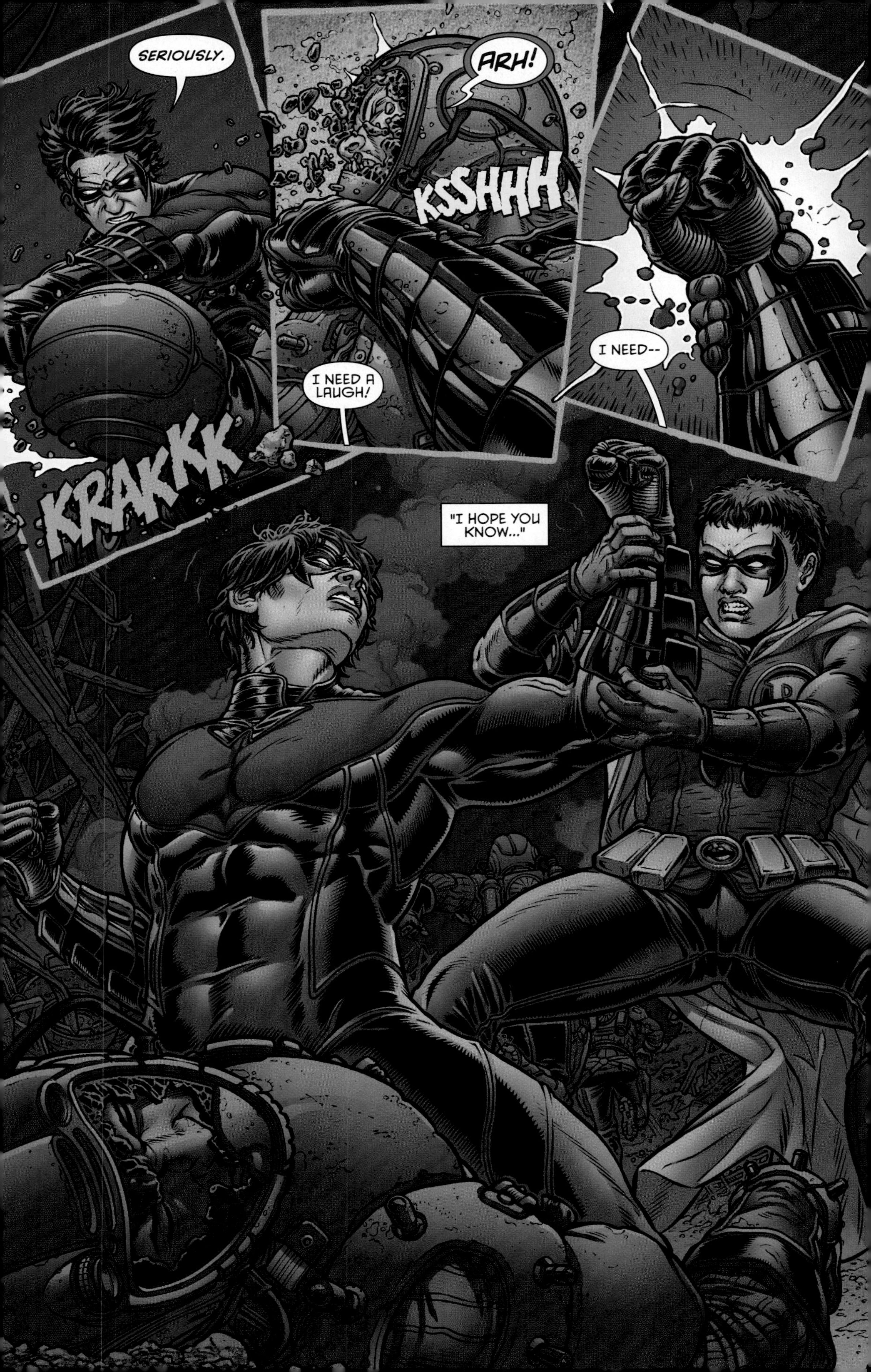

SERIOUSLY.
KRAKKK
ARH!
KSSHHH
I NEED A LAUGH!
I NEED--
"I HOPE YOU KNOW..."

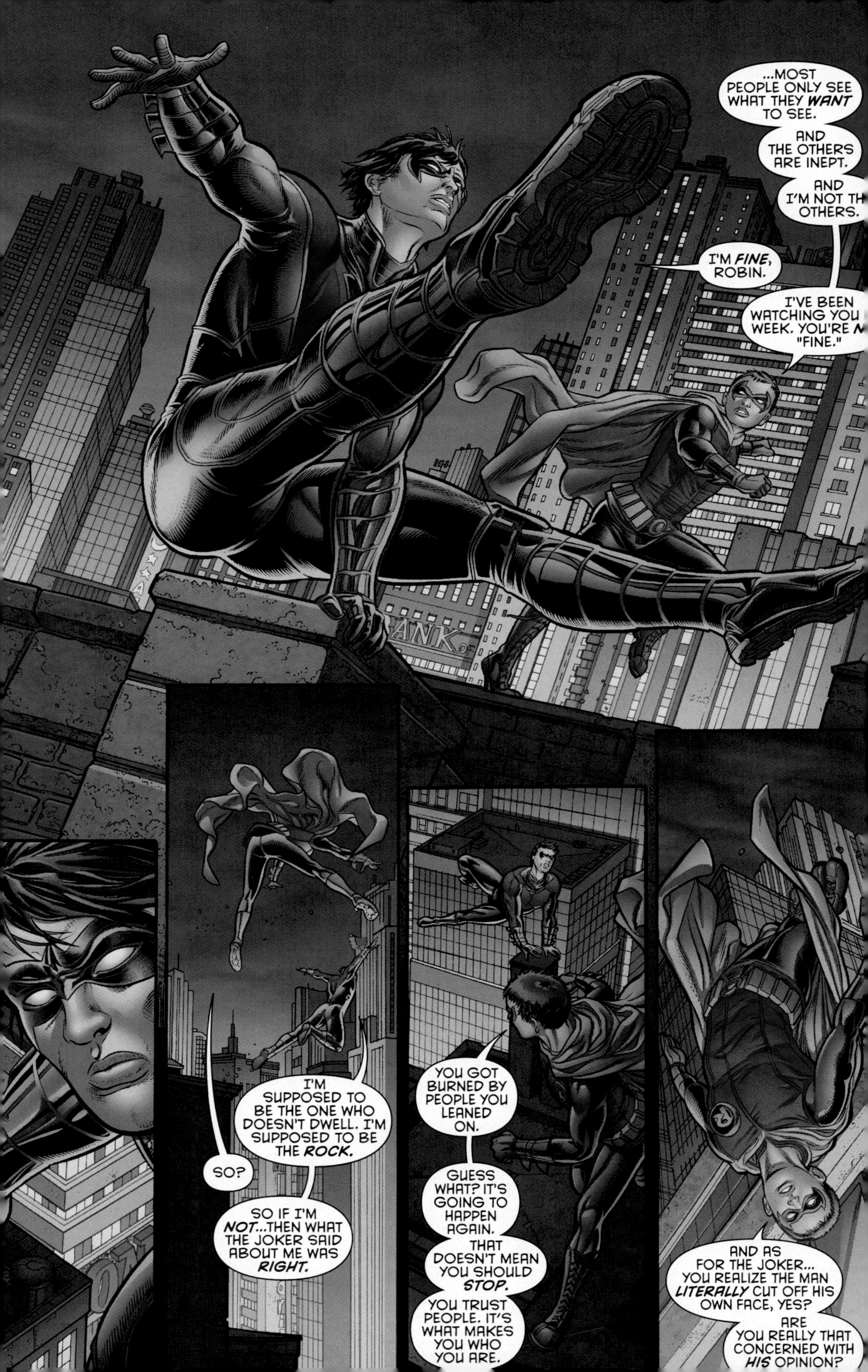
I'M *FINE*, ROBIN.
I'VE BEEN WATCHING YOU WEEK. YOU'RE N "FINE."
...MOST PEOPLE ONLY SEE WHAT THEY *WANT* TO SEE.
AND THE OTHERS ARE INEPT.
AND I'M NOT TH OTHERS.
I'M SUPPOSED TO BE THE ONE WHO DOESN'T DWELL. I'M SUPPOSED TO BE THE *ROCK.*
SO?
SO IF I'M *NOT*...THEN WHAT THE JOKER SAID ABOUT ME WAS *RIGHT.*
YOU GOT BURNED BY PEOPLE YOU LEANED ON.
GUESS WHAT? IT'S GOING TO HAPPEN AGAIN.
THAT DOESN'T MEAN YOU SHOULD *STOP.*
YOU TRUST PEOPLE. IT'S WHAT MAKES YOU WHO YOU ARE.
AND AS FOR THE JOKER... YOU REALIZE THE MAN *LITERALLY* CUT OFF HIS OWN FACE, YES?
ARE YOU REALLY THAT CONCERNED WITH *HIS* OPINION?

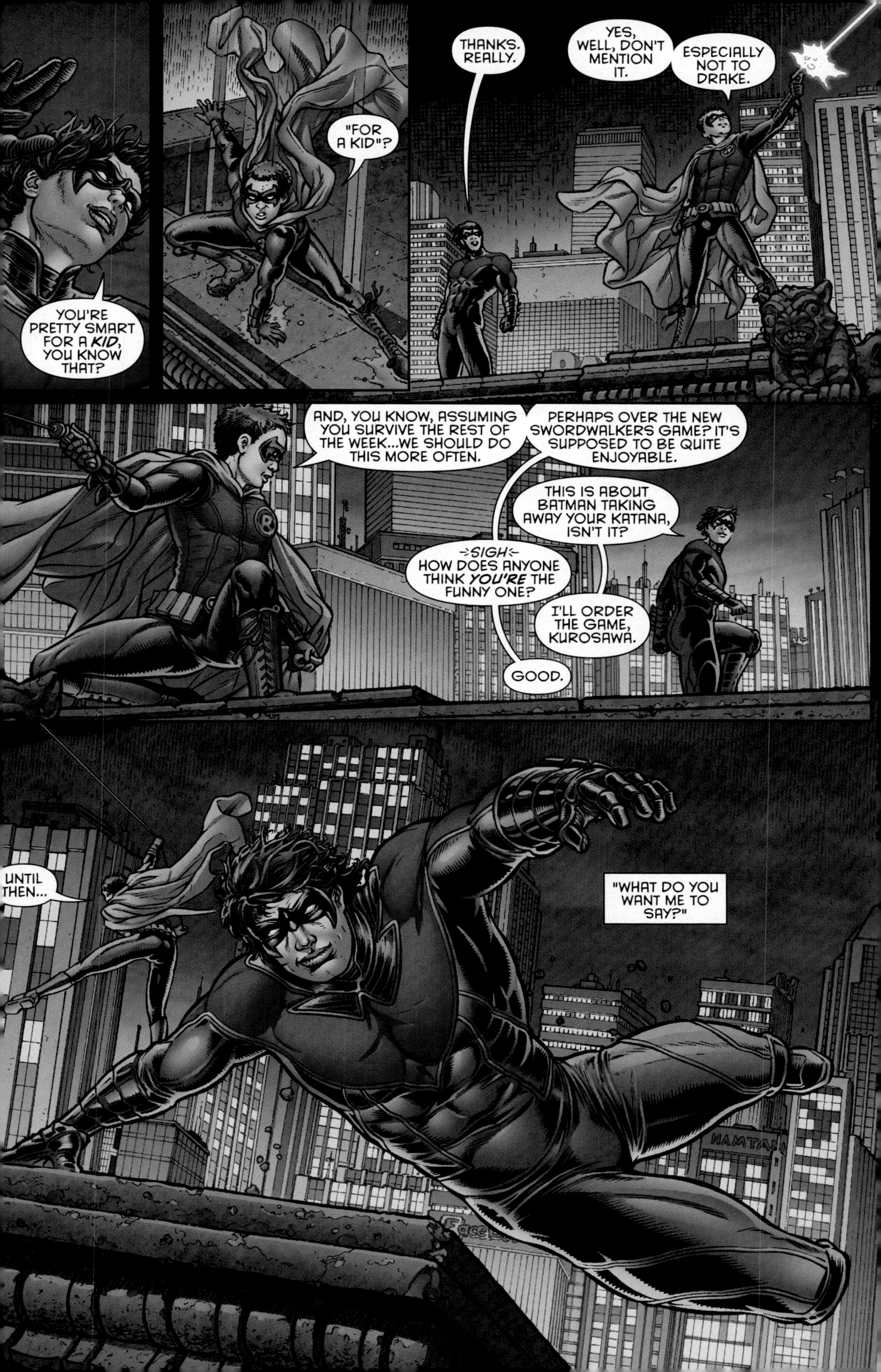
YOU'RE PRETTY SMART FOR A KID, YOU KNOW THAT?
"FOR A KID"?
THANKS. REALLY.
YES, WELL, DON'T MENTION IT.
ESPECIALLY NOT TO DRAKE.
AND, YOU KNOW, ASSUMING YOU SURVIVE THE REST OF THE WEEK...WE SHOULD DO THIS MORE OFTEN.
PERHAPS OVER THE NEW SWORDWALKERS GAME? IT'S SUPPOSED TO BE QUITE ENJOYABLE.
THIS IS ABOUT BATMAN TAKING AWAY YOUR KATANA, ISN'T IT?
-SIGH- HOW DOES ANYONE THINK YOU'RE THE FUNNY ONE?
I'LL ORDER THE GAME, KUROSAWA.
GOOD.
UNTIL THEN...
"WHAT DO YOU WANT ME TO SAY?"

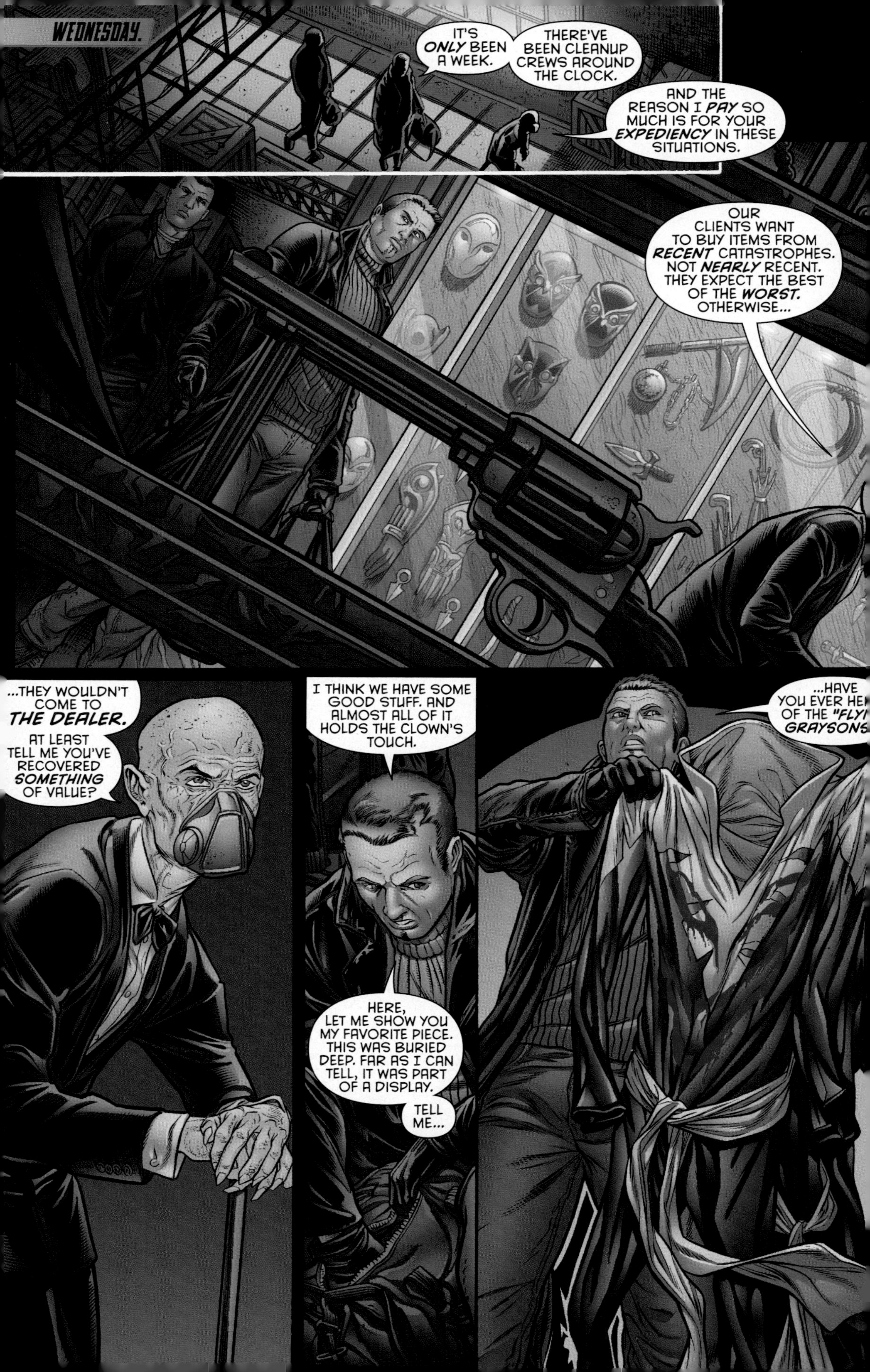
WEDNESDAY.
IT'S ONLY BEEN A WEEK.
THERE'VE BEEN CLEANUP CREWS AROUND THE CLOCK.
AND THE REASON I PAY SO MUCH IS FOR YOUR EXPEDIENCY IN THESE SITUATIONS.
OUR CLIENTS WANT TO BUY ITEMS FROM RECENT CATASTROPHES. NOT NEARLY RECENT. THEY EXPECT THE BEST OF THE WORST. OTHERWISE...
...THEY WOULDN'T COME TO THE DEALER.
AT LEAST TELL ME YOU'VE RECOVERED SOMETHING OF VALUE?
I THINK WE HAVE SOME GOOD STUFF. AND ALMOST ALL OF IT HOLDS THE CLOWN'S TOUCH.
HERE, LET ME SHOW YOU MY FAVORITE PIECE. THIS WAS BURIED DEEP. FAR AS I CAN TELL, IT WAS PART OF A DISPLAY.
TELL ME...
...HAVE YOU EVER HE OF THE "FLYI GRAYSONS

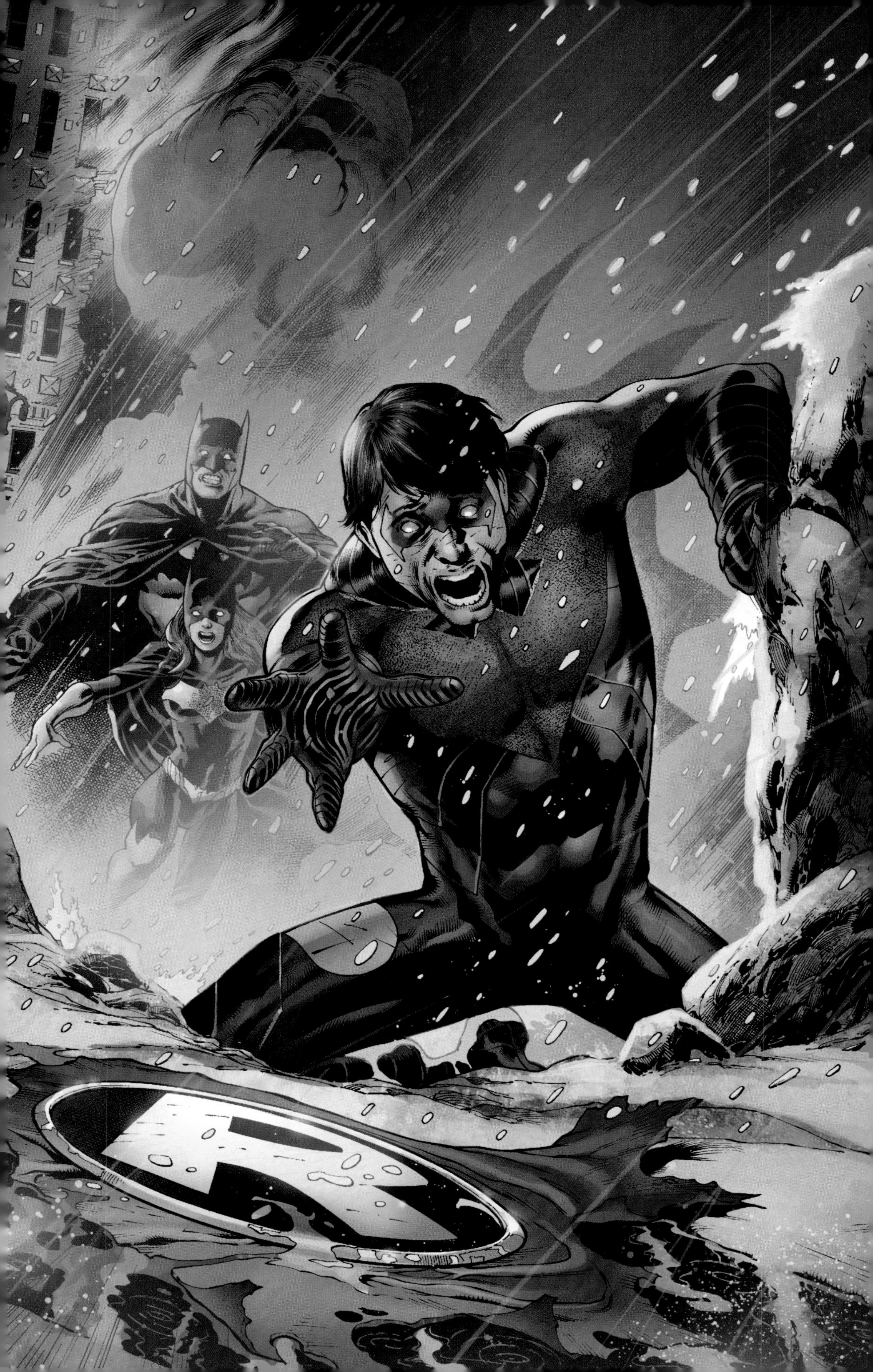

SLOW BURN

KYLE HIGGINS writer JUAN JOSE RYP penciller ROGER BONET & JUAN ALBARRAN inkers cover art by EDDY BARROWS, EBER FERREIRA & ROD RE

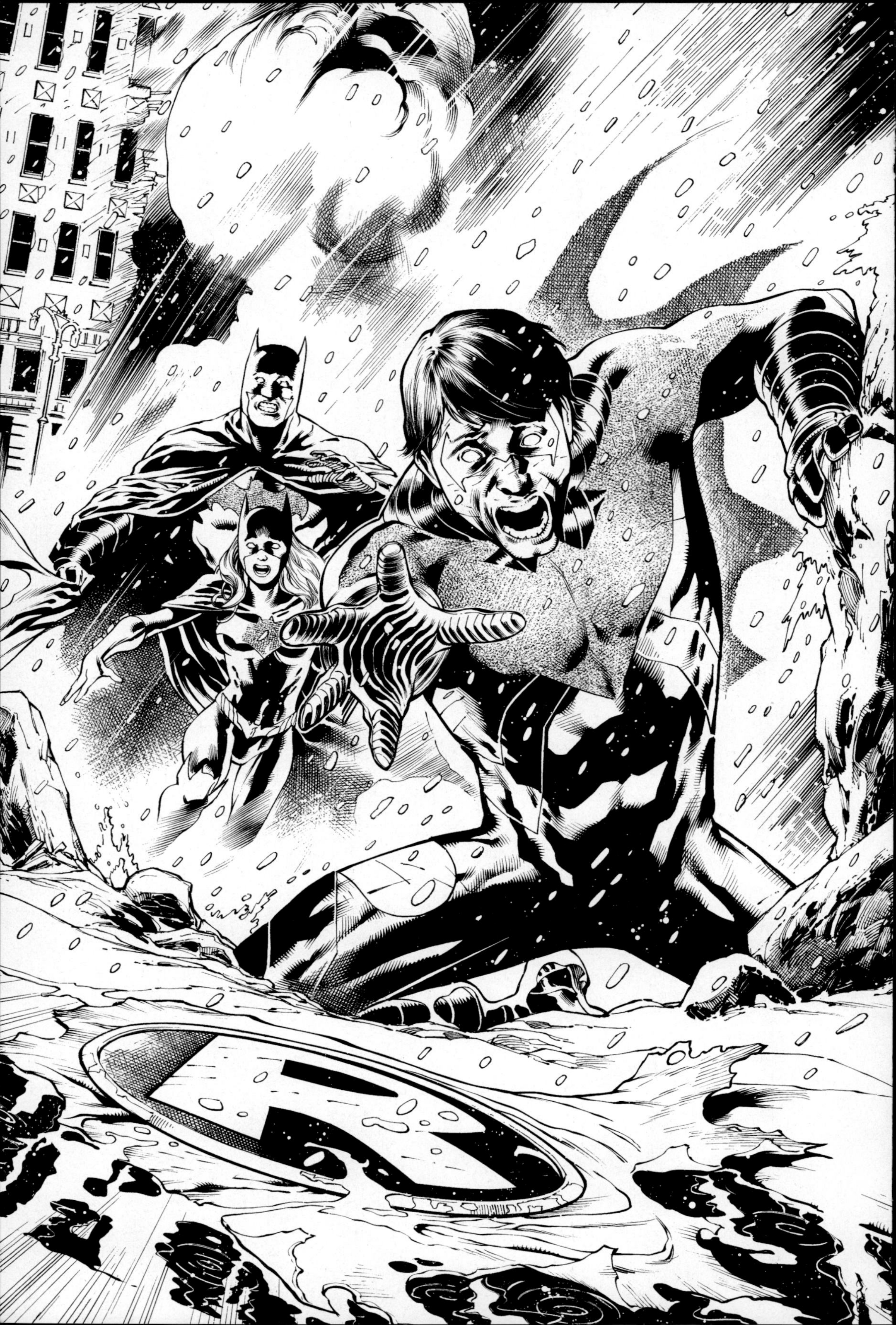

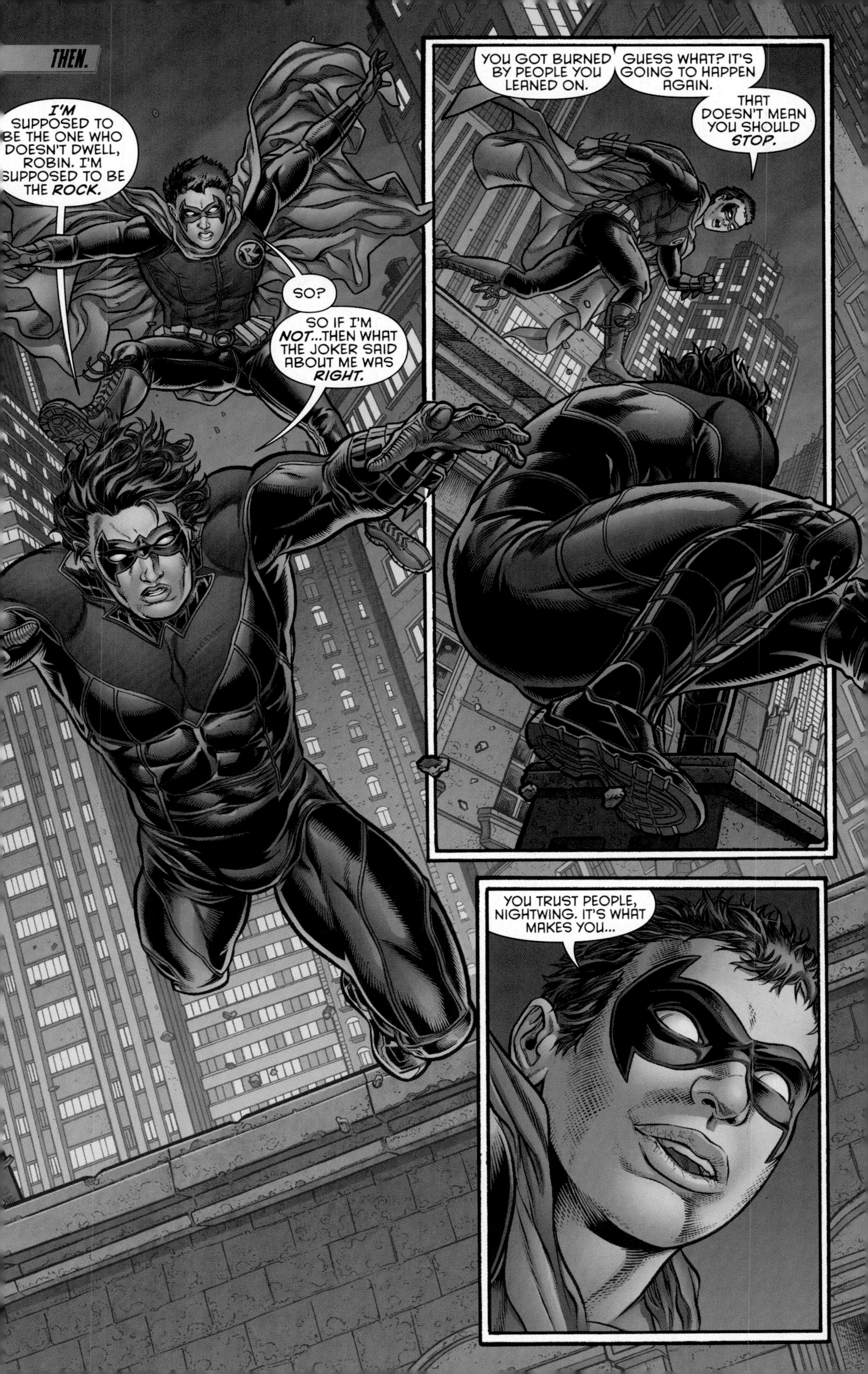
THEN.
I'M SUPPOSED TO BE THE ONE WHO DOESN'T DWELL, ROBIN. I'M SUPPOSED TO BE THE ROCK.
SO?
SO IF I'M NOT...THEN WHAT THE JOKER SAID ABOUT ME WAS RIGHT.
YOU GOT BURNED BY PEOPLE YOU LEANED ON.
GUESS WHAT? IT'S GOING TO HAPPEN AGAIN.
THAT DOESN'T MEAN YOU SHOULD STOP.
YOU TRUST PEOPLE, NIGHTWING. IT'S WHAT MAKES YOU...

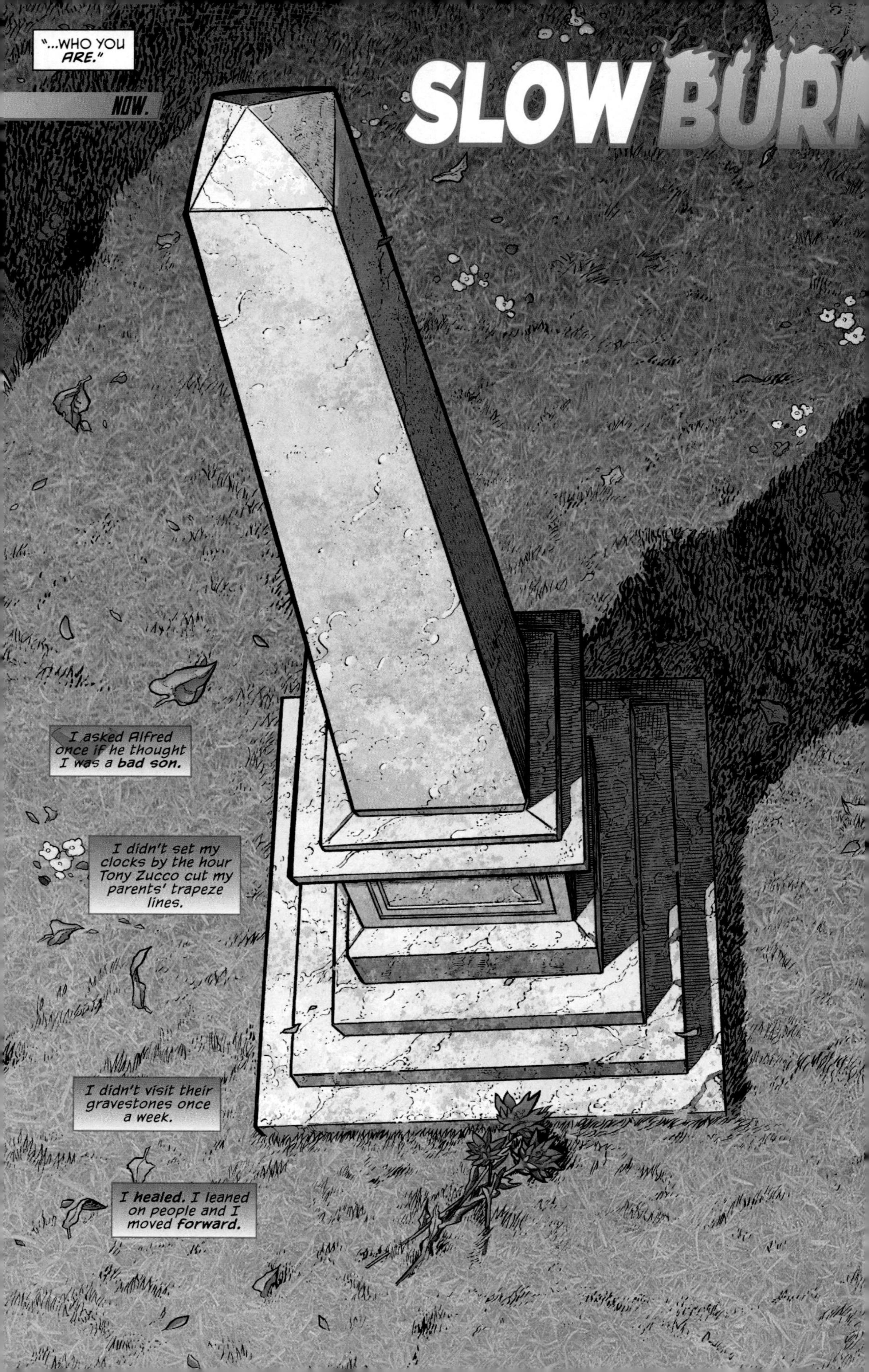
"...WHO YOU ARE."
NOW.
SLOW BURN
I asked Alfred once if he thought I was a bad son.
I didn't set my clocks by the hour Tony Zucco cut my parents' trapeze lines.
I didn't visit their gravestones once a week.
I healed. I leaned on people and I moved forward.

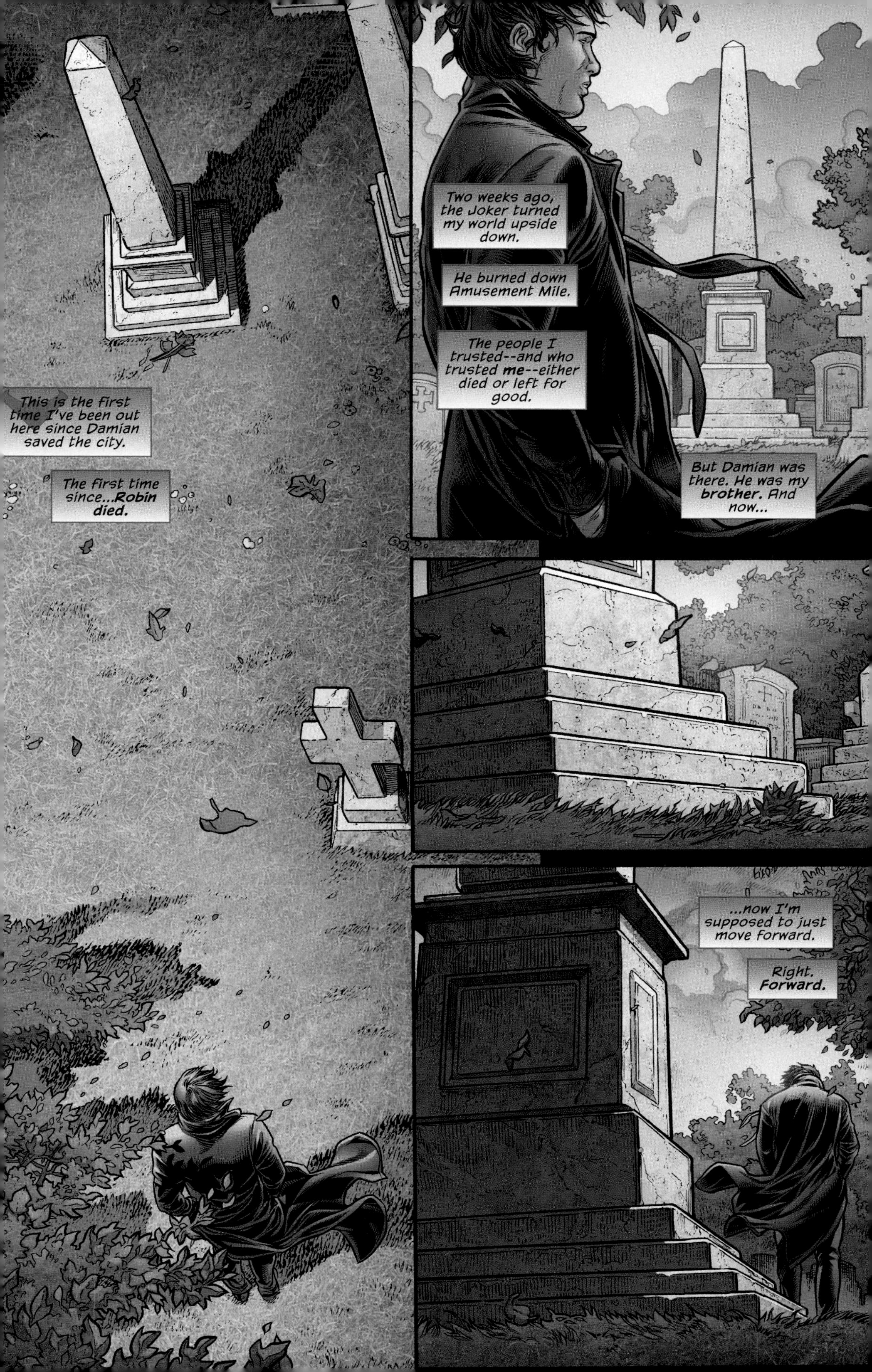
This is the first time I've been out here since Damian saved the city.
The first time since...**Robin** died.
Two weeks ago, the Joker turned my world upside down.
He burned down Amusement Mile.
The people I trusted--and who trusted **me**--either died or left for good.
But Damian was there. He was my **brother.** And now...
...now I'm supposed to just move forward.
Right. **Forward.**

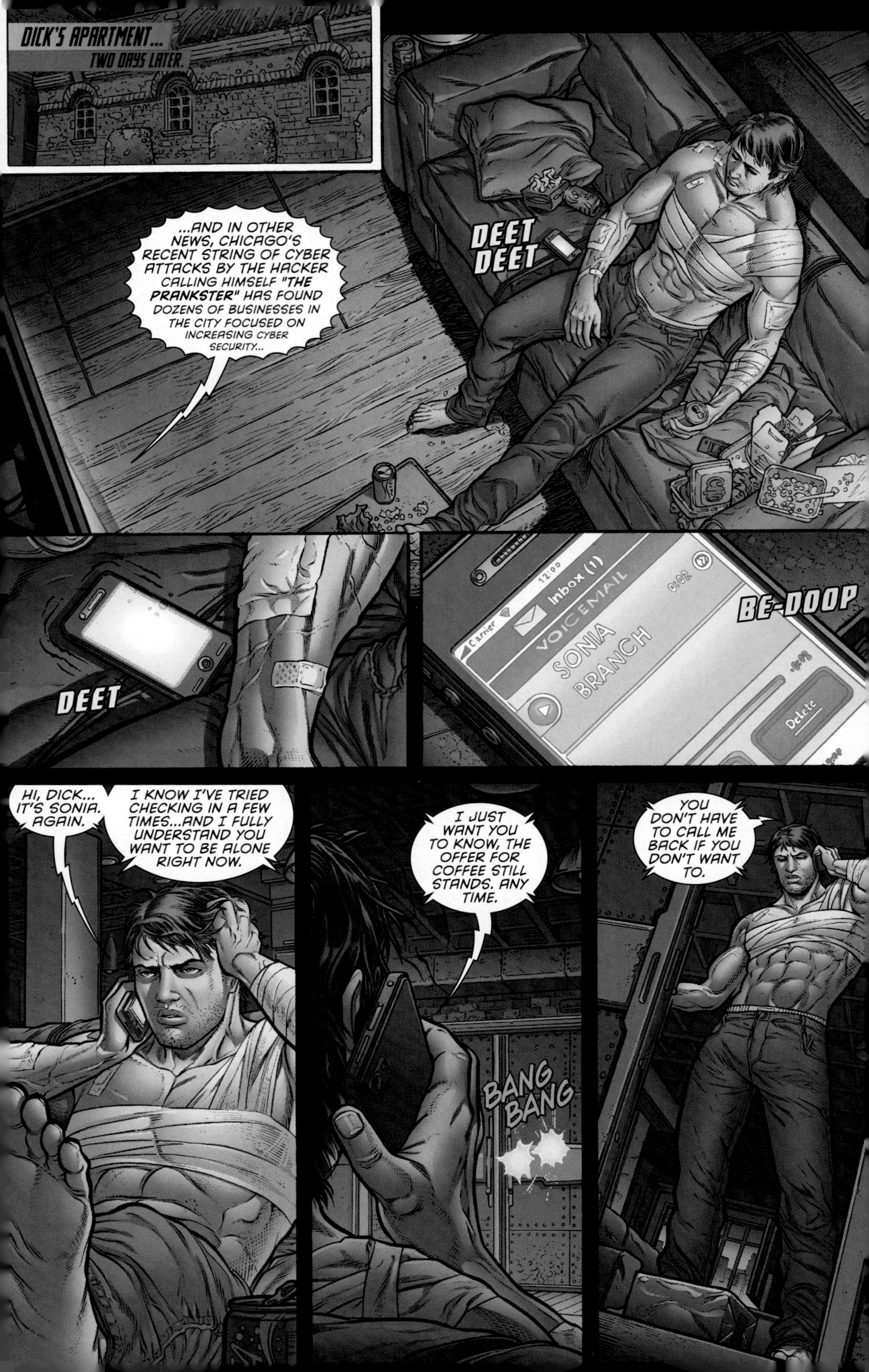

DICK'S APARTMENT...
TWO DAYS LATER.
...AND IN OTHER NEWS, CHICAGO'S RECENT STRING OF CYBER ATTACKS BY THE HACKER CALLING HIMSELF "THE PRANKSTER" HAS FOUND DOZENS OF BUSINESSES IN THE CITY FOCUSED ON INCREASING CYBER SECURITY...
DEET DEET
DEET
BE-DOOP
12:00
Inbox (1)
VOICEMAIL
SONIA BRANCH
Delete
HI, DICK... IT'S SONIA. AGAIN.
I KNOW I'VE TRIED CHECKING IN A FEW TIMES...AND I FULLY UNDERSTAND YOU WANT TO BE ALONE RIGHT NOW.
I JUST WANT YOU TO KNOW, THE OFFER FOR COFFEE STILL STANDS. ANY TIME.
BANG BANG
YOU DON'T HAVE TO CALL ME BACK IF YOU DON'T WANT TO.

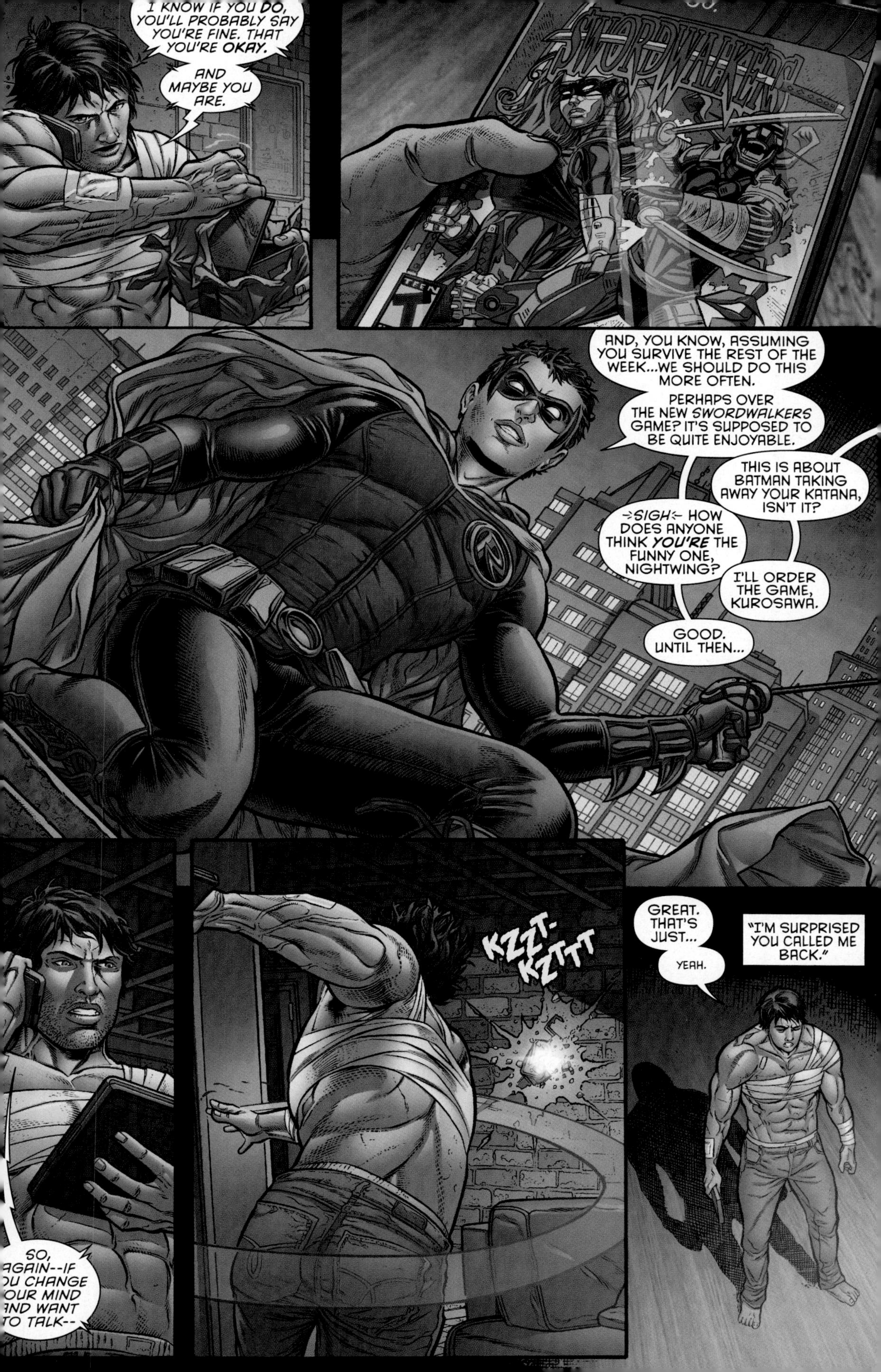
I KNOW IF YOU DO, YOU'LL PROBABLY SAY YOU'RE FINE. THAT YOU'RE OKAY.
AND MAYBE YOU ARE.
SWORDWALKERS
TEEN
AND, YOU KNOW, ASSUMING YOU SURVIVE THE REST OF THE WEEK...WE SHOULD DO THIS MORE OFTEN.
PERHAPS OVER THE NEW SWORDWALKERS GAME? IT'S SUPPOSED TO BE QUITE ENJOYABLE.
THIS IS ABOUT BATMAN TAKING AWAY YOUR KATANA, ISN'T IT?
⇒SIGH⇐ HOW DOES ANYONE THINK YOU'RE THE FUNNY ONE, NIGHTWING?
I'LL ORDER THE GAME, KUROSAWA.
GOOD. UNTIL THEN...
SO, AGAIN--IF YOU CHANGE YOUR MIND AND WANT TO TALK--
KZZT-KZTTT
GREAT. THAT'S JUST...
YEAH.
"I'M SURPRISED YOU CALLED ME BACK."

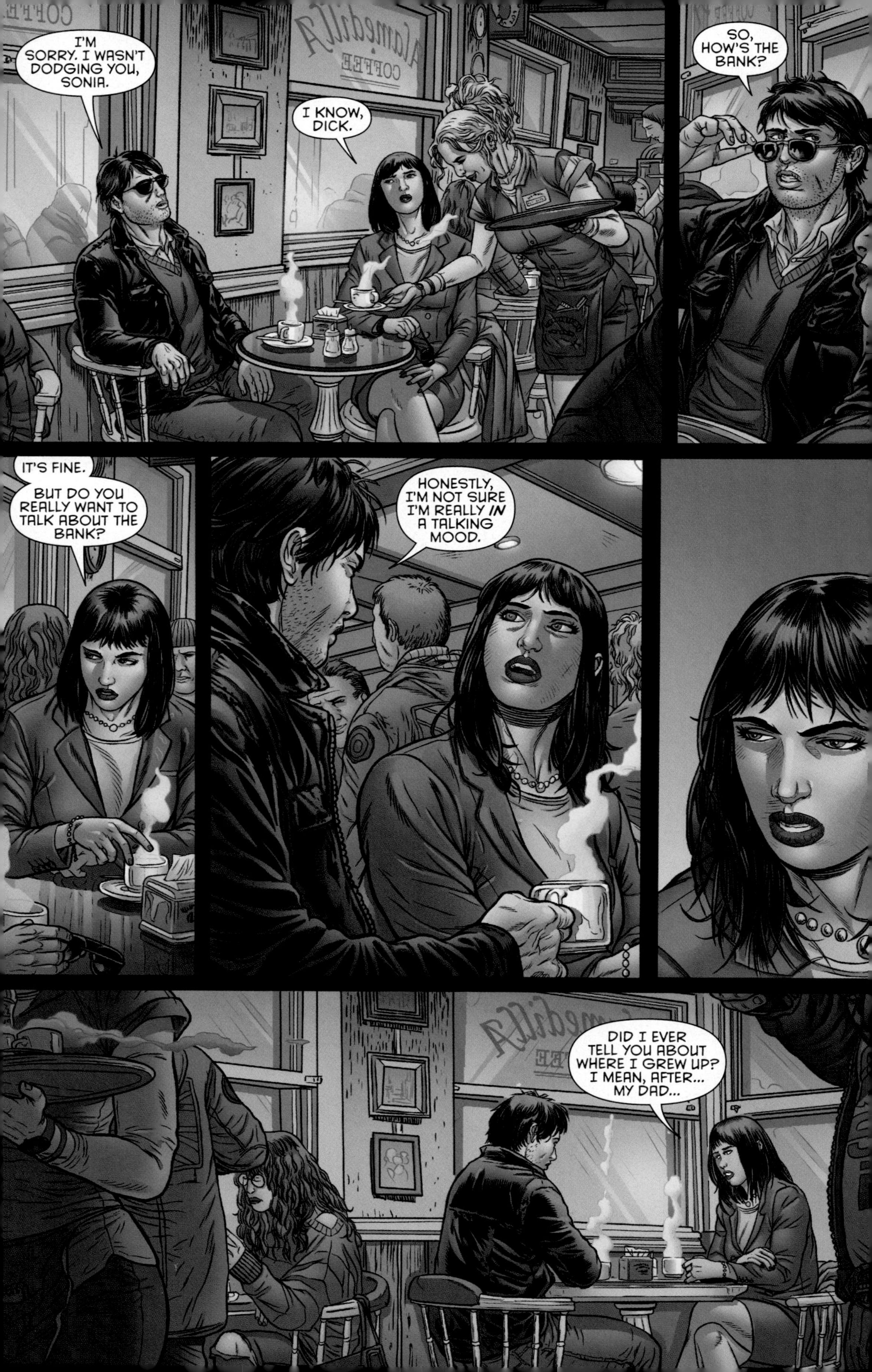

I'M SORRY. I WASN'T DODGING YOU, SONIA.
I KNOW, DICK.
SO, HOW'S THE BANK?
IT'S FINE.
BUT DO YOU REALLY WANT TO TALK ABOUT THE BANK?
HONESTLY, I'M NOT SURE I'M REALLY *IN* A TALKING MOOD.
DID I EVER TELL YOU ABOUT WHERE I GREW UP? I MEAN, AFTER... MY DAD...

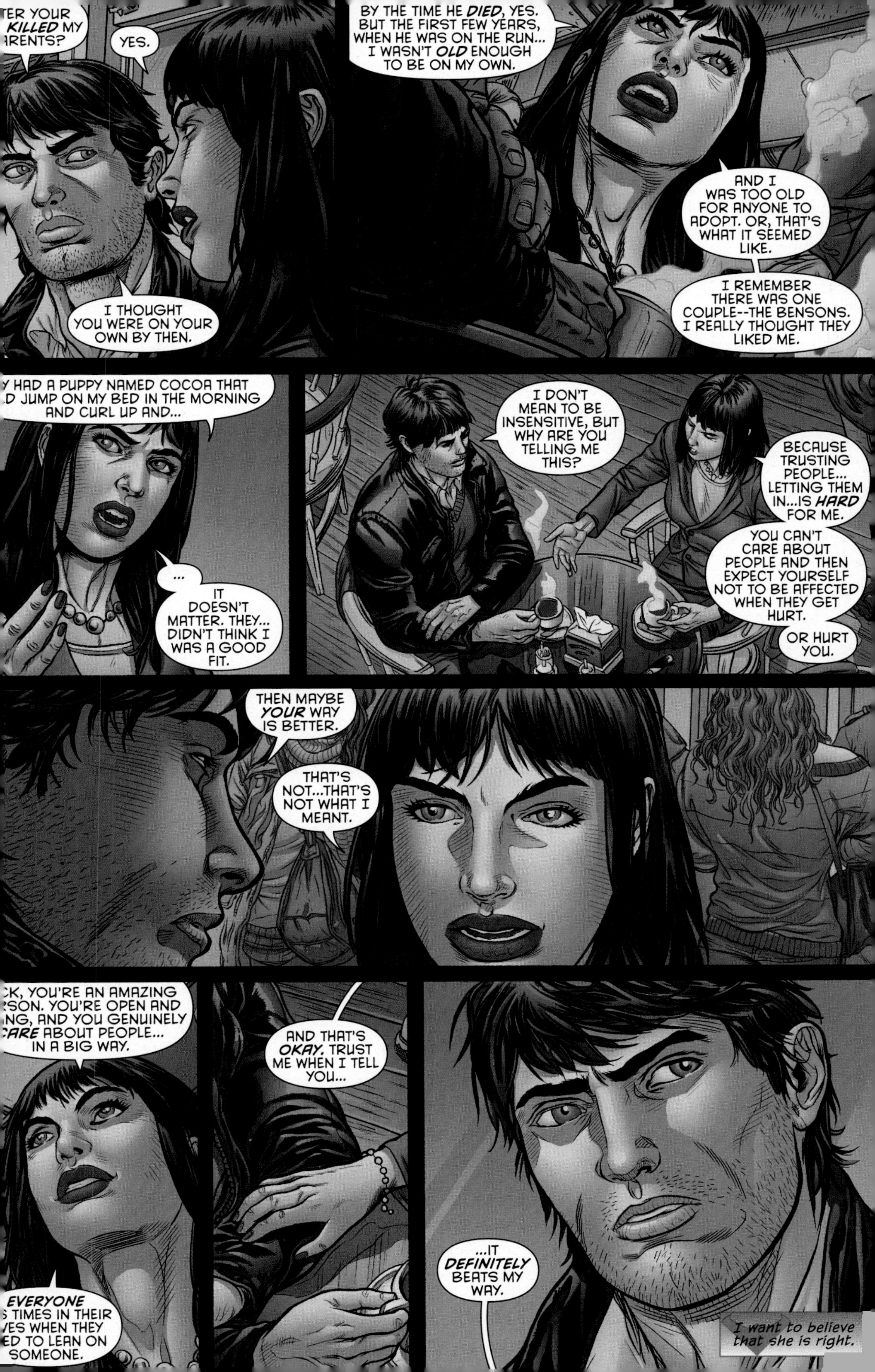
TER YOUR KILLED MY ARENTS?
YES.
I THOUGHT YOU WERE ON YOUR OWN BY THEN.
BY THE TIME HE DIED, YES. BUT THE FIRST FEW YEARS, WHEN HE WAS ON THE RUN... I WASN'T OLD ENOUGH TO BE ON MY OWN.
AND I WAS TOO OLD FOR ANYONE TO ADOPT. OR, THAT'S WHAT IT SEEMED LIKE.
I REMEMBER THERE WAS ONE COUPLE--THE BENSONS. I REALLY THOUGHT THEY LIKED ME.
Y HAD A PUPPY NAMED COCOA THAT D JUMP ON MY BED IN THE MORNING AND CURL UP AND...
...
IT DOESN'T MATTER. THEY... DIDN'T THINK I WAS A GOOD FIT.
I DON'T MEAN TO BE INSENSITIVE, BUT WHY ARE YOU TELLING ME THIS?
BECAUSE TRUSTING PEOPLE... LETTING THEM IN...IS HARD FOR ME.
YOU CAN'T CARE ABOUT PEOPLE AND THEN EXPECT YOURSELF NOT TO BE AFFECTED WHEN THEY GET HURT.
OR HURT YOU.
THEN MAYBE YOUR WAY IS BETTER.
THAT'S NOT...THAT'S NOT WHAT I MEANT.
CK, YOU'RE AN AMAZING RSON. YOU'RE OPEN AND NG, AND YOU GENUINELY CARE ABOUT PEOPLE... IN A BIG WAY.
EVERYONE S TIMES IN THEIR VES WHEN THEY ED TO LEAN ON SOMEONE.
AND THAT'S OKAY. TRUST ME WHEN I TELL YOU...
...IT DEFINITELY BEATS MY WAY.
I want to believe that she is right.

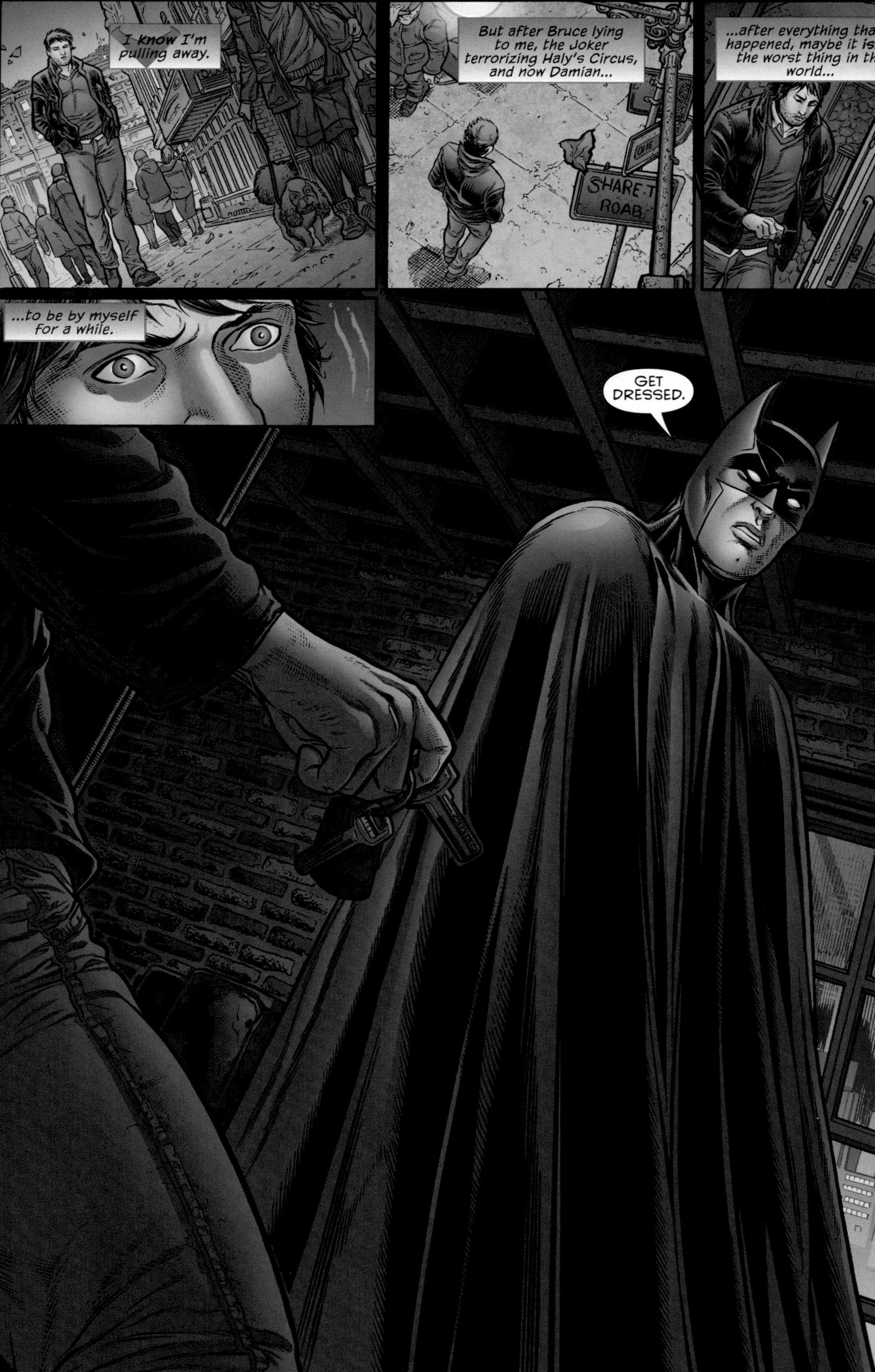

I know I'm pulling away.
But after Bruce lying to me, the Joker terrorizing Haly's Circus, and now Damian...
SHARE THE ROAD
...after everything that happened, maybe it is the worst thing in the world...
...to be by myself for a while.
GET DRESSED.

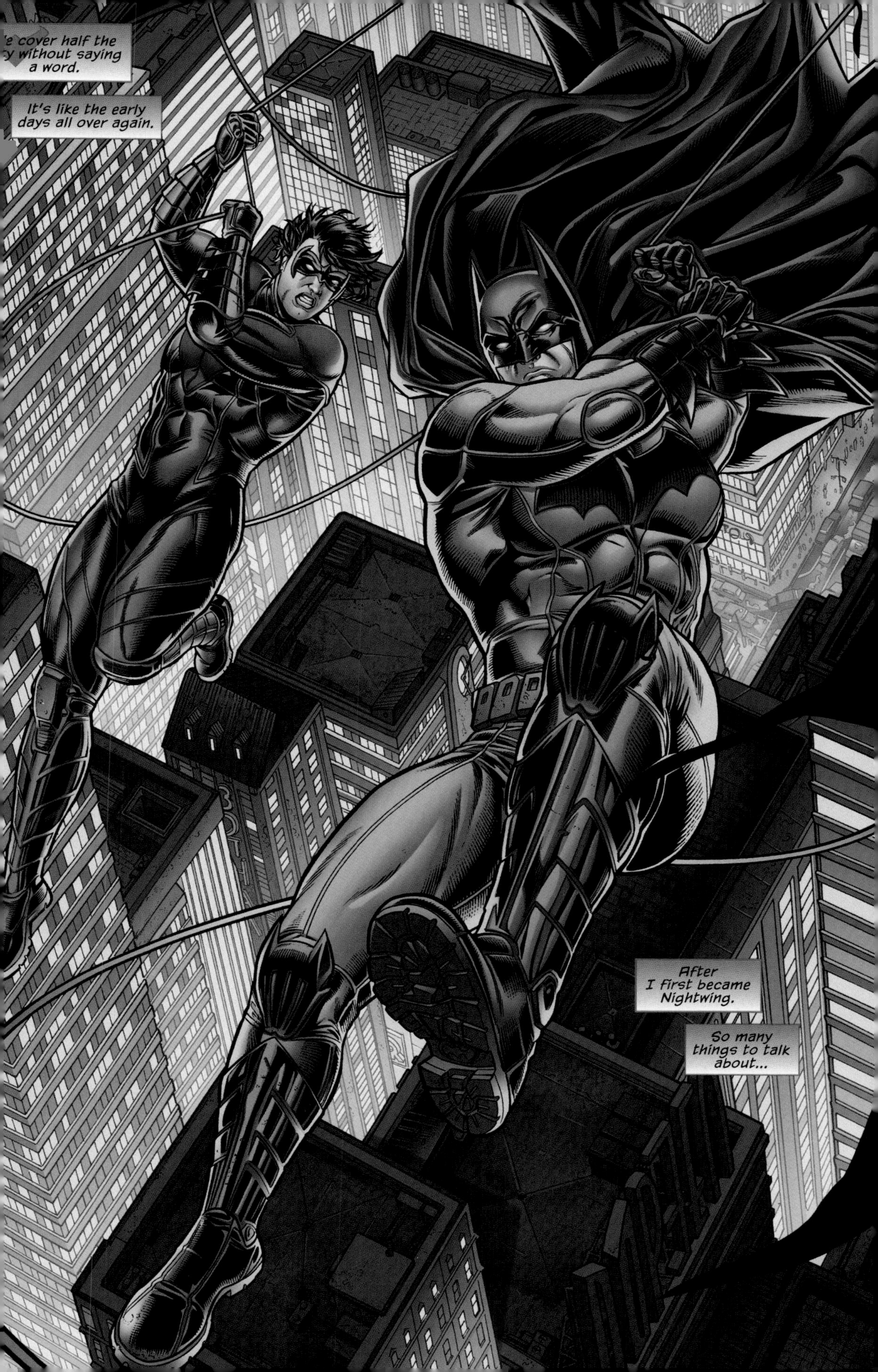
'e cover half the
y without saying
a word.
It's like the early
days all over again.
After
I first became
Nightwing.
So many
things to talk
about...

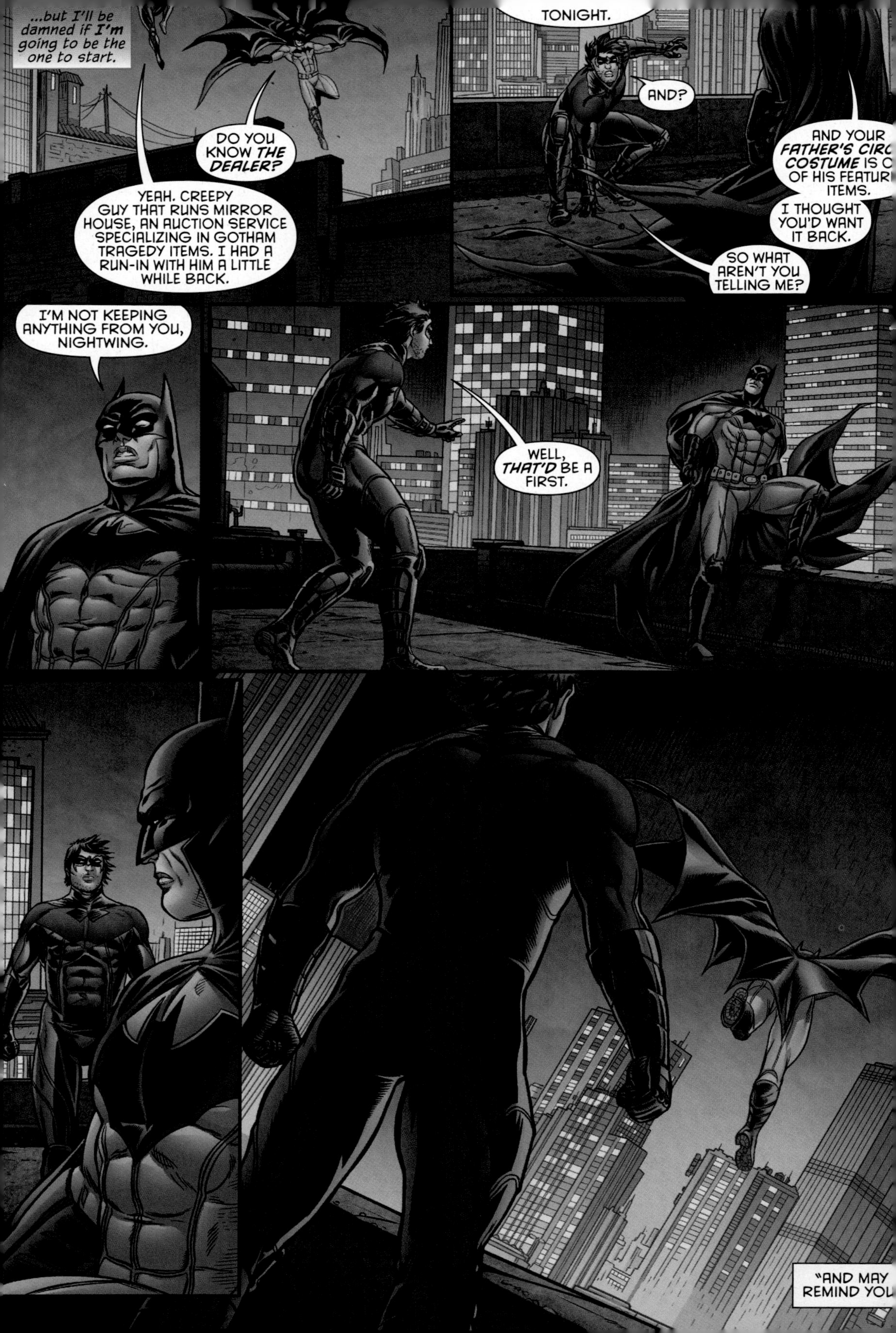

...but I'll be damned if *I'm* going to be the one to start.
DO YOU KNOW *THE DEALER?*
YEAH. CREEPY GUY THAT RUNS MIRROR HOUSE, AN AUCTION SERVICE SPECIALIZING IN GOTHAM TRAGEDY ITEMS. I HAD A RUN-IN WITH HIM A LITTLE WHILE BACK.
TONIGHT.
AND?
AND YOUR *FATHER'S CIRC COSTUME* IS O OF HIS FEATUR ITEMS.
I THOUGHT YOU'D WANT IT BACK.
SO WHAT AREN'T YOU TELLING ME?
I'M NOT KEEPING ANYTHING FROM YOU, NIGHTWING.
WELL, *THAT'D* BE A FIRST.
"AND MAY REMIND YOU

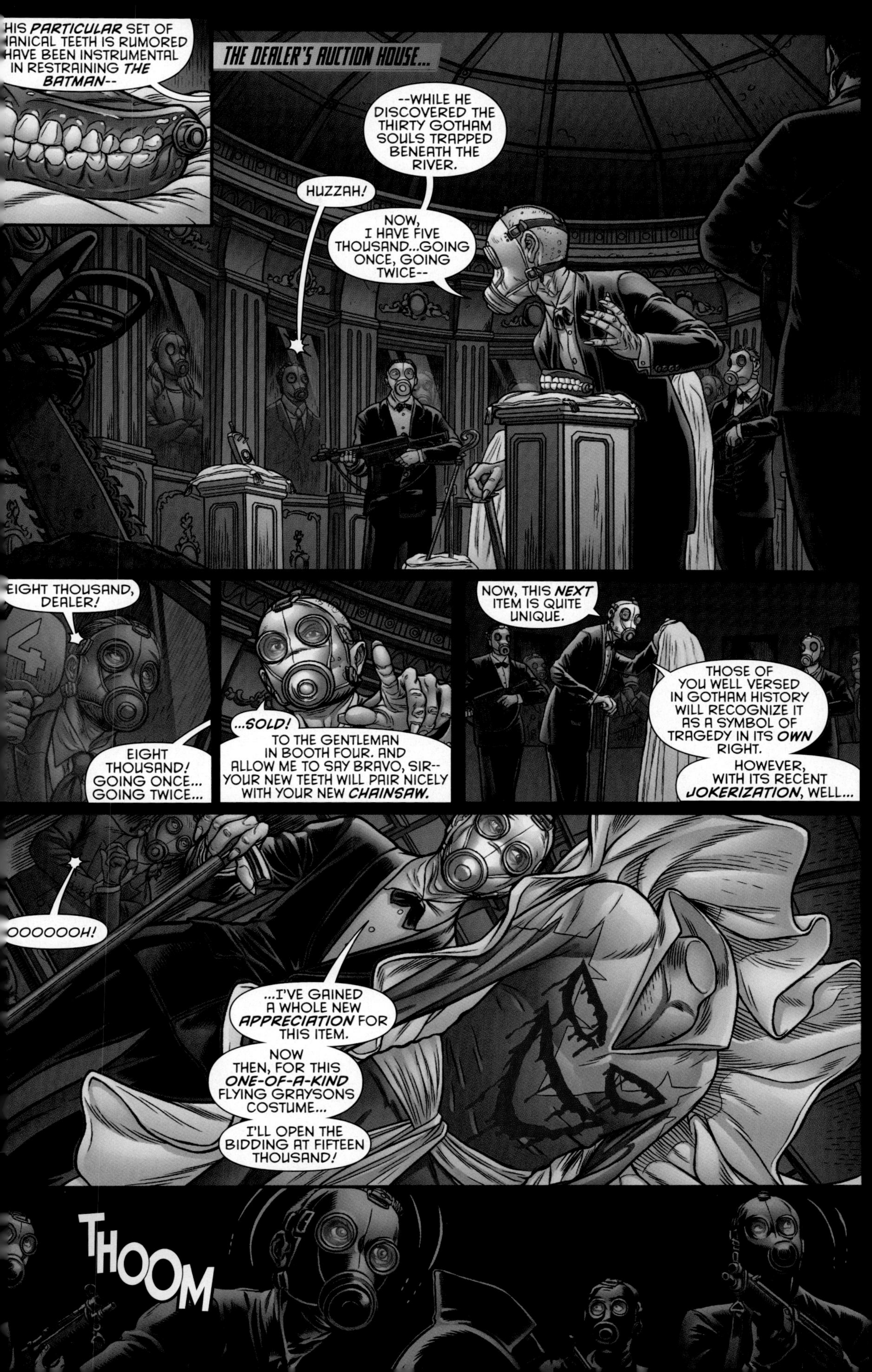
HIS PARTICULAR SET OF
ANICAL TEETH IS RUMORED
HAVE BEEN INSTRUMENTAL IN RESTRAINING THE BATMAN--
THE DEALER'S AUCTION HOUSE...
--WHILE HE DISCOVERED THE THIRTY GOTHAM SOULS TRAPPED BENEATH THE RIVER.
HUZZAH!
NOW, I HAVE FIVE THOUSAND...GOING ONCE, GOING TWICE--
EIGHT THOUSAND, DEALER!
EIGHT THOUSAND! GOING ONCE... GOING TWICE...
...SOLD!
TO THE GENTLEMAN IN BOOTH FOUR. AND ALLOW ME TO SAY BRAVO, SIR-- YOUR NEW TEETH WILL PAIR NICELY WITH YOUR NEW CHAINSAW.
NOW, THIS NEXT ITEM IS QUITE UNIQUE.
THOSE OF YOU WELL VERSED IN GOTHAM HISTORY WILL RECOGNIZE IT AS A SYMBOL OF TRAGEDY IN ITS OWN RIGHT.
HOWEVER, WITH ITS RECENT JOKERIZATION, WELL...
OOOOOOH!
...I'VE GAINED A WHOLE NEW APPRECIATION FOR THIS ITEM.
NOW THEN, FOR THIS ONE-OF-A-KIND FLYING GRAYSONS COSTUME...
I'LL OPEN THE BIDDING AT FIFTEEN THOUSAND!
THOOM

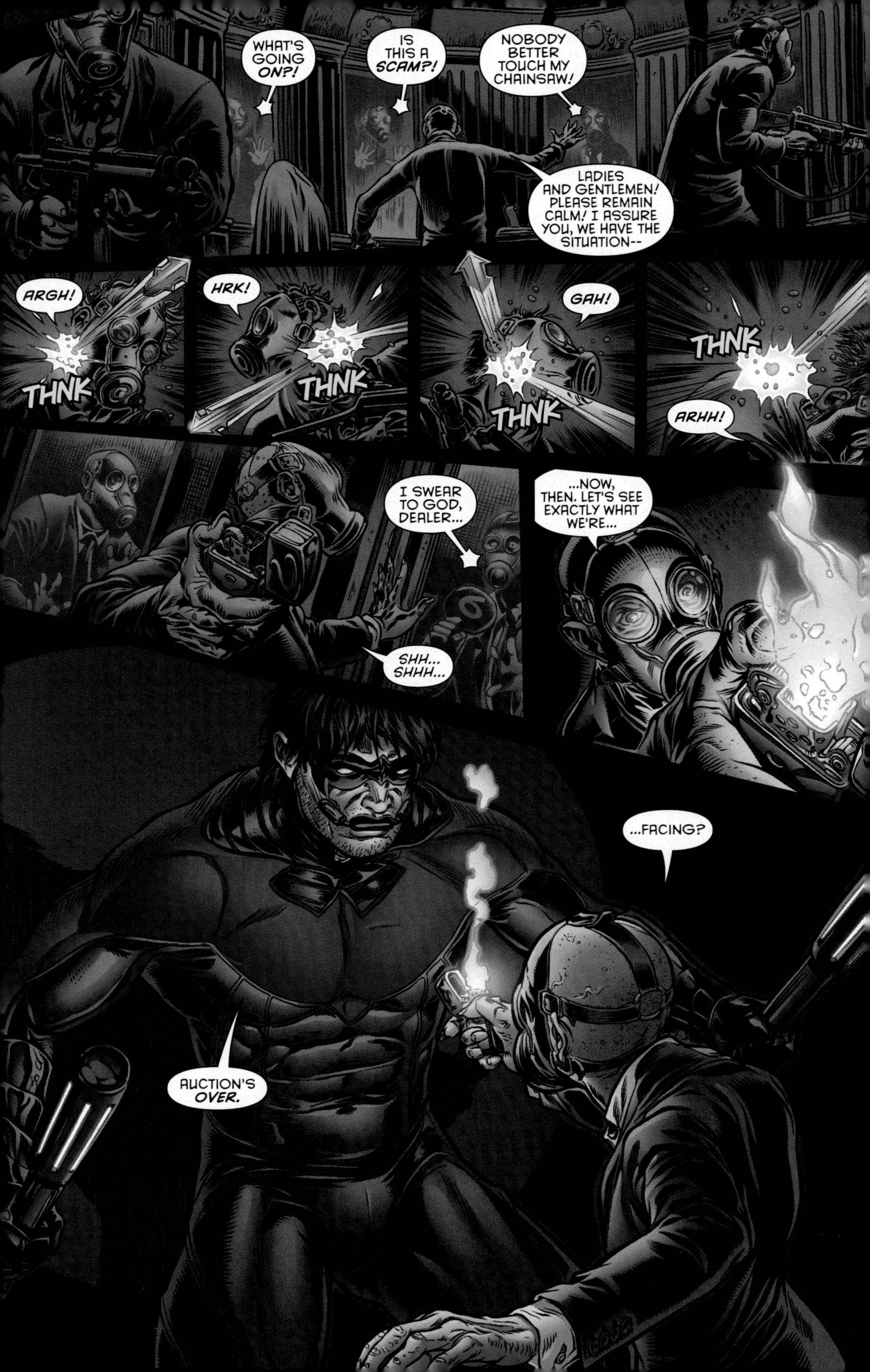
WHAT'S GOING ON?!
IS THIS A SCAM?!
NOBODY BETTER TOUCH MY CHAINSAW!
LADIES AND GENTLEMEN! PLEASE REMAIN CALM! I ASSURE YOU, WE HAVE THE SITUATION--
ARGH!
THNK
HRK!
THNK
GAH!
THNK
THNK
ARHH!
I SWEAR TO GOD, DEALER...
SHH... SHHH...
...NOW, THEN. LET'S SEE EXACTLY WHAT WE'RE...
...FACING?
AUCTION'S OVER.

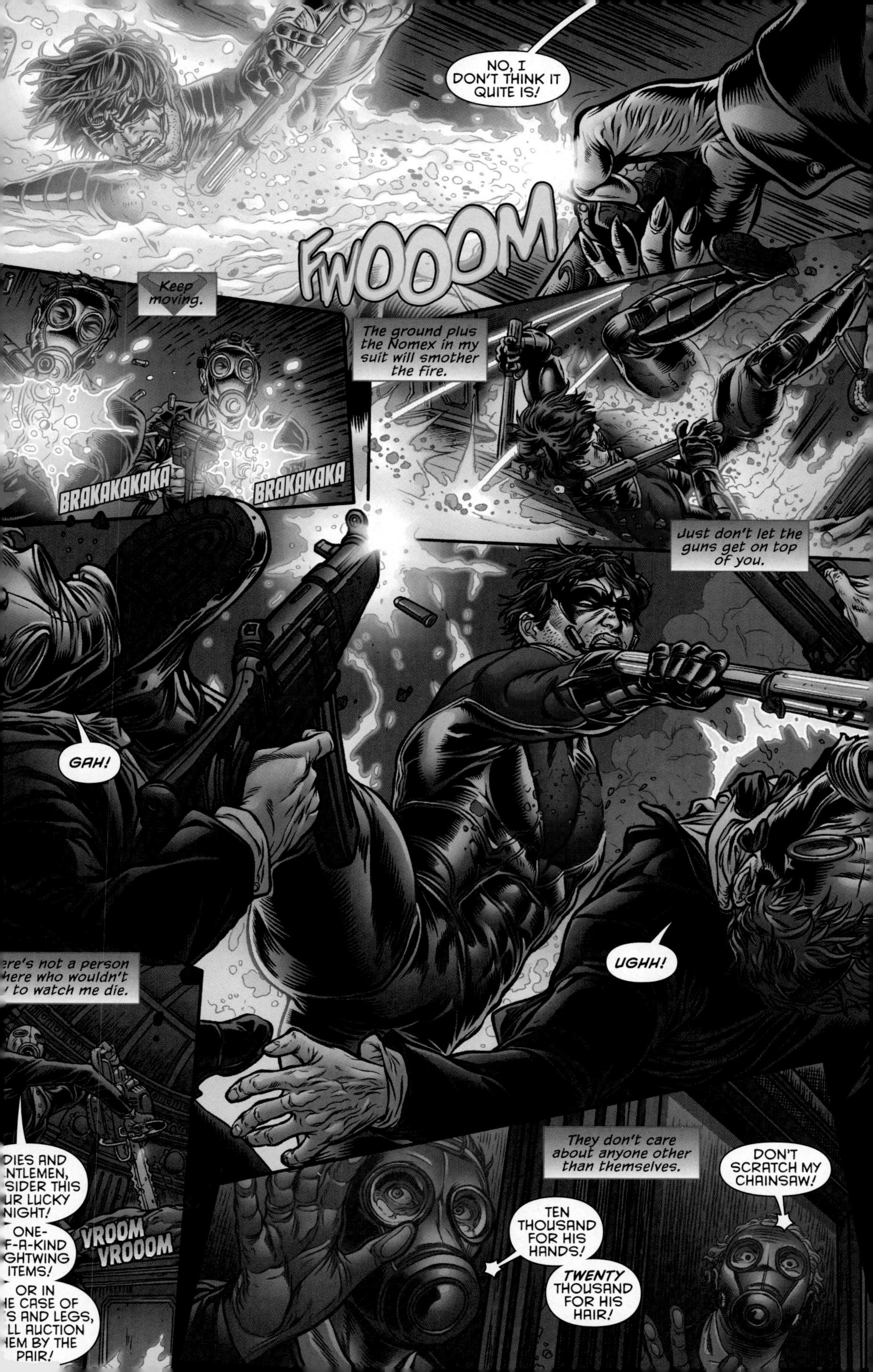

NO, I DON'T THINK IT QUITE IS!
FWOOOM
Keep moving.
The ground plus the Nomex in my suit will smother the fire.
BRAKAKAKAKA
BRAKAKAKA
Just don't let the guns get on top of you.
GAH!
UGHH!
ere's not a person here who wouldn't to watch me die.
They don't care about anyone other than themselves.
DIES AND NTLEMEN, SIDER THIS UR LUCKY NIGHT!
ONE-F-A-KIND GHTWING ITEMS!
OR IN E CASE OF S AND LEGS, LL AUCTION EM BY THE PAIR!
VROOM VROOOM
TEN THOUSAND FOR HIS HANDS!
TWENTY THOUSAND FOR HIS HAIR!
DON'T SCRATCH MY CHAINSAW!

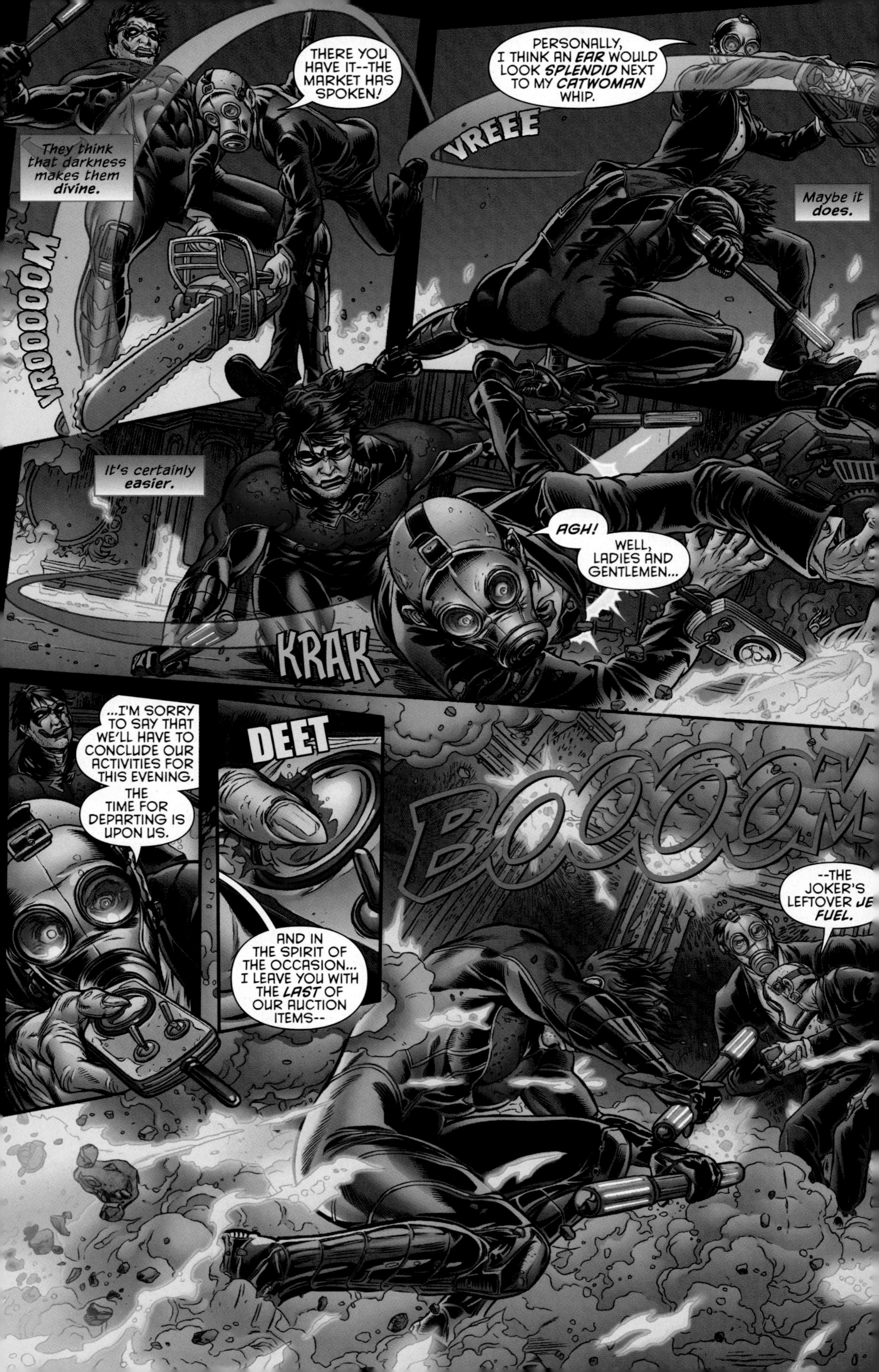

They think that darkness makes them divine.
THERE YOU HAVE IT--THE MARKET HAS SPOKEN!
YROOOOOOM
VREEE
PERSONALLY, I THINK AN EAR WOULD LOOK SPLENDID NEXT TO MY CATWOMAN WHIP.
Maybe it does.
It's certainly easier.
AGH!
WELL, LADIES AND GENTLEMEN...
KRAK
...I'M SORRY TO SAY THAT WE'LL HAVE TO CONCLUDE OUR ACTIVITIES FOR THIS EVENING.
THE TIME FOR DEPARTING IS UPON US.
DEET
AND IN THE SPIRIT OF THE OCCASION... I LEAVE YOU WITH THE LAST OF OUR AUCTION ITEMS--
--THE JOKER'S LEFTOVER JE FUEL.

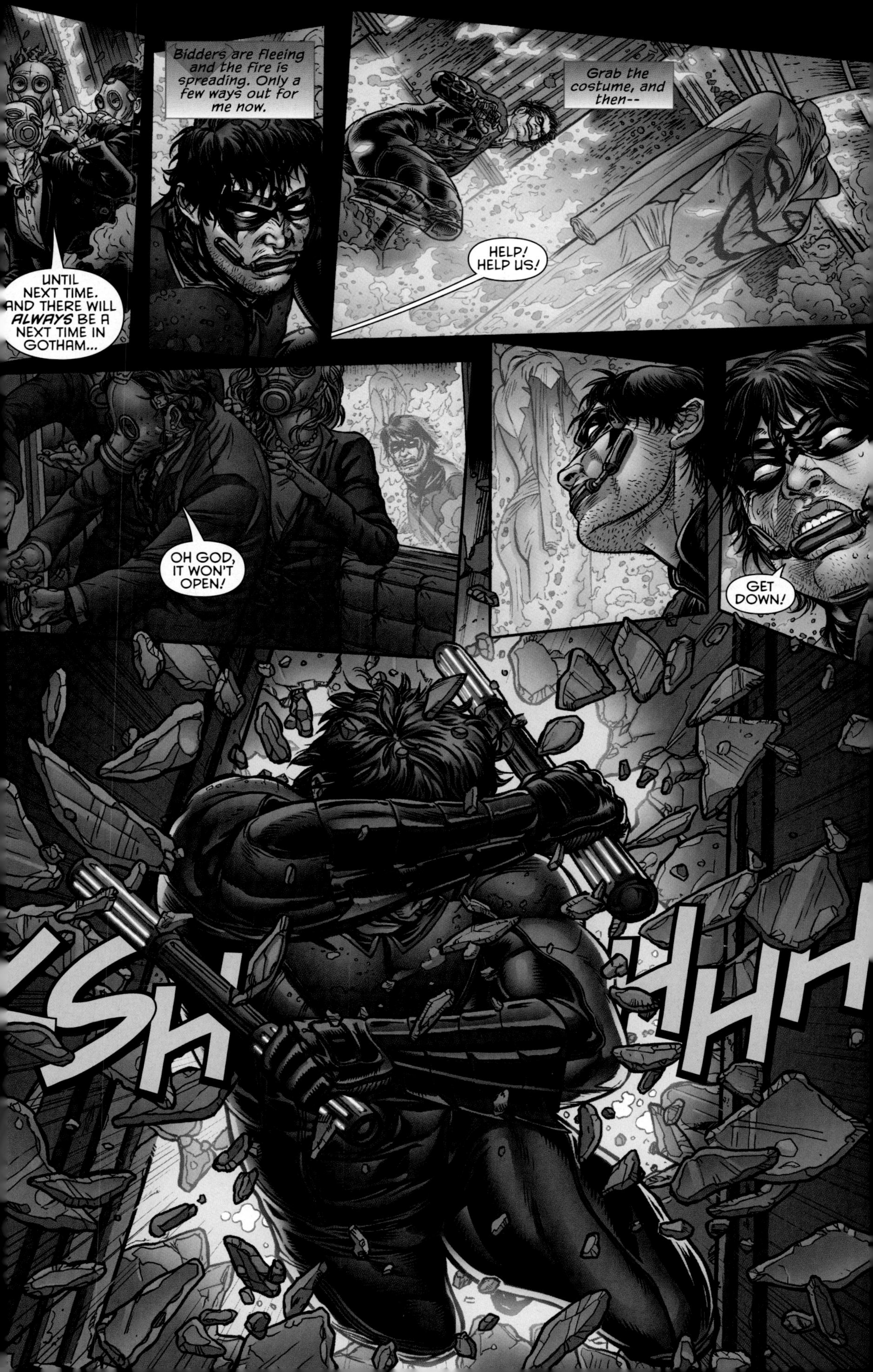
Bidders are fleeing and the fire is spreading. Only a few ways out for me now.
Grab the costume, and then--
UNTIL NEXT TIME. AND THERE WILL ALWAYS BE A NEXT TIME IN GOTHAM...
HELP! HELP US!
OH GOD, IT WON'T OPEN!
GET DOWN!
SH
HHH

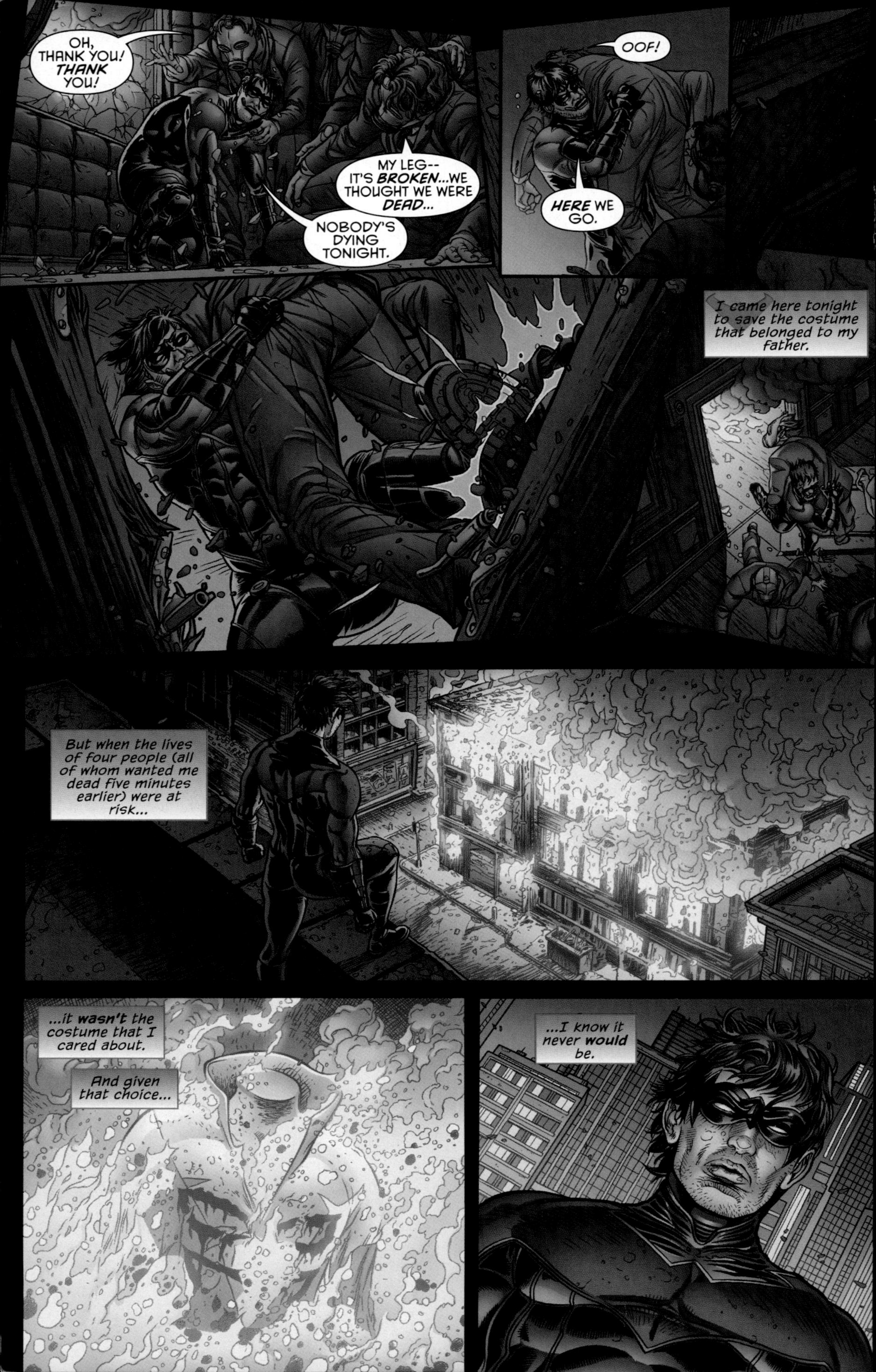
OH, THANK YOU! THANK YOU!
MY LEG-- IT'S BROKEN...WE THOUGHT WE WERE DEAD...
NOBODY'S DYING TONIGHT.
OOF!
HERE WE GO.
I came here tonight to save the costume that belonged to my father.
But when the lives of four people (all of whom wanted me dead five minutes earlier) were at risk...
...it wasn't the costume that I cared about.
And given that choice...
...I know it never would be.

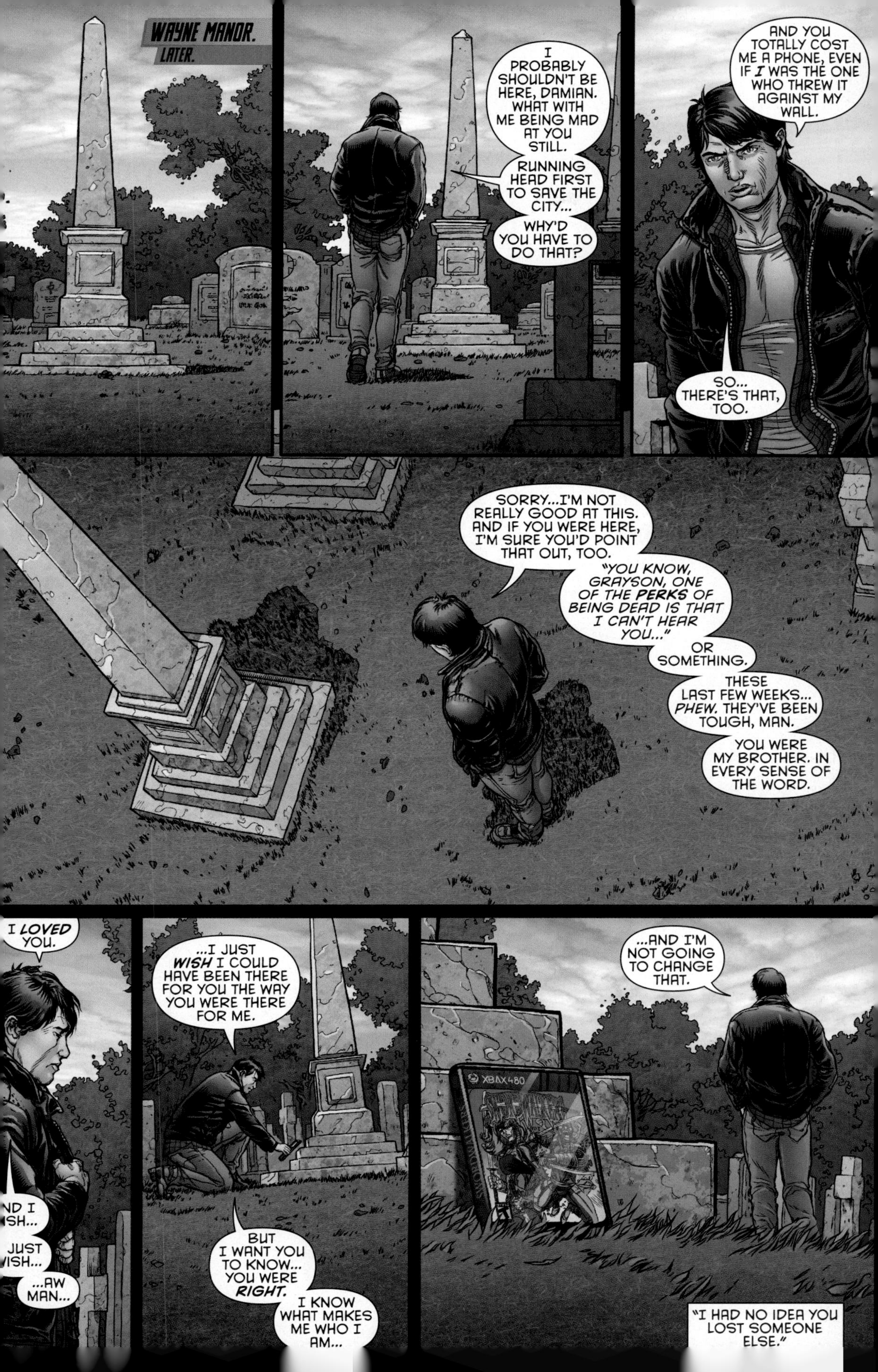

WAYNE MANOR.
LATER.
I PROBABLY SHOULDN'T BE HERE, DAMIAN. WHAT WITH ME BEING MAD AT YOU STILL.
RUNNING HEAD FIRST TO SAVE THE CITY...
WHY'D YOU HAVE TO DO THAT?
AND YOU TOTALLY COST ME A PHONE, EVEN IF I WAS THE ONE WHO THREW IT AGAINST MY WALL.
SO... THERE'S THAT, TOO.
SORRY...I'M NOT REALLY GOOD AT THIS. AND IF YOU WERE HERE, I'M SURE YOU'D POINT THAT OUT, TOO.
"YOU KNOW, GRAYSON, ONE OF THE PERKS OF BEING DEAD IS THAT I CAN'T HEAR YOU..."
OR SOMETHING.
THESE LAST FEW WEEKS... PHEW. THEY'VE BEEN TOUGH, MAN.
YOU WERE MY BROTHER. IN EVERY SENSE OF THE WORD.
I LOVED YOU.
...I JUST WISH I COULD HAVE BEEN THERE FOR YOU THE WAY YOU WERE THERE FOR ME.
BUT I WANT YOU TO KNOW... YOU WERE RIGHT.
I KNOW WHAT MAKES ME WHO I AM...
...AND I'M NOT GOING TO CHANGE THAT.
XBAX480
"I HAD NO IDEA YOU LOST SOMEONE ELSE."

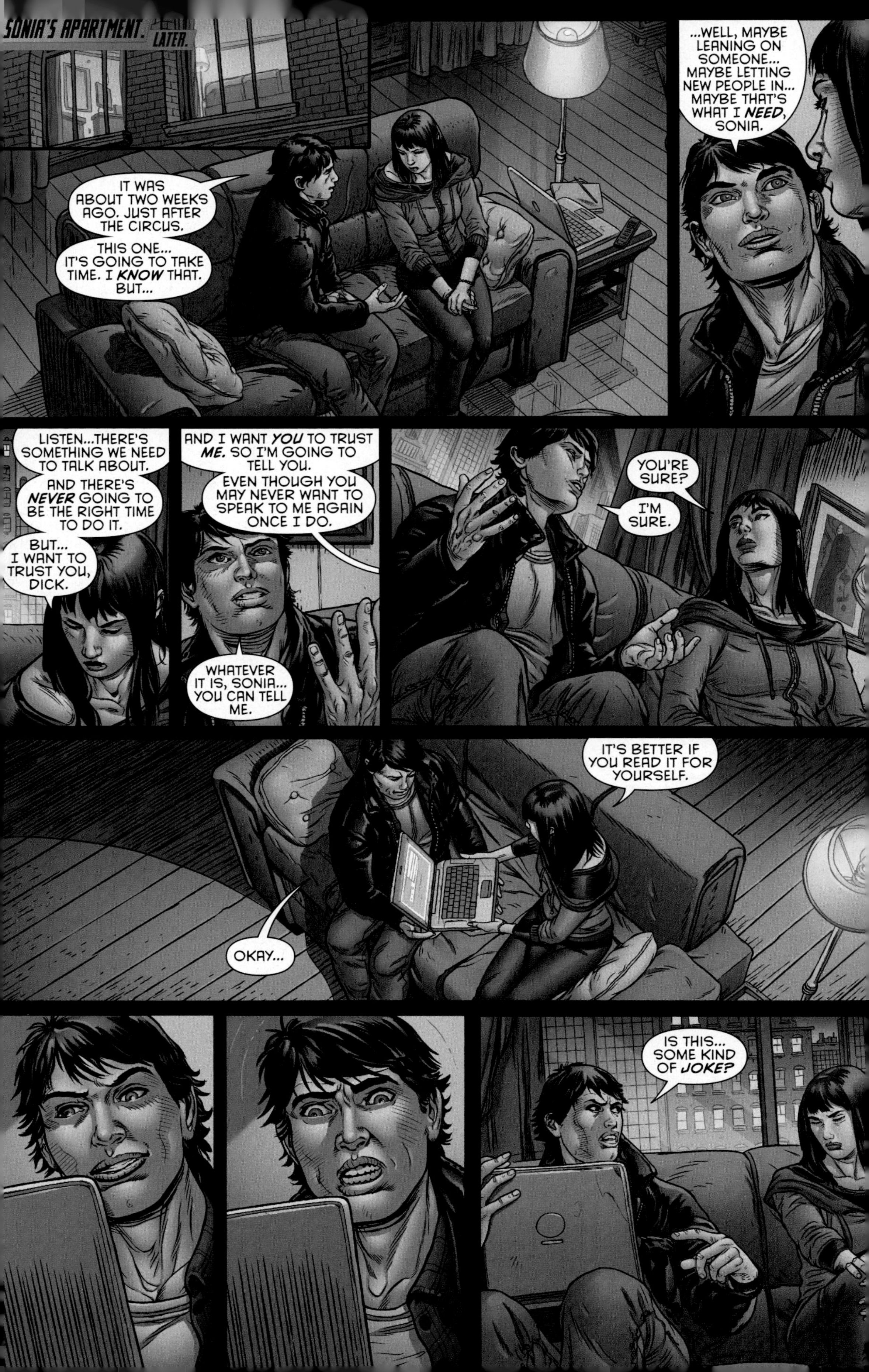
SONIA'S APARTMENT.
LATER.
IT WAS ABOUT TWO WEEKS AGO. JUST AFTER THE CIRCUS.
THIS ONE... IT'S GOING TO TAKE TIME. I KNOW THAT. BUT...
...WELL, MAYBE LEANING ON SOMEONE... MAYBE LETTING NEW PEOPLE IN... MAYBE THAT'S WHAT I NEED, SONIA.
LISTEN...THERE'S SOMETHING WE NEED TO TALK ABOUT.
AND THERE'S NEVER GOING TO BE THE RIGHT TIME TO DO IT.
BUT... I WANT TO TRUST YOU, DICK.
AND I WANT YOU TO TRUST ME. SO I'M GOING TO TELL YOU.
EVEN THOUGH YOU MAY NEVER WANT TO SPEAK TO ME AGAIN ONCE I DO.
WHATEVER IT IS, SONIA... YOU CAN TELL ME.
YOU'RE SURE?
I'M SURE.
IT'S BETTER IF YOU READ IT FOR YOURSELF.
OKAY...
IS THIS... SOME KIND OF JOKE?

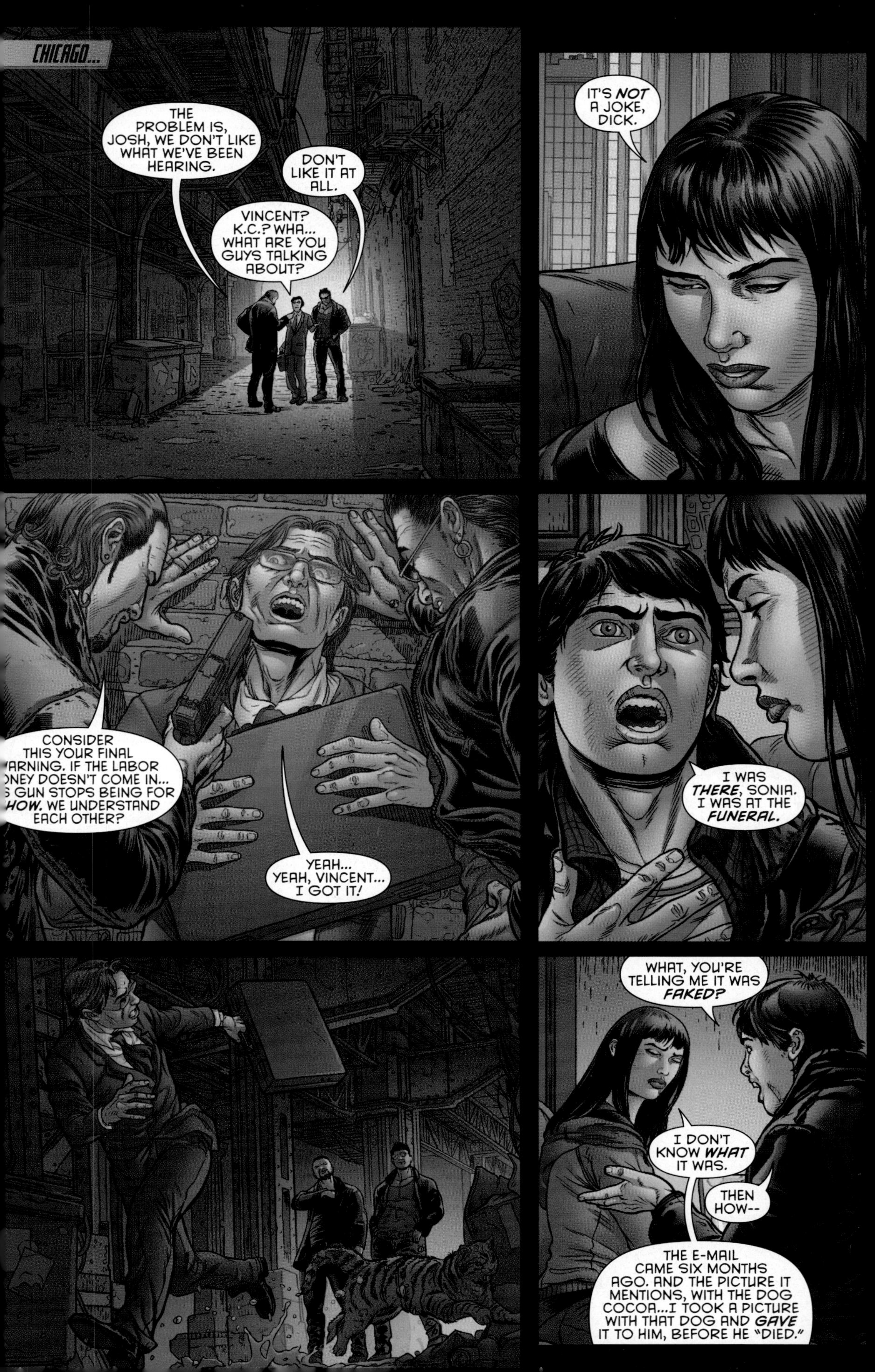

CHICAGO...
THE PROBLEM IS, JOSH, WE DON'T LIKE WHAT WE'VE BEEN HEARING.
DON'T LIKE IT AT ALL.
VINCENT? K.C.? WHA... WHAT ARE YOU GUYS TALKING ABOUT?
IT'S NOT A JOKE, DICK.
CONSIDER THIS YOUR FINAL ARNING. IF THE LABOR ONEY DOESN'T COME IN... GUN STOPS BEING FOR HOW. WE UNDERSTAND EACH OTHER?
YEAH... YEAH, VINCENT... I GOT IT!
I WAS THERE, SONIA. I WAS AT THE FUNERAL.
WHAT, YOU'RE TELLING ME IT WAS FAKED?
I DON'T KNOW WHAT IT WAS.
THEN HOW--
THE E-MAIL CAME SIX MONTHS AGO. AND THE PICTURE IT MENTIONS, WITH THE DOG COCOA...I TOOK A PICTURE WITH THAT DOG AND GAVE IT TO HIM, BEFORE HE "DIED."

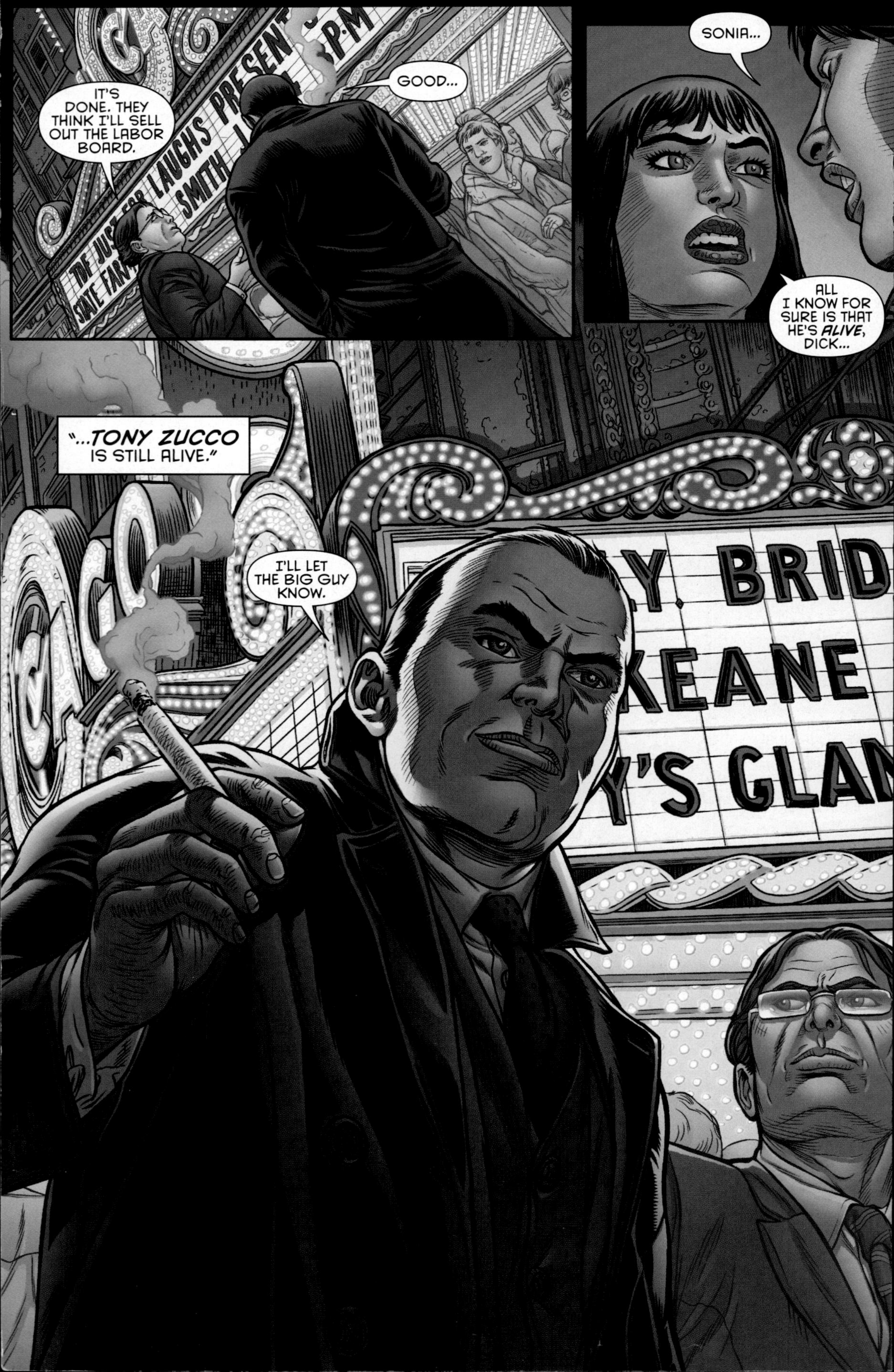
IT'S DONE. THEY THINK I'LL SELL OUT THE LABOR BOARD.
GOOD...
SONIA...
ALL I KNOW FOR SURE IS THAT HE'S *ALIVE*, DICK...
"...*TONY ZUCCO* IS STILL ALIVE."
I'LL LET THE BIG GUY KNOW.